BLACK
DEATH

BLACK DEATH

A NEW HISTORY OF THE BUBONIC PLAGUES OF LONDON

STEPHEN PORTER

AMBERLEY

First published 2018

Amberley Publishing
The Hill, Stroud
Gloucestershire, GL5 4EP

www.amberley-books.com

ISBN 978 1 4456 5685 4 (hardback)
ISBN 978 1 4456 5686 1 (ebook)

British Library Cataloguing in Publication Data.
A catalogue record for this book is available
from the British Library.

Typesetting and Origination by Amberley
Publishing.
Printed in the UK.

CONTENTS

ACKNOWLEDGEMENTS

As the historian-cum-archivist at the Charterhouse over many years I have been constantly reminded of London's history of plague. The buildings are reached across Charterhouse Square, which is the site of the city's largest Black Death burial ground. Within the complex are the outlines of the cemetery chapel built in 1349 and the grave of Sir Walter de Mauny, who bought the site for the burials of the victims and later established a Carthusian priory there. The excavations in the square for the Crossrail project confirmed both the presence of burials and the cause of death as *Yersinia pestis*, the plague bacillus. That prompted me to think that it was an appropriate time to bring together my long-standing interests in plague in London, through all the periods of the long second pandemic. The subject has changed considerably with the development of DNA analysis and historians' interpretations have necessarily been modified as well.

I am most grateful to the governors, staff and Brothers of the Charterhouse for their warm hospitality and wisdom. I am also grateful to Jay Carver and his team at Crossrail, to the many librarians, archivists and curators whose collections I have consulted over many years, and also to those editors who have made texts on various subjects readily available. I am particularly grateful to the Wellcome Collection for making so many of its images available. Plague connections turn up in many places, often unexpected ones, and my wife Carolyn has not only been alert to such associations but has deployed her diligence and expertise to great effect in drawing my attention to them. Her enthusiasm and involvement have been more valuable than I can express.

I

A REMORSELESS DISEASE

'The greatest Terror of Mankind' was how Thomas Sprat described plague in his history of the Royal Society, written in the aftermath of the Great Plague of 1665. Its reputation as one of the foulest scourges of the human population in recorded history is well deserved. At times plague has carried off more than a half of a community and its victims have endured agonies in the few days between contracting the disease and their death. Mortality on such a scale and within such a short period severely disrupted families and societies and dislocated economic life. The sheer frustration of having to endure such an affliction without being able to understand it, and so take measures to prevent it, produced vengeful behaviour and the persecution of minorities regarded as outsiders, such as the Jews. A plague epidemic was indeed socially divisive as those who could move away to avoid the disease did so, leaving most members of the community, including the poor of course, to endure the sickness. And it was spiritually challenging, for the Christian church interpreted the outbreaks as manifestations of God's wrath, inflicted as punishment on a sinful people. To assuage the guilt for wrongdoings the demoralised populace attended special services, took part in penitential processions and even indulged in physical self-torment in the form of flagellation.

The plague bacillus has been identified in skeletons in eastern Europe and the Balkans dating from the late Neolithic period and the Bronze Age, perhaps carried by migrations from the Russian and Ukrainian steppes around 4,800 years ago. Since then there have been three pandemics. The first began in the mid-sixth century in Ethiopia, reached Egypt in 540 and Constantinople in 541. The emperor Constantine re-founded the city of Byzantium in 330 and designated it the eastern capital of the Roman empire. The empire was first split into two parts and then, from the early fifth century, the western empire was overrun by Germanic tribes. Justinian I became emperor of Byzantium in 527 and his general Count Belisarius conquered Italy, Illyria, part of North Africa and southern Spain, which were incorporated into the empire. But the plague struck a heavy blow. Procopius, the chronicler of the reign, was in Constantinople when the disease hit and described its nature, the plight of the victims, and the breakdown of normal patterns, including the burial of the dead. He was understandably vague about the numbers who died, but he did write that during the four summer months in 542 'the tale of dead reached five thousand each day, and again it even came to ten thousand and still more than that'. Modern estimates are that perhaps 40 per cent of the city's population succumbed to the plague.[1] It spread across Europe; according to Procopius the disease 'always took its start from the coast, and then went up to the interior', reaching Scandinavia in the north and as far west as Ireland. He believed that it was an illness 'by which the whole human race came near to be annihilated'.[2] It recurred intermittently thereafter for more than 200 years.

There is scarcely any evidence for the British Isles during the sixth century, although a Welsh chronicle refers to the death of King Maelgwn of Gwynedd in the 'great mortality' of 547. The period 664-c.687 was punctuated by outbreaks, including two serious ones in 664-c.666 and c.684-c.687. That in 664 was said by Bede, a Northumbrian monk, to have 'depopulated first the southern parts of Britain, and afterwards attacking the province of the Northumbrians, ravaged the country far and near, and destroyed a great multitude of men'. A later epidemic c.675 also 'ravaged the country far and wide' and Bede mentioned that in the 680s 'a grievous pestilence fell upon many provinces of Britain'.[3] The death-toll in Europe during the plague of Justinian and the subsequent outbreaks has been estimated at approximately 100 million.

From the mid-eighth century Europe did not suffer from further eruptions of plague for 600 years. Because of the depredations of the first pandemic there were fewer potential victims, for its population had been much reduced since the later stages of the Roman empire, perhaps by as much as a half. The eighteenth-century historian of the empire's decline, Edward Gibbon, reached a harsh judgement on the reign of Justinian I, summing it up in a typically sweeping phrase as 'disgraced by a visible decrease of the human species, which has never been repaired in some of the fairest countries of the globe'.[4] But populations and trade began to recover before the end of the first millennium and grew further during the eleventh, twelve and thirteenth centuries as Europe's medieval economies developed, without any further onset of the disease. The consequences of that absence of the plague were that the population had no resistance to the bacterium, nor any knowledge of the form and pattern of the disease.

The second pandemic began in central Asia, probably in the 1320s, and by the spring of 1346 it had reached the region between the Caspian Sea and southern Russia. From there it spread to the port of Kaffa in the Crimea and then across the Black Sea to Constantinople and into the Mediterranean, making a landfall in Sicily. From the autumn of 1347 North Africa and the Middle East were infected and over the next six years plague engulfed almost all of Europe, killing perhaps 50 to 60 per cent of its population, according to modern assessments. Plague outbreaks recurred frequently but irregularly over the following centuries, moving along the trade routes, both by sea and overland. Between 1536 and 1670 a plague epidemic struck western Europe on average every 15 years. It continued in the Mediterranean basin until the 1830s, although never again was it to afflict the whole continent in one outbreak, as it had done in the mid-fourteenth century. But the virulence of the disease was not diminished and in some outbreaks the proportion of the population that died was as great as during that initial outbreak.

The third pandemic began in Yunnan province in south-west China around 1860 and steadily spread towards the coast. In 1894 there was a plague epidemic in Canton which was so devastating that the local administration was overwhelmed and the number of victims went unrecorded. It then dispersed through south Asia and to Africa and both North and South America: it reached North America at San Francisco in 1900 and has since extended across roughly one-third of the continent. Australia was infected at much the same time and outbreaks there occurred between 1900 and 1925. Plague epidemics continued through the twentieth century, with increased incidence where civil government was fractured, such as during the wars in Indo-China, and it still lingers on, although Europe has so far escaped the third pandemic.

During the first two pandemics contemporaries had no means of understanding the causes of the disease, but they did record the symptoms. The distinctive feature of bubonic plague is the buboes which form on the lymph nodes in the groin and armpits, and on the neck, which give the disease its name. According to Procopius 'a bubonic swelling developed; and this took place not only in the particular part of the body which is called "boubon" [groin], that is, below the abdomen, but also inside the armpit, and in some cases also beside the ears, and at different points on the thighs'. Some physicians 'supposing that the disease centred in the bubonic swellings, decided to investigate the bodies of the dead. And upon opening some of the swellings, they found a strange sort of carbuncle that had grown inside them.'⁵ Gregory of Tours described the plague in Rome in 590 as 'the groin plague', from reports sent by his deacon, who was in the city at the time; Paul the Deacon also mentioned buboes in his *History of the Lombards*.[6] Victims complained of headaches, quickly followed by a fever and vomiting. Giovanni Boccaccio chronicled the effects of the plague in fourteenth-century Florence and noted the symptoms:

> Its first sign here in both men and women was a swelling in the groin or beneath the armpit, growing sometimes in the shape of a simple apple, sometimes in that of an egg, more or less: a bubo was the name commonly given to such a swelling. Before long this deadly bubo would begin to spread indifferently from these points to crop up all over; the symptoms would develop then into dark or livid patches that many people found appearing on their arms or thighs or elsewhere; these were large and well separated in some cases, while in others, they were a crowd of tiny spots. And just as the bubo had been, and continued to be, a sure indication of fatal disease, so were these blotches for those on whom they appeared.[7]

The extremely painful blotches or carbuncles which he described were caused by haemorrhaging beneath the skin, and as the buboes formed and swelled the pain was so excruciating that some victims became uncontrollable and delirious, screaming and running wildly around the streets, and their speech was impaired. The blotches were often described by contemporaries as tokens, and plague as 'spotted death'. Scarus in Shakespeare's *Antony and Cleopatra* refers to 'the token'd pestilence where death is sure'. A foul smell emanated from the sick, repelling those caring for them, and the affliction produced such fear and revulsion that the sufferers were left unattended. As record keeping became more systematic, the numbers of dead were documented and from that information, and experience passed on by those who had experienced an epidemic, the seasonality of the disease and the likelihood of its recurrence were established. But nobody could come up with a cure. Lancing the bubo at exactly the right moment could save a patient, but if it burst inwardly the patient died. Death rates among those infected are hard to determine, but estimates of between 75 and 80 per cent are probably in order.

Few of the survivors recorded their experience; those who did so typically included it in a memoir written perhaps years later. The surgeon Guy de Chauliac was in Avignon during the first onset of the plague and recalled his experience: 'I fell into a continuous fever, with a tumour in the groin. I was ill for nearly six weeks and in such great danger that all my associates thought that I would die, but the tumour being ripened and treated ... I survived.'[8] Aeneas Sylvius Piccolomini, Provost of San Lorenzo in Milan, was at Basel in 1438 when 'there came a frightful plague which spread all over Germany'; in Basel it was said that 'they buried more than three hundred corpses in one day'. When Piccolomini contracted the disease he generously told his servants to leave, in case they should catch the sickness from him. He discovered that there were two celebrated doctors in the city at the time 'one from Paris, learned but unlucky, the other lucky but ignorant' (the descriptions reflected current attitudes to the medical profession). He chose the latter, 'preferring luck to learning – reflecting that no one really knew the proper treatment for the plague'. Despite the regimen which the doctor prescribed his fever increased and was accompanied by violent headaches until he became incoherent and his life was despaired of. Indeed, reports spread that he had died and so his post at Milan was given to someone else. But he recovered after six days, which was typical of the time between identification of the disease and the beginnings of recuperation. Twenty years later Piccolomini was elected Pope, as Pius II.

Girolamo Cardano's reminiscences were provided by members of his family, as he was an infant when he had his brush with plague. He was born in Pavia in 1501 and within his first month his wet-nurse died 'so they tell me, of the plague … Five carbuncles came out on my face in the form of a cross, and there was one on the end of my nose.' It was customary during a plague epidemic for coins to be dropped into a bowl of vinegar during a transaction, to neutralise whatever was causing the disease. The same process was applied to Cardano, for he wrote that 'When my second month was not yet run, Isidoro dei Resti, of Pavia, took me naked from a warm vinegar bath and gave me over to a wet-nurse.' Cardano survived both that experience and the plague.[9]

An epidemic erupted in Rome in the early 1520s, when the young Florentine sculptor Benvenuto Cellini was in the city. He described it as 'a plague of such extraordinary violence that many thousands died of it every day'. For a while he was not affected, although several of his friends died, but then 'a crushing headache seized me; several boils appeared on my left arm, together with a carbuncle which showed itself just beyond the palm of the left hand where it joins the wrist'. Everyone left the house, except for a young apprentice of Cellini's, whose father was a physician. He visited the house and after examining Cellini told him that 'considering the sores are so new, and have not yet begun to stink, and that the remedies will be taken in time, you need not be too much afraid, for I have good hopes of curing you'. Those remedies were followed and Cellini 'soon came well out of that dreadful sickness' and even though 'the sore was still open, with a plug of lint inside it' he went into the countryside, where he recuperated for about a month.[10]

Simon Forman was a physician and astrologer in Elizabethan London and in 1592 he fell ill with the disease, which he diagnosed from 'the plague in both my groins and … the red tokens on my feet as broad as halfpence'. He took to his bed, drank 'strong waters' and lanced the buboes himself, keeping the wounds clean. Standard medical treatment for almost all ailments included letting blood from the patient to expel corrupt matter from the body and he did this, too, but only in the early stages of the disease. He was so ill that it was 22 weeks before he recovered his health.[11]

Cardano became one of the best-known physicians of the sixteenth century, and both de Chauliac and Forman were medical men, but Ambrose Barnes was a merchant's young apprentice in Newcastle-upon-Tyne and he recalled his experience during an outbreak of plague in the late 1640s, writing in the third person. The disease 'made for some months an horrible devastation' and the carts went around the city each night collecting the bodies. Both of the maids in the household were taken ill and the merchant did not delay but 'arose immediately from dinner ... and, the same day, took ship at Shields for Hamburgh', leaving his business in Ambrose's hands. The maids died within a few hours of each other and then Ambrose fell ill, so he found himself alone 'shut up in an empty large house near the Exchange, without any living creature besides himself, but they rapt at the door when they brought him meat', which they left outside for him to collect. 'In this hideous lonely manner, he spent severall dayes and nights, but God was with him. A huge tumour rose upon his neck behind, the suppuration whereof, physitions were of opinion, saved his life.'[12]

Another survivor was Johann Dietz, who was an apprentice to a barber and was also learning about dispensing medicine; he was later to be an army surgeon. In 1682 plague broke out in Halle, where he lived with his family, and he contracted the disease 'with fear and horror', complaining of 'a violent headache'. His father took resolute action, dosing him with a 'plague essence' which Johann had prepared and locking him in a barn. 'Thereupon I began to rave, but as I was powerless to do anything, and further, had no energy to do it, the strength of the medicine resulted in a broken blood vessel, so that the blood flowed copiously from my mouth and nose.' He rolled about the barn covered in blood until he went to sleep. His father looked in from time to time and after two days Johann had recovered sufficiently to sit up, speak rationally and take some broth. His account does not mention buboes and it is his own diagnosis and his father's reaction which identify the disease as plague.[13]

What comes across from these accounts is the pain, fear and sense of desolation that the victims experienced, and the panic and revulsion that it caused in others, even family and friends, so that the sufferers were left alone. A close encounter with someone sick of the plague and the consequences were described by Paul Behaim in letters to his mother. He had left Nuremburg with two companions in 1575 to study at the University of Padua; he wrote to his mother in February 1576 to tell her that he had moved into new lodgings, sharing with a youth he had known when they were both studying at the university in Leipzig. While he was in Padua one of the worst plague epidemics of the century struck Venice. In July Paul told his mother that 'Two hundred people are now dying every day in Venice, some in the hospital, while others ... drop on the streets.' Padua had become virtually isolated because of the fear of making a journey in such conditions and because of travel restrictions. Paul and his companions moved to a village a few miles from Padua, where they lived for two weeks 'in complete comfort and good health'. Then two noblemen arrived, who they had known in the city, and wanted to share with them. Paul explained that 'Unable to deny them, we let them join us,' but three days later 'while dining, one of them fell ill with plague and died three or four days later.' As nobody was willing to take his body to the grave his companion placed it in a coffin and carted it to a village about a mile away and buried him there 'along with the cart'. As soon as the students realised that the disease was plague they hastily moved to an isolated house in a field, which Paul described as 'a shack', with a bedstead, but no bedding, so they had to sleep on straw. Paul went down with a fever and his friends obtained what little medicine they could from Padua, but Paul had to pay double the usual price for it and he commented that 'What I fear most is the physicians, who in these circumstances know only too well how to empty one's pocket.' Their food was boiled three or four days in advance and warmed a little before they ate it and Paul drank boiled barley water. This was a wretched experience and Paul suffered repeated bouts of sickness, which involved further expense, before he could return to Padua in the autumn. What should have been a period of study had turned into a nightmare of sickness, discomfort and financial anxiety, yet he had survived his close encounter with plague.[14]

Throughout the early modern period and into the nineteenth century travellers were made aware of the impact of plague by having to undergo a time in quarantine, or through the process of gathering intelligence on the presence of the disease and so the route which they should take. In 1551 a traveller on a mission to Constantinople for the French government described the practice on the island of Chios in the Aegean, where 'they do establish two persons, which by reason of their charges are called judges of health, for that specially they have a regarde that in the plague time no shippe or other strange vessel do enter into their port without first shewing a good certificat that the place from whence they come is not infected with the plague'. Another visitor to Constantinople who described quarantine in the region was Thomas Dallam. Special gifts were sent by Queen Elizabeth to the Ottoman sultan, Mehmet III, in 1599, to facilitate trade negotiations between the two countries. Paid for by the merchants of London, they included a chiming clock with moving figures that was combined with a mechanical organ, which could play for up to six hours, in a decorated case. Dallam was the maker of the organ and was one of four specialist craftsmen who took the gifts by ship to Constantinople, where the clock-cum-organ was successfully installed, to the sultan's delight. They returned overland to the western side of the Morea and then hired boatmen to take them across to Zakynthos, the southernmost of the Ionian Islands and Venetian territory. Dallam noted in his journal that they could not land on the island: 'They always do this with foreigners coming from Turkey if they do not have a Venetian or Italian health certificate. The Governor and the two Signors of Health locked us up for ten days in the lazaretto, which is a prison for travellers. If at the end of ten days anyone is sick when the Signors of Health visit, they have to stay there another ten days.' Thanks to the intervention of English merchants who traded with the island they were permitted instead to stay in a new house by the seaside. But the boatmen who had brought them from the mainland were also quarantined, at the travellers' expense, until the Signors of Health were asked if they could be released. They agreed to let the boatmen go if they would 'jump out of a window into the sea with their clothes on and washed themselves all over'. Although initially reluctant, the boatmen did so when someone produced a scimitar and threatened to cut their legs off, which 'induced them to jump out and so we were rid of them'. After that bizarre incident, the travellers then completed their period of quarantine.[15]

The Ottoman empire's reputation as being a source of plague was not misplaced. The Italian traveller Pietro della Valle was in Constantinople in the summer of 1614, during the early stages of a journey through the Levant. Unfortunately his journey coincided with a plague epidemic, which he described as 'the fury'. His figure for the death-toll was 140,000 in two months and three weeks, and as the epidemic declined 'there are still some people dying, but they no longer keep count.' Pietro's reaction was that 'As we have escaped from this great evil, it seems to me that we have reason to fear little else.'[16] More than a century later, in 1718, Lady Mary Wortley Montagu also returned home from Constantinople and explained that at Genoa she and her companions served a period of 'the Quaraintaine from which no body is exempt coming from the Levant; but ours was very much shorten'd and very agreeably passed', even though a Genoese nobleman visited them 'to see we did not touch one Another'.[17]

The historian of music Charles Burney made a visit to Italy in 1770. He had reached Naples by October but had become uneasy because of rumours that a war would break out between Britain and France and was afraid that he would be imprisoned by the French on his way home. His gloom was intensified by further rumours, as he noted in his journal at the end of the month: 'besides the war, they were talking this morning of the plague being feared in London, as 'tis supposed not only to be in the Baltic but in Holland, and ships from both these places are now obliged to perform quarentine'. Fears had run way ahead of the truth, but Burney's anxiety regarding the possibility of having to undergo quarantine reflected the continued general anxiety about plague and its impact, more than a hundred years after the Great Plague. By the early nineteenth century the quarantine process had become very boring and quite irritating, as the threat of plague receded. Henry Matthews's ship arrived at the port of Livorno in October 1817, having completed the voyage from Lisbon in 12 days. When they arrived 'A boat from the Health-office hailed us immediately, and we were ordered to perform a quarantine of ten days,' to which his objection was that 'as we had a clean bill of health … there was, in fact, no real ground for putting us under quarantine at all.' But the order could not be evaded and the days dragged, so that he was prompted to write that 'The value of liberty can only be known by those who have been in confinement.' He added that 'The quarantine laws, like most others, though originally intended for the general good, come at last to be perverted to private purposes.' He was convinced that the reason for maintaining the regulations had become the fees received by the Health Office from the quarantined vessels, because a 'number of men' were kept in employment at the expense of those they were appointed to guard. Matthews was mightily relieved when 'At last came the day of our deliverance.' Charles Dickens expressed similar sentiments in his novel *Little Dorrit*, with a scene set in Marseille during the mid-1820s. One of those impounded complained that it would be better if the travellers could go about their lawful business rather than having to undergo a period of quarantine. When it was explained to him that they were doing so 'as we come from the East, and the East is the country of the plague,' he reacted sharply: 'The plague! That's my grievance. I have had the plague continually, ever since I have been here. I am like a sane man shut up in a madhouse; I can't stand the suspicion of the thing. I came here as well as ever I was in my life; but to suspect me of the plague is to give me the plague.'[18] From Thomas Dallam to Charles Dickens, the varied practices of the quarantine process helped to focus travellers' attention on the threat of plague.

Measures such as quarantine were the only effective way to combat a disease that was not understood. Yet there were investigations, including the dissection of victims' bodies and the use of the steadily improving microscope lenses. As early as 1656 Athanasius Kircher, at the Jesuit Collegio Romano, had used a microscope to study the blood of plague victims and saw 'little worms', concluding that the disease was caused by living organisms. In his *Scrutinium pestis physico-medicum*, published two years later, he put forward this germ theory of disease and it received some support, but was also criticised, indeed ridiculed. Despite the development of bacteriology from the mid-seventeenth century, Kircher's work was not followed up.[19] Improvements to microscopes made possible observations of small creatures and in his *Micrographia* of 1665 Robert Hooke included an engraving of a flea from one of his detailed drawings. It was prominently displayed in the volume, on a plate 18 by 12 inches. But there was no knowledge or awareness to link Kircher's and Hooke's observations.

The term Black Death was not applied to the plague outbreak of the mid-fourteenth century for another 200 years, when it was used in a Swedish account; around 1600 Danish sources gave it the same title. In the context, the word 'black' could have been used to denote something terrible, or to describe the appearance of the symptoms. The term was not widely adopted and was used in English only in the eighteenth century, in specialist works, yet when Elizabeth Cartwright Penrose, the wife of an Anglican minister, wrote a history of England, in her account of Edward III's reign she included the sentence: 'Edward's successes in France were interrupted during the next six years by a most terrible pestilence – so terrible as to be called the black death – which raged throughout Europe, and proved a greater scourge to the people than even the calamities of war.' She published the book in 1823 as *A History of England from the First Invasion by the Romans to the End of the Reign of George III* with the Edinburgh publisher Archibald Constable, under the pseudonym Mrs Markham, but it did not do well. After Constable's bankruptcy in 1826 the stock of her book was bought by John Murray in London, which issued an enlarged edition in that year. She had adopted the approach of a book ostensibly written for the instruction of her children, in an accessible style and with question-and-answer sections at the end of each chapter. Under Murray's imprint it was a great success and proved to be the most popular textbook on English history through the mid-nineteenth century. She used the term Black Death again in her *History of France*, published in 1828, also by John Murray, providing a summary of the disease's progress in 1348-9. That, too, reached a large readership in Britain and America. The appearance of cholera, another mass killer, in Europe in the early 1830s also focused attention on the plague. Dr J.F.K. Hecker, a German physician, wrote an essay on the epidemic of the late 1340s which he entitled *Der schwarze Tod*, the Black Death, which was translated and published in English in 1833 as *The Black Death in the Fourteenth Century*. Hecker and his translator used the term without an explanation, as though it was already current. That essay attracted considerable, but specialist, attention, and it was Elizabeth Penrose, as author, and John Murray, her publisher, who were responsible for the widespread adoption of the term in the English-speaking world, and indeed beyond. She applied it to that first outbreak of plague, not to the subsequent epidemics of the same disease, a usage which has persisted.[20]

Cholera was defeated when the means of transmission were identified and the last outbreak in London was in 1866. But that had not been achieved for plague and so when the epidemic in Canton erupted, the world was alerted both to the danger of a major epidemic and the possibility of discovering the nature of the disease. Medical knowledge was transformed from around 1870 with the discovery that contagious diseases were caused by micro-organisms, or pathogens. Coupled with advances in microscopic optics, this raised the prospect that the disease and its means of transmission could be identified. The Japanese government despatched Shibasaburo Kitasato to Hong Kong, to which the disease had spread, while the French sent the young Swiss biologist Alexandre Yersin. The so-called 'plague race' that followed was won by Yersin, who isolated the plague bacterium, which he named *Pasteuralla pestis*, in acknowledgement of his teacher, Louis Pasteur, and the Pasteur Institute where he had trained. In 1970 it was renamed *Yersinia pestis*, the name by which it is now known. The means of transmission of the disease were discovered independently before the end of the nineteenth century. During the third pandemic, plague organisations were established to both put in place counter-measures and to record data for research. Findings based upon the records of such plague commissions in India, Algeria and Madagascar, as well as observations made by countries where the disease is present, have been analysed to greatly extend knowledge of plague and its transmission. Despite the identification of the bacillus and the means of transmission, the third pandemic has claimed many victims: 12.6 million people died of the disease in British India between 1898 and 1948. The death-toll has been much reduced by the development of modern treatments using antibiotics, notably streptomycin, and early diagnosis. In 2001 there were almost 2,700 cases worldwide and 175 deaths, by 2013 the figures were 783 cases and 126 deaths.

The means of transmission were established as rats' fleas that are parasites of the black rat. As a flea sucks blood from its infected host it squirts saliva containing partly digested blood into the bite. While the flea is feeding the ingested bacilli multiply to such an extent that they block the proventriculus, the organ at the entrance to the flea's stomach. When the rat dies the flea requires another host, usually another rat or, as the rat population is wiped out by the disease, it transfers to a human. As it attempts to feed, the passage of blood into its stomach is obstructed by the blocked proventriculus. Unable to ingest the blood, the flea becomes ravenous and persists in trying to feed, to the point where the blood is regurgitated with the saliva, carrying the plague bacilli into the bite in the skin of its host. It has thereby transferred the disease from rat to man, but in doing so ends the process, for the flea starves to death. Subsequent interpretation of the data has modified the conclusion that there was a 30-day interval between a blood-meal by the flea and the transmission of the disease; it has been shown that the transfer of bacilli from fleas can occur continuously after a blood-meal and is not dependent on blockage of the proventriculus. Once a person has been bitten by an infective flea the infection takes between three and five days to incubate before the victim becomes ill, and death typically follows within another three to five days. It comes more quickly if the bacteria break out of the buboes; they are then carried by the blood stream to the lungs and are spread in water droplets on the victims' breath. The contaminated respiratory droplets are the means of direct transmission from person to person, requiring close contact with a victim; that form of the disease is pneumonic plague. Septicaemic plague is caused by a flea bite, but the bacilli enter the bloodstream directly, not through the lymphatic system, also resulting in a more rapid death than with the victims of bubonic plague, and before buboes have formed. Both septicaemic and pneumonic plague are much less common than the bubonic form and they bring death generally within 24 hours and certainly within 48 hours; they have a fatality rate of 100 per cent when untreated.[21]

The host population of rats and their fleas needs to be large enough for an epidemic to develop, and be living close to a human population. A rat normally carries roughly half-a-dozen fleas, although a sick rat unable to groom may attract many more. Rats are agile, intelligent, resourceful and to an extent adaptable; the black rat, *Rattus rattus*, is also known as the ship rat and the house rat. The fleas are less adaptable and require relatively high temperatures and humidity, with the ideal conditions being 90 to 95 per cent humidity and temperatures of 15 to 25 degrees centigrade. In the microclimates provided by a rat's nest, stocks of grain, or textiles, which hold residual heat beyond the peak temperatures of the summer, fleas can live for up to a year and survive cold weather, especially in nests within burrows, human dwellings, or outhouses sheltering livestock. Modern observations have shown that the fleas of other burrowing animals, including mice, squirrels and marmots, can transmit the disease. The human flea and lice have been proposed as an effective vector for the transmission of the bacteria, which would explain the absence of contemporary references to dead rats preceding an epidemic in the human population. This was advocated in the early 1940s from empirical studies in Morocco and elsewhere in north and west Africa and has recently received support based on mathematical modelling, with the conclusion that during the second pandemic plague was spread predominantly through human parasites rather than rats' fleas or pneumonic transmission.[22]

Even after those discoveries, the conclusions were questioned, both on the basis of contemporary observations and uncertainty about the effectiveness, and perhaps presence, of the rat as the agent of transmission. There were even doubts whether *Yersinia pestis* was indeed the causative agent of the Black Death. Other possibilities that were suggested were anthrax or a filovirus similar to the Ebola or Marburg viruses. Neither fit the documentary evidence and, within the twenty-first century, *Yersinia pestis* has been confirmed as the cause of the three pandemics by deploying radiocarbon dating to skeletons unearthed from known plague burials sites to confirm their date, and applying the aDNA analysis to dental pulp removed from them. The technique was developed by scientists at the Université de la Méditerranée and subsequently at the University of Tübingen.[23] Dental pulp from skeletons dating from the first two pandemics taken from locations in south-west France, north Italy, the Netherlands, central Germany and, in England, Hereford, Lincolnshire and London all contained traces of *Yersinia pestis*.[24] Similar tests from other sites across Europe have confirmed those findings. In London skeletons from the Black Death burial grounds at Charterhouse Square and East Smithfield, and from the Great Plague of 1665 in the cemetery of Bethlehem Hospital, off Bishopsgate, have tested positive for *Yersinia pestis*.[25] The test has also shown that the Plague of Athens in the fifth century BC was caused not by plague but by typhus.

While society was unaware of the nature and causes of the disease it could not take decisive steps to prevent it or ameliorate its impact. Yet measures were put in place to lessen its effects and as this was a shared affliction affecting Europe, North Africa and the Middle East, governments looked abroad to discover how measures taken elsewhere might be adopted to check its progress. A part of the history of the second plague pandemic is the way in which successive generations grappled with the challenge. While the authorities evolved a strategy, Londoners developed a response to the disease that could not avert it but did allow the city to continue to function during the periodic crises which this foulest of diseases brought to their doors.

2

LONDON: A GROWING CITY

The Romans founded Londinium soon after their arrival in Britain in 43 AD and it quickly grew as a trading centre, through its position as the lowest bridging point on the Thames and the estuary's advantages as a natural harbour opening into the North Sea. It became the administrative centre of the province and the focus of its road network. It remained the principal city of Roman Britain until raids from outside the empire and political instability within it led eventually to the withdrawal of the legions in 407 and the breakdown of Roman rule shortly afterwards. Without its administrative role and in the face of disruptive incursions across the North Sea, Londinium was gradually deserted during the fifth century.

A part of the town was again occupied during the reconversion of England to Christianity in the early seventh century, when the historian Bede described it as 'the mart of many nations resorting to it by sea and land'.[1] A grant of land made in the 670s referred to 'the port of London, where ships come to land'. But that settlement was to the west of Londinium and was known as Lundenwic, which means 'old trading settlement'. It was centred on the modern Aldwych, between Kingsway and Trafalgar Square, and the Thames and Oxford Street. By 800 its population was about 4,000 and it was home to artisans as well as the traders. The landing place for ships was the foreshore and the bridge must have been partially ruined or even completely collapsed, for it did not prevent sea-going vessels from reaching so far upstream. Lundenwic may have been affected by the outbreaks of plague in the third quarter of the seventh century, which struck Kent and Essex. They brought death to the newly founded monastery at Barking, where the pestilence 'seized on that part of this monastery where the men abode, and they were daily hurried away to the Lord', and the abbess and some of the nuns also died.[2] The plague then seems to have receded and there are no further references to it after c.690.[3]

A growing threat to the town during the early ninth century was coastal raiding by the Danes, who occupied Lundenwic at least three times. But after Alfred became king of Wessex in 871 he began to stem the Danish inroads and in 886 his forces occupied London, which he then entrusted to his son-in-law Aethelred, ealdorman, or ruler, of the Mercians. Aethelred retained control of the city until his death in 911 and during his period in charge the inhabitants moved within the Roman walls of what was now known as Lundenburg, 'the fortified town', and Lundenwic was gradually abandoned.

New streets were set out on Ludgate Hill and Cornhill and between Cheapside and the river. A market space was set out in the late ninth century south of Cheapside and Poultry, its eastwards extension. East of the Walbrook, streets were built south of Eastcheap around Fish Street Hill, continuing to the Thames at Billingsgate, where a jetty was built around 1000, and the quay at Queenhithe was improved in the early eleventh century. Ships from London traded with the Mediterranean, as well as with the ports of northern France and Germany. The bridge was rebuilt and Southwark, probably unoccupied since the fifth century, revived and was first mentioned by name as one of the burhs established by Alfred. The city within the walls continued to develop, with new streets set out north of Cheapside in the tenth century, despite periodic epidemics, fires and Viking raids, which resumed in 980 and continued until 1016. From the tenth century London was England's largest and wealthiest town and it had a population of perhaps 15,000 by the middle of the eleventh century.

In 1042 Edward the Confessor became king. He re-founded the Benedictine abbey of St Peter's at Westminster, rebuilding it on a grand scale, and also built a royal palace close by. With the reoccupation of Lundenburg and the growth of Southwark, London had consisted of two components; the development of Westminster added a third. Following the defeat and death of Earl Godwine's son Harold, who had succeeded Edward, the Normans occupied London and Duke William of Normandy took the throne. The Normans built new fortifications: Baynard's Castle and Montfitchet's Tower, close together west of Ludgate, and an enclosure within the south-east corner of the city walls, where a great stone keep, the White Tower, was begun by William in 1078 and completed during the reign of his son, William II (1087-1100). The White Tower became the principal building of the Tower of London, a castle to protect the city, a restraint upon the citizens and a royal palace. It also came to function as the state prison, a military arsenal and a safe deposit for bullion and the government's records. St Paul's cathedral was rebuilt after a fire in 1087, which also destroyed 'many other churches and the largest and noblest part of all the city'. London contained more than a hundred churches, some of them pre-Norman, probably private churches from which the parish structure evolved in the eleventh and twelfth centuries. A stone bridge was built between 1176 and 1212; at just over 300 yards long it was by far the largest in England and shops lined its roadway on both sides.

William Fitzstephen's account of his native city in the twelfth century described London as having 'abundant wealth, extensive commerce, great grandeur and magnificence', and its size and affluence, with the royal palaces at Westminster and the Tower, gave it a major role as a focus of political power.[4] The citizens negotiated with the crown on such matters as the right to trade within England free from tolls and the annual levy imposed upon the city. By Fitzstephen's time the city was subdivided into 24 wards, where local courts were held under the direction of an alderman. In 1394 Farringdon was divided into two and in 1550 Southwark became Bridge Ward Without, bringing the number of wards up to twenty-six.

The first mayor was Henry Fitz Ailwin, who was described as mayor in 1194 and held the post until his death in 1212. In a charter of 1215 King John conceded the principal of an elected mayor, who was chosen annually by the freemen from among the aldermen (the term lord mayor came into use during the sixteenth century). The mayor was senior to the two sheriffs, who were appointed by the crown until John accepted that they should be chosen by the city. By the end of his reign in 1216 London had become a self-governing city, with its principal officers chosen from among its own citizens.

Another element in the city was the craft and trade guilds, the earliest of which were established in the mid–twelfth century. They became more numerous from the thirteenth century, until there were roughly 65 of them by 1300. They restricted access to their trade through apprenticeships and so controlled the numbers entitled to work, as well as maintaining the quality of the product and providing help for needy widows and children of deceased members. They came to be known as livery companies in the fifteenth century and by then they had developed an important role, as their leaders became the powerful men in the city's administration.

London's trade prospered during the thirteenth century, with imports of Baltic grain, cloth from Flanders, furs from Russia, wine from Germany and increasingly, too, from Bordeaux, following the uniting of Gascony to the English crown in 1152. Luxury items including spices, silks, gold, precious jewels and enamels were also imported. With the prosperity of overseas trade and the output of London's skilled artisans, the city's economy grew, as did its population, which may have been 80,000 by 1300. That was to be a peak, for the new century was to bring crises and sudden death on an unprecedented scale.

London's growth was part of a steady increase in population in England and across Europe. Between 1100 and 1300 England's population rose from about 1.25 million to roughly 5 million, producing pressure on food supplies. For the higher levels of population to be sustainable, good, or at least sufficient, harvests were essential. From around 1300 the climate of much of Europe became wetter and the bad weather produced poor harvests; the consequent shortages resulted in high prices for grain and, when diseases struck farm livestock, meat, too, became dearer. It may be that farmland was being over-cultivated because of the pressure to produce cereal crops, perhaps with the area set aside as fallow each year being reduced and so fewer livestock being raised, generating less manure to replenish the soil's fertility. Lower crop yields and hence higher prices reduced the nourishment of the poorer citizens' diet, making them susceptible to disease.

Poor harvests for three consecutive years around 1310 led to high prices for corn and other foodstuffs, but they then fell back, before rising steeply in 1317. Almost incessant rain during the summer and autumn of that year caused a terrible harvest across much of northern Europe and the Chronicle of London recorded, in macabre terms, that there was 'a gret derthe of corn and other vitailes ... and the poure peple eten for hunger cattes and hors and houndes ... stal [stole] children and eten them, and thanne anon after there fille a gret pestilence among the peple'.[5] The price of grain in London rose to almost three times the level of the preceding few years. The famine and epidemic lasted through the next two years, but grain prices then fell before another, although less severe, rise in the early 1320s, during which 52 men, women and children were crushed to death in a crowd of desperate people pressing forward at a distribution of alms in London. But that crisis was not a prolonged one and the record of grain prices in the city's markets shows no appreciable problems with supply between the mid-1320s and the late 1340s.[6] Those who were not bound by manorial labour services, or who could escape from them, might have been drawn to London when food supplies were reduced and prices were high, if only because both civic and national governments took steps to ensure that the city was adequately provisioned. Such incomers helped to ensure that its population was not greatly reduced by subsistence crises.

The city recovered from the problems of the 1310s and early 1320s and increased its share of England's overseas trade. In 1275 Edward I had introduced a levy on wool, effectively initiating a national system of customs, and the quays on the north bank between the bridge and the Tower became the Legal Quays, where goods liable for customs duties were loaded and unloaded, and where a custom house was built c.1382. Edward also intervened in English trade when, in 1270, Flemish merchants were arrested during a dispute between England and Flanders. They had considerable control of the export of wool, which they preferred to ship to the cloth-making towns of Flanders from Lynn and Boston, rather than London. By the time that they were readmitted to the trade seven years later Italian merchants and those from the Hanseatic ports had taken their place; they operated through London. Boston's share of the export trade in wool fell as London's rose. The Hanseatic League was formed in 1241 as a loose grouping of north European cities trading abroad, directed by a Diet that met in Lübeck. German merchants were operating in London by the 1150s and were granted concessions in 1194, 1260 and 1303, which included the freedom to trade throughout England and partial exemption from taxation. The merchants of Hamburg, Lübeck and Cologne had their own trading stations until they merged in 1282 to form the Steelyard, or Stahlhof, alongside Dowgate, between Blackfriars and London Bridge.

Italian merchants already had a toehold in the English economy as the collectors of papal taxes and they began to exploit the openings left by the Flemish, both in wool exports and the import of luxury items, such as spices and expensive textiles, fruit and alum. Members of Edward III's lavish court were profitable customers for textiles and other finery. In the mid-fourteenth century the king's Great Wardrobe was in Lombard Street. The street took that name in the early fourteenth century, from the merchants from Lombardy and elsewhere who had settled there. Furs accounted for 42 per cent of the Great Wardrobe's budget in 1344-5 and those wealthy citizens who could afford to do so tried to imitate the courtiers, while the 'Common lewd women' were forbidden from wearing fur-lined and trimmed garments, so that everyone 'may have knowledge of what rank they are'.[7] The Italian and north European merchants also took over some functions, such as the granting of loans, from the Jewish community, who suffered from both official and more general persecution from the mid-thirteenth century. In 1275 the Statute of the Jewry prohibited them from taking interest on loans and granting mortgages and in 1290 Edward I expelled the entire community from England.

London's reputation as a city where Italian merchants could prosper was reflected in a tale by Giovanni Boccaccio, in which three brothers in Florence, sons of a very wealthy father, squandered their wealth and to recover their fortune sold up and went to London. There they took a small house and lived frugally, lending money at interest, so that within a few years they had earned a great deal. They returned to Florence, sending a nephew to England to continue the business, while they drew on the profits which it made. But a civil war in England brought disruption and the business foundered, so the nephew had to leave. In fact, it was not civil war but Edward III's need to bankroll his overseas campaigns which made the financial business a hazardous one, especially for those lending to the crown, as several Italian banking houses did. When he defaulted on his repayments in 1343 the Peruzzi family business went bankrupt and in the following year so did that of the Bardi, although in truth they were also over-committed elsewhere and were hit by the beginnings of an economic recession in Italy. The king was already taking loans from a wider range of merchants, from the Hanse cities and the Flemish towns of Brussels and Mechelen.[8]

Finance, the wool trade, wine imports, supplying the aristocratic demand for luxuries, a range of everyday trades and the provisioning of the inhabitants contributed to London's economy. The city was crowded, with most of its population living and working in the area between the Temple and the Tower and northwards to the city wall. A few suburbs straggled out beyond the gates, and Westminster and Southwark were more substantial communities, but it was in the City where most Londoners were housed. Even so, it had space for gardens; a lease of property in the parish of All Hallows, London Wall granted in 1348 included the proviso that the lessees were entitled to a half of the fruit from the trees growing on the premises.[9]

At the edge of the City's western boundary the Temple and other groups of buildings nearby came to be occupied by lawyers during the early fourteenth century; those were the beginnings of the development of London's legal quarter. Other neighbourhoods had their own specialities, indicated by street names, such as Rope Street, Ironmongers' Lane, Garlick Hill, Cordwainer Street and Pudding Lane. The skinners were clustered around Dowgate Hill and their company received its first charter in 1327. The Vintry, upstream from the bridge, was where wine imports were landed, to be stored in a large building in Thames Street, one of many storehouses in the street that connected the quays along the riverside. Parallel to Thames Street were Watling Street and Candlewick Street, which became the focus of the drapery trade. Newgate Street was a centre for the butchers, a corn market was held in Gracechurch Street, Eastcheap was 'a place replenished with cooks', while the names of the streets off Cheapside reflected the prominence of stalls and shops of those supplying provisions: bread, milk, honey, wood and poultry. As well as the markets held in the streets, by the early thirteenth century Cheapside was lined with small shops, resembling modern booths. Behind the frontages were yards containing bazaars, known as selds, each of which had 20 to 30 traders' places, where they stored and sold their wares. In 1300 the street had as many as 400 shops and up to ten times that number of traders' spaces in the selds. Property values in and around Cheapside fell during the 1330s but rose again in the following decade, suggesting that the city's economy was still buoyant.[10]

The city was well supplied with fresh water. Within Cheapside were two conduits, the 'little conduit' at the west end and the 'great conduit' at the east and a fountain called the Standard. Water was piped from Tyburn to the 'great conduit', a long rectangular building close to the junction with Poultry, built in 1236-45 and rebuilt in 1286. Water also came from the Thames and its tributaries the Fleet and the Walbrook, but they did not necessarily contain clean water. In 1344 there was a complaint that two men had combined to reduce the width of the Walbrook by three feet in the parish of St Margaret, Lothbury, and built sties for pigs and other animals above it, supported on piles, presumably so that the effluent could easily be deposited in the watercourse. They were ordered to remove the sties within 40 days.[11] All watercourses were tempting places for the disposal of rubbish and effluent, whether in an organised way or by casual dumping. By 1383 the Walbrook was said to be 'stopped up by divers filth and dung thrown therein by persons who have houses along the said course, to the great nuisance and damage of all the City'; the aldermen of the wards through which the stream flowed were to investigate if there were stables or other houses from which manure could fall into it. They were also to check the number of latrines along the stream, but not to order their removal, because 'it shall be fully lawful for those persons who have houses on the said watercourse, to have latrines over the course, provided that they do not throw rubbish or other refuse through the same, whereby the passage of the said water may be stopped'.[12] Odours and health were closely associated in the public mind. In 1354 complaints were made about butchers at Newgate who were using a wharf on the River Fleet and nearby pavement for cleaning animals' entrails, creating a smell which was 'so bad as to be injurious to the health of the inhabitants of the free prison of the Flete and neighbourhood'. They should have followed an arrangement by which they carried out such cleansing at 'a certain public place of the City ... where the Thames ebbs and flows'.[13]

The city was dotted with wells, but they, too, could be contaminated by seepage, as they were not the only holes in the ground among the buildings. There were also cess-pits and rubbish pits, where much of the city's effluent and garbage were deposited. Some were as large as 12 feet across and 12 feet deep and were lined with wattles or stone. Regulations specified that the cess-pit of a privy lined with stone should be 2½ feet from a neighbour's property boundary and for an unlined one the distance should be 3½ feet; the rule applied to all pits, whether they contained clean or dirty water. But some privies, although separate and on different plots, shared a cess-pit with another, and seepage was a hazard, so that the foulness of the deposits caused complaints. In 1341 Isabel Luter objected that Henry de Ware had a window and four other apertures in his wall overlooking her tenement in St Antholin's parish, through which the stench from his cess-pit infiltrated to her tenement. In the same year William and Alice de Fulham complained that William de Braybrok had a pit too close to their stone wall, into which the rainwater drained, and that slops and other filth were thrown into it by his household, saturating their wall to such an extent that the buildings were in danger of being ruined. Five years later Sir Hugh Blount grumbled that water from his neighbour's tenement in the parish of St Mildred the Virgin, in Poultry, ran onto his buildings and walls, causing the upper parts to rot. Furthermore, his tenants drew water from his well and the overflow from it, with the sewage and other refuse which they threw outside his tenement, had rotted the foundations of Sir Hugh's walls.[14]

In some places poor or neglected drainage or guttering were causing problems with overflowing water or waste, rather than there being any malicious intent to use adjoining properties for dumping rubbish. Clearance of garbage had become such a problem that in the summer of 1345 the aldermen responded to complaints by the beadles of various wards that they could not keep Cheapside and other streets clean by ordering that no one should deposit rubbish in the streets. They also allocated the beadles of two wards two assistants each, but warned the beadles that they could be imprisoned if they did not keep the streets clean. In the same year the aldermen imposed a toll on those using Dowgate Dock; the receipts were to be allocated to cover the costs of cleaning the dock, which had become so foul that the water-carriers were no longer able to take water from it.[15]

The house of a vintner in Candlewick Street Ward close to the Thames, recorded in 1337, was typical of a London artisan's dwelling. It was of two storeys, timber-built, but with party walls of stone. On the ground floor was a living-room and a kitchen, with a separate hall that had an oriel window at one end, probably projecting towards the street, the upper part of which was glazed and the lower part closed with shutters. A steep stairway, or perhaps simply a ladder, led to the upper room, which was used for sleeping, with a bed and mattress, three feather beds and two pillows. The room also had a large cupboard where the linen was stored and the clothing, kept in six chests, included some fine and cheerfully coloured garments, as well as a suit of quilted leather armour. Curtains were hung against the street door for warmth, there was a green carpet, cushions, a candlestick, a frame for holding candles, brass pots, basins, an iron cooking spit, a frying pan, other kitchen utensils and plates. The valuables consisted of a cup with a base and cover of silver, valued at £1 10s 0d, another cup and six silver spoons. In the buttery at the rear of the house were six wine casks, valued together at £4, there were two cellars, and the property had its own cess-pit. The furniture and clothing were valued at £12 18s 4d, so the vintner and his wife were comfortably off.[16]

Londoners were protective of their privacy, despite the crowded buildings. In the case of Andrew and Joan de Aubrey that was understandable, because their privy was enclosed with boards and roofed, so that the seats in it were concealed, until their neighbours removed both the wall and roof 'so that the extremities of those sitting upon the seats can be seen, a thing which is abominable and altogether intolerable'. Most of the complaints about intrusive windows were that they allowed the occupants to peer into the house next door, watching the neighbours go about their daily business. In the case of the allegation against John le Leche, a fishmonger in St Antholin's, it seemed that he was just plain nosey, using a leaden watch-tower on his house in which he and his household stood to look into the adjoining premises. The sense of insecurity revealed by such cases extended to fear of crime. In 1346 a complaint was lodged that because Walter de Eure had not fenced a plot of land in the parish of St Bartholomew-the-Less 'malefactors and disturbers of the king's peace and robbers lurk there by night and waylay passers-by, attacking, beating and wounding them and stealing their goods'. He was ordered to fence the ground within 40 days. Dark and constricted lanes may also have caused anxiety. Fishingwarf Lane in St Mary Somerset parish was too narrow for carts to use and Desebourne Lane in the same parish was 215 feet long and seven feet wide, narrowing to just under four feet at its southern end, towards the river.[17]

This crowded and busy – but not necessarily badly contaminated – city was the focus of much English economic, political and cultural life and so it had regular contact with most of the country. As a centre of international trade, it also had connections with many continental ports, as well as those parts of northern France and Flanders where Edward III's armies and garrisons campaigned from the late 1330s, in the early stages of what was to become the Hundred Years War.

3

THE BLACK DEATH

The source of the second pandemic may have been as far east as the Gobi Desert and as early as the 1320s. In 1334 plague struck a community close to Lake Ysyk-Köl, in modern Kyrgyzstan, and the disease then spread to the area north-west of the Caspian Sea. This is a region of steppe landscapes and was crossed by routes followed by merchants trading with central Asia along the Silk Road. European traders had been banned from using the route by the Kipchak Khanate of the Golden Horde, the Mongols who ruled the region, after the khanate had converted to Islam in 1313. The plague did not enter Russia from the khanate's lands, suggesting that trade links between the two regions had been effectively cut, but it did travel south-west, perhaps assisted by military action to expel Christian merchants from their trading posts.

A Russian chronicle related that in 1346 'God's punishment struck the people in the eastern lands, in the town of Ornach and in Khastorokan, and in Sarai, and in Bezdeh.' Ornach is on the estuary of the River Don where it flows into the Black Sea and the other places mentioned are along the lower reaches of the rivers Don and Volga. The mortality was so heavy that 'they could not bury' the dead; the victims were 'among the Bessermens, and among the Tartars, and among the Armenians and the Abkhazians', who were peoples living on the eastern side of the Black Sea, although the

Bessermens were in north-eastern Russia and so not part of the population of the Caucasian region. The victims were also 'among the Jews, and among the European foreigners', indicating that the merchant communities on the Black Sea were affected. An Arab writer, Ibn al-Wardi, was told by Muslim merchants that in the autumn of 1346 an epidemic was raging in the land of the Uzbeks, a term which then described the territory of the Golden Horde, and that it spread to the Crimea. Gabriele de Mussis, in Piacenza in Lombardy, also collected information on the origin of the epidemic and he, too, placed it in the lands of the Golden Horde. The disease may have reached the region of the steppes from northern Iraq or Kurdistan.[1]

For an epidemic to develop from that region's plague reservoir the disease had to emerge from animal burrows to infect the human population. Analysis of data collected in the twentieth century in the Kazakhstan desert has shown that plague erupted roughly two years after a rise in the number of inhabited gerbil burrows. Plague epidemics develop after a surge in its host populations of rodents and other burrowing mammals, for their larger numbers allow fleas to transfer more readily from one host to another, and the bacteria thrive.[2] An increase in the numbers of rodents may follow wetter winters and springs, which increase the numbers of plants and insects on which the animals feed. With the greater number of hosts, infected fleas were more likely to come into contact with herdsmen, or those passing through as traders and camping for the night. Travelling there in the early 1330s, the Moroccan Ibn Battuta found that the merchant caravans set out after dawn and halted in the mid-morning, resuming their journey after noon and then stopping in the evening. The wagons were pulled by two or more horses, or by oxen or camels: the one which he rode in was pulled by three camels. When the travellers halted 'they loose the horses, camels and oxen from the waggons and drive them out to pasture at liberty, night and day'. That allowed the caravan's animals to wander through areas where the rodents' burrows were, and the environment in the wagons was warm because the wooden frameworks on them were covered with 'felt or blanket-cloth' to protect the passengers; those carrying the baggage were also 'covered with a form of tent'. The region contained 'large numbers of animals ... without keepers or guards'.[3] Infected fleas could transfer from rodents to the travellers' animals and then into the warmth of textiles or grain in the covered wagons.

An army provided a far larger and more concentrated mobile group, consisting of soldiers, support troops and camp followers, with their riding and draught animals, moving and camping together. When undertaking a siege they remained encamped for weeks or months, while the defenders were trapped in one place maintained by a diminishing stock of food and fuel; the conditions of both besiegers and besieged deteriorated the longer that the siege continued and they created ever-larger deposits of filth. Throughout the pandemic armies were blamed for spreading plague.

In 1343 Janibeg, the Khan of the Golden Horde, resolved finally to end trade with the Christians and he expelled them from Tana, at the mouth of the River Don, where the Venetians were based, and then moved on to besiege the fortified port town of Kaffa (now Foedosiya) on the Black Sea. Kaffa was a Genoese colony which had expanded considerably over the previous hundred years or so; in 1332 Ibn Battuta described it as 'a great city along the sea coast inhabited by Christians, most of them Genoese'. He admired its markets and the 'wonderful harbour with about two hundred vessels in it, both ships of war and trading vessels, small and large, for it is one of the world's celebrated ports'.[4] Janibeg failed to take the town in 1343 but tried again in 1345 and that siege dragged on into 1346, when plague erupted in the Mongol army and spread to the Genoese and Venetian defenders. Contemporaries took this to be the origin of the epidemic in Europe, for some of the besieged broke the blockade and sailed away, stopping at Constantinople to replenish their supplies before setting out for home through the

Bosphorus and into the Mediterranean. De Mussis wrote that the Mongols 'worn out with this pestilential disease ... ordered the corpses to be placed upon their engines and thrown into the city of Kaffa'. That is not improbable, but whether it was the effective or sole way by which the disease was spread to the defenders, and hence into the Mediterranean basin, may be doubted. Thwarted by the stubbornness of the defenders and the plague ravaging his troops, Janibeg was forced to raise the siege and withdraw the remnants of his army. Plague broke out in Constantinople in July 1347 and over the next couple of years spread across Asia Minor and the Levant to Egypt and the Nile valley, through Mesopotamia to the Persian Gulf, into the Arabian peninsula, and to Cyprus.[5]

The Venetian galleys from Kaffa sailed into the Adriatic and probably touched at Venice's colonies on the Dalmatian coast. Plague broke out in Split and Dubrovnik before reaching Venice itself in January 1348. The Genoese had sailed on and in late September 1347 landed at Messina, Sicily's largest city. The plague outbreak which followed was the beginning of the Black Death epidemic in Europe. As it developed the inhabitants fled from the city and, according to a Franciscan friar, Michael of Piazza: 'the people of Messina dispersed over the whole island of Sicily and with them the disease, so that innumerable people died'.[6] Sardinia and Corsica were infected before the end of the year, as was Reggio di Calabria on the mainland, and by early 1348 the plague had reached Pisa and Genoa. It then spread remorselessly across the Italian peninsula, afflicting both cities and the countryside. By the end of the year it had reached Piedmont; only Milan among Italy's larger cities appears to have escaped lightly. Seaborne traders had carried the disease to Marseille by November 1347. With a population of perhaps 15,000, the city was an important commercial hub, with trading connections to the ports of Italy and the western Mediterranean, and into France along the Rhone valley. Plague was reported in Aix-en-Provence about a month later and before the end of the year had reached Avignon and Arles and, crossing from the Mediterranean littoral to that of the Bay of Biscay, it had reached Bordeaux by the spring of 1348. The papacy had been resident in Avignon since 1309; the pope, Clement VI, survived the epidemic.

The pattern was set in those early months as the epidemic rolled across the landscape, jumping between towns but invading the rural communities as well. Only a few areas may have been left unscathed by the 'great mortality'. Awareness of the terrible death-toll and perhaps the speed with which it advanced ran ahead of the disease. Governments maintained contacts in other countries and merchants kept a wide-ranging network of agents to provide the news and information that were essential to their businesses. Yet the dreadful tidings which were passed on were not enough to encourage effective preventative measures to be taken. No strategy could be devised by governments, civic or national, in the time available and with the knowledge which they possessed. Other epidemics had struck occasionally, but, however deadly, they were far less devastating and widespread than the plague. Perhaps the practice of isolating infected houses had been deployed in such outbreaks and could have been the reason for Milan's relatively light mortality in 1348. But that example was not followed, even if it was known beyond the city, and only the threat of the disease itself could halt commercial traffic, for no international co-operation to prevent it was feasible. The entire continent was overrun by the plague, which in 1353 reached the Russian lands bordering on the Kipchak Khanate, having, as it were, gone full circle around Europe.

Death tolls were difficult to establish, even in general terms. Statistics of births and deaths were not kept and where lists of households were compiled they related to taxpayers and not to the whole population. Even so, contemporaries felt the need to estimate the numbers who died and the proportion of the population which succumbed to the disease, as a way of illustrating the scale of the disaster and its impact. Some writers put the proportion as high as

90 per cent, such as Gilles li Muisis in Tournai, who wrote that in many cities, towns and settlements, where there had been 20,000 inhabitants before the outbreak, scarcely 2,000 survived, and in smaller towns and villages a population of 1,500 was reduced to barely 100. His later summary moderated this estimate, yet he noted that the mortality 'was so great that in many places a third of the population died, elsewhere a quarter or a half, and in several areas only one or two people out of ten survived'.[7] A letter from the papal court at Avignon believed that at least a half of the city's population had died and that in the suburbs 'one might imagine that there is not one survivor'. In England a letter from Edward III to the bishops written in August 1349 referred to 'the few people who still survive'. Thomas Walsingham, a monk at St Albans abbey, noted that it was 'calculated by several people that barely a tenth of mankind remained alive', and that was supported by the estimate of John of Reading, a monk at Westminster, who wrote that 'Scarcely a tenth of the population survived'. A chronicle of the cathedral priory of Rochester was more plausible, with the judgement that the epidemic 'destroyed more than a third of the men, women and children' and a chronicler at Malmesbury abbey thought that over England as a whole a fifth of the men, women and children were 'carried to burial'.[8] Without even mildly credible estimates for a city or region, a continent-wide estimate would surely have seemed impossibly difficult, yet Clement VI did ask for such an assessment and he received it, suggesting that however bad things were in some places, the church's organisation remained effective. The totals produced in response to his request were a pre-plague population of Europe of 75 million and a death-toll of 23,840,000, or roughly 32 per cent.[9]

People responded in a variety of ways to the likelihood of imminent death, after an agonising illness and almost uncertainly unshriven, as the priests could not attend so many people within the short time between the appearance of the symptoms and death, and they themselves were victims. Giovanni Boccaccio used the plague as the setting for a collection of stories published as *The Decameron*. In setting the scene for the telling of the tales he described how the citizens of Florence reacted to the epidemic, identifying several types of behaviour. Those who could leave the city and had somewhere to go went away, arguing that going to the countryside would allow them to avoid 'the disgraceful example set by other people and live virtuously' in fresh air, with nature all around them and provisions available. They were aware that 'the labourers in the fields are dying just as the townsfolk are; but as there are fewer houses and fewer people about than we have here in town, it's all that much less distressing', and better than 'staring at the empty buildings in this city!'. Boccaccio described those who left the city as 'totally ruthless ... heedless of anything but their own skins', while admitting that they 'no doubt chose the safest option'.[10]

Some of Florence's citizens stayed in the city and formed a group, establishing themselves in a house free from all plague victims where 'they would refrain from speaking to anyone or from gleaning any news from outside that related to deaths or plague-victims'. That approach should have helped them to maintain their morale, but it required resources, because there they would 'enjoy the good life, partaking of the daintiest fare and the choicest of wines – all in the strictest moderation – and shunning all debauchery ... rather did they bask in music and such other pleasures as were at their disposal'.[11]

Others behaved in quite a different way, on the basis that 'the surest remedy to a disease of this order was to drink their fill, have a good time, sing to their hearts' content, live it up, give free rein to their appetites – and make light of all that was going on'. Day and night they could be found in a tavern or similar establishment drinking 'like sponges' and 'carousing all the more in other people's houses', wherever they could have fun, 'as if there were no tomorrow'. Most people had stopped protecting their property, or it was empty because the occupants had died or fled, and so there were many houses which anyone could walk into from the streets and make themselves at home 'just as if they owned the place'. Indeed, they included 'the great palaces, the fine houses and gorgeous mansions that once boasted full households, now bereft of their masters and mistresses, abandoned by all, down to the humblest menial!'. But those who enjoyed such dissolute living were nevertheless wise enough to avoid all contact with the sick. Nobody was likely to be punished because the normal orders could not be enforced; the magistrates were dead or had been taken ill, or they had been deprived of those officers who would normally have implemented their orders, and the collapse of authority 'left everyone free to do precisely as they pleased'.[12]

Between those who withdrew to lead a quiet life and those who preferred to carouse were many others who 'adhered to a middle way ... neither following the frugal regimen of the first group nor letting themselves go in the drunken, dissolute life-style of the second. They partook of their fill but no more and, instead of shutting themselves away, they would go about holding flowers to their noses or fragrant herbs, or spices of various kinds, in the belief that such aromas worked wonders for the brain (the seat of health)'. The nosegays helped them to avoid the worst effects of the noxious atmosphere, 'charged with the stench of corpses, it reeked of sickness and medication'.[13]

In each of those groups some fell sick and 'those whose health remained sound left them to languish unattended. One citizen avoided the next, there was scarcely a man who would take care of his neighbour, kinsmen would seldom if ever call on each other, and even then would keep their distance.' Worse than that 'a man would desert his own brother, uncle would forsake his nephew, sister her brother, and often a wife her husband'. It was even the case that parents would avoid visiting and caring for their children. Yet the sick were 'a number beyond counting' and they needed nursing and care; perhaps they were able to call upon their friends or servants, although Boccaccio believed that many succumbed who might have recovered if they had received help. He was critical of the servants, who were 'few and far between, even though they were recruited with absurdly inflated wages', while admitting that 'Quite often in the course of his duties the servant lost his life along with his wages.' They were 'men and women of the commonest sort, for the most part totally untrained', who did little more than handing to the patient such objects as he or she asked for, or watching the patient die, and yet 'all too many passed away without so much as a single witness'. The absence of family and friends, and the shortage of servants, led to an unprecedented practice, for when a woman fell ill she did not object to being tended by a man, and he could be 'any male, never mind his age, and displaying to him any part of her anatomy without embarrassment, just as she would do with another of her sex, if her invalid condition required it'. Because of the death-toll 'the survivors were virtually forced to engage in practices which were totally at variance with the traditional Florentine way of life.' Normal funeral rituals and procedures had to be abandoned. Grieving was replaced by 'quips and jollity more suited to a festive gathering' and few people accompanied the coffin; perhaps no more than ten or a dozen neighbours did so, preceded by only half-a-dozen clergy, but sometimes 'none at all'. The pall-bearers were no longer prominent and distinguished citizens and the function was undertaken by 'a tribe of pallbearers, people of the commonest sort who liked to call themselves undertakers' who were doing the task for money. Burial was at the nearest church, not the one which the deceased had requested, and the corpse was deposited in the first grave which could be found with enough space 'without too much effort being wasted on a lengthy or solemn requiem'.[14]

The poorer people could manage only to place the body in the street, helped by bearers if they could find any, so that someone going along it, especially early in the morning, would see any number of corpses. Few coffins were available and planks had to serve in their place on which to place a corpse, and a bier might carry two or three bodies. Priests who left a house to accompany a body to the grave often found that several pall-bearers joined their procession along the way, so that they had half-a-dozen or more bodies to bury when they reached the burial ground. Corpses arrived at the churches daily, indeed 'practically hour by hour', and as the graveyards became filled enormous pits were dug, in which bodies were interred 'by the hundred; here they were packed in layers, the way goods are stowed in a ship's hold, and each layer would get a thin covering of earth until the pit was filled up'.[15]

Florence itself was Boccaccio's chief concern, but he also described conditions in the countryside. Those in the market towns were little different from the situation in the city, albeit 'on a smaller scale'. In the remote villages and in the fields the labourers, those 'poor penniless wretches, and their households died like brute-beasts rather than human beings; night and day, with never a doctor to attend them, no sort of domestic help, they would pass away, some indoors, others out on the roads or among their crops'. Their behaviour became like that of the feckless citizens of Florence, neglecting their affairs and possessions, their crops and livestock, not taking in the harvest and letting animals roam the fields to scavenge, while they 'bent their best efforts to dissipating whatever came to hand'.[16]

Boccaccio's account is the most coherent and considered of the descriptions of a community under severe stress during the Black Death, but other chroniclers told of similar reactions elsewhere. The chronicle of the monastery of Neuberg, in south Austria, recorded that there, as in Tuscany, the nobles and citizens 'seeking to escape death, took themselves to safer places', but as they were infected before they left that was to no avail, and they died. That chronicle also noted that 'thoughtful men resolved that they should try to cheer each other up with comfort and merrymaking, so that they were not overwhelmed by depression'. That should have been helped by the fact that the best wine was now easily obtainable, but 'all those who indulged in it to excess behaved as if they were mad, beating and abusing people for no reason'.[17] The great chronicle of France kept by the monks of Saint-Denis recounted that two of their number passed through a town where the strategy of cheerfulness was being employed and the inhabitants were dancing and making merry. They explained to the monks that they were aware that in nearby places people were dying of the plague and they hoped to keep it away by their merrymaking. But when the monks returned they found very few people and were told that a hailstorm had hit the town and killed some of the citizens, which had ended the jollifications.[18]

The more common reaction to the pestilence was resentful aggression rather than cheerfulness. To the medieval mind events such as epidemics or natural disasters were the result of a conjunction of the planets, or were sent by God as a punishment that was inflicted on a sinful people, and as a warning to repent. Flagellation to appease God's wrath and so lessen the suffering had emerged as the millennium had approached and again in 1260 in Italy at a time of stress, spreading to Germany, where it developed as an anti-clerical and anarchic movement, reappearing intermittently thereafter. During the Black Death the practice again began in Germany, extending into the Low Countries and parts of France. It drew the opposition of the church and was condemned by the papacy; associated with the movement were outbursts of anti-Semitic fervour and horrific massacres of Jews. The persecution was justified on the assumption that foul water from poisoned wells was the source of the disease and that the Jews were carrying out the poisoning. Governments, as well as the church, were alarmed at the mass enthusiasm which was aroused by the flagellants and by attacks on the Jews, and took steps to prohibit the movement, insofar as they were able. The pope banned the flagellants in October 1349.

Neglect of the sick was common. The pope's personal physician, Guy de Chauliac, recalled that the plague was 'most humiliating for the physicians, who were unable to render any assistance, all the more as, for fear of infection, they did not venture to visit the patients, and if they did could do no good and consequently earn no fees'.[19] In Padua it was said that priests refused to visit the sick, as did the notaries and judges, and so the victims could not make a will. Changes in burial practices under the pressure of the numbers of dead and the fear of the unknown disease were commented on by several chroniclers. Gabriele de' Mussis in Piacenza wrote of the mass funerals and lack of burial space, so that 'pits had to be dug in colonnades and piazzas, where nobody had ever been buried before'. He also noted that no one would nurse a sick victim of the disease, even close friends, and the physicians would not visit them, while priests 'panic stricken, administered the sacraments with fear and trembling'. The social equals of the dead would not attend a funeral for fear of being struck down, only a short service was held, without a mass, and there was no 'prayer, trumpet or bell' to summon mourners.[20] In Padua many corpses 'at a price, were buried by poor wretches, without priests or candles'. At Tournai, Gilles li Muisis noted that 'they died especially in the streets in the market areas, and more people died in narrow lanes than in broad streets and open squares'. The civic authorities there tried to maintain funeral practices as they had been before the epidemic, ordering that the body should be buried in a coffin or box, the bell tolled in accordance with the deceased's status, and the customary masses sung on Sundays. This could not be sustained as the numbers rose and another proclamation issued soon afterwards accepted that no bells were to be tolled or pall placed over the bier, no mourners were to be invited to a funeral and only two people were to pray for the dead and attend the vigils and the mass. A stipulation was included with those orders which was aimed at curtailing the citizens' sinfulness, with the direction that no one was to make or sell dice, or play any game which involved rolling or using dice, and when playing games 'there should be none of the usual swearing by God or the saints'.[21]

Those who survived should perhaps have been lifted by a great sense of relief and have been aware that, in cold mercenary terms, they were better off, for wealth and property were now distributed among fewer people. Yet Jean de Venette's account of the plague in France included the assessment that 'after the plague men became more miserly and grasping, although many owned more than they had before. They were also more greedy and quarrelsome, involving themselves in brawls, disputes and lawsuits.' The chronicle of Neuberg used similar terms in describing similar reactions: 'Survivors of the plague, apparently putting the terrible experience right out of their minds, embroiled themselves in many disputes and quarrels over the wealth of the dead, or shamelessly went beyond the bounds of decency and, in many cases, lived with no reference to the law.'[22] Social norms had been discarded during the epidemic and it took time for them to be re-established.

The Neuberg chronicle also noted that foreigners were blamed for the disease and so they were not allowed to stay in the inns, and it was ordered that the merchants 'by whom the pestilence was being spread' should leave the area immediately. In the Padua region 'cities banned the entry of all outsiders, with the result that merchants were unable to travel from city to city'. Ordinances issued in the Tuscan city of Pistoia in 1348 forbade access to the city to those coming from an infected area or anyone carrying or transporting linen or woollen cloth, reflecting the suspicion that the disease emanated from textiles. Venice established a sanitary council in the same year, which had powers to intercept infected ships and detain them, their crews and passengers at an island in the lagoon. All the city gates of Marseille were kept closed, except for two small posterns, which must have seriously restricted movement in and out of the city.[23] Isolation and restrictions on travel were to become fundamentals of plague policies in the future, aimed at preventing the spread of the disease, or at least restricting it. These were the first steps towards the development of a policy, although taken after the onset of the disease rather than in anticipation of its arrival.

No such measures were adopted in England, despite the inexorable advance of the disease across France towards the Channel ports. On 1 July Edward III's fourteen-year-old daughter Joan, on her way to marry Peter, heir to the Castilian throne, died in Bordeaux of the plague.[24] Commercial interests would have opposed a prohibition or even restriction of trade across the Channel, the Bay of Biscay and the North Sea. The trade from Gascony alone was carried in between 150 and 200 ships annually, and as roughly a half of the wine from the region was shipped to London, it is reasonable to suppose that was reflected in the number of vessels. Even though the city's merchants would have been as aware of the growing threat of contagion as the court, they would have objected to a ban on shipping so that they could complete as much business as possible before the disease struck. Most seaborne trade was conducted during the summer months, avoiding the seasonal risks of stormy seas, and so there would have been little chance of prohibiting shipping during the summer of 1348. The government's own interests were tied to the continuance of sailings between London and the continent, so that its forces and garrisons in France would continue to be supplied during the phase of the Hundred Years War that followed Edward III's victory at Crécy in 1346 and the capture of Calais in the following year.

Edward planned to keep Calais and consolidate the English hold on the town and the surrounding area, known as the 'pale', by maintaining a substantial garrison. He also encouraged English people to settle there and so make it a predominantly English town, and granted it commercial privileges. Calais was both prepared as a base for future campaigns and raids into enemy territory and developed as an English colony. Its stocks of provisions and military stores were built up, requiring frequent voyages from London and the ports of south-east England, especially Sandwich, to the town, as most vessels could carry only a small load on each voyage. Ships transporting horses could carry on average only 13 men, while the capacity of those without horses averaged fewer than 20 men. Even as the plague spread, both English and French governments planned military activity in response to events in Flanders, where those elements in the cloth-making towns who in 1339 had defied the Count of Flanders and declared Edward III to be their king were gradually being suppressed. Edward was concerned for the security of Calais and at the end of September 1348 despatched a force of 400 men there; early in the following month more troops were summoned and ships were commandeered to transport them. Edward himself arrived at Calais in the middle of November. Clearly, there had been no sense of a need to sever communications with the near continent and extend the earlier military truce, even though the plague had erupted in Paris during the summer. It reached Calais in December.[25]

A quite separate consideration was that a government which attempted to prevent the plague from reaching England could be regarded as trying to thwart the divine purpose of punishing a sinful people. That would risk provoking hostility from its own subjects and the church as well as the deity. The clergy and members of the monastic orders needed to look no further than the court in recent years for the kind of sinfulness which could have provoked the wrath of God. In 1328 Edward III married Philippa, daughter of William, Count of Hainault. From relative financial stringencies during the early years of their marriage, she came to develop a taste for fashionable clothes and luxuries, although of course she was doing no more than maintaining the dignity and splendour expected of the court. As is the way with such things, what the queen did, so did the members of her entourage, some of whom had come with her from Hainault, and those who sought to emulate them. The ladies' clothes now in favour were in the French style and more figure-hugging than the loose gowns previously worn. Those styles of dress and the behaviour which was assumed to go with them attracted unfavourable comment, as new fashions usually do. In 1344 the Westminster chronicler wrote that:

> Ever since the arrival of the Hainaulters about eighteen years ago the English have madly followed outlandish ways, changing their grotesque fashions of clothing yearly. They have abandoned the old, decent style of long, full garments for clothes which are short, tight, impractical, slashed, every part laced, strapped, or buttoned up, with the sleeves of the gowns and the tippets of the hoods hanging down to absurd lengths, so that, if the truth be told, their clothes and footwear make them look more like torturers, or even demons, than men.

Even the clergy had adopted those fashions. The women dressed in such tight clothes that 'they wore a fox tail hanging down inside their skirts at the back, to hide their arses'. This the chronicler judged to be 'the sin of pride' which 'must surely bring down misfortune in the future'.[26] Things got worse, according to Thomas Walsingham, who wrote that in the aftermath of the victories in France in 1346-7 and the ransoms received for high-ranking French prisoners: 'Then began the English ladies to wax wanton in the vesture of the French women; and as the latter grieved to have lost their goods, so the former rejoiced to have obtained them.'[27]

The citizens could see the court's exuberant dress and lavish expenditure at the tournaments and feasts favoured by Edward III, which indeed were a major part of the royal displays which he promoted and in which he took an active part. They were held around the country and in London itself, in Smithfield and Cheapside. The king favoured exotic and fanciful themes for the events; at a tournament in Cheapside in 1343 he and 12 companions dressed as the pope and cardinals. Ladies accompanied their knights and were adorned in fancy dress appropriate to the theme of the event. Tournaments continued to be held during 1348, despite the fact that the plague was spreading through France: at Reading and Bury St Edmunds in February, at Lichfield and Eltham in May, at Windsor in June and at Canterbury in July.[28] While they provided good business for the London merchants who supplied fine fabrics, jewels and accessories, as well as food and drink, moralists took a dim view of such proceedings at a time when abstinence and penitence were surely called for, if God's wrath was to be assuaged. Henry Knighton recorded the popular reaction: 'A murmuring and great complaint arose among the people, because whenever and wherever tournaments were held a troop of ladies would turn up dressed in a variety of extraordinary male clothing, as if taking part in a play.' As many as 40 or 50 of them would participate 'representing the showiest and more beautiful (but not the most virtuous) women of the whole realm'. Wearing bright tunics and short hoods, with belts studded with gold and silver and daggers in pouches, they rode horses with 'elaborate trappings' to the site where the tournament was to be held. From this Knighton moved on to a judgement of their morals: 'They spent and wasted their goods and (according to the common report) abused their bodies in wantonness and scurrilous licentiousness. They neither feared God nor blushed at the criticism of the people, but took the marriage bond lightly and were deaf to the demands of modesty.' He interpreted the heavy rain and thunderstorms which struck a tournament as divine punishments, but in hindsight the plague could be judged to have been the real chastisement for such sinfulness.[29]

Unlike the court, the church did react to the crisis. The plague was first noticed in England at the small port of Melcombe, in Dorset, probably a few days before 24 June, although Knighton placed its first appearance at Southampton. It would have taken time for the nature of the disease to be recognised and for the news of its arrival to spread, and so an instruction issued by the Archbishop of York, William Zouche, on 28 July, may not have been a direct response to intelligence from the west country. He required that devout processions were to be held twice a week throughout the diocese and that a special prayer should be included in the mass every day 'for allaying the plague and pestilence'. In the preamble was the observation: 'There can be no one who does not know, since it is now public knowledge, how great a mortality, pestilence and infection of the air are now threatening various parts of the world, and especially England; and this is surely caused by the sins of men.' Perhaps prompted by this, or by his own chaplains and clergy, Edward III requested the Archbishop of Canterbury, John Stratford, to compose prayers against plague for use throughout the province of Canterbury; after Stratford's death on 23 August the prior of Christchurch, Canterbury, carried out the task. He wrote that he was afraid that England 'because of the growing pride and corruption of its subjects, and their numberless sins' would suffer 'the pestilences and wretched mortalities of men which have flared up in other regions'. On 28 September he sent the prayers to the Bishop of London, who was to ensure that they were 'effectively observed' within his own diocese and to distribute them to the other dioceses of the province.[30] As his letter was dated on a Sunday, it is likely that it was on the next Sunday, 5 October, that most Londoners heard those prayers for the first time, in the parish churches across the city. That was all that could be done in the face of the impending catastrophe.

4

LONDON'S AGONY

The chronicler Henry Knighton's response to the wet summer of 1348 was that God had punished the people's merrymaking by 'opening the floodgates of heaven with rain and thunder and livid lightning and by unwanted blasts of tempestuous winds'.[1] London's population was generally well supplied, although prices inevitably rose after a poor harvest, which must have been expected as the rain continued to fall. Yet the far greater menace that had spread inexorably across Europe had arrived at the south coast ports of Melcombe and Southampton. The disease dispersed inland across Dorset and Hampshire during that sodden summer. A chronicler of Malmesbury abbey wrote that the plague 'wretchedly killed innumerable people in Dorset, Devon and Somerset', and that 'very few were left alive' in Bristol. It advanced northwards from Bristol along the Severn valley and the citizens of Gloucester attempted to keep it out by closing their gates against travellers, but to no avail.[2] Either along the road network from the west and south-west, by coastal vessels, or perhaps by a separate source of infection from the continent, London was vulnerable to the disease.

Towards the end of October 1348 plague reached this densely packed and busy city, where 'people superabounded' and numerous rodents and their parasites could also subsist. Extant records for the summer and early autumn contain nothing to suggest that life was other than normal and a letter issued by William Edington, the Bishop of Winchester, from his palace in Southwark on 24 October, mentioned that the disease had begun 'a savage attack on the coastal areas of England' and added that 'We are struck by terror lest (may God avert it!) this brutal disease should rage in any part of our city or diocese.' His diocese included Southwark and had the disease been present there or in the city anywhere he would surely have been aware of it and have said so. Robert of Avesbury was a commissary clerk on the Archbishop of Canterbury's staff at Lambeth Palace and he stated that the pestilence 'arrived in London at about the feast of All Saints [1 November]'.[3] On 14 November a papal indult was issued permitting Londoners of both sexes to choose death-bed confessors, a recognition that their parish priest may have been incapacitated or have died before their own death became imminent. It reflected the experience of areas already afflicted and news that the disease had reached London must have been sent in early November in order to have reached the papal court at Avignon by the middle of the month.[4] Geoffrey le Baker was a clerk at Swinbrook in Oxfordshire and he dated the beginning of the outbreak in London to 'around Michaelmas [29 September]', but that does not match the other sources and may have been a case of assigning such an event to one of the year's quarter days, because he was uncertain when the outbreak had actually begun.[5]

Wills proved in the city's Court of Hustings were drawn up by only a few citizens, not a representative cross-section of the population. Nevertheless, those who made such wills were as affected by the pestilence as the rest of the inhabitants and so the dates on which the wills were drawn up provide evidence of the onset and progress of the plague. Of the six wills with dates in October 1348, four were compiled in the last five days of the month, ten were made in November and then 27 in December. The usual practice was for a will to be drawn up when the testator was close to death, not well in advance. The coming of the epidemic presented the citizens with the stark choice of anticipating death and making the legal preparations for it, or waiting until the symptoms showed themselves, with the risk that no-one would be prepared to come to the infected house to draw up the document. In the case of John le Hicchen, a pepperer of St Anthonin's parish, the traditional practice was followed, for his will was dated 28 November and he died on 2 December.[6]

Because of the speed and scale of the mortality in the final couple of months of the year there was concern that the churchyards would soon be filled. In normal conditions bones could be lifted and transferred to an ossuary to clear space for new interments, but the urgent need for such an unprecedented number of burials presumably did not allow time for that to be done. Churchyards in the City centre were small, reflecting the size of the parishes and their population, but those outside the walled City were larger. Whatever the space that was available and the arrangements followed, in London 'so great a multitude eventually died there that all the cemeteries of the aforesaid city were insufficient for the burial of the dead. For which reason very many were compelled to bury their dead in places unseemly and not hallowed or blessed; for some, it was said, cast the corpses into the river.'[7]

New and larger cemeteries were urgently needed and three were brought into use, all of them outside the city walls. In East Smithfield, to the north of the Tower, an area of about four acres was made available by John Cory, a clerk in the royal service, who had been acquiring sites in the area since 1346, probably on the king's behalf. He acted 'at the instigation of substantial men of the City', yet initially his plans were opposed by the king, possibly because the land had been acquired with the intention that he would found a monastery there. When that opposition was removed Cory then required the agreement of the prior of Holy Trinity as owner of part of the ground, which he obtained, and so the site was designated the New Churchyard of Holy Trinity.[8] It was dedicated by the Bishop of London, Ralph Stratford, who had been bishop since 1340 and was a nephew of John Stratford, Archbishop of Canterbury, who had died on 23 August 1348. The bishop himself acquired three acres of land for a burial ground, which he 'inclosed with a wall of brick'; known as Nomanneslond, it lay north-west of the City, to the east of St John's priory. This may have been in use before the end of December 1348.[9]

The third of the new burial grounds was Spitalcroft in West Smithfield, just south of Nomanneslond, and it was by far the largest of the three. The site was acquired by the prominent courtier and soldier Sir Walter de Mauny, who was a boon companion of Edward III. He had arrived in England from Hainault with the queen and by the late 1340s he was on the way to making a considerable fortune, based on the king's favour and his success as a commander in the Hundred Years War, which yielded booty and ransoms. Given that the Hainaulters' conduct and mode of dress at court was thought to have provoked God's wrath, it may have been thought that one of the most prominent of them should provide a resting place for the victims as an act of penance as well as charity. When de Mauny asked his staff if they knew of a suitable site, one of them told him, 'The master of the hospital of St. Bartholomew in Smithfield and his brethren have a place enclosed outside Smithfield aforesaid which is called Spitell Crofte where you might very well be able to obtain the accomplishment of your devotion.' He came to an agreement with the priory and took a lease of the land; the arrangements were completed around the turn of the year. Sir Walter later recalled that he had established the cemetery for 'poor strangers and others', which may imply those who were not long-term residents and so were outside the parish system. It covered 13¼ acres and until then had been open to the citizens for recreation and sports. The Bishop of London went with Sir Walter and 'a great multitude' in a 'solemn procession' to bless the cemetery, which was in use by 26 January 1349. The site was dedicated to the Holy and Undivided Trinity and the Annunciation of Our Lady and a will of 3 March referred to a chapel there, although that anticipated its erection, for it was not until the Feast of the Annunciation on 25 March that the bishop, de Mauny, the mayor (John Lovekyn), the sheriffs, aldermen 'and many others, nearly all barefooted and with a most devout procession', went to the cemetery. The bishop preached a sermon on the word 'Hail' and he, de Mauny and the mayor laid the foundations of the chapel, which was 'begun to be built on the day of the Annunciation'.[10] Spitalcroft was taken for the purpose because it was available immediately and its size and position, just outside the City, were ideal. So was its configuration; a gently sloping plot of land which drained south-westwards to a brook at the side of Smithfield. The fact that the three burial grounds were brought into use around the turn of the year suggests that the benefactors reacted to a concerted request, rather than acting independently on their own initiative.

The king returned from France on 7 November 1348 and on the 23rd ordered that the port of London and the other principal harbours around the south and east coast should be closed; that was a case of shutting the stable door after the horse had well and truly bolted and perhaps could have been implemented much earlier. He also issued writs for a parliament, but it did not meet and on 1 January he postponed it until April, because the plague 'has so grown in strength that men are fearful to go there [Westminster] safely'. The hearings of the courts of King's Bench and Common Pleas were suspended in January; the king wrote to the justices explaining that because of 'the terrible pestilence of vast deadliness, daily increasing in the city of London and neighbouring parts, we do not wish any danger to threaten you, your serjeants, clerks and other officers'. The king's letter of 10 March further postponing the meeting of parliament justified his decision on similar grounds, because the pestilence 'is increasing with more than its usual severity, in Westminster and in the City of London and the surrounding districts'.[11] The king and Bishop Edington, his Treasurer, may have stayed in London during December. Edward then went to the priory of Merton to celebrate Epiphany, when the celebrations included jousts and games, which suggests that the courtiers were not unduly restrained despite the unfolding disaster.[12] Edington also left London after Christmas and spent the rest of the winter at his rural manor houses. He and the king both survived the epidemic, as did de Mauny, Lovekyn and Stratford, who died in 1354.

The archbishops of Canterbury did not fare so well. The new archbishop was John Offord, who was nominated by the king on 24 September 1348. He died at Tottenham on 20 May in the following year, perhaps of plague. His successor was Thomas Bradwardine, who held the position for 38 days before succumbing to the pestilence in Canterbury. Simon Islip was then appointed, despite not having held a bishopric; the number of suitable candidates was limited because of deaths of senior clergymen during the epidemic. In April the prior of Westminster Abbey died, as did 26 of the monks, and his successor, Simon de Langham, was promoted to abbot only seven weeks after being appointed prior. He served as abbot until 1362, when he was appointed Bishop of Ely and four years later he was translated to the archbishopric of Canterbury. The deaths of the senior clergy during the epidemic provided vacancies and rapid promotions for the survivors.

That applied to other organisations. London's shearmen submitted ordinances for approval by the mayor and aldermen; of the eight names appended to the document, six were struck through and marked as dead, sick, or living outside the City.[13] During 1349 eight of the guild of cutlers' wardens died. All six wardens of the hatters' guild died between December 1347 and July 1350 and all the goldsmiths' guild's wardens between 1347 and 1349; the grocers' guild's first fatality was on 2 December 1348 and its overall loss during the epidemic was just under 30 per cent of the membership. Three of the mercers' wardens who left office in June 1348 survived and the fourth died; of their replacements, one certainly died and another survived, and the other two may have survived.[14]

   The painters in London experienced a high death-toll. They were
well enough organised before the end of the thirteenth century to
have come together in a body which in 1283 issued ordinances
as 'the goodmen of the painting craft of London'. Many of them
lived in Cripplegate Without and became associated with the
Guild of St Luke at St Giles's church. During the early fourteenth
century the Stockwell family gained some prominence within the
craft, with five of them recorded as painters in the first half of the
century. Walter Stockwell made his will in 1348 and it may be
that the family, or at least its menfolk, was wiped out by the Black
Death. Walter's eight-year-old daughter Agnes was committed to
the guardianship of Thomas de Bourneham, also a painter, which
implies that no member of the family was left to take care of
her. The Porkele family of painters was also a large one and its
members, too, disappear from the records after the middle of the
century. John de Mymmes, an 'ymaginour', or painter, and his
wife Mathilda, who was also a painter, lived some distance away,
in the parish of St Mildred, Bread Street, adjoining Cheapside. He
made his will on 19 March 1349 and had died by 10 April, when
Mathilda's will was drawn up, bequeathing the best one-third of
her tools and copies for picture-making to her apprentice, William,
who was to be sent to work under a Brother at Bermondsey
Abbey. John had appointed Roger Osekyn, a pepperer who was a
neighbour in Bread Street, as guardian of one of their daughters,
Isabella, but Roger's will was dated just three days after Mathilda's
and he died in the epidemic, along with John and Mathilda and
probably their other daughter, Alice. Isabella survived to maturity;
the fate of William the apprentice is not known.[15]

   The chroniclers described the progress of the plague in general
terms. Robert of Avesbury wrote that in London it 'daily deprived
many of life' and Thomas Walsingham, in St Albans, may have
been describing the situation in London when he commented that
the pestilence 'grew so strong that men and women dropped dead
while walking in the streets, and in innumerable households and

many villages not one person was left alive'. John of Reading's summary was also presented in a broad way: 'And there was in those days death without sorrow, marriage without affection, self-imposed penance, want without poverty, and flight without escape. How many who fled from the face of the pestilence were already infected and did not escape the slaughter.'[16]

Around the end of September 1349 more than 120 men practising flagellation arrived in London, most of them from the Low Countries. Thomas Walsingham was so fascinated by their practices that he described them in some detail. They processed through the streets twice a day, four of them singing and the remainder chanting the responses. They went barefoot, wearing only a loin-cloth which reached to the ankles and a hood painted with a red cross on both the front and the back. Each of them carried a whip with three thongs, and each thong was knotted, with a sharp implement that projected on both sides, with which they struck themselves. Three times during each procession they prostrated themselves and while continuing the singing, each would step over the others, lashing the man beneath him with his whip, until all of them had been hit in this way. When they put on their usual clothes and returned to their lodgings they continued to wear their hats and carry their whips. Walsingham described them as 'noble men of foreign birth, who lashed themselves viciously on their naked bodies until the blood flowed, now weeping, now singing'.[17] The group in London seems not to have attracted support and, as the Jews had been expelled more than half a century earlier, there was no community in the city on which to heap blame and resentment. According to Jean Froissart, the flagellants' rules 'forbade them to sleep more than one night in each town and the length of their goings-out was fixed by the thirty-three and a half years which Jesus Christ spent on earth'. So their visit to London should have been a short one and provided a bizarre footnote – and almost a postscript – to the epidemic.[18]

By the time that the flagellants arrived in London the epidemic had virtually come to an end. In January, 38 wills had been made which were enrolled in the Court of Hustings, in February the number was 50, in March 89 and in April 104, including seven on Easter Sunday. This was many times the figure compiled in a normal year; the number of enrolments in April was over forty times the pre-plague average. But in May the number of wills made fell to 56 and in June it was only nine, in July just six. The court was suspended during August and September and the number of wills drawn up during those months were three and two respectively. The dates of the making of wills are a more reliable guide to the chronology of the epidemic than those of the enrolments, as there was a delay before they were enrolled. Deaths of tenants on the Bishop of London's manor of Stepney, to the east of the City, peaked in February. Robert of Avesbury gave Pentecost as the date for the ending of the plague in London, which in 1349 fell on 31 May. An entry in the City's letter-books in July referred to the 'recent' pestilence and the Chronicle of London recorded that it lasted 'unto the monthe of August'.[19]

By then the city's business was returning to normal. On 21 May the mayor's court considered a case of an outstanding debt owed by a woolman of St Mildred, Poultry. Eight days later the Assize of Nuisance met for the first time since 26 September and heard a complaint that a tenant had refused to rebuild a ruinous earthen wall, 80 feet long, in the parish of St Mary Axe; the court ordered that it should be repaired. On 10 August those responsible for measuring and transporting salt landed at Queenhithe made a formal statement of their charges for the aldermen. Before the end of the month six fishmongers brought to Guildhall illegal fishing nets belonging to three fishermen of Greenwich. The nets contravened the regulation regarding the fineness of their mesh, so that the fish caught in them were 'useless owing to their smallness', and the aldermen ordered that they should be destroyed. Such proceedings were routine and provide no hint of the major crisis from which the city was beginning to emerge. Those city officers who had died were replaced, usually within a few weeks, enabling business to proceed with little delay. The chamberlain died on 25 April and his successor was sworn in on 19 May and other officers took their oaths at ceremonies on 25 March and 19 April, during the worst of the crisis, then on 11 and 24 June.[20] The grocers' guild's meetings resumed in June and July. At Westminster the south cloister walk of the abbey was begun in 1344 and was vaulted in 1349, which suggests that enough craftsmen and workmen of the existing team had survived to complete that specialist task during the building season, from spring to autumn, despite the death of the monks in the abbey.

On the other hand, trade had ground almost to a halt. One of the principal victims was Walter Chiriton, from a Warwickshire family, who by the 1340s was described as a 'merchant of London' and was closely involved in the international trade in wool, and through that with the crown's finances. He was one of the merchants who were farmers of the customs, that is, paying a fixed rent to the crown in return for the right to collect the customs, making a profit from the sums collected over and above the rent. In May 1346 he took a three-year lease of the customs, in partnership with Thomas Swanland, at an annual rent of £50,000; it may be that the rent was rather high as Edward strove to maximise the revenue from the wool trade to finance his military expenditure. Chiriton was also a lender to the crown, claiming that he had advanced 100,000 marks (£66,600) towards the cost of the siege of Calais. When the trade in wool was halted because of the Black Death, Chiriton had to borrow to maintain his payments to the crown, taking loans of more than £53,000 while paying the king at least £126,000. Some of those loans, which were from sources in York, Dortmund and Bruges, were at ruinously high rates of interest. That could not continue and in April 1349 Chiriton and Swanland went bankrupt; in June they were imprisoned and their landed property was confiscated by the crown. Attempts to recover Chiriton's money continued into the 1350s, but seemingly to no avail. Other financiers suffered losses from their dealings with the crown and the collapse of trade because of the plague and the complete ban on the export of wool, which was in force from 15 March until 10 June 1349. Wool exports recovered after the ban was lifted, but that was too late for Chiriton and his associates.[21]

Although bankrupt, Chiriton and his partners had at least survived, as had members of the Chaucer family. Probably because of their involvement with the wine trade, the family had moved from Ipswich to London and settled in the district of Vintry, where John Chaucer, father of the poet Geoffrey, had a house in Thames Street. During 1347–9 John was in the royal service as assistant royal butler at Southampton and so may have been living there rather than at his London house during the epidemic, but both places were badly stricken by the plague. Yet John and the young Geoffrey emerged unscathed; John died in 1366 and Geoffrey in 1400. Others were not so fortunate. Probably eight of the twenty-four aldermen were victims of the pestilence and the incumbents of nine out of sixteen City parishes also died; in some of them more than one incumbent perished. The aldermen's administrative duties and the pastoral care of the clergy had doubtless brought them into contact with the victims and so with infective fleas and lice. The chronology of the epidemic and several descriptions from across Europe suggest that pneumonic plague, transmitted by water droplets, was an element in the outbreak. The aldermen and parish clergy were high-risk groups, but that was not the case for the wealthy citizens, who may have had the opportunity to leave the city, or at least sequester themselves, as had those in Florence described by Boccaccio. Of a group of 359 well-to-do citizens identified from taxation records, some 29 per cent died during the epidemic and a further 33 per cent disappear from the record. It may be that some of those who cannot be traced had gone away, or the records are missing, but it is equally likely that some had died, raising the proportion of plague victims to perhaps one-third or more. Some families suffered the loss of several members. William and Richard Shorditch were goldsmiths, and both died during the epidemic. When Johanna Elys drew up her will on 5 February her husband had already died, so she provided for the future security of their two children by making her mother their guardian, assigning them rents from tenements in St Bride's and St Dunstan-in-the-West, and allocating them household items. She died within 72 hours of making that will. A chandler's daughter in St Botolph Aldgate made her will on 8 February and within five days she had died, for her sister referred to her as deceased in her own will, drawn up on 13 February. A shipwright who lived near the Tower died within 24 hours of making his will, as his wife then made hers, describing him as dead.[22]

The practice followed by the burial parties in the cemetery at St Mary Spital during an epidemic in the late thirteenth century was to place the bodies in trenches, closely packed in layers. They were correctly aligned west-east and carefully laid, with the head to the west, in the conventional way. Christian teaching held that the body would rise at the resurrection of the dead, and so would be facing east.[23] The systematic way of interring the dead shown by that excavation was described in an account of the plague epidemic that ravaged Paris in 1418, when 'so many people died so fast that ... they had to dig great pits in the cemeteries of Paris and lay thirty or forty in at once, in rows, like sides of bacon, and then a bit of earth scattered over them'.[24]

Excavation of the East Smithfield burial ground has shown that similar methods were applied during the Black Death, with the dead buried in an orderly way in both parallel rows in trenches and in individual graves. Those in trenches were placed in as many as five layers, on a west-east alignment, and they had not been interred in haste or in a negligent way. The use of coffins in more than one-quarter of the burials also suggests that those interments were not carried out hurriedly or without due preparation; indeed, it indicates a considered and organised response to the crisis, in arranging the supply of timber and employment of enough carpenters to have far more coffins made than would ordinarily have been required. No similar frequency of burials in coffins has been discovered at other excavated sites from the period in Britain, which suggests that there was an opinion that the corpses of those who had died from the disease should be enclosed, to contain the corruption. Of 490 skeletons that could be analysed, 26 per cent were those of females, of whom 11 per cent were young, and 74 per cent were male. Of the male victims, 39 per cent were infants and children, 12 per cent were young men and 23 per cent were mature or elderly. A section of trench had been prepared but was not needed, so those organising the interments had anticipated future need and were prepared for it, not struggling to make room for corpses being delivered to the site for burial. The continued interment of victims there until the end of the epidemic shows that there were enough able-bodied adults to methodically carry out the work of collecting, preparing and interring the bodies, and overseers to organise the gathering of the corpses and their carriage to the cemetery. One pit that contained eight victims probably was for those buried earlier, or perhaps abandoned unburied, who had been brought to the cemetery some time after death.[25] That may have been part of a general process of gathering hastily buried bodies into the cemeteries, perhaps as the epidemic subsided. If carried out assiduously, the practice would have removed all the victims to the consecrated burial grounds. The report that some bodies had been thrown into the river may have been hyperbole, to emphasise the drama of the epidemic. Most bearers would have passed close to a churchyard before reaching the river and would surely have left the corpse there for burial rather than going further and then face the difficulty throwing it into the river; only with a child's body would it be easy to do that.

Much of Spitalcroft may have been used for burials, for a geophysical survey has shown that the northern part, within the later Carthusian priory, contained graves, although widely spaced and not necessarily made during epidemics. During digging for a new sewer in Charterhouse Square in 1834 'vast numbers of bones and skeletons were found', the southern end of the area was taken for the extension of the Metropolitan Railway, which opened in 1865, and in 1885 excavations on the west side of the square for the erection of buildings given the generic title of warehouses, uncovered a 'large number of human skeletons', which had been interred in trenches. In 1998 a small excavation within the square uncovered a single skeleton of a child under ten years old, probably from the Black Death period. The digging of a shaft in the open space on the west side of the square in 2013 uncovered 25 skeletons, 11 of them from the Black Death period, two from a second phase of burials, also in the mid-fourteenth century, and 12 from a third phase, dated to the fifteenth century. Burials from all three phases contained evidence of *Yersinia pestis*. All but two of those buried in the first phase were adults and of the 16 within the shaft for which the sex could be identified 13 were males and three were females, which is a striking imbalance of 4.3:1, whereas at East Smithfield the ratio from a much larger sample was 1.77:1. Those in the first two phases were in individual graves; in the third phase there were two graves with multiple burials. The alignment of the burials in the first two phases was south-west to north-east, while those in the third phase were on the correct west-east alignment, perhaps with reference to the chapel built close by in 1349, which was on the true west-east orientation. One child may have been buried in a coffin, evidenced by the nails found, but no other fragments of coffins have survived and the individual uncovered by excavation in 1998 was not buried in a coffin. Remains of at least five others were exposed in the shaft and other trenches during the works for Crossrail and a community dig on a part of the square. Of the remains of ten people suitable for analysis, four probably had moved to London, one after the age of five, one after the age of eight and two after the age of sixteen, which indicates that during the difficult mid-fourteenth century period London was, as usual, drawing in people from the regions around the city.[26] The burial parties would probably have worked inwards from the most accessible parts of the perimeter of the cemetery, which were in the south-west, approached across Smithfield, and the north-east, where the cemetery adjoined the road leading from Aldersgate. Some of the area was not used for burials and in some parts the density of graves was low.

Because of Spitalcroft's continued use after 1349, possibly largely, or even exclusively, as an epidemic cemetery, some of the burials uncovered by excavation were later than the Black Death period, which may also apply to some shown by the geophysical survey. Allowing for those later burials, the evidence of the geophysical survey and excavations indicates a figure of 5,000 burials there during the Black Death. The fuller excavation evidence for the density of burials in the four acres of the East Smithfield burial ground implies that roughly 2,400 victims were interred there.[27] Applying a similar density to Nomanneslond suggests that a further 1,800 were interred in that cemetery. That provides a total of 9,200 for the three burial grounds, which can reasonably be adjusted to 10,000.

In addition, there were the interments in the City's churchyards and that of St Paul's, which were the only burial places available before the emergency burial grounds were opened. The north-east of the cathedral churchyard became known as Pardon Churchyard; the name signifies remission of a punishment, suggesting its use as a burial ground during the epidemic. The same designation was given to Nomanneslond. Roughly one-fifth of wills made during the epidemic were drawn up in its first four months, before the three cemeteries came fully into use, and the wills have been used to estimate a sixteen-fold increase in the death rate over the period of the epidemic. A presumed 'normal' death rate of 3.5 per cent across the population of approximately 75,000, somewhat down from its medieval peak of 80,000, produces an annual pre-plague toll of 2,625 deaths, and a multiplier of 16 raises that to 31,500 deaths during the epidemic. Adjusting that total according to the chronology indicated by the wills suggests that there were roughly 6,300 burials in the churchyards before the cemeteries were opened.[28] Interments in them would have continued thereafter, where space was available, if only because for many bearers it was easier to move corpses the shorter distance to a local churchyard than to one of the cemeteries. As there were over 110 parishes in London and Southwark, a figure of 10,000 in the churchyards is possible. Adding the 10,000 for the cemeteries produces a death toll of 20,000, roughly 26 per cent of the pre-plague population; substantially lower than the figure derived from the wills.

Fourteenth-century Europe was not accustomed to recording numbers of deaths; figures given for unusually high mortality, such as on a battlefield, were greatly exaggerated throughout the Middle Ages. This was so well recognised that the Italian commander Galeotto Malatesta devised a formula to apply to the numbers reported, which would give an idea of the true figure of casualties in a battle.[29] In a society which did not record the numbers of victims, contemporary evidence of numbers is of course unreliable. They are included in the account by Robert of Avesbury, who in one passage reported that on a single day '20, 40, or 60 bodies, and on many occasions many more, might be committed for burial together in the same pit'. He does not specify that this related to London, but from the numbers and the fact that he was based at Lambeth Palace, that is probable. The mention of a single pit, or trench, must refer to one of the three cemeteries, not a churchyard. This is tantalising, for he does not indicate the place or length of time to which his comment applied. He was more specific in another statement, that between 2 February and 12 April 'more than 200 corpses were buried almost every day in the new burial ground made next to Smithfield', which suggests a total of almost 14,000 in Spitalcroft. As that cemetery continued to be used beyond 12 April the figure is incomplete and revising it in proportion to the numbers of wills compiled provides an estimate of almost 23,000 burials. When that is added to the figure of 4,200 for the other two cemeteries the total for the three becomes 27,200; with the 10,000 burials in the churchyards this indicates a total of approximately 37,000, equivalent to almost 50 per cent of the population.[30] But Avesbury's numbers for daily burials was qualified by his phrase that they occurred 'almost every day', and the pattern of interments revealed by recent excavations is less dense than the numbers based on his comments would suggest. His figures could have repeated hearsay reports of the scale of the burials; he was not an eyewitness if he remained at his duties in Lambeth Palace and did not venture as far as Aldersgate and Smithfield often enough to estimate the daily numbers.

Sir Walter de Mauny's own figure of 60,000 for Spitalcroft was given in a petition to the pope of 1352; a later memorial on the site put the number at more than 50,000. Those numbers are implausibly high in the context of the city's population. Exaggeration of the scale of the recent mortality was a feature of the post-plague period and de Mauny's figure should be interpreted in that context. It may have been consciously set at a high level to reflect the scale and importance of his charity in acquiring the land; the more burials, the greater the significance of his contribution. A lower number was included in a bull issued by Urban VI in 1384, which refers to Spitalcroft as a place where 'twenty thousand and more dead are buried', and by then victims of the epidemic in 1361 had also been interred there.[31] Employing Urban's figure of 20,000 for Spitalcroft, but reduced by 5,000 to allow for burials after the Black Death, suggests that the proportion of the total population that died was roughly 40 per cent, considerably higher than the percentage suggested by the density of burials.

The mid-point figure of the two estimates for the Black Death in London, one derived from the excavated burials and the other from Avesbury's figures for Spitalcroft, is 28,500 deaths, which would represent a fall in the population of approximately 38 per cent.

An estimate based on a sixteen-fold increase in the number of wills produces a higher notional death-toll of 31,500, or 42 per cent of a population of 75,000.[32] But over the longer term the annual average number of wills enrolled in the Hustings Court was 23 in 1338–48 and 16 in the period 1351–9, a fall of 26 per cent in that small sample, and in 1357 Londoners claimed that one-third of the city's properties were standing empty, a figure that was made in the context of a plea for the reduction of their tax burden and so not likely to be understated.[33]

These conjectural estimates are based on limited and varied evidence, but the proportion of the population that died which they suggest, roughly in the range of 25–40 per cent and perhaps around one-third, is in line with estimated losses in other cities. A much higher proportion than one-third would seem to be unlikely, if only because of the systematic way in which the burials were organised and normal business, not at all related to the epidemic, was so readily resumed, while a lower figure would not accord with the mortality levels among the guildsmen, aldermen, clergy and some families. There is no suggestion that the kind of breakdown of social norms that Boccaccio described in Florence occurred in London. That may be because the city did not experience such a reaction, or that it lacked a Boccaccio to chronicle it.

The range of estimates of both numbers of deaths and the percentage of the population which they represented indicates the uncertainty of the available evidence, but the traumatic impact on the city's society is surely not in doubt. Yet the *Chronicle of London* described this catastrophe with the laconic comment that in 1348 'was the grete pestilence at London'. Writing in retrospect, Froissart, chronicler of much of the fourteenth century, also gave it only a passing mention, observing merely that 'in that time of death there was an epidemic of plague'.[34] As the hoped-for repentance and moral reform to assuage God's wrath did not materialise, pessimistic moralists feared a return of the epidemic.

5

THE AFTERMATH

Whatever the proportion of the population killed by the epidemic, the scale of the mortality was large enough to be obvious without an enumeration or systematic investigations. The king and his council reacted swiftly to the crisis by issuing orders to deal with the impact of the deaths and restrain changes which they feared may ensue. Most obviously, the shortage of labour would produce a demand for higher wages, which employers would find difficult to resist, for should their journeymen or servants reject a wage increase they could simply defect to another master, who would be glad to retain them and offer them improved terms. In the countryside those who owed labour services would now be able to leave their manorial lord and find employment which did not have such an irksome element to it, and perhaps move to a town. Landlords reduced their rents, to retain or attract tenants, and remitted labour services, but their incomes fell because of the lower rents. The government's concern was collecting taxes so that the costs of the war could be met, and a fall in income among the tax-payers was therefore a great concern.

More immediately, the shortfall in manpower during the coming summer would reduce the quantity of grain and other crops that could be harvested. It could also have an adverse effect on the sowing of the winter grains of wheat and rye during the autumn and so impact on supplies during 1350. Henry Knighton, writing later in the century, gave a gloomy summary of the effects of the pestilence, commenting that in the following winter labour was so scarce that farm livestock wandered around without a shepherd, and that 'all victuals and other necessities were extremely dear'.[1] Of course, there were now fewer consumers, but the reductions in supply may not have matched the fall in population, or corresponded geographically, and the marketing of produce was dislocated, at least temporarily, by the shortage of manpower. The imbalance should have seen an adjustment through the prices at the markets, but in London that would place undue pressure on the mayor and his officers when they set the key prices for the season ahead. They would need to be mindful not only of the likely quantity of supplies, which would be difficult to predict, but also the changing levels of wages, which could be in a state of flux. Waiting to see what price and wage changes brought was a risky strategy, for that could lead to acute shortages and so to unrest. For that reason the government was especially concerned about London's food supply.

The prime objective was to prevent inflation of wages and prices. After consulting with prelates, nobles and other 'learned men' the king issued the Ordinance of Labourers on 18 June 1349. The epidemic was only just subsiding in London and had not yet ravaged all the kingdom and so the measure was a prompt response to the crisis. Its preamble noted that with the shortage of labour, especially of agricultural workers, many people were refusing to work unless they were paid 'excessive' wages. Anyone under 60 years of age who was not living by trade or a craft, or had an independent income, and was offered a job 'consonant with their status' was obliged to accept that job, at the pre-plague wage level. Those already in employment for a fixed term must serve the whole period. No employer was to offer higher wages than those prevailing before the epidemic and if they had done so before the ordinance was issued they were not bound to pay them. Skilled artisans and their labourers were also to remain 'in the place where they happen to be working' and at the wages they were receiving before the plague. That was specified to be in 1346: the abnormal harvest in 1347 made it unsuitable as the year to be used as the standard. Sturdy beggars were making a living from begging alone, not from a mixture of casual work and gratuities, and passing their time 'in idleness and depravity, and sometimes in robberies and other crimes' and so it was forbidden to give them charity or alms. The penalties were harsh. Anyone declining employment, or leaving it before their term was completed, or was receiving higher wages than in 1346, was to be imprisoned, as was someone giving charity to sturdy beggars. Landlords or their officials who broke the terms of the ordinance were to be proceeded against in the courts.[2]

The ordinance also addressed the problems of supply with the order that all dealers in foodstuffs should sell their produce 'for a reasonable price, having regard to the price at which such food is sold in the neighbourhood'. The seller was to be allowed a moderate 'but not excessive' profit, allowing for the distance which the produce had been transported. Urban officials were required to investigate complaints about prices and impose the specified penalty of twice what the seller had received to be paid to the customer or the person bringing the prosecution.[3]

London was not exempted from the policy, and a writ was delivered to the sheriffs of the City and Middlesex instructing them to proclaim the ordinance 'regulating the wages of servants and artificers, and forbidding the enhancement of victuals in consequence of the recent pestilence'.[4] In the month following the issue of the ordinance, 21 people working for bakers were proceeded against for combining to obtain higher wages. With their case before the mayor and sheriffs, the bakers then took the opportunity to require all journeymen working for them to agree to three-monthly periods of employment. Some wine-drawers were imprisoned for demanding higher wages and 60 of the shoemakers' employees admitted that they had colluded to demand a specific daily wage; they were imprisoned for 12 days.[5] In November the mayor and sheriffs were commanded to issue a proclamation 'against artificers and others demanding higher wages than the average they were receiving before the pestilence, in accordance with the terms of a previous ordinance', which indicates that there were difficulties in enforcing the ordinance in London. That was acknowledged in 1350 by the issue of further orders 'for the redress of loss suffered by the inhabitants of the City during the past year through masons, carpenters, and other labourers demanding unreasonable wages'. Clearly, workers in the building trades had defied the terms of the ordinance and had managed to obtain higher pay.[6] It could scarcely have been otherwise, for the complexity of the city's economy and the size of its population made it difficult to oversee such matters as the wages and terms of employment of the many tradesmen working there. Enticing workers from other masters was an existing problem, but one which became more common because of the labour shortage.[7] Quality of work was also an issue. The shearmen had fixed their rate for piece-work, but returned to the court to ask permission to punish the piece-workers 'who did their work in a slovenly manner'. Specifically, they 'do so greatly hurry over the same, that they do great damage to the folks to whom such cloths belong; by reason whereof, the masters in the said trade have great blame and abuse, and take less than they were wont to do'.[8] John of Reading complained in the 1350s that workers now worked less and more poorly.

The government was concerned to restrict the movement of people, to prevent them from moving elsewhere to obtain higher wages. London was a magnet for those who were freed from labour services and were looking for other work. In December 1349 the mayor, sheriffs and aldermen were granted an indemnity for their actions in 'arresting misdoers who had flocked to the City after the cessation of the pestilence and threatened the peace of the City'. Restrictions on movement also applied to those travelling abroad. On 1 December the mayor and sheriffs were instructed to make a proclamation 'against any leaving the kingdom except well-known merchants, inasmuch as the country had become so much depopulated by the pestilence and the Treasury exhausted'. Anyone trying to leave the country without the king's permission was to be arrested; in October 1350 the prohibition was even extended to those setting out on a pilgrimage to Rome.[9]

Prices attracted official attention, as well as wages. Wine-drawers were alleged to be asking double the accustomed price and some brewers were said to have complained about regulation by the mayor and aldermen, because they should be free to set their own terms. The shoemakers' guild was sued for the prices which its members were charging for shoes, but they passed the blame on to their suppliers, the curriers and tanners, for selling cowhides at inflated prices. A few curriers and shoemakers were sentenced, in November 1349, but the case surely had too many ramifications for the court to follow it through in detail. A smaller case was the dispute between the saddlers and the fusters, who supplied them with wooden frames. The fusters were a small and specialised group of tradesmen who were in a weak position because they were wholly dependent on the saddlers to take their product. Nevertheless, they put up a fight, claiming that the wood which was their raw material was now more expensive and the prices of food and ale had risen. They added that they had worked all their lives, were older and weaker than they had been, and were unable to find apprentices or journeymen to do some of the work. If they accepted the prices which the saddlers were trying to impose on them, they would need to work three times as long to maintain their present level of income. The court tried to achieve a compromise.[10]

The fusters' complaint about the increased cost of food and drink reflected the struggle which the authorities were having to keep the provisions in London's markets at reasonable prices. In 1350 a detailed list of prices and wages was issued by the mayor and aldermen, even covering such a matter as the costs of shoeing a horse, at the rates charged before the epidemic: 'for a horse-shoe of six nails 1½d., and for a horse-shoe of eight nails 2d.; and for taking off a horse-shoe of six nails or of eight, one halfpenny; and for the shoe of a courser 2½d., and the shoe of a charger 3d.; and for taking off the shoe of a courser or charger, one penny'.[11] The aldermen's efforts included enquiries into the organisation of the salt trade and the charges made 'according to the ancient custom of the City'. They also tried to prevent the forestalling of the markets by suppliers. In April 1350, 22 poulterers were convicted of the offence; one of them who had previously been convicted of a similar fault was condemned to stand in the pillory and the others were sent to prison.[12] A royal writ issued in March 1351 required the mayor and sheriffs to 'make diligent search for and punish any victuallers, wholesale or retail, they find enhancing the price of victuals, under cover of a recent statute'. That is, the butchers, fishermen and poulterers were using the stipulation in the Ordinance of Labourers referring to the free supply of markets, without interference by municipal officers, to try to circumvent the traditional controls exercised by the mayor's officers. That aspect of the ordinance was contrary to the mayor's authority and it had to be made clear that it did not apply to London. Another writ in the following December required the sheriffs to proclaim that the export of corn from the city was forbidden, without special permission; that was repeated a month later.[13]

The arrival of adequate quantities of supplies in London's markets remained a paramount concern for a generation. Those places where fish were to be sold were specified and penalties were prescribed for brewers and taverners who were selling ale and wine by false measures, including Rhenish and wine from Crete. Quality also mattered and in April 1350 two butchers were arrested by the sheriffs and convicted of offering putrid meat for sale in the parish of St Nicholas at the Shambles; they were condemned to stand in the pillory and the meat was to be burned at their feet, so that they had to endure the stench rising from it. Taverners and vintners were warned not to mix new wine with old and imported wine was not to be stored in cellars or sold before it had been tested by the king's gauger of wines or his deputy, 'according to custom'. The prices of Rhenish and Gascony wines were fixed.[14]

As the measures were not seen to be successful, in February 1351 Parliament enacted a Statute of Labourers, which was a more detailed version of the royal ordinance. Attempts to enforce the stipulations continued. In September 1353 the officers of the dyers' guild were instructed to see 'that no one took more for his labour than he was accustomed to take before the Pestilence'. And in the following year there was a general instruction that victuallers should continue to follow their trade as they had done before the plague.[15] No major crisis occurred with the supplies available in London, whether because of the government's swift actions or an adjustment of both production and supply in the changed circumstances. Nor did higher prices lead to falls in charitable giving to the hospitals. Before the Black Death roughly 5 per cent of testators bequeathed funds to them and in the 1350s the proportion was 15 per cent, with the amount of the average bequest being around 40 per cent higher.[16]

In other matters the government could be satisfied. The pestilence made the collections of the subsidies granted to the king in 1348 more complicated than they otherwise would have been, with a flood of requests for relief or exemption, but the level of arrears was only slightly higher than normal.[17] Although the populations of England and France had both been ravaged by the disease, the war could be resumed. The ensuing campaigns culminated in the English victory at Poitiers in 1356, when the French king John II was taken prisoner. He was brought to London in 1357 and the procession was greeted by the members of the guilds in their liveries, watched by thousands of curious

Londoners lining the streets, refreshed with free wine, while young maidens sprinkled gold and silver leaf over the parade.[18] The citizens' morale had not been so subdued by the plague and its aftermath that they could not rouse themselves to celebrate such an occasion, and profit from it. Other festive events followed, including jousts in 1359 to celebrate the marriage of John of Gaunt to Blanche of Lancaster, when the king, his four sons and nineteen nobles were disguised as the mayor and aldermen, willing to take on all comers.[19]

The spirit of the age drew criticisms from melancholy observers, such as John of Reading, who disliked the styles now favoured by the fashionable and wondered at 'the empty headedness of the English, who remained wedded to a crazy range of outlandish clothing'. He saw this as a manifestation of society's ills, condemning 'useless little hoods, laced and buttoned so tightly at the throat that they only covered the shoulders'. Extremely short garments were also in vogue 'which failed to conceal their arses or their private parts'; they were worn with a very long hose that was tied to the garments with laces. Shoes had very long toes, the caps were twisted into the shape of hose or sleeves, and knives were hung between the thighs. Some of this clothing was so 'misshapen and tight' that the wearers were unable to kneel without great discomfort 'to God or the saints, to their lords or to each other'. It was also highly dangerous in battle, although surely those fashionable clothes would be discarded before a fight for something more appropriate. Robert Rypon, a Benedictine monk, also censured those men whose clothes were 'so short that they barely hide their shameful parts, and certainly, as it appears, to show women their members so as to provoke lust'.[20]

Such views by writers who were critical of the corrupt times through which they were living were not unusual. The poet John Gower lived from the 1370s in St Saviour's priory in Southwark and he looked back to the old days when 'people behaved properly, without deceit, and without envy. Their buying and selling was honest, without trickery.' Greed had become widespread; even the apothecaries in the city were deceitful and colluded with the physicians to over-charge their patients. In his General Prologue to the *Canterbury Tales* of c.1380, Geoffrey Chaucer drew attention to physicians conniving with apothecaries, with the observation that his physician, who was 'a really fine practitioner',

> Knowing the cause, and having found its root,
> He'd soon give the sick man an antidote.
> Ever at hand he had apothecaries
> To send him syrups, drugs and remedies,
> For each put money in the other's pocket –
> Theirs was no newly founded partnership.

Physicians made money from the plague and were not reluctant to display their wealth. His physician was 'dressed all in Persian blue and Scarlet', lined with 'taffeta and fine sarsenet':

> And yet was very chary of expense.
> He put by all he earned from pestilence;
> In medicine gold is the best cordial,
> So it was gold that he loved best of all.[21]

Thomas Brinton, Bishop of Rochester from 1373 until his death in 1389, complained in a sermon that 'False merchants ... infringe the rule of justice. Throughout the whole profession such great falsehood is practised in measures, charging interest, weights, scales, adulteration, lies and false oaths, that each studies to deceive the next man.' An anonymous writer observed bitterly that 'the subtlety of merchants shifts into fraud'. Nostalgia for the period before the plague extended to the way in which those with social ambitions now dressed inappropriately for their station in life. Robert Rypon complained that the clothing 'of those who were once noble are now divided as spoil … among grooms, and maid-servants and prostitutes'.²²

Those who considered that the duty of the post-plague generation was to re-people the country expected married couples to have children. Some of child-bearing age who had lost their spouse to the disease chose to re-marry and start a new family; that became a common pattern after a plague outbreak, with successive peaks in the numbers of deaths, marriages and births. But the sexual conduct of others who were not fulfilling that obligation attracted hostile comments. John of Reading was quite vicious:

> Infected by malice, cunning, deceit and evil, perverting every convention, decency and standard in their deeds, gestures and words, men considered that to deflower virgins and violate the chastity of wives and widows was doing them a favour, not an injury. Men did not have sexual intercourse with their wives, or married women with their husbands, but preferred to get bastards on strangers.²³

Boccaccio included a tale in *The Decameron* which related the adventures of a general handyman who pretended to be a deaf mute so that he could obtain a job in a nunnery. He became friendly, and then very friendly, with two of the nuns. They agreed between themselves that as they broke so many of their vows there was no reason why they should not break this one. Others began to take notice of what was going on and were happy to join in, and eventually the abbess realised that something was afoot, and she, too, was willing to accept his attentions. This produced a contented community of abbess, nuns, children and handyman, and when he felt that it was time to leave he was showered with thanks and enough gifts to make him comfortably off. This was Boccaccio's pleasantly disapproving comment on those who chose celibacy at a time when procreation was required to replace those who had died.

The clergy came under attack for other reasons, including greed and selfishness, when they should be comforting their parishioners. The author of a poem known as 'On the pestilence' complained: 'Alas! rectors and vicars have changed their ways, they're hirelings now, not true shepherds, and their works are motivated by the desire for money.' The poet William Langland probably would have agreed. He was aware of the beneficed clergy trying to leave their parishes, which were poor since 'the pestilence time', by petitioning their bishops for a licence to go to London, where they could sing masses for payment, 'for silver is sweet'. Bishops and those holding degrees in divinity also went to the city, where some served the king in a financial post, or pleaded in the Exchequer and Chancery courts to recover his debts from orphans who were wards and the local wardmote councils, and from 'waifs and strays'. In other words, mulcting those who could ill afford to pay. Some became chaplains to lords and ladies, and acted as their stewards. Such positions drew the clergy from their pastoral duties in the country, while helping to renew London's population. Its role as the focus of church, law and government ensured that it recovered to a certain extent from the death-toll.[24]

To those and other writers the nub of the problem was that nowadays society was riven, because everyone was dissatisfied with their lot. Unsuitable clothing, verging on the indecent, sexual misconduct, social pretension, selfishness and greed provided manifest evidence of the unhappy situation. With such behaviour and fashions, it should not be a surprise if the population was punished by further plague outbreaks. Scholars writing in the aftermath of the Black Death were not able to assuage such fears by offering convincing reasons for the disease, and hence remedies. The University of Paris's medical faculty was called upon by King Philip VI in 1348 to provide an explanation and it pointed out that at one o'clock in the afternoon on 20 March 1345 there had been a conjunction of

Saturn, Jupiter and Mars. A conjunction of Saturn and Jupiter was held to bring death and depopulation, while Jupiter, as a warm and humid planet, drew up foul vapours from earth and water, and Mars was a very hot and dry planet and so set fire to the vapours. The great heat and dampness favoured pestilential vapours, which were a likely cause of the plague. The Paris faculty's report became widely accepted; the faculty was, after all, the most distinguished of the six principal medical faculties in Europe. Yet it could be argued that no planetary conjunction lasted more than two years and as the epidemic had continued beyond that, perhaps it was not the true cause.[25] Other factors were put forward by various writers, including the weather – especially the bad effects of warm air and the benefits of cold air – and earthquakes and volcanic eruptions in the years immediately preceding the epidemic, which had ejected subterranean miasmas into the atmosphere. The University of Paris explained earthquakes as caused by 'decaying matter piled up in the interior of the earth'. To escape the plague, the avoidance of bad smells, bloodletting and prescriptions for a variety of concoctions were all suggested by the tractate writers to their readers. Into the sixteenth century a southerly aspect for a house was regarded as hazardous, especially if it had many doors and windows facing that direction, because of winds carrying unfavourable warm, damp vapours. A house's windows should ideally face north. From the first years of the plague's onset in the 1340s, corrupt air, caused by stagnant water, in pools, lakes or wells, or by putrid and decaying matter, was in the forefront of thinking about the cause and spread of the disease.[26]

The scholarly community had been depleted by roughly a third, the same proportion as the population generally, and the medical theory of the time did not provide a framework for the radical new thought that was required. It rested largely on the work of the second-century physician Galen and the notion that the human body was comprised of four humours, blood, black and yellow bile, and phlegm; disease was caused by an imbalance between the humours. The nature of plague and its spread did not readily fit into Galenic theory. Some physicians whose curiosity and courage had taken them into sick rooms to observe the nature and progress of the disease were likely to have succumbed themselves, and so many of the writers on the subject were probably repeating information received at second-hand, rather than summarising their own experiences. They were not invariably wrong with their descriptions of the symptoms because of those circumstances, but they were unable to assemble that evidence in such a way as to provide enlightenment for the medical profession itself, or the lay public eager for explanations and solutions. Observations did lead to an awareness that those who took the bedding or clothes of the sick contracted the disease, that it erupted in a place after someone arrived there from an infected community and that those communities which were able to exclude the sick could escape the epidemic. Ibn Kātimah of Almeria in Andalusia, who wrote a tract in February 1349, noted those facts and observed that someone who succumbed after contact with a sick person displayed the same symptoms as they did, which was also the case among members of a household, and therefore they were afflicted by the same disease, but he did not conclude that the disease was infectious; a plague was punishment sent by God. Yet Ibn al-Khatib, a physician and statesman of Granada, did accept the theory of infection, based on experience, including autopsy. Christian writers were also inclined to accept infection, warning against contact with the sick, especially coming within breathing distance, which suggests the presence of pneumonic plague.[27]

To avoid the plague, flight was obviously the best course of action. But other steps could be taken, such as lighting fires in the streets to circulate the air, recommended by Gentile of Foligno, a distinguished physician who was in Perugia at the time of the Black Death. They could be made from the material from dirty houses and streets. Within the houses, burning aromatic woods and herbs was favoured, although they could be expensive, and in the summer fragrant plants and flowers should be spread around, preferably sprinkled with vinegar and rose-water. When out in the streets or other public places carrying sweet-smelling herbs close to the nose, perhaps in a pomander, was suggested. Another recommendation was washing with vinegar and one writer of a mid-fourteenth century tractate mentioned using it to swill out the mouth. Hot baths were not advised because opening the pores allowed corrupt air to enter, but a quick dip in tepid water should be not too dangerous. Physical exercise was not favoured, either, because it drew too much air into the body, and that air could be corrupt. The favoured antidotes to poison – theriac, mithridate, bol Armeniac and terra sigillata – were now pressed into service to ward off plague, together with pills of aloes, myrrh and saffron, and eating figs and rue before breakfast was commended, but onions should be eaten only by strong men.[28] Other concoctions were developed and sold over the years and many measures recommended at the outset of the second plague pandemic were to be practised in the following centuries.

In 1361 the apprehensions of those who feared a new affliction to chastise their unrepentant society were realised, with a new plague epidemic. The *Chronicle of London* recorded that 'in this yere was the second gret pestilence'.[29] Other chroniclers mentioned that it afflicted the young 'with great mortality among children, youths and the wealthy'. They also believed that men died in greater numbers than women during the outbreak. The plague began in the spring of 1361, just after Easter, which that year fell on 28 March. Two chronicles remark that it started in London: the continuation of Ranulf Higden's *Polychronicon* noted that in 1361 'a great pestilence of men began in London and then it steadily advanced from the south of England to the rest of the country killing many men but few women'.[30] A royal order issued on 30 April closed the ports to everyone except merchants and by 10 May the outbreak had become so serious that the sittings of the courts of law were suspended. The death-toll rose rapidly through May and into June, which may have seen the peak, and the epidemic continued through the summer before the number of deaths declined; the epidemic ceased around the end of October.[31] This was unlike the pattern of the initial plague outbreak in 1348–9, which had erupted in the autumn, with the number of deaths increasing through the winter and peaking in the spring. Nor was it entirely typical of the characteristic pattern of subsequent epidemics, which was that plague symptoms were first recognised in the spring and the number of deaths increased thereafter, with high mortality through the summer, peaking in August or September, and a slow decline during the autumn, with the epidemic ending in the winter.

The prior of St Bartholomew's died in the 1361 outbreak, as did the Master of St Thomas's hospital and his successor, and by December all but one of the Brothers of the hospital were also dead. In the high-risk groups, parish clergymen, the almoner of St Paul's and at least two apothecaries were victims of the pestilence. In the Tower, the master of artillery, the king's smith, the keeper of the royal wardrobe and a Scottish hostage who was being held there all died. The total death toll may have been ten times the annual average. Allowing for some recovery in London's population since 1349, this suggests that the second plague saw a further fall of roughly 10,000, reducing the number of inhabitants to approximately 45,000, a drastic decrease since the mid-1340s.[32]

The number of victims of the outbreak in 1361 required the use of the earlier plague cemeteries. The churchyard of Nomanneslond perhaps was full after the Black Death, but Pardon churchyard adjoining St Paul's continued to be used. A part of the land at East Smithfield was now occupied by a monastery, although its buildings were incomplete, but the burial ground remained administratively separate until 1364 and victims were interred there in 1361. Almost one-third of the burials were of children and 40 per cent were of females. The burial customs were similar to those in 1349, with coffins used in almost a half of the cases excavated, although a greater proportion of child burials were in a coffin than had been the case 12 years earlier. The practice of coffining the bodies of plague victims was to continue and during an epidemic at Tewkesbury in 1603 all those who died of plague 'to avoid the perill, were buried in coffins of bourde'.[33] Interments also took place in the burial ground at Spitalcroft in 1361. The chroniclers' description of this second plague as being an epidemic in which children suffered disproportionately seems to have been incorrect so far as London was concerned.

The monastery at East Smithfield was St Mary Graces, a Cistercian house founded by the king in 1350. Its initial endowment consisted of property in the district and £13 13 4d per annum out of the Treasury, but that was soon found to be inadequate. The house was given more property in 1353 and the king paid for the initial work on the buildings; the endowment was increased again in 1358 and the king made a further donation before his death in 1377. It maintained its royal connections and before the end of the fourteenth century had attracted considerable aristocratic patronage. Even so, it probably never contained more than a dozen monks, although the king had intended that it should have twice that number. The cemetery chapel of 1349 served as the monastery's chapel until a new one was built after 1361. Construction of the other buildings was slow and the infirmary was not erected until the early 1390s.[34]

Sir Walter de Mauny did not immediately try to emulate the king by establishing a monastery on Spitalcroft, although in 1351 he obtained papal approval for the establishment of a college with a warden and 12 secular priests. He did not proceed with the plan and by 1354 a hermitage had been built close to the cemetery chapel for two anchorites, who were to offer continual prayers for those buried there. A pulpit house was also built, adjoining the hermitage on the south side of the chapel, so that sermons could be delivered to congregations in the cemetery. The area, which became known as New Church Haw, was used for playing games and filth was dumped there, until both were prohibited by Gregory XI during the 1370s.[35]

The early history of the London Charterhouse was chronicled in the late fifteenth century in an account which states that de Mauny was persuaded to establish the Charterhouse by the efforts of Michael Northburgh, who succeeded Ralph Stratford as Bishop of London in 1355. Having been impressed by the Chartreuse in Paris, which he visited several times, Northburgh was especially keen to see a Carthusian house in London, and gave de Mauny 1,000 marks (£666) towards its foundation. In 1361 the two men came to an arrangement by which de Mauny was designated the principal founder of the priory, yet gave Northburgh leave to act as he thought fit.[36] But Northburgh died four months after the agreement was made and, despite his legacy of £2,000 and a dozen properties in London, a considerable delay followed before the scheme was revived. It was taken up by John Luscote, prior of the charterhouse at Hinton in Somerset, who enlisted the support of Simon Sudbury, Northburgh's successor as Bishop of London. Luscote's role proved to be an important one, both before the Charterhouse was founded and afterwards, as its first prior.

Edward III granted a royal licence for the foundation of the Charterhouse in February 1371, and de Mauny's foundation charter followed in March.[37] Its name, the House of the Salutation of the Mother of God, derived from the service of dedication of the cemetery chapel on the Feast of the Annunciation in 1349. The London Charterhouse was the fourth and, as a double house of 24 monks and a prior, the largest of the Carthusian houses established in England thus far. It occupied the whole of New Church Haw, the freehold of which had been acquired from St Bartholomew's by de Mauny, who died in January 1372 soon after the house was founded. A further four acres were obtained from the priory of the Hospital of St John in 1377.

St Mary Graces and the Charterhouse were visible reminders of the Black Death and members of the laity chose to be buried in their chapels. Clearly, there were no reservations about building them on the sites of plague cemeteries. Yet they were the only examples in London, and perhaps in Europe, of the placing of a monastery on or adjoining a burial ground.[38]

Successive plague outbreaks after 1361 were chronicled, but only cursorily; contemporaries came to realise that the disease was not an affliction that struck once, and then a second time, but a recurring scourge. An outbreak in the summer of 1368 prompted the suspension of the courts of King's Bench, Common Pleas and the Upper Exchequer between 22 May and the end of September. That seems to have been less severe than the epidemic in 1361, although the proportion of deaths is uncertain. The next eruption was in 1375, a year which was remembered for its very hot summer, during which 'a large number of Londoners, from among the wealthier and more eminent citizens, died in the pestilence'. Yet that outbreak lasted only from late May until the middle of August, a shorter duration than the earlier ones and so producing a lower death-toll. In 1390 'a great plague ravaged the country' but may not have struck London. After the initial outbreak of 1348–9, plague epidemics did not afflict the whole country in the way that it had done.[39]

Despite the plague outbreaks London had continued to follow the routines of administration and civic functions. The streets were cleaned, nuisances were reported and orders were issued for their correction. The response to the outbreak had led the city's government to take a close interest in its economic life, through the enforcement of regulations on labour, pay and prices. But in the longer term it passed through a turbulent time, in Edward III's later years and during the reign of Richard II, from 1377 until his deposition in 1399. Wealth from plunder and ransoms was no longer flowing in, as it had done during the middle years of the century, especially after the battles of Crécy (1346) and Poitiers (1356). The French monarchy had gradually recovered its authority and its forces were recapturing territory taken by the English and expeditions despatched to France to remedy the situation achieved nothing except to empty the Treasury. At sea, pirates sent out by the French and their Castilian allies were capturing English vessels, to the distress of the merchants. More organised naval expeditions raided and burned towns along the south coast and in August 1380 a Castilian force had the effrontery to enter the Thames, reaching Gravesend and Tilbury, which were burned. That incident must have caused great anxiety in London and added to the existing discontent with a government which levied taxes yet could not protect the city's commerce. Londoners were prominent in the attacks on the government in the Parliament of 1376, which became known as the Good Parliament. Sir John Philpot, mayor in 1378-9, took direct action and fitted out a fleet to curb the pirates, which did succeed in capturing several ships and one of their leaders.

As well as the military problems and commercial depression, the late 1370s saw political turmoil in the city, with changes to the elections to Common Council and the introduction of a rule that aldermen should be elected for only one year, not for life, which undermined their authority. Then during the Peasants' Revolt in 1381, a popular uprising provoked partly by the imposition of a poll tax, the rebels ran amok in the city, looting the shops, destroying 'several fine houses', attacking the Archbishop of Canterbury's palace at Lambeth, capturing the Fleet and Marshalsea prisons, burning John of Gaunt's palace of the Savoy and the lawyers' books at the Temple, and threatening to 'burn and destroy everything'. They broke into the Tower, released prisoners and murdered Simon Sudbury, Archbishop of Canterbury and Chancellor. Perhaps as many as 150 people were beheaded across London in one day. The revolt petered out after its leader, Wat Tyler, was wounded during a meeting with the king at Smithfield and subsequently executed.

The revolt was a short, if sharp, jolt to London, and the contentious electoral changes were reversed, but divisions within its elite continued to simmer. When the lords who challenged the king's authority gained control of the city the mayor, Sir Nicholas Brembre, a supporter of the king, was tried by Parliament and executed in 1388. Richard survived the crisis and punished the city for its support of his opponents by suspending its government and levying from it the huge fine of £10,000. But after Henry Bolingbroke took the throne as Henry IV the city's elite again took unchallenged control and political stability returned. That was not before London's streets were disturbed by clashes among the apprentices. According to the lawyer and chronicler Adam Usk, during Lent in 1400, 'The lads of the city of London, often gathering together in thousands and choosing kings among themselves, made war upon each other, and fought to their utmost strength; whereby many died stricken with blows, or trampled under foot, or crushed in narrow ways.' Usk went on to write that 'From such gatherings could they not be restrained, until the king wrote to their parents and masters with grievous threats to prevent them.' The citizens wondered what such subversive behaviour by the young men mimicking their elders and betters might portend; Usk's interpretation was that it presaged 'the plague that happened [in 1400] … wherein the greater number of them departed this life'. In that year 'a great plague prevailed through all England, and specially among the young, swift in its attack and carrying off many souls'.[40] The victims included the abbot of Chertsey and 13 monks there, and probably Pierre Blanchet, a French envoy whose hectoring manner had made him unpopular with his English hosts. The French cried foul and alleged poison, but it seems more likely that he was a plague victim.

France, too, suffered a destructive outbreak of plague during this period, lasting from 1398 to 1403, with high mortality in Paris in 1399, when the royal court took refuge at Rouen. Overall, the country may have lost roughly one-quarter of its population during those years, and its level of economic activity may have fallen by a greater proportion, perhaps one-third.[41] Whether England experienced such levels of death and disruption is unknown, but plague not only ushered out the old century, but opened the new one as well.

Above: Skeleton of a young female, in a single grave, excavated in Charterhouse Square. © Crown copyright, NMR

Below left: The black rat, an etching by William Samuel Howitt. © Wellcome Collection

Below right: The human flea, *pulex irritans*. © Wellcome Collection

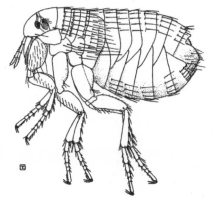

Left: Flagellants carried out their punishing rituals during the Black Death and a group of them came to London. © Stephen Porter

Below: Knights and ladies riding to a tournament in London. An illustration from Jean Froissart's *Chronicles*. © Stephen Porter

Right: A sick patient with his attendants, 1460: a devil which has knocked over the table in the foreground indicates that all is not going well. © Stephen Porter

Below: A citizen meets Death, from a Dance of Death, Lübeck, 1489. © Stephen Porter

Above left: A fifteenth-century funeral; the body is not in a coffin. © Stephen Porter

Above right: Plague was a disease of the trade routes and was brought to England in vessels such as this one. © Stephen Porter

Below: An apothecary's shop depicted by Quintorius Joannes. © Stephen Porter

Above: A Dance of Death; a woodcut of 1493. © Stephen Porter

Right: A fashionably dressed young man of the fifteenth century is confronted by Death; his coffin is nearby. © Stephen Porter

A plague victim is attended by his
nurses and a physician, who stands
as far away from him as possible.
From *Fasciculus Medicinae*, 1493.
© Stephen Porter

Plague as one of the Four
Horsemen of the Apocalypse in the
Book of Revelation by Albrecht
Dürer. © Stephen Porter

Right: St Sebastian suffering with arrow wounds and so protecting those behind him, by Urs Graf. © Stephen Porter

Below: The clean and orderly bedchamber of a well-to-do householder in the early sixteenth century. © Stephen Porter

An apothecary's shop in
the early sixteenth century.
© Wellcome Collection

klop duuel klop

The devil knocking on a
door in a town; Cologne,
1508. © Stephen Porter

Right: The Classical
physician Galen,
depicted in a
woodcut of 1582.
© Stephen Porter

Below: Death
disrupts a printers'
workshop and
appears at the
counter as a
customer: a drawing
published in 1499.
© Stephen Porter

Two Soldiers and a woman enjoy a conversation, while Death looks on from the nearby tree, by Urs Graf. © Stephen Porter

UTOPIAE INSVLAE FIGVRA

Plan of Thomas More's imagined ideal commonwealth of Utopia. © Stephen Porter

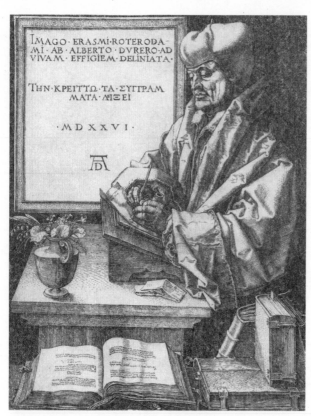

Left: Desiderius Erasmus
by Albrecht Dürer, 1526.
© Stephen Porter

Below: King Death, by
Albrecht Dürer, 1505.
© Stephen Porter

Above and below: Dance of Death of the women, by Guy Marchant, 1486.
© Stephen Porter

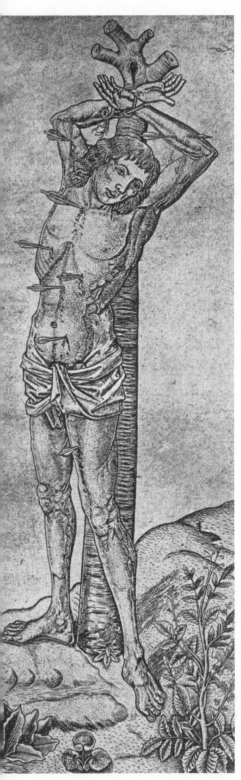

Above: A king plays chess with Death, but his expression suggests that he has lost the game. ©
Stephen Porter

Left: The martyrdom of St Sebastian, by Hans
Holbein the Elder, 1516. © Stephen Porter

Death comes to all, illustrated in this troubled death of a monarch, attended by saints yet pestered by demons. © Stephen Porter

A leper, drawn by Hans Holbein the Younger. As the incidence of leprosy declined, leper hospitals could be used for plague victims. © Stephen Porter

Left: Death enters the bedroom of a sick man, who is being pestered by demons while an imp sorts through his worldly wealth in his chest. By Hieronymus Bosch. © Stephen Porter

Below left: Hans Holbein, *Dance of Death*: a corpulent abbot is dragged away by Death, despite his protests; there is an hourglass in the tree. © Stephen Porter

Below right: Hans Holbein, *Dance of Death*: an advocate is attended by Death in the street just as he is receiving a sum of money from a wealthy man; a poor suitor looks on. © Stephen Porter

Above left: Hans Holbein, *Dance of Death*: an astrologer sits in his study consulting a celestial globe, but Death offers him a skull to study. © Stephen Porter

Above right: Hans Holbein, *Dance of Death*: outside a large building which may be a hospital or almshouse a neglected beggar covered with sores lies on some straw. © Stephen Porter

Above left Hans Holbein, *Dance of Death*: a duke outside his palace averts his gaze from a poor woman asking for alms, but Death has seized his cape. © Stephen Porter

Above right: Hans Holbein, *Dance of Death*: a gambler has been grabbed by both Death and an imp; while one of his companions intervenes the other counts the money. © Stephen Porter

Above left: Hans Holbein's *Dance of Death*: merchants checking their goods on a quayside are accosted by Death. © Stephen Porter

Above right: Hans Holbein's *Dance of Death*: Death intervenes as the judge makes a ruling between two litigants. © Stephen Porter

Above left: Hans Holbein's *Dance of Death*: Death carries a large lantern as he accompanies a parish priest leaving his church. © Stephen Porter

Above centre: Hans Holbein's *Dance of Death*: Death helps himself to handfuls of a miser's gold from the table; the miser, dismayed, is powerless to intervene. © Stephen Porter

Above right: Hans Holbein's *Dance of Death*: Death carrying a large flask of urine for examination comes between a physician and his elderly patient. © Stephen Porter

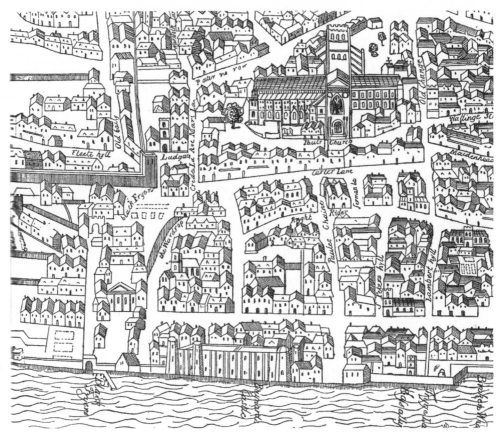

Above: Blackfriars and the area around St Paul's, depicted on the 'Agas' plan of the mid-sixteenth century. © Stephen Porter

Right: A woman and her children evicted from their home, depicted by Joris Hoefnagel in London in 1569. © Stephen Porter

Above: The crowded buildings of Westminster in the early seventeenth century, drawn by Alexander Keirincx. © Stephen Porter

Left: The playhouses were closed when plague threatened; this is a drawing of the Swan Theatre in 1596. © Stephen Porter

A mouse trap being investigated by a potential victim.
© Stephen Porter

VENVS
AND ADONIS

Vilia miretur vulgus : mihi flauus Apollo
Pocula Castalia plena ministret aqua.

LONDON

Imprinted by Richard Field, and are to be sold at
the signe of the white Greyhound in
Paules Church-yard.
1593.

When the playhouses were closed because of plague, in 1593 Shakespeare turned to writing poetry, including *Venus and Adonis*.
© Stephen Porter

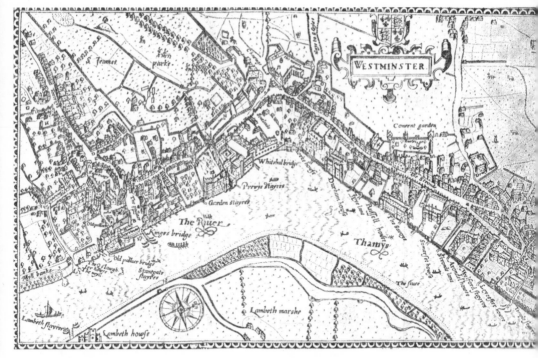

John Norden's plan of Westminster, 1593. © Stephen Porter

The ill treatment by country people of those fleeing the plague in London was illustrated in this woodcut of 1641. © Wellcome Collection

The rat-catcher calls at the door to collect his fee for the rats he has killed and is taking away on his pole; an etching by Rembrandt of 1632. © Stephen Porter

6

A PESTILENTIAL AGE

Plague recurred periodically during the fifteenth century, with some outbreaks on a national scale and others confined to London and its immediate environs. Its role as a major port made it vulnerable to repeated introductions of the bacillus. In contrast to the late fourteenth century, the epidemics did not leave a clear trace in the records. Chroniclers mentioned some of them and others can be identified from official documents and personal letters, although the allusions are often almost incidental, as though an outbreak of the pestilence was such a customary occurrence that it needed no great comment. That did not apply to new diseases, which erupted with unexpected suddenness from time to time.

The peaks in the numbers of wills registered in the hustings court which marked the fourteenth-century plague outbreaks do not occur so sharply after 1375. That may have been because of negligent record keeping, with some wills not entered when there was an upsurge in numbers, or perhaps many of those who made wills attempted to avoid death by leaving when an epidemic threatened and did not return until it was over, or they died away from London. With such vagueness in the records even the scale of the outbreaks is uncertain, despite the impact which the disease continued to make. The death-toll in a severe epidemic in London in 1407, for example, was recorded by Thomas Walsingham, who reported that the 'furnace blasts of death' claimed 30,000 victims in the city, and a Venetian merchant who left towards the end of September 1464 wrote from Bruges that plague was then killing 200 victims per day in London.[1] While those are clearly exaggerated numbers, they reflect a death-toll which must have been in the thousands in both years.

After the deadly outbreak of plague in 1407, the disease hit London again in 1413 and 1426, and in 1433, 1434, 1437, 1438 and 1439, during a decade which was also marked by several harsh winters. In 1433 the sittings of parliament were suspended because of an outbreak of pestilence in London and its suburbs, and in the following year there was a 'grete pestilence in London, both of men, women and children; and namely of worthy men, as aldermen ... and also thrugh England the peple deyed sore, bothe pore and riche'. The high mortality from pestilence in the late 1430s was accompanied by famine, with 'a sekenesse called the Pestilence universally through this youre Roialme more comunely reyneth than hath bien usuell bifore this tyme' and 'great dyrth of corne' throughout England in 1439. The 1440s may have seen epidemics in London in each year between 1442 and 1445, and another in 1449, according to the Rolls of Parliament. There was 'great death' in London in 1452, when the sittings of parliament were again adjourned because of the 'infectious air', and in 1454 William Paston wrote to his brother Sir John, in Norfolk, 'Here is great pestilence. I purpose to flee into the country.' There was then a short hiatus until epidemics on a national scale in 1463 and 1464: that in 1464 was especially virulent in London and, in the autumn, was one of the most severe outbreaks of the century. Another outbreak in London followed in 1467 and one in 1471, which was widespread, if John Paston's evidence is accurate, for he wrote in the middle of September:

I fear there is great death in Norwich and in other borough towns in Norfolk; for I ensure you it is the most universal death that ever I wist in England, for by my troth I cannot hear by pilgrims that pass the country, nor by none other man that rideth or goeth any country, that any borough town in England is free from that sickness. God cease it when it pleases him.[2]

This shows how an individual, admittedly a member of the gentry, could gain a picture of the extent of an outbreak and the level of danger without any official proclamation, by questioning those who travelled around what conditions were like elsewhere. It also reveals the continued acceptance that an outbreak was attributable to God's will.

The plague recurred in the mid-1470s and in 1479 it was reported that 'the sekenese ys sore yn London' producing 'an huge mortalyte ... To the grete mynysshyng of the people of all maner of agys'; the legal term was 'deferrd from Ester to Myhyhlmas [29 September] be cause of the grete pestelens', which may have been the worst in the entire fifteenth century.[3] In October Sir John Paston went to London, where conditions were such that he feared for his well-being, if not his life, writing: 'I have been here at London a fortnight; for the first four days I was in great fear of the sickness, and also found my chamber and stuff not so clean as I thought it was, which worried me very much.' His fears proved to be well founded, for he died in the city in mid-November and was buried in the Carmelite priory of the Whitefriars, south of Fleet Street. His brother, the third John Paston, went to London to sort out the family's affairs and he, too, was fearful, but in December was able to write to his mother: 'thanked be God, the sickness is well ceased here, and also my business putteth away my fear'.[4] That epidemic made such an impression on one chronicler that he was moved to compare it with the impact of the Wars of the Roses, writing that 'by reason of great heate and untemperate aire, happened so fierce and so quicke a Pestilence, that fiftene yeres warre past, consumed not the thirde part of the people, that onely foure monethes miserably and pitifully dispatched, and brought to their sepulture'.[5] The 1470s was the worst decade for epidemics since the 1430s, in a century punctuated by plague and other maladies.

A new disease struck England at the very outset of Henry VII's reign in 1485, 'which by the accidents and manner thereof they called the sweating-sickness'.[6] This scourge 'swept the whole country; it was a baleful affliction and one which no previous age had experienced' and to that extent it resembled the onset of the Black Death. But the symptoms were quite different and could not be confused with those of the plague, for a 'sudden deadly sweating attacked the body and at the same time head and stomach were in pain from the violence of the fever'. In any case, for its 'sudden sharpenes and unwont cruelnes [it] passed the pestilence' and it acted quickly, so that it was said that it 'immediatly killed some in opening theire windowes, some in plaieng with children in their strete dores, some in one hour, many in two it destroyed, & at the longest, to those that merilye dined, it gaue a sorowful Supper'. Some victims removed the bedclothes to reduce the heat that was tormenting them, while others added more covering to the bed to try to sweat out the disease. Neither strategy worked, for 'all alike died, either as soon as the fever began or not long after, so that of all the persons infected scarcely one in a hundred escaped death'.[7]

The outbreak began in London around 21 September and on the 23rd the mayor, Thomas Hill, died. His replacement was Sir William Stokker, but he died on 28 September and John Warde was then chosen. He survived the short period until the end of the mayor's annual term, but four aldermen and 'many worshipfull comoners' also died in the epidemic.[8]

The notion that the corrupt matter causing the disease could be expelled from the body through heat was also a solution attempted in the case of another new disease, recognised in Europe about ten years after the sweat and known as *Mal Francese*, or the French Pox.[9] The sweat soon became known as the English Sweat, *Sudor Anglicus*, for no outbreaks were detected on the continent, except in 1529, when it swept through much of northern Europe and Germany, and as far south as Austria and Switzerland. Its recurrence in England was variously explained by the damp climate, with frequent fogs, bad diet and poor standards of cleanliness. Both the sweat and the pox were regarded by contemporaries as recent afflictions, while plague was an existing, recurrent one.

The speed of the sweat's onset and the rapidity with which it claimed its victims were alarming aspects of the affliction, not giving time for the citizens to leave, but it did not recur during the last years of the century. Leprosy remained a problem and in 1472 Edward IV ordered that all lepers found within the city were to be removed to the isolation hospitals; by the sixteenth century London had as many as eight such houses for lepers. The mayor and aldermen duly issued a proclamation that 'No lepour nor any persone enfecte with the same sikenesse of lepour entre or come wtin the libertee of this Citee of London upon payne of lesyng of his horse if he come ridyng on horse bake and of his gown or upper garment of his body accordyng to the lawes and usages of this Citee.'[10]

Plague returned before the end of the century and the increased number of wills, once more an indicator of numbers of deaths, peaked in 1498 and remained high in the following two years. Indeed, one of the worst outbreaks of the disease during the late medieval period struck in 1500 with 'a great plague of pestilence wherof men died very sore in many places, especially in and about London, where died in that whole yeere (as it was thought) about the number of 30000 people'. Robert Fabyan, a London draper, put the death-toll at a more modest 20,000.[11] Both estimates are implausibly high, given the total population, and a reasonable approximation is 10,000, which, even so, was roughly one-fifth of the inhabitants. The turn of the century was marked by a major plague epidemic, which had also been the case a hundred years earlier.

The problem of space for burials in London recurred during the epidemics and the churchyards were again insufficient. The stench of pestilential death could be unsettling. In 1431 a petition to the Bishop of Rochester claimed that the cemetery on the east side of the church of St Michael Paternoster Royal produced such smells that the Master could no longer sleep in the church.[12] Spitalcroft was again used for plague burials in the early fifteenth century, perhaps during the outbreaks in 1407 and 1433–4.[13] That was in the southern part of the space, which had become the outer precinct of the Carthusian priory. In 1481 a chapel was built there, dedicated to the Virgin Mary and All Saints, which was intended as a gate-chapel for those visiting the cemetery and was part of the ongoing attempts to keep the laity away from the original chapel, which had been adapted as the priory's church. The outer precinct also contained its flesh-kitchen, for preparing meat dishes for guests, the Carthusians themselves being vegetarians. In 1500 hangings for beef and bacon were made in the roof of the flesh-kitchen 'for defence agenst ratts'.[14] Householders across London faced the same problem of safeguarding their provisions from the depredations of those agile and voracious rodents, helped by cats, with their unquenchable instinct to catch rats and mice. Chaucer's *The Maunciples Tale* acknowledges their role, with the lines:

Let take a cat, and foster him wel with mylk
And tender fleish, and mak his bed of silk,
And let him see a mous go by the wal,
Anon he wayveth mylk and fleish, and al,
And every deyntee which is in that hous,
Such appetit hath he to ete the mous.[15]

The church had attempted to suppress cats, especially black ones, regarding them as evil because of their supposed role as witches' familiars. In 1233 a papal bull identified cats with Satan and countless numbers were tortured and killed over the following centuries. But the number of representations of cats from the late Middle Ages, including carvings in churches, shows that the church's efforts were in vain, and they played a part in keeping the number of rodents down. Late-medieval townspeople were also pestered by parasites, however assiduous they were in cleaning themselves and their premises, and however thorough the street sweepers were. As the Breton poet Jean Meschinot wrote in the late fifteenth century, 'Fleas, scabmites and so much other vermin Make war upon us.'[16]

Without either totals for the city's population or the numbers who died in epidemics, it is difficult to chart London's demographic pattern during the fifteenth century. If it matched the national trend, then it experienced a slow decline during the first three-quarters of the century followed by a period of stagnation and then a slow rise thereafter. Land values of sites in and around Cheapside were stable through the fifteenth century, with a dip during the 1490s and 1500s, although London recovered from the serious and widespread mid-century recession quicker than did the provinces.[17] By the end of the fifteenth century London's population was roughly 50,000, within a national figure of 2.6 million. Not only had there been high mortality levels since the Black Death, chiefly through epidemic disease, but fertility had been low, with couples raising small families. So the population barely maintained its level from generation to generation. Among London's merchant class, 45 per cent of the generation of 1378–1407 lacked a male heir at death, a proportion which fell to 37 per cent for the generation of 1408–37 and was 38.7 per cent 1438–67, and then it fell further, to 28 per cent for the generation of 1468–97.[18] As well as a higher average age of first marriage by women, and so a relatively small number of births, the figures reflect high infant and childhood mortality. Despite the improvement during the last third of the century, these are low levels and if they were replicated across the whole of metropolitan society they explain the stagnation of London's population.

The reproduction rate of the city's inhabitants was only a part of its demographic structure and with the end of the feudal system and ensuing greater freedom of movement for labour, London was well placed to attract internal migrants, eager to make good. Then, as later, those with spirit and ambition were drawn to the city and its challenges, and the potential rewards which it offered. This was the age of Richard Whittington, the third son of a minor Gloucestershire landowner, who had established himself in London before the end of the 1370s through an apprenticeship, and he went on to succeed as a mercer and merchant. He amassed a fortune, much of which was donated to charities, and acted as a civic servant, as Master of the Mercers' Company three times and as an alderman, holding the office of mayor of London on four occasions before his death in 1423. The legend of Dick Whittington and his cat may not have become current before the early seventeenth century, yet he and others, less celebrated, were models for the success that an individual could achieve in the great city. But the effect of plague in the provinces was such that there was no great surplus population from which the city could draw incomers; metropolitan and provincial populations necessarily moved more or less in step.

England's economy underwent a considerable change after the mid-fourteenth century as its wool increasingly was used to manufacture cloth at home, rather than exported to provide the raw material for cloth-making towns in Flanders. Wool exports steadily declined as cloth exports rose, with an eightfold increase during the second half of the fourteenth century, and then quadrupled by the 1490s, an overall rise from 5,000 to 160,000 cloths per year. The trade increasingly was in the hands of London merchants and the cloth was finished and prepared for sale and shipment in the city. Plague appears to have had little impact on the trade, for in only one plague year between 1400 and 1485 were cloth exports below the totals of both the preceding and succeeding two years. That was in 1467. Overseas trade was largely carried on during the summer months, to avoid the uncertain and sometimes dangerous weather in the North Sea and English Channel between October and April; summer and autumn were the seasons when plague was at its most virulent. It seems from the figures that the city was not shunned, either by those supplying cloth to it from the cloth-making areas in East Anglia, the West Country and Yorkshire, or by the merchants and the mariners who transported it. Nor was the trade greatly interrupted by official prohibitions of vessels arriving at and leaving London, or the harbours with which the trade was carried on, to try to prevent the disease from arriving at their port. It seems that neither the national nor the metropolitan economies were greatly impeded by plague, at least in respect of this important and growing sector.[19]

London contained a plethora of trades and during this period the guilds were emerging as the livery companies, regulating the trades and their members. Apprenticeship was one area where the companies set down rules and they did not exclude the enrolment of women; in the fifteenth century many London citizens made provision in their wills for their daughters to be apprenticed. Those who went on and became established in their craft could maintain themselves without marriage, while some widows took over the business after their husband's death. It was the custom of the city that freemen's widows were recognised as freewomen. That close involvement of women in the urban economy reflected a shortage of labour, with not enough young men either growing up in the city or being drawn to it to meet the demand.[20] Despite the plague, London's was a developing economy through much of the century and as new trades emerged, with greater specialisation and innovation, a company absorbed those practising it until a new company was eventually created. There were 78 livery companies by 1500, with a clear order of precedence, their status and self-confidence increasingly marked by the construction of halls for administration and ceremonial events.

Civic policy concerning plague was based on orders for cleanliness in public places because polluted air was thought to be where plague lurked. The duties of the Serjeant of the Channel were to keep the streets clean, and each ward employed rakers to collect the garbage. A proclamation issued in 1461 forbade the 'casting of dung or rubbish into the open streets or lanes'. Attention continued to be given to badly sited and smelly latrines and in 1462–3 the City decided to vault over the Walbrook, which was partly paid for by a donation from Robert Large, mercer and former mayor. Those charged with throwing filth into the River Fleet were to clean that part of the river adjoining their premises by Christmas, with a rather stiff fine of £10 for those who did not do so. Yet another order was required in 1477, that no latrine should be placed over the Walbrook or any of the city ditches; a levy of 5d was imposed on all householders to pay for a man in each ward to clean those ditches. In 1466 the city awarded a contract for ten years to John Lovegold to clean out the latrines; he was to take no more than 2s 2d per ton of ordure removed and sold. Lovegold had petitioned for the contract on the basis that the business had been 'hitherto imperfectly performed by others at an exorbitant charge'. Attention was given to the Thames, with an order in 1472 that all dunghills and rubbish between the Palace of Westminster and the Tower on both sides of the river should be removed, and the mayor and sheriffs of London and Middlesex were ordered to keep the river free from rubbish. That was not easy: in 1477 the foreshore in the parish of St Peter's, Paul's Wharf was said to be covered with the entrails of beasts and other filth at low tide. As well as through orders from the city's government, cleanliness was maintained by citizens, who included clauses in leases requiring the emptying of privies. A lease granted in 1469 of a tenement and shop in Bucklesbury placed the obligation of cleaning its privies on the lessors and three years later a lease of a property straddling the parishes of St Mary-le-Bow and St Mary Aldermary directed that all the privies there were to be 'voided clensed and made clene as often as need shall require'. The impression is that by the late fifteenth century the city was cleaner than it had been a century earlier.[21]

There was still no government or civic policy on plague, even though well considered counter-measures had been put in place in many European cities and towns, including those in northern France, which the English merchant community must have been aware of. Essentially, they consisted of isolating the sick and restricting movement, especially of merchants and their goods, particularly textiles, because plague was recognised to be a disease of the trade routes. Implementation of the regulations could be disruptive and required manpower resources and administrative organisation. Despite such problems, it seems that the measures were enforced with increasing thoroughness from the 1470s, perhaps in response to a rise in the number of outbreaks and perhaps to greater levels of trade. Although England did not have a formal policy, considered views were held on how to manage the outbreaks of the disease, and they were circulated. A manual of advice on plague was sent to the mayor by the 'masters and doctors of Oxford' in 1407, although it probably had been written 20 years earlier.[22]

The citizens themselves were not short of advice. The plague tracts issued in the aftermath of the Black Death were early examples of a genre that developed from the mid-fourteenth century. They circulated throughout Europe, in both Latin – the language of scholarship, including medicine – and the vernacular. Probably more than a thousand were produced between 1348 and 1500; a few popular ones reached beyond the medical professions to literate merchants, artisans and others.[23] The medical professor known only as John of Burgundy wrote a tract in or soon after 1365 that circulated in five languages. Some of these must have reached the London citizens and following the invention of printing with moveable type by Johannes Gutenberg in the mid-1450s, introduced into England in 1476, the number of tracts in circulation was greatly increased. One written in 1364 by Johannes Jacobi, Chancellor of Montpellier University and a papal physician, circulated in manuscript and a version was printed in London in 1485 as *A passing gode lityll boke necessarye & behovefull agenst the Pestilence*. The first medical work printed in England, it was also the first English book to have a title page; hitherto printed books had followed manuscript practice of having the subject matter revealed in the opening words on the second leaf. This innovation may have been because its printer, William de Machlinia, thought that it would have a wide appeal, as indeed it did, for it was reprinted several times during the sixteenth century and an edition of 1536 claimed that its recommendations had been 'practised and proved in mani places within the City of London, and by the same many folks have been recovered and cured'. A new translation in the 1520s by Thomas Paynell was issued as *A Much Profitable Treatise against the Pestilence*; it included 'A remedy for the frenche pockes'. John of Burgundy's tract was also printed in English and remained current to around 1580.[24] There was a growing market for printed works among an increasingly literate public, with some livery companies requiring newly enrolled apprentices to be able to read and write.[25] William Caxton's assistant Wynkyn de Worde had taken over the printing business in Westminster after his master's death and in 1500–01 moved it to Fleet Street, close to St Bride's church, despite the epidemic; plague did not completely hamper business decisions. That was the beginning of the district's dominance in the English printing industry, which was to last until the late twentieth century.

With the greater availability of plague texts the citizens could choose their own treatments to some extent. For those who had contracted the disease the writers of the texts recommended the common practices of letting blood, lancing the buboes and applying specially prepared plasters to the plague sores. Paynell's text recommended taking exercise, and that 'if a manne fele hym selfe to be grevyd with any impostume, he muste avoyde slepe, And seke for good merye companye, or elles walke'. That contradicted the earliest advice on plague, but tract writers generally followed their predecessors when advocating actions to be taken to avoid contracting the pestilence, especially warding off foul air by sniffing herbs in pomanders (poorer people used bread or a sponge soaked in vinegar); keeping a house clean by strewing pleasant-smelling herbs and plants; having rooms clean and aired; eating a moderate diet; and avoiding crowds, especially those likely to contain smelly beggars and other ne'er-do-wells. South-facing windows should be kept closed and the south winds avoided 'for naturally they cause moche infection and daungerous putrifaction', but the north and east windows of a chamber where someone was being treated for the disease should be opened. Places where 'putrified ware' was sold and those which were malodorous because of rotting and decaying matter should be shunned, including 'stables, pryveys, and above all other the infection of deed carein [dead carrion], and of longe standynge waters, the infection of olde sinkes, that cause such corruptions, that the inhabitours of suche houses do die, theyr neyghbours continuyng in helth & prosperite'. The belief that the disease was infectious was reflected in the recommendation that crowds should be avoided and that 'a man shulde not bayne nor wasshe him amonge moche company, for the breth of one infectid person may infect a hole'. Washing in a mixture of water and vinegar was still recommended, with the hands then sniffed, for 'it is helthsome to smel to suche thinges, as be sharpe & tarte'.[26]

Some remedies were the familiar home-made ones for treating common ailments and living a healthy life, which came from herb gardens and the kitchen. Nevertheless, one such preparation was apparently given the royal approval, for it came to be known as 'Recipes for Edward IV's Plague Medicine' and was said to have been written during one of the 'reyning sekneys' during his reign. The person making up the concoction should take

...a hanfull of rewe, a hanfull of marygoldis, halfe a hanfull
of fetherfev, a hanfull of burnet, a hanfull of sorell, a quantite
of dragenys - the crop or the route – then take a potell of
ryngyng water. Fyrst washche them clene and let then seethe
easily tyl yt be a-moste cum from a potell to a quartre of
lekker; then take a clene clothe, and strayne ytt and drynke
yt; and yt be bitter, put ther-to a lytel suger of candy, and thys
may be dronkyn ofttyme; and yf yt be dronkyn before eny
purpel a-pere, by the grase of god their schall be no perell of
no dethe.[27]

The 'suger of candy' was included to make the potion a little
more palatable. Considerable quantities of sugar were imported,
chiefly from Sicily, and it was included in the more refined and
expensive treatments, together with drugs and spices brought
in from abroad. The mixtures and potions were dispensed by
apothecaries and spicers, who came together in 1346 as the
Fraternity of St Anthony and emerged as the Grocers' Company
in the early 1370s. Their concoctions were made agreeable by
the inclusion of the sugar, as suggested in Edward IV's plague
medicine, together with cloves, ginger, cinnamon and nutmeg. By
the end of the fifteenth century Venetian galleys were bringing
more than 40 pharmaceutical commodities to London. The most
highly regarded was theriac, or 'treacle', which had remained
popular since the fourteenth century, for it was commonly thought
to have provided protection against plague, was believed to have
wide medicinal effects and was recommended 'as wel for hole and
seke folks' during epidemics.[28] Specialist dealers in treacle had
emerged by the early fifteenth century in London and Westminster.
In 1479 John Paston asked his brother 'I pray you send me, by the
next man that cometh from London two pots of treacle of Genoa;
they shall cost 16d.' Yet trust in the physicians' prescriptions was
not universal, even within his family. In 1464 Margaret Paston
wrote to her husband, 'For God's sake beware what medicines ye

take of any physicians of London; I shall never trust them because of your father and mine uncle, whose souls God assoil [absolve].'[29]

The Grocers' Company oversaw the quality and authenticity of its members' products, including those of the apothecaries, which may have gone some way to assuaging the scepticism of customers such as Margaret Paston. In 1432 Robert Sewale was fined for the sale of 'false treacle' and in 1456 John Ashfield was fined 6s 8d for making an 'untrue' powder containing ginger, cinnamon and saunders. The 'saunders' in his prescription was powder from the sandalwood tree, which appears in cooking recipes in the fifteenth century, as well as in medical applications.[30] In 1471 the mayor, William Edward, intervened in the trade and seized 'certain barrels and pots of treacle … as being unwholesome, the same having been brought to London in galleys'. Sure enough, a panel of experts consisting of two physicians and seventeen apothecaries condemned the shipment as unwholesome, and it was publicly burned on bonfires in Cheapside, Cornhill and Tower Street 'as a warning to others'.[31]

The apothecaries were located especially in the upmarket shopping streets of Cheapside and Bucklesbury; the value of the imports of spices and sugar also indicates that at least some of their trade was directed to well-to-do customers, from both London and the provinces. The onset of an epidemic provided a potentially rewarding opportunity for the apothecaries, as those who could afford their recipes sought assurance by taking them, or filling their pomanders with the concoctions which they sold, and perhaps by burning the fumigants that were also available. But that was also a dangerous time for the apothecaries, who could meet that demand only by remaining in the pestilential city, while physicians could leave, following their wealthy patients. In any case physicians were unlikely to be approached for treatment by the great majority of Londoners, for a visit from a physician, with the drugs and potions which he prescribed, was far beyond their means, and so during a plague epidemic the apothecaries were the members of the medical profession who found themselves in the front line of risk. Some citizens would not have consulted either a physician or an apothecary, in the belief that, as death was a punishment from God, intervention through treatments and prescriptions was an attempt to thwart the divine purpose.

Unquestionably, the best way to be safe was to leave as soon as plague threatened and not to return until after the epidemic had subsided. That was recommended throughout the second pandemic and was the course of action commonly followed. In 1465, Leo of Rozmital, in Bohemia, set out with his retinue on a perambulation of western Europe. After leaving Braga and continuing on through Portugal they travelled through a region suffering very badly from plague and 'rode through a market or village which was quite deserted and desolated ... We had to buy wine and bread from people who lay ill, or had sick people in the house, and lodge with them.' The sick and their nurses seemed to be the only people left there, the other inhabitants having died or left. When Leo and his companions reached Avignon they had a similar experience, for the plague 'was very bad there and most of the people had fled, so that the town was quite deserted'.[32] Londoners behaved in the same way and during the epidemic of 1443 many of them were said to have left for the countryside, including a draper who, with all his household, departed 'from the said citie for this dethe'. In 1479 it was said that 'meche pepyll of the sete [city] ys yn to the contre [country] for fere of the sekenese' and in 1490 Edward Plumpton, an attorney, wrote, 'They begin to die in London, & then I must departe for the tyme & other men do.'[33] The citizens scarcely required expert advice to choose such an obvious way of self-preservation, but leaving raised the tortured question of the morality of such behaviour. It posed a dreadful dilemma: survival set against Christian duty and civic responsibility. Abandoning one's fellow citizens who were unable to move away worsened their plight, depriving them of help, if not through nursing and comforting the patients, then by organisation and administration, for instance supervising the collection and distribution of charitable funds to aid the sick. Those who left would have been acutely aware of this predicament and needed to find ways of appeasing their consciences.

The literature of plague in fifteenth-century London includes poems by John Lydgate, intended as invocations to ward off the disease and probably written during the epidemic of 1434. His advice to escape the plague was to be cheerful, avoid bad air and infected places, drink good wine and eat wholesome food, smell sweet things and 'walk in cleene heir [air]'. In addition, he added a stanza to his verse, 'How the Plage was Syd in Rome', which was also intended as a means of warding off the plague. The original had been inscribed over a votive picture in the church of St Pietro in Vincoli in Rome. Plague was alluded to in some of Lydgate's other poems, such as the protection of God and the saints from 'the deluge of mortall pestilence' mentioned in his *Pain and Sorrow of Evil Marriage*.[34] Also circulating during the fifteenth century were prayers and anthems for those hoping for protection from the pestilence; penance and confession were strongly recommended. When one of Sir Robert Plumpton's correspondents heard that a servant of his had 'decesed of the sicknes' in 1499, he urged Sir Robert and his household to observe a fast on the eve of St Oswald; Sir Robert annotated this with the comment, 'A reminder for preventing of the plage'.[35] Awareness of the plague was a thread which ran through late-medieval culture.

Civic morale and pride remained high despite epidemics and the threat of plague did not inhibit ceremonial, such as the feasts of the livery companies and the City's own celebrations, especially the procession and feasting to mark the annual election of the new mayor. Those festivities associated with royal entries to celebrate coronations, military success and returns from overseas visits had a long history but became quite frequent during the early fifteenth century. London Bridge and the principal buildings were lavishly decorated, pageants were made and erected and crowds turned out in large numbers to both witness and participate in the revelries. In the fourteenth century such a celebration was held roughly every seven years, but in the fifteenth century the interval was down to around five years. They gave the City the opportunity to display its loyalty and its craftsmen the chance to show off their skills to the courtiers and other members of the nobility, who were a wealthy clientele whose affluence was increased by the military successes of the English during that phase of the Hundred Years War.[36]

Two figures who played an active part in the organisation of the celebrations were John Carpenter, who held the post of Common Clerk of the City from 1414 until 1438, and John Lydgate. Carpenter was an important figure in London's civic life for more than 20 years in the early part of the century. Among his achievements was the compilation of a record of the City's ordinances and customs, known as the *Liber albus*, which was completed in November 1419, when his friend Richard Whittington was serving as mayor. As the preface explained, its compilation was prompted by the plague, which had claimed many of the City's most experienced rulers and administrators, removing their involvement and memory of how things had been done, so that 'their successors have, at various times, been at a loss for written information and disputes have arisen as to what decisions should be taken'.[37] That implies that the City's officers stayed in London during epidemics and succumbed to plague, rather than giving in to the temptation of moving away.

The sudden death that periodically wiped a part of the city's collective memory lay behind another of Carpenter's projects, which was the commissioning around 1430 of a series of boards depicting the Dance of Death. The images were copied from those in the Cemetery of the Innocents in Paris, which had been painted in 1424–5, during the English occupation of the city. They were the first examples of the genre and were accompanied by inscriptions by Lydgate, which were based on his translations of the texts in the Cemetery of the Innocents. Unlike the French version, Lydgate's verses stress the impact of plague, asking:

Where is your reason, where is your wisdom
To see in advance the sudden violence
Of cruel Death, who is so wise and knowing
Who slays all of us, by the stroke of pestilence
Both young and old, of low and high degree.

The boards were hung in the north cloister of St Paul's and came to be well known, as the 'Dance of Paul's'.[38] Death comes to everyone, regardless of rank, position or wealth, and is likely to strike at any time, so that the figures are shown going about their normal tasks, with death poised to intervene. Such an unanticipated fate was surely a reference to epidemic disease. The large and artistically accomplished Dance of Death series on the wall of the Dominican convent's lay cemetery at Basel was probably painted following the plague outbreak in the city in 1439. Sudden death did not allow victims to make proper provision for their worldly goods or their posterity, and there was a danger that the soul would be sent on its journey without due preparation. Within that prevailing mood of anxiety, Dance of Death images were powerful ones and became increasingly popular from the mid-fifteenth century in the form of printed books and prints, as well as monumental murals. The images typically were accompanied by a text emphasising the moral depicted by the image. Death could be a seductive figure who helped his victim to pass his or her leisure time, such as a musician or dancer, or a player of games. One such image depicted a king on the point of losing a game of chess with Death, watched by a sad group of courtiers and prelates. In another a finely dressed young lady is in a garden, where she is accosted not by a handsome suitor or a cupid, but by Death, with his arrow raised. Guy Marchant's Death of the Women, produced in Paris in 1486, shows that Death does not discriminate according to social background, for the dancing figures of Death are paired with women from several backgrounds: a housewife, perhaps a servant, in an apron, a well-dressed and bejewelled lady.[39]

Plague was represented – along with famine and war – as one of God's mortal arrows which he could unleash to punish sinners or send as warnings to repent. An epidemic did indeed resemble the effect of a cloud of arrows or darts fired into a crowd, killing some at random and leaving others untouched. The clergy and moral writers continued to condemn the population for its woeful behaviour and plead for repentance and reform, so that God would relent and end the plague. Expiatory services and penitential processions were held and the saints were beseeched to intercede so that a community would be spared before being completely wiped out. Some saints were particularly venerated for their influence in times of plague, especially Saint Sebastian and, from the mid-fifteenth century, Saint Roch. Saint Sebastian had survived being pierced by arrows, which inflicted the sharp pain characteristic of the disease, only to be pummelled to death, and Saint Roch, a hermit, had been succoured by a dog in the wilderness after he caught the plague and so had survived. Artists and woodcarvers commonly depicted Saint Sebastian wounded by pestilent arrows, thereby saving others who could have been the victims, but those who depicted Saint Roch made a more direct reference to the plague by showing him with a large bubo on his thigh.[40]

Funerary monuments, too, displayed more realistic depictions of death in the tomb effigies, even having cadaverous figures in place of the formal depictions of individuals. That is difficult to substantiate for London because almost all such monuments were destroyed in a burst of tomb-wrecking that occurred in the mid-sixteenth century, or in the destruction of the churches during the Great Fire in 1666. But the late-medieval period saw an increase in the number of monuments in churches commemorating the lives of the elite and the wealthy, which, through their growing wealth, included the well-to-do London citizens. As well as stone effigies, such memorials were in the form of 'brasses', large and small, which were produced in their hundreds in London workshops, through which the capital influenced the style of monumental imagery around the country.[41]

Such depictions and an awareness of the danger of sudden death during an epidemic clearly did not subdue the city's essential nature and contemporaries commented on aspects of its character which were in evidence at almost any period. Its boisterousness, expense and casual criminality – and the sheer bewilderment of a visitor – were conveyed by the author of *London Lickpenny*, written around 1410, shortly after the serious epidemic of 1407. The tale is that of a man from Kent who goes to London to obtain legal redress in some matter, but he came to realise that he did not have enough money to pursue his cause. Arriving at Westminster he found himself in such a crowd that he lost his hood, presumed stolen, and inside Westminster Hall he was unable to find a lawyer willing to take the case because he could not afford their fees. When he emerged he was thronged by people from the Low Countries, tempting him with their goods, including fine felt hats, reading glasses and other 'gay gere'. Then he was offered food and drink at fast-food stalls, 'good brede, ale, and wyne ... Rybbes of befe, bothe fat and fine', but he could not afford them. So he went into London and there he was tempted with peascods, strawberries, cherries, and pepper, cloves, saffron and rice flour. He found that Cheapside contained 'moche people', and there he was asked to buy linen, fine gauze, thread, cotton and a cap. In Candlewick Street, a neighbourhood dominated by drapers, he was offered bargains in cloth, but also food again, such as sheeps' feet, cod and mackerel, and in Eastcheap, where there were butchers' shops and cook-stalls, the cry was 'Ribes of befe, and many a pie!' The mood there was enlivened by music: harp, pipe and psaltery, with busking singers. He found that stolen goods were for sale in Cornhill, where he recognised the hood that he had lost that very morning, but he could not afford to buy it back. Eventually he bought a pint of wine from a taverner for a penny, but without enough money to satisfy his hunger he decided to return home. The author presents this day's wandering through London as a salutary experience for someone from the country in the big city, which he acknowledged 'bearethe the prise', in other words, it was the best.[42]

Nor had plague suppressed London's prosperity in the eyes of visitors, who were impressed by its wealth and trade. In 1466 a German visitor, Gabriel Tetzel, described it as 'a powerful and busy city, carrying on a great trade with all countries. In the city are many people and many artisans, mostly goldsmiths and cloth-workers, also very beautiful women, but food is dear.' The Parisian scholar Domenico Mancini spent several months in London in 1482–3 and noted that it was inhabited by 'diverse sorts of craftsmen'. Artisans dominated the city, not the nobility or the church, and their premises were 'spacious depositories, where goods are heaped up, stowed and packed away as honey may be seen in cells'. Along the riverside were to be found 'all manner of minerals, wines, honey, pitch, wax, flax, ropes, thread, grain, fish, and other distasteful goods'. In the line of streets running eastward from St Pauls, beginning with Watling Street, 'you will find hardly anything for sale but cloths', while in Cheapside, in contrast, 'there is traffic in more precious wares such as gold and silver cups, dyed stuffs, various silks, carpets, tapestry, and much other exotic merchandise'.[43] To Mancini and other visitors London was a prosperous and impressive city and the ravages of plague were not mentioned. It may be that the periodic epidemics had become just one of the unpleasant aspects of metropolitan life, to be dealt with when they occurred.

7

A POLICY FOR PLAGUE

By the turn of the sixteenth century attitudes to plague had been modified since the first epidemics in the 1340s. While the wrath of God or the conjunction of planets were still widely regarded as the causes of plague, other possible reasons for the disease, such as floods of frogs or serpents, wild weather, or earthquakes, no longer attracted much support. Beyond the middle of the fourteenth century an outbreak of plague was not accompanied by hysterical reactions such as those which produced the flagellant movement. The nature of the disease had altered somewhat because the pneumonic and septicaemic plagues seemingly present in the first onset of the disease probably did not recur in the later visitations, in which the bubonic form predominated; the numbers dying within 24 to 48 hours had been reduced as a result. Physicians and others had begun to try to understand the causes of the disease from observations and considered deductions, and regulations restricting movement and isolating the sick had been introduced across much of Europe.

Admittedly, regulations were not always well received by the populace, who put their trust in their own practices during epidemics and in the powers of a religious relic to keep the plague at bay. The Holy Shroud, believed to have been the one in which Christ's body was wrapped after his crucifixion (now known as the Turin shroud), was in Chambéry, the capital of Savoie, from the mid-fifteenth century. Not only did it benefit the town because 'vast numbers of people flock from near and far to see it', but the citizens believed that since it had been there they had hardly ever been struck by plague 'as it used to be, when outbreaks occurred annually', and they were afraid that if it should be taken from the town they would again be subject to the plague.[1] London did not contain such a powerful relic.

The conclusions of those who studied the disease were not wholly pessimistic and they did not passively accept the views put forward in the immediate aftermath of the Black Death. Gentile da Foligno's opinion was that the explanation for plague was to be found not in the movements of the planets but in the bodies of the sick, and suggested that it was due to 'a certain poisonous material which is generated about the heart and lungs'.[2] Among the early fifteenth-century writers, Giovanni di Pagnolo Morelli, professor of medicine at the University of Padua, wrote that 'because of the present plague, and others that we have lived through, there are now cures ... I truly believe that some remedies work'. He thought that the doctors' advice should be heeded and described a number of remedies, while admitting that their efficacy could not be assured. Not only had a more rational view of the possibilities of surviving the plague emerged, but so had ideas on its nature and transmission. The humanist philosopher Marsilio Ficino (1433-99), the son of a physician, speculated that dogs and cats carried the disease from house to house; as they hosted fleas, he was some way towards the truth, without of course being aware of that. Efforts to understand the disease continued through the sixteenth century. Maximilian II, Holy Roman Emperor from 1564 until his death in 1576, encouraged scholars and scientists to base themselves at his court and, according to Johannes Crato, one of the emperor's own physicians, Maximilian himself compiled a catalogue of 'experiments' to facilitate investigations into a cure for plague.[3] Within the intellectual straitjacket of Galenism two general schools of thought gradually emerged. One was that the disease could be transmitted from person to person, and the other was that the disease was carried by venomous atoms which were conveyed in foul and polluted air, and could lodge in merchandise such as textiles, especially those with a thick texture, such as woollen cloth. The debate between the contagionists and the anti-contagionists was to continue, sometimes in passionate terms, until the late nineteenth century.

Enough victims survived to encourage the view that resources should be put into the care of those sick from plague. Medical and nursing staff were appointed and buildings were erected in which the sick could be isolated and nursed. Those lazarettos, or pest-houses, were similar in conception to the lazar houses for lepers which many cities had built, but by the sixteenth century the incidence of that disease was declining. London's corporation maintained two of its lazar houses into the sixteenth century, at St Giles-in-the-Fields and Kingsland, on the edge of the City. In 1515, £400 was allocated for their repair and the institution at Kingsland was still staffed in the early 1540s.[4] Lazarettos were to evolve into isolation hospitals for those suffering from infectious diseases. They were set up in some continental cities from the early fifteenth century, the best-known and most widely admired of them being Milan's Lazaretto di San Gregorio, built in 1488, and the plague hospital on Lazaretto Vecchio in the Venetian lagoon, erected shortly after an epidemic in the city in 1485; an older lazaretto in Venice had been built in the early fifteenth century. Several Italian cities decided to invest in such a building in the years after 1550, although some were slow in erecting them; Genoa took that decision in 1467 and the lazaretto was not completed until 1512.[5] The Hospital de San Antón was established in Madrid rather earlier, in 1438, while plague hospitals were founded in Lyon in 1474, in Marseille in 1476 and Toulouse in 1514. Henry IV founded the Hôpital Saint Louis in Paris in 1607, but cities in northern Europe were slow to erect pest-houses. Long-term care for plague victims was not required, as the epidemics were intermittent, the mortality rate was very high and those who survived the disease recovered after a few weeks.

Those people who succumbed to the Great Pox, on the other hand, did require long-term care, and were known as the *incurabili*. That disease erupted in Italy in 1496 and was blamed by the Italians on the French armies which had invaded two years earlier, while the French attributed the outbreak to voyagers returning to Naples after the discovery of the Americas. The earliest responses seem to have been to banish the sufferers from the town, as was ordered in Aberdeen and Edinburgh in 1497, and as the disease was of a venereal nature it provided an opportunity to roust out the prostitutes. But when it did not disappear some authorities set aside buildings to house the victims, as Paris did, and in 1565 a hospital for them was built in Venice.[6] In 1540 surgeons in London were reproved for treating in their houses 'diseasid personnes as ben infected with the pestilence, great pockes, and such other contagious infirmities', because they also cut hair, washed and shaved their customers on the premises, 'which is very perillous for infecting the Kinges people resorting to their shoppes and houses'.[7]

Where pest-houses for plague victims were erected, they were commonly placed just outside the built-up area, as they could serve both as isolation hospitals, to which victims were taken when they exhibited the symptoms of the disease, and as places where those who survived could be nursed. That was not always the case, however, and at Delft, for example, the buildings of the convent of Maria Magdalen within the city were adopted as the municipal pest-house before the Reformation in 1572 and retained thereafter. London did not erect a pest-house before the last decade of the sixteenth century, even though the aldermen came under pressure to do so as the government evolved a policy to deal with the impact of the disease. In 1583 the Privy Council admonished the corporation for not having erected a pest-house and attempted to play on civic pride by pointing out that they had been provided by 'cities of less antiquity, fame, wealth, circuit and reputation'.[8] The aldermen resolved to do so and chose a site for it, but it was not built until 1594 and they did not appreciate the credit to be gained by building an architecturally admirable response to plague, as Milan and Paris had done. London's pest-houses were small and short-lived. Apart from the expense of erecting and maintaining such a building, there was the inescapable fact that if it was to be reserved for plague sufferers then it would stand empty for most of the time, while if it were used as a hospital or poor house in non-epidemic years, then the occupants would have to be displaced and accommodated elsewhere when the disease erupted, just when the city was trying to deal with the immediate effects of the outbreak.

England was indeed slow to adopt a policy to deal with plague and its impact, even though by the end of the fifteenth century many European cities were no longer simply passive sufferers during plague outbreaks, but were learning to adjust to the special circumstances which an epidemic imposed on them, recognising the early signs of its onset and being aware of how it would develop. They were attempting to evolve strategies so that their citizens had other options than facing the stark choice of either leaving or being condemned to remain and take their chances. In France and Spain measures were adopted locally, before central government brought them together as an evolving set of orders, but in the Italian states the steps taken against the plague were generally initiated by the government, and were then applied locally in cities and towns. England was to follow the latter model, but with London acting separately, albeit under the Privy Council's stern and critical gaze.[9]

Mortality in London was high during the first two decades of the sixteenth century, with a peak in 1503–4 and another plague outbreak in 1506, which continued into the winter, for at the Inner Temple 'the gentlemen of the house dare not tarry for Christmas on account of the plague'.[10] Henry VIII succeeded his father in April 1509, and in that year there was 'a great Pestilence in the toune of Caleys, and muche people died'. Perhaps mercantile traffic between the town and England, and maintenance of its garrison, spread the disease to England, where 'The same yere the plague was greate, and reigned in diverse partes of the realme, the kyng kept his Christemas at Richemond.'[11] The young king's reign had begun with an epidemic, as had his father's.

The sweat returned in 1508–9 and again in the spring of 1516 and during the second half of 1517; outbreaks of plague occurred intermittently into the 1520s. In 1513 'began a great mortalitie in London and other places wher much people died'. It continued in London from the spring until the autumn; during the summer the Venetian ambassador was prompted to remark that in London 'deaths from plague occur constantly' and he reported in October that the death-toll was still as high as between 300 and 400 each day. At the Inner Temple 'everyone was discharged from commons' at Midsummer, after the death of one of the butlers there from plague, and that was continued through the autumn.[12] Plague struck the house of the Poor Clares at the Minories during an epidemic in 1515 and 27 nuns and some of their servants died, almost the entire house. Such a death-toll was unusual in a plague epidemic and suggests that, once the disease had been identified in their community, the nuns may have agreed that they should all remain within the site and not risk spreading the disease by fleeing.

Desiderius Erasmus's parents died of plague, his mother when she was living in Deventer, caring for him while he was at school. When he was in the third form 'the plague, which was raging there, carried off his mother, leaving her son now in his thirteenth year. As the plague grew daily more and more severe, the whole house in which he lived was deserted, and he returned to his native place.' Plague touched many families and made many children orphans but, as Erasmus's career shows, that was not in itself a bar to success in renaissance Europe. Not surprisingly though, he was very wary of diseases. In 1511 he was lecturing in Cambridge and early in October wrote to John Colet that he would be in

London in early December, if the plague did not frighten him off. He followed that with a letter to his friend Andrea Ammonius in London, to tell him that he would visit the city during the coming winter, if the frost had cleared off the plague. Ammonius had recently been appointed Latin Secretary to Henry VIII and would have been a reliable source of information on the prevalence of diseases. He replied that the plague was decreasing but he was worried that there might be a famine and wood prices were high, which suggests an interruption to trade during the summer and early autumn, when fuel supplies were stockpiled. By the end of November he could report that the plague had entirely gone, and Erasmus, reassured, arrived from Cambridge, but not until February. Contemporaries would not have been tempted to smirk at Erasmus's fastidiousness and anxiety, for those who travelled from place to place depended for their safety on reliable news on the presence of disease, notably plague and the sweat. He remained wary of conditions in England and in 1518 wrote that 'in England nothing is safe from the plague', but Germany was little better, for there 'besides the usual robberies there is also plague to deter me'.[13]

That such a widely-travelled humanist scholar should reproduce crude national stereotypes, such as Germans being robbers, may be surprising, but they were commonplace even among Europe's intelligensia. Germans were also inclined to insolence and drunkenness, Erasmus characterised the Dutch as 'mean and uncultivated' and they despised 'humane studies' (and he was from Rotterdam!), the Spanish were abstemious with regard to food and drink, while the English, in contrast, were self-indulgent. Erasmus repeated the tale that Charon, who rowed the dead across the Styx, preferred to ferry Spaniards because they were lean, whereas Englishmen were so corpulent as to risk upsetting his boat.[14] Diet was a prominent element in English recommendations against the plague and sweating sickness, the two things clearly being associated in the opinions of medical writers. So were personal cleanliness and health, and the Venetian Andreas Franciscus, who travelled through Europe to England in 1497, wrote when he was in the Netherlands: 'In Germany nearly all the men and most of the women and children are very dirty; in this country such a condition is strongly disapproved of.'[15]

Franciscius was also critical of the condition of London's houses. Because they were all 'so badly paved that they get wet at the slightest quantity of water' from rain and spillages by the water carriers, a 'vast amount of evil-smelling mud is formed, which does not disappear quickly but lasts a long time, in fact nearly the whole year round. The citizens, therefore, in order to remove mud and filth from their boots, are accustomed to spread fresh rushes on the floors of all houses.' Erasmus criticised that practice, because although the rushes were renewed occasionally, that was done 'so as to leave a basic layer, sometimes for twenty years, under which fester spittle, vomit, dogs' urine and men's too, dregs of beer and cast-off bits of fish, and other unspeakable kinds of filth'.[16] He would have set his standards by the towns of the Low Countries. Antonio de Beatis wrote in 1517 that the Flemish were 'so meticulous about not dirtying the floors in their houses that in every room, before you go in, there is a cloth to clean your feet with, and the floors have a dusting of sand'. Londoners clearly did not match that degree of domestic cleanliness.[17]

Being at court did not confer immunity and the king was as anxious as anyone else in the realm. Rules for Edward IV's court had included the stipulation that there should be 'no perilous sykeman to lodge in this courte, but to avoyde within three dayes' and the king's physician, or 'Doctour of Physicke', was responsible for keeping infected persons out of the court. Despite the attention given to the court's safety from disease, in the spring of 1514, when the plague 'is kindling sparks everywhere here [London], and looks like becoming a roaring blaze any day now', the disease 'even had the effrontery to force its way into the royal palace itself, causing two or three deaths'.[18] Two years later a suspected case of plague in Sebastiano Giustinian's house meant that he was not admitted to Cardinal Wolsey's presence to deliver the diplomatic letters from the Venetian Council of Ten entrusted to him, and he withdrew to Putney for his own safety.[19]

In September 1517 Giustinian reported that he had left London to avoid the plague. News of that outbreak 'in London and other places' was deployed to deter Luigi d'Aragona from visiting England. Known as the Cardinal of Aragon, he was one of the wealthiest and best-connected of the Italian cardinals and was undertaking a tour which began at Ferrara and took him and his entourage of more than 35 people across Germany, then through the Low Countries and France, before returning to Ferrara across northern Italy. His progress was noted, but the purpose of the journey was unknown, leading to speculation that it may have had some covert diplomatic purpose, or that he was scheming to enhance his own position, which might pose a threat to Cardinal Wolsey's diplomatic arrangements and plans. He would therefore be unwelcome in England and Sir Richard Wingfield, the Deputy in Calais, was instructed to put him off. Yet the weather was fine and the cardinal's attendants had arranged a ship. Some delays could be caused by taking the cardinal hunting, but that would not serve as an excuse for very long. Then Sir Richard received a letter which contained news of the plague outbreak in London and he told the cardinal of this 'knowing how much the Italians are afraid of coming into a place where there is danger of death' and, sure enough, he cancelled the voyage and continued into France, and did not return. His chaplain, Antonio de Beatis, kept a journal and he wrote that Wingfield 'told Monsignor that large numbers in that island [England] were dying of a disease they call the sweating sickness because it kills by making men sweat, within 24 hours at the most, and is highly contagious, and that in London, the capital of that kingdom, 500 had died of it in a day'. In any case, an audience with the king would have been difficult, because he 'keeps aloof at Windsor to avoid the sickness', and Wolsey had gone even further away, to Walsingham in Norfolk. Two months later ambassadors from France did arrive in London, but could not gain access to the king 'through fear of the plague'. Diplomats' travels and negotiations were seriously disrupted by plague and the sweating sickness, which could also be used as pieces in the diplomatic chess game.[20]

In 1517 Ammonius died of the sweat during an epidemic that killed the courtiers lords Clinton and Grey, as well as 'many other knights and gentlemen', and, more alarmingly, two pages in the royal household. The young Lord Grey's burial cost £10, which was paid out of the royal coffers, when he was described as 'late the King's henchman'.[21] Ammonius made his will on 17 August and he died during the night, 'carried off by the sweating-sickness in the space of eight hours'. Thomas More wrote to Erasmus, telling him the news, and explaining that Ammonius 'saw himself very well protected against the contagion by his modest manner of life, thinking it due to this that, though he rarely met anyone whose whole household had not suffered, the evil has so far attacked none of his people'. That a member of the European intellectual elite such as Ammonius sought refuge from the disease in his lifestyle and diet indicates that there was no other accepted method of avoidance, and he probably felt unable to leave London because of his official duties. Members of More's household had suffered but had recovered, including his eldest daughter, Margaret. The physicians, 'of whom she had divers, both expert, wise, and well learned, then continually attendant upon her', were unable to keep her awake, which was thought to be important for her recovery, 'so that both the physicians and all the others despaired of her health and recovery, and gave her over'. Her father was very attentive and had the idea of applying a clyster, or enema, to her as she slept, to expel the contents of the rectum. That was done, but when she awoke she displayed 'God's marks, undoubted tokens of death', yet she recovered. Perhaps based on the experiences in his family and household, More repeated the current opinion that 'this sweating-sickness is fatal only on the first day' and went on to make the wry comment, 'Of this I can assure you: one is safer on the battlefield than in the city.'[22] John Colet endured three attacks of the sweat, which exacerbated a liver condition, before succumbing in July 1519. The Venetian ambassador wrote that the king was dashing about from one place to another to avoid the disease and had dismissed both his own and the queen's courts, retiring to the countryside with just three gentlemen and his favourite musician, Dionysius Memo. The citizens were displeased when the court remained away from Westminster and London over the Christmas holidays, depriving them of the courtiers' profitable business. Giustinian reported that 'general discontent' had developed because of the absence of the court 'on account of the plague, which had somewhat abated'.[23] As late as the following March the king had not returned and he asked Wolsey whether any of the royal palaces near London were infected. He was at Richmond in the middle of the month, where three pages in his household were said to have died of the plague.[24]

Those frequent outbreaks, affecting the royal household as well as the city, coincided with the acceptance in high places of humanist ideals and endeavours to improve conditions, reflected in the first organisation of the medical profession, and a government under Cardinal Thomas Wolsey that was prepared to act on social matters. Wolsey's career blossomed after Henry VIII's accession in 1509. He was created Bishop of Lincoln and Archbishop of York in 1514, Bishop of Bath and Wells in 1518, Bishop of Durham in 1524 and of Winchester in 1529; the pope made him a cardinal in 1515 and the king appointed him Lord Chancellor in December that year. He was as close to being all-powerful as any statesman could be under the early Tudors. Education was a priority of the reformers and Erasmus's friend and collaborator John Colet re-founded the school at St Paul's in 1510, having been made dean of the diocese of London in 1505. Colet's friend Thomas Linacre was a member of the humanist circle and the key figure in terms of the organisation of health matters. He had taken a degree in medicine at Padua in 1496 and in 1509 he obtained an appointment as royal physician to Henry VIII. His reputation came to rest chiefly on his translations of Galen's works from Greek into Latin, for he was no innovator. Galen's work remained supreme and those few physicians who suggested other ideas were harassed, if not persecuted, by the profession. Linacre was Wolsey's personal physician and would have needed to secure the cardinal's support when he proposed to create an institution for physicians in London.

Linacre, five other physicians and the theologian Thomas Cranmer petitioned Henry VIII for the establishment of a college for physicians in London; through their efforts the College of Physicians came into existence by royal charter in September 1518, with Linacre as its president. It was authorised to license and oversee medical practice, and to punish unlicensed practitioners and prevent them from practising in the City of London or within seven miles of it. That had already been forbidden in an Act of Parliament of 1511, which was intended to prevent 'the grievous Hurt, Damage, and Destruction of many of the King's liege people, most especially those that cannot discern the cunning from the uncunning', which was inflicted by those without any medical knowledge or skill who 'take upon them great Cures and things of great Difficulty, in the which they partly use sorcery and Witchcraft', and inappropriate medicines.[25] The college also came to provide advice and information respecting plague in London. Its supremacy in London in medical matters was confirmed by an Act of Common Council of 1525, which also ordered that apothecaries should provide medicine only on a prescription issued by a licensed physician. The physicians were to engage in a long struggle with the apothecaries to maintain their exclusive right to diagnose patients' illnesses and issue prescriptions. But their skills were not universally acknowledged. When the Venetian diplomat Andrea Badoer arrived in London in 1512 he was stricken with a fever which kept him in bed for more than five weeks. He wrote that 'I had two physicians, each of whom chose to receive a noble [6s 8d] per diem ... and their coming was as beneficial to me as if they had stayed away'. The physicians' charges and seeming ineffectiveness partly explains why Londoners preferred to go directly to an apothecary. Writing from London in 1517 Giustinian reproved Erasmus for taking pills 'which that fool of a doctor gave you'; he added the general advice to 'Give the physicians a wide berth; they treat a man and his horse, and don't know the difference. Fees and not physic is what interests them.'[26]

In January 1518, while attention was focused on medical matters but before the college was founded, a royal proclamation drafted by Wolsey was issued addressing the problem of plague. It declared that the 'resorting of persons not infected with the pestilence to other persons infected doth daily cause the increase of further infection, to the great mortality and death of many persons which, by reason of such resort one to another, have been ignorantly infected with the said pestilence'. To limit such contacts it required that any house in London containing a plague victim should have a bundle of straw hung outside it, on a pole at least 10 feet long overhanging the street, so that passers-by and would-be visitors would know there was plague in the house. Everyone from an infected household was to carry a white rod, four feet long, whenever they went out. The pole on the house was to remain there for 40 days after the last appearance of the symptoms among the occupants, a period which was probably chosen because of its biblical connotations. Furthermore, a plague victim's clothes were not to be worn for three months after their death. The distinguishing marker on an infected house proved to be too elaborate and in September 1521 the bundle of straw was replaced by a headless cross, known as a St Anthony's Cross, again fixed on the front of the building.[27]

These were the first regulations concerning plague in England and in issuing them the government acknowledged that it had a role in public health matters. They came at a time when other measures were being taken to improve London's environment. In January 1517 a deal struck by the City with the Fraternity of St Katherine, the Carmen's organisation, included the arrangement that they would 'clense, purge and kepe clene all the Stretes and lanes of this Citie and Suburbes of the same of Donge and other filth ... for such sumes of money and at suche prises as the wardes be now appointed and assessed to paye'. This was to be done 'for the avoiding of contagious infections'.[28] A year later a new appointment was made, of an official whose duties included searching for able vagabonds and beggars; the 'impotent' beggars, that is the infirm and the elderly, were to be licensed, and those suffering from the Great Pox were to be taken to hospital, proof that the disease was present in the city and creating a problem that needed to be addressed.[29]

That burst of activity aimed at improving conditions in London coincided with a period when the king was without satisfactory accommodation there. The residential quarters of Westminster Palace had been destroyed in a fire in 1512 and were not rebuilt and Henry did not favour the palace within the Tower. He used instead the accommodation in Baynard's Castle, near Blackfriars, which had been improved by his father. The new Bridewell Palace was begun in 1515 but took eight years to complete, and it was not in a favourable setting, alongside the River Fleet and close to the Thames, in an area afflicted, it was thought, with damp and unwholesome air. That was not an ideal environment for a monarch who was nervously anxious about his health and was the kind of setting condemned by writers from the fourteenth century onwards as potentially unhealthy. The court was peripatetic for much of the time, but when the king needed to be in London the accommodation available to him was within the crowded and built-up city itself.

Wolsey's regulations concerning plague were not well received by Londoners. They were issued during the winter, when the disease was usually quiescent, and the more immediate threat was the sweat, yet within three weeks the Londoners' reaction was hostile, to such an extent that it was said that they 'have murmured and grudged and also have had seditious words whereby commotion or rebellion might arise within this city'. The seditious words were directed against the proclamation and against the king himself, for having fled from the city.[30] Setting up a pole on a house and carrying a wand or stick could be regarded as inconvenient at a time when households were afflicted by disease, but surely were not irritating enough to prompt such a strong response, so it may be that it was the disruptive impact of the 40-day rule which provoked the objections. Regardless of such protests, the household quarantining of victims and those in contact with them was to become the cornerstone of the government's plague policies for the next 150 years, and the period of 40 days, although varied from time to time, was generally adhered to. Wolsey's orders were aimed at containment, not prevention, and were to have long-term consequences, provoking controversy and confrontation in the years ahead.

In April the king was at Woodstock and Thomas More was regulating matters in Oxford, where, towards the end of the month, he reported that three children had died of the sickness, but no others. He had instructed the mayor and common council of the city 'that the inhabitants of those houses that be and shall be infected shall keep in, put out wispes and bear white rods', as Wolsey had ordered for Londoners. The Council approved More's orders and debated whether the fair to be held at Oxford in a fortnight's time should be allowed to go ahead. It was apprehensive that if it was banned 'there should ensue grudges and murmurs amongst the King's subjects; specially in London, where they would think that men went about utterly to destroy them, if, with other their misfortunes, they should also be kept from their fairs and markets'. Clearly the rumbling discontent in London had been noticed, and the fair was allowed.[31]

More's account of the ideal commonwealth of *Utopia* described the environmental regulations in its chief city of Amaurote. They included a rule that nothing 'filthy, loathsome, or uncleanly to be brought into the city, lest the air, by the stench thereof infected and corrupt, should cause pestilent diseases'. Despite the precautions and the city's four hospitals, which were 'so big, so wide, so ample, and so large, that they may seem four little towns', the island had twice experienced 'a great pestilent plague'.[32] More wrote that part of the book in Bruges in 1515 and it was published in Louvain in 1516, in Latin; the first English translation appeared in 1551. He was evidently aware of the measures taken in some European cities, but may not have had an input into the compilation of the orders in the king's proclamation.

To assess the extent of the risk and to gain an indication of whether the policies were effective, the government required information on the number of plague cases and if they were increasing or declining. In 1519 the mayor was directed to compile the necessary statistics, presumably based on the number of houses that were marked, in accordance with the proclamation of the previous year. At the end of August a return was made to Wolsey of the numbers who had died of the 'common sickness' since the beginning of the enquiry, with the Court of Aldermen paying John Ward's expenses 'for boat hire to my Lord Cardinal's and to Mr Lark with the bill of the number of such persons as be deceased of the common sickness since the beginning of the search thereof'. This is the first use of the word 'bill' in connection with the compilation of statistics of the victims, which were shortly to become known as the Bills of Mortality. This marked another step in the evolution of the government's plague policy.[33]

Outbreaks of plague continued and in 1521 there was 'a great pestilence and death in London and other places of the realme'; the following year 'was not without Pestilence nor Derthe of Corne' and in the winter of 1525–6 'was greate death in London, wherefore the Terme was adjorned, and the king for to eschew the plague, kept his Christmas at Eltham with a small nomber, for no manne might come thether, but suche as wer appoynted by name: this Christmas in the kynges house, was called the still Christmas'. Yet Wolsey spent Christmas at Richmond, where he 'kept open housholde, to lordes, ladies, and all other that would come, with plaies and disguisyng in most royall maner'. It seems that the cardinal was not afraid to risk outshining the king at such a popular season; that brought a reaction, for it 'sore greved the people, and in especiall the kynges servauntes, to se hym kepe an open Court, and the kyng a secret Court'. Fear of the plague had shown a division within the ruling elite, which was apparent to the citizens.[34]

In 1528 the level of mortality was so high that figures were compiled of both the number of plague deaths and the parishes which were free from the disease. By April the French cardinal and diplomat Jean du Bellay was so concerned that he wrote 'I intend to remove a mile hence for some time, as the plague is in the neighbourhood, though not from any great fear of it'. On 5 June Brian Tuke admitted that he had fled to Stepney 'for fear of this infection, a servant of mine being ill at my house in London'. That was also a year with an outbreak of the sweating sickness; the Bishop of Lincoln excused himself to Wolsey with the comment that he had remained in his house in London while many were dying of the sweat and 'tarried till it came to my house, and then was forced to flee'. The Bishop of Exeter wrote to the cardinal, 'God preserve you from the pestilent air about London.'[35] Even the greatest in the land contracted the disease: the king told Anne Boleyn of five members of the royal household, including the apothecary, who had been afflicted by it yet had survived, and both Anne and Wolsey recovered from an attack. Anne's brother-in-law William Carey and his fellow courtier Sir William Compton did not escape and both died in June. Thomas Cromwell's wife Elizabeth also died during that outbreak and their two daughters in the following year, possibly of the disease.

Du Bellay wrote to France in the middle of June 1528 to explain that the sweat had appeared within the previous four days, yet he estimated that about 2,000 people in the city already had been attacked by it. The outbreak had caused great alarm and everyone 'is terribly amazed'. The Milanese ambassador had left his lodgings 'in great haste because two or three had been suddenly attacked'. It was, du Bellay wrote, 'a most perilous disease. One has a little pain in the head and heart; suddenly a sweat begins; and a physician is useless, for whether you wrap yourself up much or little, in four hours, sometimes in two or three, you are despatched without languishing.' Those who feared that they had contracted the sweat could be seen 'as thick as flies hurrying out of the streets and the shops into the houses, to take the sweat the instant they were seized by the distemper'. That is, they were rushing home to wrap themselves up and get hot, to try to sweat out the disease. Du Bellay added that 'the priests there have a better time of it than the physicians', presumably referring to fees received for burials, and not for treatments, because the disease acted so quickly. He explained that there had not been an outbreak like it for 12 years and then 10,000 had died within 10 or 12 days. The current epidemic had begun in a more alarming manner and if it continued food prices would fall, because of the reduced demand. His fears and his statistics were both exaggerated, but the alarm, fear and disruption that the outbreak caused were clearly expressed in his account.

The king was also guilty of passing on misleading information when he wrote to reassure Anne Boleyn that 'Few women have this illness; and moreover, none of our court, and few elsewhere, have died of it.' He also told Brian Tuke 'how little danger there was if good order be observed; how few were dead of it' and recommended that everyone should eat 'small suppers' and drink little wine. He did not practise what he preached, for according to du Bellay the king 'shuts himself up quite alone. It is the same with Wolsey. After all, those who are not exposed to the air do not die.'

In a postscript he explained that the king had eventually stopped 20 miles from London at one of Wolsey's houses 'finding removals useless', and had made his will and taken the sacraments 'for fear of sudden death', while the cardinal had 'stolen away with a very few people, letting no one know whither he has gone'. Du Bellay went on to give some more of his dubious statistics, reporting that the disease had attacked 40,000 people in London, but 'only 2,000 are dead'; he also repeated the current fear that 'if a man only put his hand out of bed during twenty-four hours, it becomes as stiff as a pane of glass'. In early July another of Henry VIII's reassuring letters to Anne Boleyn could have been read by her as actually quite alarming, for he wrote that five people had contracted the sweat 'in this house'; they had recovered, but it showed that 'the plague has not yet quite ceased here', before adding rather lamely that 'The rest of us are well.'[36]

Du Bellay mentioned that the astrologers were predicting that plague would follow the epidemic of the sweat. That did not happen, but astrologers continued to foretell onsets of the plague. So long as they were vague about when the outbreaks would occur they could not be wrong, for one would happen eventually. Londoners were willing to listen to those predictions, even though they increased their apprehension. Everyone knew that plague would strike again, the only doubts were when, and how destructive of life and prosperity it would prove to be.

The practice of recording the number of deaths when they were abnormally high became an established feature of epidemics. In October 1532 the Council ordered the mayor 'to certify how many have died of the plague', the disease having broken out 'in sondry partes in London' including Fleet Street, so that the Serjeants at Law and the members of the Inner Temple had broken up. The return showed that three-quarters of the 126 recorded deaths across the city were attributed to plague.[37] By then Wolsey had fallen from power and his protégé Thomas Cromwell was in the ascendant. This did not produce a change in policy respecting plague. In the summer of 1535 Cromwell asked mayor Sir John Champneys for lists of the victims and he duly provided the numbers of those who had died from plague and from other causes. Champneys's covering letter summarised the situation: 'there be dead within the city of London of the plague and otherwise from the 6th day of this month of August to the 14th day, which be eight days complete, the full number of 152 persons (105 of them from the plague)'. He promised a similar account for the following week. By recording the parishes where plague deaths had occurred, the districts within the capital which were affected could be identified. The Bills of Mortality were beginning to emerge as a useful tool for the government and the city, with the parish churchwardens given instructions to 'write or cause to be written weekly certificate of all such people as shall die within the City of London and the liberties'.[38]

The recording of vital information was extended in 1538 when Cromwell, as Vicar General, ordered that a record be kept of the baptisms, marriages and burials in every parish. Some clerks chose to note the cause of death, especially plague, in their parish register, and in 1555 this became a requirement when they were directed to make returns of the numbers 'of all the persons that do die and whereof they die'. The parish registers provided a continuous record, whereas at that stage the Bills of Mortality were compiled only intermittently, when plague was detected and an epidemic threatened.

Despite the greater amount of information available, disagreements arose regarding the implementation of policy, and a row broke out over whether to allow Bartholomew Fair to go ahead in 1535, a plague year. In mid-August Cromwell was told that the plague 'rages in every parish in London' and again, in early September, he was informed that the plague 'rages in the city' and was increasing, as the mayor's certificate of the numbers showed. A new house was being built for Cromwell at the Austin Friars and in late September a mason living near his 'great gate' was reported to be sick of the plague.³⁹ As with the discussion over the fair at Oxford in 1518, the economic consequences had to be weighed against the risk of allowing so many people from a wide area to come together; not only was Bartholomew Fair much larger, but its catchment area and economic significance were much greater. The mayor defied Cromwell and refused to cancel the fair, claiming that the extent of the disease was exaggerated, being 'nothynge so grete, as yt ys bruted yn the contry, by the sayenges of suche persons as resorte to the seid Citie at this present tyme'. And if the fair was not held he was afraid that those who brought their cloth to the city to sell, which would then provide work for London's artisans, would not be able to find buyers in the current economic climate. Rather than cancel the fair he asked Cromwell for a loan of £10,000 from the crown, which the city would use to promote sales at the fair and so create employment in the capital. Perhaps his scheme was not favoured, for he assured Cromwell, 'I knowe none yn London, of whom I mought boroo, for this purpos, £100 in money.' His arguments carried the day, but a few weeks later Lord Audley, the Lord Chancellor, was afraid to enter the city on his return from Colchester, having earlier heard that 'they dy of the plage in dyverse parishes in London', and he wrote from Old Ford, in Essex, that 'I lye verey nygh London, to my daungier'.

Business was disrupted by the outbreak, and the French ambassador, who was entrusted with a verbal message to the king, was not allowed within six miles of the court because a French merchant who had followed him had died, it was suspected of the plague. At last the ambassador was instructed to go to a field where the dukes of Norfolk and Suffolk and Cromwell went to hunt, and he delivered his message to them there, in the open air and away from any company. At the end of September Cromwell warned the Imperial ambassador that the plague was so severe in and around London that someone who went from there to visit the Princess Mary 'might seem wanting in attention'; that is, he should not do it.⁴⁰

Intermittent epidemics continued to be in the forefront of the awareness of the royal household and the Privy Council, while the Londoners, too, could scarcely have been ignorant of the threat when they heard of outbreaks, not only in their own city, but elsewhere in England or on the continent. The Council, London's rulers and its citizens should, it seems, have had much common ground in devising and implementing measures to reduce the spread of the disease when it did occur, yet in practice that often was not the case. Fear, disruption, economic need, the practicalities of everyday life, social divisions, and a host of considerations of individuals and their households combined to make plague not only a destructive element in London life, but also a divisive one.

8

PLAGUE AND SWEAT

Londoners felt aggrieved and economically damaged by the measures taken when plague was prevalent, notably the cancellation of the law term and the transfer of the courts to other towns, the proroguing of Parliament and proclamations forbidding anyone going from London to court. All of them were sources of tension between the Privy Council, the corporation and the citizens. Parliament met only intermittently, but its sittings became more frequent from the 1530s. Members of both houses and those attending the courts took the opportunity to buy fashionable and expensive apparel, jewellery and other luxuries, household furnishings and fine horses, making them profitable customers for London's merchants, dealers and artisans. They also consulted their lawyers about ongoing cases in the courts, titles to property and marriage settlements. When their meetings and hearings were held elsewhere, that business was lost to London, and those who regularly supplied the courtiers were thwarted when they were not allowed to go to court, to take orders, supply goods or collect payment.

Henry VIII remained nervous of the plague, the sweat and his health generally throughout his reign. By the early 1540s the royal household paid five physicians, four surgeons and three apothecaries, and inadvertently may have helped to guard against the plague by employing a rat catcher, John Willis, described as 'rattaker', at 4d a day.[1] The Privy Council kept a close eye on the risk posed by London, where mortality levels in the city fell during the second half of the 1520s and remained low throughout the 1530s, despite the anxieties of 1528 and 1535, before rising towards the end of the decade and peaking in 1540. Several years of high mortality followed and concerns for the king's safety were renewed.[2] An outbreak of plague in the spring of 1543 continued through the summer. In August it was described as 'the raging pestilence' and in October the law term was moved to St Albans because London was 'sore infected with the pestilence'. All but one of the 19 deaths in St Pancras, Soper Lane during the year were attributed to plague.[3]

The epidemic in 1543 caused a flurry of activity. In early August the Privy Council wrote to the corporation on the king's behalf complaining that the disease increased daily and blaming this on 'slowthe and negligens' and the actions of those who had fled from their houses, rather than the corruption of the air. This in turn was the fault of the authorities, so the Council directed that a number of actions should be taken and the corporation duly issued them as orders. All infected houses were to be marked with a cross; the practice of using a pole and bunch of straw had been abandoned. Everyone who was infected should not go into others' company 'for a season', if by doing so they could still gain their living, which was a significant qualification, presumably designed to avoid provoking opposition and creating the practical difficulties of providing for those who had no income when confined at home. But it risked the possibility that most infected people would claim exemption from being quarantined in their houses by asserting their need to go to work, seriously weakening the efficacy of that order. Those who did go out were to carry a white rod, two feet long, for 40 days after they had first been infected. A further order was that dogs should be taken out of the city, or killed and their bodies deposited in the common rubbish dumps. Hounds, spaniels and mastiffs were exempted from this order and were to be allowed as 'necessary for the custody and safe keeping of the houses', but they must be kept on the premises and not allowed to roam in the city, as they were thought to be a means of spreading the infection.[4]

Cleanliness was addressed, too, with orders that greater thoroughness should be used in sweeping and washing the streets, carrying away filth deposited in them and drawing water from the wells. Straw and rushes were not to be thrown into the streets but burned on the premises, and if that was not feasible the householder should 'truss it up close' and take it during the night to designated sites in the fields around the city, where it would be burned. The clothing of people who had died was not to be aired by being hung from a window but taken to the fields. One of the orders ruled that no householder should put a sick person out into the street or elsewhere unless arrangements were made for them to be looked after in some other house. This was the most chilling of this set of rules, because it suggests that it was the practice to do so; why else would it be mentioned?[5]

The Council continued to monitor the situation in London and in October it again complained to the corporation of its 'slaknes used at this present'. It ordered that it should be sent weekly returns of the numbers of deaths from the disease so that 'his highness may surely knowe howe the sykenes dothe augment or decrease'. The indignant mayor protested that he had sent those figures weekly 'as his predecessors did' and now would forward the returns from 27 April. But he struck a shrewd blow at the Council's own restrictions by pointing out that his officers would have mixed freely 'among people of the city' to obtain the information and so could not be admitted to court; he asked for a rendezvous, where the paperwork could be handed over without breaching the order that no Londoner should go within seven miles of the court, which was then at Woodstock.[6] The outbreak in 1543 had therefore prompted a revision and extension of the plague orders for London, developing those issued a generation earlier.

Plague recurred in the capital in 1545 and again in 1547, when the aldermen were to direct all householders whose houses contained someone who had been afflicted by the plague to 'cause to be fyxed upon the uttermost post of their Strete dore A certein Crosse of saynt Anthonye devysed for that purpose', which was to remain in place for 40 days. The aldermen were also 'to cause all the welles & pumpes within their seid wardes to be drawen iij tymes euerye weke, that ys to saye, Mondaye, Wednesdaye, & fryday. And to cast down into the canelles att everye suche drawyng, xij bukkettes full of water att the least, to clense the stretes wythall.' In the following year the mayor's court was suspended in August 'by reason of the vyolence of the plage'. During the year the number of deaths was three times the average and the plague orders were extended to interments, with the instruction to all 'curates and others having to do with burials' that no corpse should be buried between five o'clock in the evening and six o'clock in the morning.[7] Henry VIII died in 1547 and was succeeded by his son, as Edward VI. Anxiety about the safety of the court remained high and in 1548 when plague was identified at Boulogne, in English hands since 1544, the Privy Council ordered that no-one who came from there was go to court 'untill suche tyme as they shall have been abrode and ayred', that is, effectively to have served a period of quarantine.[8]

Following Wolsey's fall from power Henry had appropriated his palace of York Place in Westminster and adapted it for royal use, with a programme of building work on both sides of the roadway which bisected the site. It had been the custom to take the bodies of parishioners of St Margaret's who had died in St Martin-in-the-Fields along that roadway for burial in their own parish church, close to the abbey. But in 1534 a royal decree banned the practice, on the grounds that

Sundry & often times by recourse of much People resorting from Sundry Parts of the World unto us often times great Sickness doth Raign in both those Parishes ... [and] the same Corps of the Dead Persons be brought & borne Earley & late nightley & Dailey throughout our Said Mannor to their Buriall & Parish Church to be buryed to no little Jeperdy of us & of all other our Subjects & Trayne as well in their goeing & comeing by the Infect Persons accompying the Dead Persons & Bodys as by the Infection of their Cloaths.

In future, the victims were to be buried in the parish in which they died.[9]

In the early 1530s two new gatehouses were built, King Street Gate and the Holbein Gate, partly so that the roadway could be closed and partly to bridge the thoroughfare and so provide access between the two parts of the palace without having to cross the street. The roadway was to become Whitehall and the conglomeration of buildings served as the principal royal palace, as Whitehall Palace, until it was destroyed by fire in 1698. Hampton Court to the west and Greenwich to the east of London also came to be favoured by the Tudor and Stuart monarchs. They provided the court with rather more security from epidemics than when it had been within the city, yet were not regarded as safe havens and it remained the practice to move further away from London during a plague outbreak; in 1548 the court went to Hatfield.

Merchants opposed restrictions on travel and the movement of goods, yet were subject to some restraints when plague erupted elsewhere. Bristol experienced an epidemic in 1535, a 'great plague' in 1544–5, which was said to have lasted for a year, and another in 1551–2, which caused 'the greatest mortality by pestilence that any man knew'. Reading suffered in 1537 and again in 1543–4, Worcester in 1528, 1545 and 1553, and among the larger cities Norwich and Exeter experienced plague

outbreaks in the mid-1540s.[10] The ports around the coasts of
northern Europe were obviously of great interest because of
their trade connections with London, especially those in the Low
Countries, where Antwerp was London's chief trading partner
until the 1560s. The English community in the city around the
middle of the century numbered 300 to 400 people, mainly
engaged in trade. Elsewhere, Lübeck experienced epidemics in
1543 and 1548 and Hamburg in 1537 and 1547; Rouen suffered
in 1530 and Amiens in 1545, while mortality during epidemics
in Paris in 1531, 1533 and 1534 required the setting out of a
new cemetery for plague victims. News of such outbreaks was
a concern for the merchants and for the many citizens whose
livelihoods depended on trade.

In 1554 the Venetian envoy Giacomo Soranzo wrote that
there was 'some little plague in England well nigh every year, for
which they are not accustomed to make sanitary provisions, as it
does not usually make great progress; the cases for the most part
occur amongst the lower classes, as if their dissolute mode of life
impaired their constitutions'.[11] His impression was formed during
his stay over the previous three years; the social division that he
hints at between the poor, thought to be likely victims of plague,
and the well-to-do, reflected an accepted opinion. Of course,
the poor were more susceptible than the wealthy because there
were more of them, but other reasons were adduced for their
vulnerability to plague. Those who lived in the densely populated
parts of the growing city were assumed to be dirtier than their
prosperous fellow-citizens, creating conditions which produced
the foul air which harboured the plague venom. In fact, they were
more subject to the disease because they lived closer to the rodents'
nests and runs than did the better-off Londoners, whose servants
carried out the chores which brought them into dangerously close
contact with rodents, fleas and other parasites. Moreover, the
poor were unable to leave as an epidemic developed, not having
an alternative means of support, no resources to tide them over

the dangerous time, and simply nowhere else to go, while those with wealth and contacts or family away from the city, who were willing to provide a refuge, could escape from the danger. But the assumption that the poor's deplorable way of life caused the disease created a social bias in the making and implementation of policy.

The sweating sickness, on the other hand, struck both rich and poor. The outbreaks of the disease were monitored and, with the new practice of collecting statistics, the numbers of victims were recorded. In 1551 there was another epidemic of the sweat, which 'commenced in Wales, and then traversed the whole kingdom, the mortality being immense amongst persons of every condition'. Its progress from Shropshire was tracked, to Ludlow, Presteigne, Chester, Coventry, Oxford and 'other tounes in the Southe', reaching London on 7 July. Edward VI wrote in his journal under 9 July: 'At this time came the sweat into London, which was more vehement than the old sweat,' referring to the attack of the disease in 1528. He explained that 'if one took cold, he died within three hours, and if he escaped, it held him but nine hours, or ten at the most. Also, if he slept the first six hours, as he should be very desirous to do, then he raved and should die raving.' It struck swiftly and the Venetian envoy wrote that the alarm which was caused 'was great and universal', especially at the royal households.[12] The king noted that 'One of my gentlemen, another of my grooms, fell sick and died – [so] that I removed to Hampton Court with very few with me.' As chance would have it, a French delegation under Monsieur le Maréchal arrived in London, landing at Rye, rather than Dover, to avoid Flemish pirates. He was formally received on 11 July at Tower Wharf and lodged at Durham House in the Strand, but the sweat was taking an increasing number of victims and so two days later he moved to Richmond 'where he lay with a great band of gentlemen, at least 400, as it was by divers esteemed'. According to the Chronicle of the Grey Friars 'there dyde a grett multitude of pepull soddenly thorrow alle London'. No deaths were recorded for the 8th and 9th of the month, 761 died of the disease between the 9th and the 16th, and when the sweat briefly reappeared at the end of July it claimed a further 142 victims.[13] Other figures were given, but were not significantly different from these, and the death-toll was below 1,000 in London; the victims there included 'rich yong men' and the epidemic was said to have claimed the lives mainly of men 'and those also of the best age, as between 30 and 40 yeeres, fewe women, nor children, nor olde men died thereof'. The disease had ceased in England by the end of September.[14]

That outbreak was characteristically short, but the nature of the illness, the speed of death and the loss of those who had seemed to be 'in best health' made such an impact that the epidemic was remembered as 'a terrible time in London'. John Caius, a physician who had trained at Padua, published a tract on the disease and attributed its virulence to the state of the air and that of the victims' bodies, suggesting that 'they which had thys sweat sore with perille or death, were either men of welthe, ease, & welfare, or of the poorer sorte such as wer idle persones, good ale drinkers, and Taverne haunters'. That was because 'by the great welfare of the one sorte, and large drinkyng of the other, heped up in their bodies moche evill matter: by their ease and idlenes, [they] coulde not waste and consume it'. Those who worked hard or ate little were less likely to contract the disease, and so 'persones of all contries of moderate and good diete, escape thys Englishe Ephemera, and those be onely vexed therewith, whiche be of immoderate and evill diete'. He outlined a healthy diet and his recommended treatment for those who had the disease was the familiar one of getting them so warm that they would sweat the disease out, while ensuring that they were not exposed to the least cold. Caius's work was the first account of a single disease to be written and published in English and was very influential. But its recommendations could not be tested, for the epidemic in 1551 proved to be the last outbreak of the disease.[15]

Although the sweating sickness did not reappear, it was not forgotten. John Stow mentioned the epidemics in his *Annals* of English history, and Sir Francis Bacon described its initial onset in 1485 in his history of the reign of Henry VII, published in 1622. Drawing especially upon Caius's work, Bacon wrote that it was a new disease; it had 'a swift course' so that those who survived for 24 hours after displaying the symptoms 'were thought almost assured'. He described it as 'a pestilent fever' but the victims did not develop a carbuncle, purple or livid spots, in other words, not the symptoms displayed by plague sufferers. The remedies which he described were the common ones of keeping the patient at 'an equal temper[ature], both for clothes, fire, and drink moderately warm, with temperate cordials, whereby nature's work were neither irritated by heat nor turned back by cold'. Yet he admitted that 'infinite persons died suddenly of it, before the manner of the cure and attendance was known. It was conceived not to be an epidemic disease, but to proceed from a malignity in the constitution of the air, gathered by the predispositions of the seasons; and the speedy cessation declared as much.' Bacon did not treat the sweat as a medical curiosity of the past so much as a dangerous disease which had 'reigned in the city' in 1485 and one that his readers should be aware of.[16]

Writings on plague were becoming more common, dealing not only with the disease and its treatment, but also with the morality of people's reactions. Thomas Paynell, in 1534, questioned why it should be that in the same house 'one dothe dye, and another not'. His answer to the question followed the orthodox medical line that some people were 'humourally imbalanced' and so succumbed to the venomous air. Yet his practical advice suggested that he thought that the disease was infectious, recommending that the individual should 'avoyde greate multitude and congregation of people. For in a greatte multitude maye be some one infectyd the which may infecte manye.'[17] The lawyer and physician Thomas Phayre's opinion in his *Treatise of the pestilence* of 1545 was conventional in acknowledging that the plague was God's punishment of wicked people, that the conjunctions of the planets should be studied, that one cause of the plague was 'the stynch and filthy savours that corrupte that ayre whiche we lyve in' and that diet and lifestyle were important. But he also wrote that when 'a corrupt & venymous fever of pestilence' had infected a person's body, it was 'very contagious to all that are about them, for the venymous ayre it selfe, is not halfe so vehement to enfect, as is the conversacion or breathe of them that are enfected already'.[18]

Changes introduced by the religious reformers during Henry VIII's later years, and more especially in Edward VI's reign, were seen by those who were conservative in theological matters as provoking divine wrath, and so causing plague and sweating sickness. These had included changes to the interiors of churches, in the removal of the rood and statues, the ending of processions bearing statues around the streets and changes to the liturgy. A parishioner at St Martin Ludgate during the sweating sickness in 1551 vented her wrath on the curate, claiming that it was 'such as he is [that] was the occasion that God did plague the people so sore, because that they would not suffer them to pray upon their beads [rosaries] ... And that men did die like dogs because they cannot see their maker borne about the streets as they have seen it in time past.' The reformers accepted that sin was a cause and feared that Englishmen had especially offended, hence the appearance of the sweating sickness almost exclusively in England. But they blamed selfishness and lack of charity, which one preacher summarised as 'that greedy and devouring serpent of covetousness'. The increasing use in trade of credit, bills of exchange and money lending, which was still condemned as usury, together with the visible wealth of the merchants, fuelled their uneasiness. Avarice and self-indulgence were adding to the sins of society and so increasing the danger of plague.[19]

For those looking for hope rather than to cast the blame on others, Psalm 91 offered reassurance and could be read in the bibles in English that were not only available from the 1530s, but were officially endorsed. Miles Coverdale produced a complete English bible in 1535, and that was followed by another in 1537, edited by John Rogers and known as Matthew's Bible. Rogers's version gained royal approval and carried on its title page the clear statement: 'Set forth with the king's most gracious licence.' By an order of 1538 an English bible was to be placed in all churches and a new Great Bible was issued in 1539. A part of Psalm 91 reads:

> I will say of the Lord, He is my refuge and my fortress: my God; in him will I trust. Surely he shall deliver thee from the snare of the fowler, and from the noisome pestilence ... Thou shalt not be afraid for the terror by night; nor for the arrow that flieth by day: Nor for the pestilence that walketh in darkness: Nor for the destruction that wasteth at noon-day. A thousand shall fall at thy side, and ten thousand at thy right hand; but it shall not come nigh thee. Only with thine Eyes shalt thou behold and see the reward of the wicked. Because thou hast made the Lord, which is my refuge, even the most High, thy habitation: There shall no evil befall thee, neither shall any plague come nigh thy dwelling. For he shall give his angels charge over thee, to keep thee in all thy ways.

Daniel Defoe described the effects of the psalm in his fictitious, but well-researched, *A Journal of the Plague Year*, covering the Great Plague of 1665 and published in 1722. In the early stages of the epidemic the narrator is uncertain what to do and looks through his bible hoping for guidance, stopping at that psalm and reading the appropriate verses before noting 'I scarce need to tell the Reader, that from that Moment I resolv'd that I would stay in the Town, and casting my self entirely upon the Goodness and Protection of the Almighty, would not seek any other Shelter whatever.'[20]

In practical terms, cleanliness, public and personal, remained a key way to ward off plague, for foul miasmas were still widely believed to carry the disease. To avoid the dangerous smells of insalubrious alleys and corners, and equally odiferous people, surely the safest course was to leave. But that raised once again the disturbing questions about the morality of such a selfish action, deserting one's fellow citizens when the community's needs were greatest. John Hooper, Bishop of Gloucester, issued a homily in 1553 'to be read in the time of pestilence'. His advice on treatments was to be cautious and well-informed, for 'the greater and more dangerous the sickness is, the more circumspect and wise the sick man must be in knowledge and choice of the medicine, lest haply he seek a remedy inferior and too weak for the greatness and strength of the disease'. A religious reformer, Hooper's views on the causes of plague were nevertheless traditional ones: that it was not caused by the corruption of the air or 'the superfluous humours within man', but by sin and the transgression of God's law. The remedy was to repent of one's sins, believe in the gospel, and live a godly and virtuous life. While the securest course was to flee, he emphasised that some could not do so, such as 'the poorer sort of people, that have no friends nor place to flee unto, more than the poor house they dwell in'. As well as those who could not leave, there were others who should not do so because they held offices of trust, including 'the bishop, parson, vicar, and curate, who hath the charge of those that God pleaseth to infect with the pestilence; and if they forsake their people in this plague-time, they be hirelings and no pastors; and they flee from God's people into God's high indignation'.[21]

William Bullein addressed the issue in the form of a dialogue between husband and wife. The husband becomes very anxious as an epidemic unfolds, marked by 'the daily jangling and ringing of the bells, the coming in of the Minister to every house in ministring the communion, in reading the homily of death, the digging up of graves, the sparring in of windows, and the blazing forth of the blue cross'. When he asks his wife what they should do she gives the rational reply that they are still young and have lives to live, they have already sent their children into the country, the only reason to stay is to earn money, but what use is that if they die? Her conclusion is to leave the city and only return when the epidemic has come to an end.[22]

Fear of plague was indeed universal, from the king to the courtiers, merchants, aldermen and the citizens. The reactions to the disease was one of the subjects addressed by Andrew Boorde, a prolific writer on health, diet and a range of related matters. Boorde was born in Sussex around 1490 and, after an upbringing at Oxford, in 1515 joined the Carthusian monastery in London. The members of the order had a reputation for piety and strictness and, tiring of their regime's rigidity, and alleged to have been 'conversant with women', in 1528 he was granted a dispensation from his vows. His objective was to train in medicine and he travelled across Europe, visiting as many universities as possible. He had returned to England by 1530 and began to practise, the Duke of Norfolk being among his patients. He then undertook a second tour through Europe, in 1532, visiting Normandy, Orléans, Poitiers, Toulouse, Wittenberg, Rome and Santiago de Compostela, seeking out the medical men in the centres of learning. Boorde was back at the London Charterhouse by 1534, where he took the Oath of Conformity, although some of his fellow monks and lay brothers obdurately refused to do so. He had been noticed by Thomas Cromwell, who realised the potential usefulness of his continental travels and sent him on an extensive journey around Europe in 1535 to gauge the reaction to England's policies and the impending break with Rome. From his experiences Boorde wrote for Cromwell *The Itinerary of Europe, a diary describing each region*. He was in Scotland in 1536 and then returned to London before setting out on another tour in 1538, going to Venice and then on to Jerusalem, returning via Naples and Rome, before settling in Montpellier, where the university had a distinguished medical faculty. While he was there he had produced by 1542 *The Brevyary of Helth*, which was followed by *The Dyetary of Helth*, dedicated to the Duke of Norfolk. On his return to England he may have lived for a time in St Giles-in-the-Fields and was said to have had many patients in London. But in 1547 he was accused of keeping three prostitutes in his chamber and, with his former sponsors dead, he was vulnerable to the charges brought by the Bishop of Winchester, Stephen Gardiner, and was confined to the Fleet prison, where he died in April that year.[23]

Boorde divided Europe into high and low regions. His summary of the common response to plague was that 'When the plague of the pestilence or the sweating sickness is in a town or country, with us at Montpellier, and all other high regions and countries that I have dwelt in, the people flee from the contagious and infectious air; preservations with other counsel of physic notwithstanding.' In other words, nothing devised by the medical profession was convincing enough to dissuade those who could from departing when the disease threatened. He did draw a contrast with the 'lower and other base countries' where, when an epidemic erupted, houses in cities and towns were closed, both doors and windows, and the occupants were not permitted to leave, even to go to church or the market, or to 'any house or company, for [fear of] infecting others the which be clean without infection'. He was describing the policy of household quarantine, which was steadily becoming the bedrock of plague policy in England; indeed, his account could be read as justifying that practice, for it indicated that the procedure was generally followed abroad. Boorde was definite about the risk:

A man cannot be too ware, nor can not keep himself too well from this sickness, for it is so vehement and so parlous, that the sickness is taken with the savour of a man's clothes the which hath visited the infectious house, for the infection will lie and hang long in clothes. And I have known that when the straw and rushes hath been cast out of a house infected, the hogs which did lie in it, died of the pestilence.

For those unable or unwilling to leave and so avoid the 'contagious air' he recommended daily use of juniper, rosemary, bay leaves, marjoram, frankincense, or bengauyn (an aromatic resin-like substance) to sweeten the air. The occupants of the house should keep a fire burning in their chamber, 'of clear burning wood or charcoal with-out smoke' and they should be careful not to catch a cold.[24]

Much of Boorde's book dealt with diet and the domestic environment, and his recommendations for those hoping to avoid plague were to take 'temporate meats and drink, and beware of wine, beer and cider'. The 'temporate meats' were 'those the which be light of digestion', not the 'gross meats'. The air in a house should be 'fresh, pure and clean'. Among those things which could corrupt the air were 'the influence of sundry stars, and standing waters, stinking mists and marshes, carrion lying long above the ground', and so a house should not be built close to marshy ground, smelly ditches, gutters or channels, 'nor corrupt dunghills, nor sinks, except they be oft and divers times mundified and made clean'. The air could also be polluted by overcrowding when there were 'much people in a small room lying uncleanly, and being filthy and sluttish'. He warned his readers to 'beware snuff of candles, and of the savour of apples, for these things be contagious and infective', although he especially recommended eating stewed or baked pears. Cleanliness about the house was of the first importance, especially in the buttery, cellar, kitchen and larder. His advice on sleeping arrangements was similar to his other recommendations: 'beware that you do not lie in bed chambers which be not occupied, specially such chambers as mice, rats, and snails resorteth unto. Lie not in such chambers the which be deprived clean from the sun and open air; nor lie in no low chamber except it be boarded.' Boorde's advice on plague was not innovative but rather a rational summary of the practices and recommendations then current, and his recommendations on diet, housing and healthy practices were substantially those current in the mid-fourteenth century, as described in the tractates of the post-Black Death period. Many of them would have been familiar to those who knew Peynell's edition of Johannes Jacobi's text of 1364. If there had been new thinking on such matters, Boorde's work did not reflect it. Even so, he made those notions available in English in a coherent form, and no-one without direct experience of the disease could take it lightly after reading Boorde.[25]

The danger preoccupied members of the intelligensia, whose rational responses to most issues crumbled when plague threatened, throughout the century. They would have been aware that the morality of staying or leaving dictated that anyone who could help to alleviate the disaster should stay. But set against that was the strong instinct for self-preservation. According to the comments of Michel de Montaigne, that varied from person to person. His grandfather lived until he was 69 and his father until he was nearly 80; neither of them had ever taken any kind of drug and the 'very sight of medicine horrified my father'. Montaigne, on the other hand, was very concerned for his health and well-being: 'I believe health to be so precious that I would buy it at the cost of the most agonizing of incisions and cauterizations.' From that remark it should be no surprise to learn that when plague threatened Bordeaux, where he was mayor in 1585, he left home, with his elderly mother, wife and daughter, fearful that he was 'relentlessly pursued by a thousand different pestilences'. His courage in other situations had never been in doubt and when the city was threatened by hostile troops during the Wars of Religion he had organised the defence and served his turn as a lookout on the walls, night and day. But such a challenge was unlike that of the plague. Both he and Erasmus, two of the towering intellects of sixteenth-century Europe, displayed tremendous moral courage, yet scampered away when plague threatened, such was its threat. Montaigne may have felt subsequently that he was justified in leaving, for the outbreak in 1585 slew 17,000 people in Bordeaux, or a half of the city's population. But he also explained the problems of becoming a health refugee: 'Friends are terrified of you, you terrify yourself, the people with whom you seek shelter are gripped by panic and you might be forced to change your abode without warning, when one of the company complains of a pain at the tip of a finger.'[26] Such reactions were typical and would have been encountered by those fleeing London during any of the epidemics in the city. And would mortality have been so high if the leading citizens had stayed behind in their localities to organise those trying to carry out the orders? Scarcely any other issue provoked such fear and revulsion, selfishness and guilt as did plague.

The Venetian envoy in London in the early 1550s, Giacomo Soranzo, noted that the city was 'much disfigured by the ruins of a multitude of churches and monasteries belonging heretofore to friars and nuns'. The Reformation had indeed brought many changes, including the removal of the Dance of Death boards at St Paul's, and the destruction of the cloister where it hung, which was carried out in April 1549. That was done to obtain materials for a new palace in the Strand for the Duke of Somerset, the Protector during Edward VI's minority. The Dance of Death genre had continued to be popular into the sixteenth century, even though Thomas More believed that the fantasy of death in the imagination was more powerful than such images, or even seeing a row of skulls in the charnel house. Printed books disseminated the depictions of death to a far wider audience than the panels in St Paul's or Paris. Indeed, drawings of the Paris panels were issued as a pamphlet in 1485.[27]

The most successful set of Dances of Death was produced by Hans Holbein, who arrived in London from Basel in 1526. He returned to Basel in 1528, but the opportunities open to him there had worsened and he was back in London by the summer of 1532. He settled there and was appointed the king's painter in 1535. Around 1526 Holbein created a series of woodcuts entitled 'Pictures of Death', which was published in 1538 and became commonly known as 'The Dance of Death'. It followed the established tradition of illustrating how imminent death was, showing Death closely engaged with its intended victims in everyday life, not detached from them. Holbein's Death is a skeleton with considerable character, in several of the illustrations he is holding an hour-glass, to indicate the inexorable passing of time. Holbein's images are sharply critical of elites, in the church, society and the professions, for their pomposity, indolence, corruption and lack of charity, in other words not practising the Christian virtues, while the poor are seen to suffer as a result. Several scenes could have applied to Londoners, including merchants on the quayside examining bales of goods newly unloaded from ships when Death accosts them, an advocate, a judge, a miser, a preacher, a parish priest who is being taken from his church by Death, carrying a lantern, an old man and a child of poor parents. Such images captured the anxiety of the time that sudden and hideous death could strike everyone, from the emperor and the pope to the friar, the nun and the ploughman. Nor could scholars escape, for an astrologer at his desk with his books, studying his astrolabe, has Death confronting him, holding a skull, and Death comes between a physician seated at his desk and his elderly patient, offering the physician a large flask of urine for examination. The physician's role generally was said to be 'lookinge of folks waters that weare sicke'.[28] Neither astrologers nor physicians had been able to predict, prevent or cure the plague, and they were as subject to unforeseen death as everyone else. And so, of course, were artists; Holbein succumbed to the disease in London in 1543. His set proved to be very popular and 16 editions had appeared in Lyon by 1562 and 15 by 1573 in Venice and Cologne, even though the genre itself was gradually losing its appeal.

Artists continued to depict society's problems in other forms. Joris Hoefnagel was in London in 1568–9 and in 1569 produced a set of drawings which he entitled Patientia. One of them shows a woman and her two young children who have been evicted and are now in the street with their household possessions, which are being inventoried. This looks to have been a sudden calamity, from the quantity of her belongings; if the problem had crept up on her gradually, she would surely have sold some of her goods and so there would have been little left by the time that she lost her home. Perhaps her husband was a plague victim? What other reason could there have been for the sudden death, which surely had brought her problems to a head? But all is not lost; the porter who has removed the goods indicates to her the doorway of the poor house, where she will be helped. That was better than the street but it represented a major loss of status and dignity for someone who had been intent on bringing up her children in comfort and respectability.

Care for the destitute and the sick, including the infirm, was maintained after the Reformation. Anticipating the possible closure of London's hospitals when the monasteries were dissolved, the mayor, in 1538, and the Court of Aldermen, in 1539, petitioned the crown, asking that they and their endowments should be granted to the City. That did take place, but after a long delay. St Bartholomew's priory was dissolved in 1539 and the hospital continued to operate, although in a reduced condition, so that by 1546 it had just 40 bedsteads and not enough bedding for all of them. In 1544 and 1545 Henry VIII nominated new masters for St Bartholomew's, effectively re-founding the hospital, although probably with the intention that it should be a shelter for the poor rather than a place for the treatment of the sick. Then, in 1546, it was presented to the city, to be governed by the four aldermen and eight common councillors who had negotiated the transfer to the city, including most of its existing property. The hospital was served by three surgeons, a matron and twelve sisters, who were to tend the sick poor, keeping them 'sweet & clean as in giving them their meats & drinks'. The post of physician was created later.[29]

The re-founding of St Thomas's Hospital in Southwark also took a long time to achieve. In 1538 it was investigated by Richard Layton, the king's commissioner, who discovered that the master had sold some of the silver plate and other items, and that he had taken excessive fees. Layton also accused him of living immorally and described the hospital as 'the bawdy hospital of St Thomas's in Southwark'. The hospital was closed in 1540 and the staff and the 40 patients were dispersed. Sir Richard Dobbs, the mayor, and the Bishop of London, Nicholas Ridley, presented an appeal to Edward VI in 1551 and that achieved a positive response. The site and any of the estate of the medieval foundation that had not been disposed of were transferred by the crown to the corporation, which then re-founded the hospital, with St Thomas the Apostle adopted as its patron. Its modest endowment was increased by the transfer of the estate of the hospital of St John at the Savoy after it was suppressed in 1553, as well as all its beds and bedding. St Thomas's had ten wards and initially 250 patients were admitted, but that number was soon reduced to around a hundred.

Despite the nursing provided in the hospitals after the Reformation, they were quite ineffectual during an outbreak of plague. They could not accommodate or nurse so many victims, nor could they isolate the sufferers, and so admitting them would have put the existing patients at risk. Plague policy rested on separating the sick from others and that was not practicable in the hospitals. With the physicians powerless to offer adequate treatment, either cures or palliative care, and nursing care in hospitals unavailable, the medical profession was seen to be inadequate in combating the disease. On the other hand, the church's hierarchy maintained that it could point the way. After the Reformation, the Church of England accepted God's role in sending and withdrawing the disease, and the Book of Common Prayer of 1559 included a collect which recited that in the time of King David, God in his wrath had sent 'the plague of pestilence', which had slain 70,000 people, and yet in his mercy he had spared the rest. It now entreated the almighty to 'have pitie upon us miserable sinners, that now are visited with great sicknesse, and mortalitie, that like as thou diddest then command thine Angel to cease from punishing: so it may now please thee to withdraw from us this plague, and grevous sickenesse, through Jesus Christ our Lord'. Fasts and special services continued to be observed during epidemics, despite the prohibition of other gatherings for fear of spreading the disease.

The plague policy that was in place in London by the mid-sixteenth century was largely invisible outside the plague years themselves. Those measures were revived when an epidemic struck, and the Bills of Mortality were compiled only when the onset of the disease had been recognised. A critic of the procedures in the mid-sixteenth century might have judged that greater continuity and coherence were required. But perhaps the lack of a more forceful implementation of policy was not so obvious, for the economic impact of the epidemics was imperceptible. The author of *A Discourse of the Common Weal of this Realm of England*, writing around the middle of the century, complained that 'greate desolation and povertie' were affecting 'the most parte of all the townes of England, London excepted'.[30] It had steadily enlarged its share of both internal and international trade and the cloth industry, the most important of its occupations, experienced a boom during the 1530s and 1540s. Nicander Nucius, a Greek, was in London in 1545 and wrote, 'In this city there dwell men from most of the nations of Europe, employed in various mercantile arts ... somewhere about the middle of the city a certain place is set apart, where there is daily an assemblage of merchants, from which there arise very extensive barterings and traffic.' He was referring to Lombard Street, where the merchants met twice each day; from 1527 it was pedestrianised while they were meeting, by drawing a chain across it. Nucius described the process by which merchants used bills of exchange to transfer money, adding that 'in London, and in Antwerp in Flanders, more than elsewhere, such transactions take place'. Giacomo Soranzo was impressed by the numbers of vessels on the Thames: 'Up to London Bridge it is navigable for ships of 400 butts burden, of which a great plenty arrive with every sort of merchandise.' The city itself he described as having 'a dense population, said to number 180,000 souls; and is beyond measure commercial, the merchants of the entire kingdom flocking thither'.[31] His estimate of the size of the population was greatly exaggerated, but by the time of his visit it probably had reached 80,000, roughly the level at which it had stood before the Black Death 200 years earlier.

9

THE GREAT SICKNESS OF 1563

Consistency of enforcement of the plague policy was made easier when Southwark became one of the City's wards from 1556, but the suburbs were not brought within its jurisdiction and remained the responsibility of the county justices. In any case, the sweat and plague were not the only mass killers of London's citizens and further heavy mortality came with an outbreak of influenza across the country in the late 1550s. In 1558–9 the mortality rate was more than twice the long-term average and the late 1550s probably was the only period between 1540 and the 1650s when the increase in England's population was checked and there was a decline.

In the early eighteenth century John Strype summarised the accounts of the Tudor chroniclers:

What diseases and sicknesses every where prevailed! the like whereof had never been known before, both for the lasting and mortality of them: which being hot burning fevers, and other strange diseases, began in the great dearth 1556, and increased more and more the two following years ... In 1558, in the summer, about August, the same fevers raged again in such a manner, as never plague or pestilence ... killed a greater number.

Sir Thomas Smith, commenting in 1561, saw the mortality of those years as a reflection of God's disapproval of Queen Mary's policies and especially her marriage to Prince Philip of Spain.[1] The loss of Calais to the French early in 1558 could also be interpreted in those terms: the diarist Henry Machyn's reaction was that this was 'the hevest tydyngs to London and to England that ever was hard of'.[2] While Londoners were absorbing the news of the capture of England's last territory on the continent, they were also enduring the epidemics, during which at least 8,000 people died in London, but neither plague or the sweat were identified as the cause of those deaths. The survivors were unsettled by the experience. In July 1558 the astrologer John Dee wrote to the cartographer Gerard Mercator telling him that an 'extremely dangerous illness' had caused his health to be 'dangerously shaken for a whole year now'.[3] The response was, once again, to blame the lack of cleanliness; the scale of the problem could be judged from the smell. In 1557 Sir Philip Hoby, at Bisham, urged William Cecil to leave London and 'not to tarry so long ... in such a stinking city, the filthiest in the world'.[4] Hoby had personal experience of many European cities, having served as a diplomat in France, the Netherlands and the Empire, and he knew London well, for he owned houses in Carter Lane, Dowgate and Bread Street, so his opinion was a damning one.

In November 1558 Mary died and was succeeded by her half-sister Elizabeth. The early years of the new reign were free from epidemics and plague may have been almost completely absent from London. But that was a calm before a storm, for in 1563 an epidemic erupted which was to be the worst plague outbreak in the city since the Black Death, in terms of the number of deaths, and the most destructive epidemic of the sixteenth century. Its cause was attributed to the English military expedition to Le Havre, in support of the Huguenots during the first of France's religious wars. Elizabeth's government hoped that the English occupation of the town might induce the French to return

Calais in exchange for the English evacuation of Le Havre. An English force occupied Le Havre in October 1562, but found itself besieged there in the following May and it had to be withdrawn at the end of July, without any diplomatic gains. Movements of armies were recognised as one of the commonest ways in which plague was spread and the disease appeared in Le Havre during June. The government realised that those supplying the troops and the wounded and other soldiers returning to England from this ill-fated expedition could bring the disease with them. In August it issued an order that every city and town should set aside 'somewhere remote' for plague victims who were from Le Havre. Whether they were the cause of the outbreak in London is uncertain, but by the beginning of June it was claiming victims in Holborn.

The corporation reacted by implementing the measures already in place. In mid-July the lord mayor ordered that blue crosses on white paper should be fixed to the doors of houses in which anyone had been infected within the previous six days. The crosses were enclosed with the order and after they had been fixed they were to be checked daily; if one had been pulled down 'by anye malicious persones', then the alderman and officers of the ward were to replace it at once. Anyone discovered pulling down a cross was to be liable to a fine of £2 or 20 days imprisonment and, rather harshly, the clerk could be fined £1 for not replacing it and churchwardens and constables who did not assist the clerk were liable to be fined £2 or given 14 days' imprisonment. The corporation ordered 200 crosses on 1 July and followed that up with further orders on the 6th and the 8th. In his *Chronicle*, the printer Richard Grafton conveyed the speed with which the plague spread and threatened to overwhelm the system: 'These crosses increased so sore and the citizens were crossed away so fast, that at length they were fain to leave their crosses, and to refer the matter to God's good merciful hand.' Those within the closed houses were required to stay indoors for one month after the death or infection of anyone in the building; one uninfected person was to be allowed out to buy provisions, carrying a white rod, two feet long, with a fine of £2 if they did not carry the rod, or imprisonment for 20 days if they were too poor to pay. In mid-August the lord mayor further ordered that anyone infected with the disease 'with the plague sore running upon them' who went out of their house, or just into their shop and so met customers, was liable to a £5 fine, levied on the master of the household, or 40 days' imprisonment. It seems unlikely that the victim would have survived for 40 days and taking offenders to prison through the streets meant that they might come into contact with others, which the policy was designed to prevent. The harsh punishments of fines and imprisonment were almost impossible to enforce on the poor and sick at such a time, and reflect the desperation of the corporation that its policies should be implemented, with an awareness of their continuing unpopularity. Yet there was no other means available of enforcing them. This was the application in full of the policy of household quarantine to which the government and the city were committed; in the absence of pest-houses there was no other practical way in which the sick could be kept separate from the rest of the population.[5]

Another mayoral order, in July, required that fires were to be lit in the streets on Friday, Monday and Wednesday evenings, which were to be 'competent and cleare burning fyers' of wood. Henry Machyn noted this as an order that 'evere man in evere strett and lane for to make fires iij tymes in the weke'. Dogs were again blamed for spreading the plague as they went around the city, and there were too many of them, causing offence by their barking during the night, which was 'a grete disquietnes and troble' to Londoners, disturbing their rest and causing disputes. And so no dog was to be allowed out unless on a lead, with a fine of 3s 4d for each offence, and the dog to be killed. It was noted that a man had been appointed to kill as many dogs as he could find in the streets, with a fee for doing so 'every day and nyght'.[6] A note in the Annals of the College of Physicians suggests that the reason that dogs were killed during this epidemic was that all the members of one family had died, along with their three dogs, so the connection was made that the dogs were somehow the cause, hence all dogs were to be killed, and so were cats.[7]

Some 320 deaths were attributed to the disease in July and the number then rose alarmingly, with 299 in the first week of August and 976 three weeks later. In mid-August the death-toll was said to be more than 1,000 in a week. Yet the lord mayor wanted St Bartholomew's Fair to go ahead and to make that acceptable ordered that in the four parishes adjoining Smithfield, where it was held, houses and shops were to be kept closed for five days before the beginning of the fair and five days after it had ended. No such leeway was granted for legal proceedings and the forthcoming legal term was postponed by royal proclamation; in December it was transferred to Hertford. The court had left London for 'places far distant' and Parliament was prorogued on 2 October. As in the past, those actions impacted on the Londoners who were dependant on supplying the royal household, the courtiers and the Members of both Houses of Parliament 'to the greate decay, losse and hinderance of a number of honest cytezens ... as well Inholders and other victuellers as also of many artificers and handy craftsmen'. The queen informed the newly elected lord mayor, Sir John Wright, that no celebratory procession and feast would be held that year for the incoming mayor because 'thorough bringing together such a multitude, the infection might increase'. The livery companies also cancelled their annual feasts. Those cancellations, too, reduced the level of business for the citizens.[8]

The number of deaths continued to rise, despite the efforts of the lord mayor and officers. The situation was so desperate that in some parishes those who were buried were unknown to the parish officers and so were recorded in the register without a name. But at least the registers were still being kept and compilation of the Bills of Mortality throughout the epidemic indicates that many parish officers remained and fulfilled their duties. At St Dionis, Backchurch the clerk, John Webb alias Clarke, was appointed in 1516 and was so diligent that during almost 50 years in the post 'he never lay nyght owt of the same p'ishe ... but allwayes watyng on hys sarvyse'.[9] Christ's Hospital took in some victims of the epidemic, including a youth 'turned out in the plague time', presumably an apprentice evicted by his master, and a boy of 15 who was 'taken up in the street all comfortless'. The mother of a baby girl, only 14 days old, 'did comfort ... one Moore', but he, his wife and their child died, and so did the baby's mother.[10]

A mayoral proclamation of 16 August implied that the clergy were neglecting their duties, for it required that they should officiate at divine service every day at eight o'clock in the morning until further order. The churchwardens were also to ensure that at least one person from every household attended each service and remained for at least an hour. A few weeks earlier the Bishop of London, Edmund Grindal, had written instructing the parish clergy to exhort their parishioners to attend services in their parish churches not only on Sundays but also on Wednesdays and Fridays. Those services were to be preferred to larger assemblies because of the smaller size of their congregations than gatherings such as those at Paul's Cross. Families were also to 'use private prayer, fasting and abstinences with other the fruits of faith and true repentance' at home. To adapt the churches to the dangerous conditions churchwardens were to keep the buildings clean and thoroughly swept, and 'some competent part' of the glass windows was to be removed to allow 'clear and wholesome air' to circulate. Furthermore, tavern keepers and 'common victuallers' were not to permit eating and drinking on their premises while services were taking place, and the connection between undesirables and plague prevention was made clear with the order that 'mynstrells bowlers archers and other gamesters' were not to use their 'Arts Scyences and games' at those times.[11]

The Dutch community of around 1,600 members reacted promptly when it became apparent that a full-blown epidemic was under way. In July the consistory appointed a surgeon and would appoint another, should the need arise. They were to look after the poorer members of the community in particular; the wealthier members were to pay the surgeon directly. Paid watchers and nurses were appointed to assist the ministers with their visits to the sick to provide solace and practical care, including making their wills. Prejudice was not entirely absent despite the scale of the unfolding crisis, and word that the French-Walloon community's surgeon was being helped in his attendance on the sick by a prostitute caused the Dutch consistory to refuse to recommend him to its own members.[12] That the French were generally unpopular was implied by a comment that the 'common people grudge at the Frenchmen and want them out of the realm'.[13] That might have been due not only to the suspicion that the plague had been brought from France, but also to lingering resentment over the loss of Calais, coupled with the failure of the Le Havre campaign, as well as a long-term simmering dislike of immigrants for taking jobs. In truth, no more than 5 per cent of London's population in the 1560s were aliens and three-quarters of them were from the Low Countries; only 15 per cent of its foreign residents were French.

The shortcomings of the City's plague policy were revealed now that it was being put to the test. No financial support had been arranged for the victims and those quarantined in their houses and the corporation recognised that some had been forced to lie in the streets to beg, or had died in their houses, because of the lack of provisions. Evidently some parishes had responded by calling meetings of the parishioners and appealing for a collection and provisions for the sufferers. In early September the lord mayor issued a proclamation stating that some plague victims were so impoverished that they were faced with the stark choice of lying in the streets to beg or wasting away in their own houses. He ordered that the practice in some parishes of taking a collection should be extended across the city, so that those which had not so far arranged such assemblies and collections should do so. If a parish had no need to provide for its own poor, or was not afflicted by plague, then it should make such collections anyway and donate them to those parishes which were in need. Recognising that some of the wealthy parishioners may have 'departed from you into the country for fear of the sickness', the proclamation directed that their servants and housekeepers should be given notice of the collections, so that the wealthy householders could be informed of the process and contribute to the collection. In fact, not all the senior officers remained, for by 26 August 'a greate number' of the aldermen had left, so that the lord mayor, Sir Thomas Lodge, ordered that the Court of Aldermen would not meet again for three weeks, unless there was some emergency. When it did reassemble it ordered that the chamberlain should disburse £60 to help the poor, because those with any wealth left in the city 'are not well hable to releve & succour the poverty in the same city in many places thereof'. The Common Council itself had to admit that its strategy did not work very well and that 'the execution of such diligence therein towards the poores releif hath taken no such good successe as was hoped for'. The response was to order the clergymen and churchwardens of every parish to make a collection every week and to take 'gentle monition' with those who failed to contribute.[14]

Although the number of plague deaths had begun to fall, Common Council noted at the end of October that the disease 'dothe more and more encrese' and it re-issued its orders, and added new ones to prevent an influx of people from outside the city who might spread the infection. It ordered an enumeration of empty properties from which the inhabitants had left, or in which they had died, especially those in alleys and 'back lanes', with the instruction that landlords were not to let them again without licence from the lord mayor. Nor should anyone take in a lodger who had not lived in London for three months, with the penalty of four months' imprisonment. Someone who had come into the city with a plague sore was to be 'whipped out of it'. The orders issued in the autumn express the exasperation of the corporation with those poor who, without consideration for others, and only 'hoping of gayne and lucre and very little or nothing fearing the great plague' came into the city and took lodgings in infected houses. They were to be prevented, while the officers were to allow those who had been away for their own safety to return. Such orders were difficult to enforce, especially as the influx of outsiders was prompted by a search for work, because the economic disruption caused by the epidemic extended beyond London into the surrounding areas.[15]

Common Council also gave attention to the effects of hasty burials. The parish clergy and churchwardens were to ensure that the graves dug during the epidemic were of the accustomed depth used before the crisis, so that no exhalations might 'break out or ascend' from the bodies. Those graves and pits used for burials during the epidemic that were too shallow should have more earth piled on them. Pressure on burial space during the epidemic was so severe that the corporation opened the New Churchyard outside Bishopsgate in 1569, anticipating future need, and the entitlement to use St Paul's churchyard was reduced, from 23 to 13 parishes. A general cleansing was felt to be necessary in the aftermath of the plague and in January 1564 the aldermen were instructed to inform the occupants of their wards that they should 'ayre, clense & purge theyre howses, beddynge & apparrell, for the daunger of thinfeccion of the sycknes of the plague'. But that was not to include any bedding or clothing which may have been infected by the disease, or been in contact with it, and bedding should not be beaten out of a window facing a street. Of course, not all householders would have carried out those tasks, but the association of dirt with plague and the wish to cleanse the city so that the disease would not recur in the new year, coupled with the close administration of the City in wards, parishes and precincts, the smallest units, suggests that many would have done so, producing a mass spring-cleaning of London's houses in the spring of 1564. Fear of the return of plague saw the continuation of the regulations and in February stage plays and interludes without a licence from the lord mayor were banned. That was because people assembling frequently and being 'pressed together' risked spreading infection, although that seemed to contradict the orders to attend church.[16]

The peak number of deaths in 1563 came in the week ending 1 October, with 1,828 recorded. The total number of deaths in the City and surrounding parishes during the year was 23,660, of which 20,136, or 85 per cent, were attributed to plague, with an overall mortality rate of roughly 20 per cent of the total population. Within the City the number of burials was almost eight times the pre-plague level. Indeed, the worst affected parishes were within the walls, while the least affected were the large ones on both the west side of the City and in the north-east, including St Botolph Aldgate and St Botolph Bishopsgate. In St Mary, Aldermanbury, close to Cheapside, there were 119 burials in the year, 99 of them within the four months from July to October and six of them on one day, 27 September. The register of St Dionis, Backchurch, recorded eight burials from January to July, then 33 in August, 65 in September and 40 in October, with just 13 during the last two months of the year. The total for 1563 was 158 burials; there had been 74 in the four previous years and there were to be 61 in the following four years. At St Mary Aldermary the epidemic lasted rather longer than in St Dionis, for there were 13 burials in August, 32 in September, 39 in October, 21 in November and 15 in December. The annual average for 1559–69, excluding 1563, was just under 13 burials. Those were common experiences, for 1563 was by far the worst year for deaths in the period 1560–72 in every one of a sample of 26 London parishes.[17]

During the epidemic the queen remained at Windsor and even there she was not entirely safe, for a rumour spread that one of her maids-in-waiting had contracted the plague. Concern for her security prompted the Marquess of Winchester to recommend that she should be kept away from Hampton Court and Richmond palaces, and he suggested more distant ones, such as Oatlands, Eltham, Woodstock and Farnham. She must not be allowed near Syon, where the exchequer had been temporarily located, because people would go there 'from all places in the realme wherof may grow perell'. The courts of Wards and Liveries and the Duchy of Lancaster were moved away from Westminster to Sheen. Robert Dudley took refuge at Bagshot and William Cecil, who had emerged as the queen's leading minister, presumably stayed at the family seat at Hatfield.[18] The government's revenues were reduced, especially as much was derived from the customs, and trade from London was diminished during the second half of the year. Sir Thomas Gresham continued to have oversight of the government's affairs at Antwerp and he wrote to Cecil in mid-August that he was loath to return to London 'considering the great sickness I understand is yet ther'. He was still in contact with the city and told Cecil that 'this plague tyme, there is noe money nor creadit to be had in the streat of London [Lombard Street]: for I understand by my servant Chandeller, that everie man is afraide to speke one with another'. But he was confident that 'hereafter, when the plague is passid, and everie man falls to his trade agayne, monny will be better to be had'.[19] He could not have anticipated a diplomatic blow which was to fall that autumn, which delayed economic recovery after the epidemic.

Anglo-Spanish relations had deteriorated since Elizabeth's accession and the transfer of the throne of Spain by Charles V to his son Philip, Mary Tudor's consort and now installed as Philip II of Spain and ruler of the Netherlands. That deterioration was partly caused by protectionist measures introduced by Elizabeth's first Parliament, which restricted imports from the Netherlands with the aim of promoting English industries, and partly by the queen's espousal of Protestantism, which was seen as a threat to the Catholicism which Philip sought to impose on his domains. Heretical ideas and literature flowed from England to the port cities of the Netherlands, and emigrants left those ports to sail to England. As the largest city in the trade between England and the Netherlands, Antwerp was regarded with especial suspicion by the royal government in Brussels, which consisted of the Regent, Margaret of Parma, her chief minister, Cardinal Granvelle, and the Council of State. Antwerp was a cosmopolitan trading city and attracted heterodox religious groups, while the city fathers maintained a measure of independence from Brussels in respect of the freedom of their own citizens and a sluggishness in the implementation of unpalatable royal policies. An embargo on trade with England was an attractive option for the regent and her council because it could serve two purposes: it would demonstrate to the English government its reliance on the trading connection with Antwerp and hence its need for the goodwill of Spain, while also diminishing that city's rulers by emphasising its economic dependence on the processing of English cloth. Both of those factors were obvious ones, but there was no loss in drawing attention to them. Granvelle complained in October 1562 of the ingratitude of Antwerp's citizens and pointed out that they should be aware that the king could bring ruin on their city simply by a stroke of the pen. Subsequent negotiations between Philip's representative and the English government had broken down in May.[20]

In November 1563 Philip's consent to an embargo on trade between England and the Netherlands was received in Brussels, but that was not to include cloth and wool, the two most important items in the trade. The plague epidemic gave the regent and Granvelle the opportunity to take the more drastic step of banning all trade without consulting the king, justifying their action by 'the danger of the plague' and the urgent need to keep the disease away from Antwerp. News of the ban reached the city on 29 November, before the fleet carrying the English cloth exports for the year had left the Thames. The English merchants asserted that their cargoes would not transfer the infection because they consisted of cloth, lead and tin that had not originated in London, but their arguments were ineffective. In any case, Elizabeth responded by forbidding the export of woollen cloth, and so the 40 ships of the fleet now had to be unloaded, for the cloth would spoil if it was kept in their holds over the winter. Seeing the ships moored in the river for week after week would have been a gloomy sight for those many Londoners who earned their living from some aspect of the cloth trade, for no income would be forthcoming until the cargoes had been delivered, but to see them unloaded at the quays would have been even more demoralising, for there was no prospect of finding an alternative outlet for them that year. Both the failure to deliver the consignments of 1563 and the continued uncertainty of how and when the trade would resume indicated the strong likelihood that there would be no demand for one year's output of cloth. Diplomatic manoeuvres, trade and religious policies may have been the reasons behind the embargo and Elizabeth's counter-embargo, but the actual pretext was plague, and the policy did have a rational justification in attempting to exclude the disease. But the timing of the epidemic in London had played into the hands of the regent and her council, who could use it to both warn the English not to permit heretics and heretical materials to go to Flanders, as well as showing their own recalcitrant citizens that they should enforce the king's policies and crack down on religious dissent. The English merchants found an alternative outlet for their cloth in 1564 at Emden, outside the Netherlands (in Lower Saxony), although conditions there were not ideal, and in 1565, after a period of hardship in the cloth industry in both England and Flanders, the trade between them resumed, only to collapse later in the decade as the religious disputes intensified, leading to unrest in Antwerp which provoked a military response from Spain.[21]

John Stow's summary of 1563 was that 'The poore Citizens of London were this yeere plagued with a three fold plague, pestilence, scarcitie of money and dearth of victuals: the miserie whereof were too long heere to write, no doubt the poore remember it, the riche by flight into the countries made shift for themselves.'[22] Economic recovery in 1564 was impeded by the problems of marketing that were confronting the cloth industry and was also hindered by the extent of the epidemic across the country in the following two years. Plague struck communities from Kent to Yorkshire, in the Midlands and the West Country. Leicester, Salisbury, Hastings, Rye, Lichfield and Coventry all suffered high levels of mortality. Burials in Stratford-upon-Avon in 1564 were roughly five times the normal level and in Bristol interments in nine parishes in 1565 were between five and ten times the norm during this 'great plague', the city's annals put the number of deaths at 2,070. Germany and the Low Countries also suffered high levels of mortality in those years. In such circumstances, the government's revenue fell, as did its credit.

John Geynes, a fellow of the College of Physicians, was one of those who died of plague in le Havre during the siege, when 'the streets lay even full of dead corpses, not able to be remooved, by reason of the multitude that perished'. A doctor of nearly 30 years' standing before he was admitted to the College in 1560, he was summoned to appear before the fellows 'because he had been accustomed to declare in public that Galen had erred'. When he refused to attend he was ordered to do so by the sheriffs of the city 'or else be committed to jail'. He sensibly relented and went to the College and presented his views on Galen; the ensuing discussions lasted for three days, until Geynes, unable to justify his claims, made a public declaration that Galen was not at fault.[23] The College was the bastion of medical orthodoxy and the experience of such a severe epidemic as that in 1563–4 did nothing to alter the belief in medical circles regarding the cause and spread of the plague.

In his *A diall for all agues*, published three years after the epidemic, John Jones reiterated the common Galenic belief that corrupt air caused the humour of the body to corrupt and putrify. That corruption was the result of 'pestilent exhalations', which 'although they do contaminate and infect by touching, by the companye of men & society of life, yet their origin and most puissant force, consytyth in the ayre which we breth and from thence they proceed'. He repeated the view that the worst air was that carried by winds from the south and south-west, but some areas were at greater risk than others because of the activities carried on there. That applied, for example, to parts of St Sepulchre's parish, in the north-west of the City, because rotting or over-ripe fruit corrupted the air and the parish contained 'many fruterers, pore people, and stinking lanes, as Turnagain laine, Secolayne, and such other places, there dyed most in London, and were soonest infected, and longest continued, as twyce sence I have knowen London, I have marked to be true'. One of those periods of high mortality to which he refers to must have been 1563 and the other perhaps was the outbreak of influenza five years earlier.[24] Foul air was still regarded as providing the greatest risk for contracting plague. Nothing could be gained in practical terms from such a restating of previous views, but the re-appearance of plague later in the decade did cause some policy changes in the light of the 1563 epidemic.

IO

THE TIME OF
PESTILENT PLAGUE

Those who issued the plague orders were not wholly inflexible and
introduced modifications based on experience and probably arising
from the intermittent exchanges between the Privy Council and the
City. Even such a fundamental aspect of the policy as the duration
of household quarantine was subject to variation. The City's rulers
must also have been aware how their declarations conflicted with a
whole range of motivations: altruism, compassion, neighbourliness
and family loyalty, indeed the web of personal social contacts and
patterns of everyday life, which were not abandoned because of
the plague orders, or the dangerous threat of the disease itself.
Attitudes were slow to change and long-standing concerns about
rich living and indulgence were added to fears of social criticism
and disorder emanating from the new theatres, with plague seen as
a punishment for such depravity.

It is likely that awareness of the difficulties of providing for a
quarantined household for a long period prompted the drastic
reduction of the period of closure to just 12 days when an order
was issued in 1569. But that must have met with disapproval,
for later that year 40 days was reinstated. The regulations of
1569 also ordered that those who were incarcerated were to
be cared for by two 'honest women', who would attend the
sick, and one other person would supply provisions and fuel.

Surgeons from the hospitals would also be available and those poor sick people who were 'lyinge under stalls or at menns dores' were to be taken into St Bartholomew's and St Thomas's hospitals, which had been instructed to receive them. This was a far more developed and humane arrangement than hitherto and was to be financed by weekly collections among the 'rich and wealthy'; evidently a compulsory rate was not approved of and so voluntary contributions were to be relied on. Cleanliness was not overlooked, with the instruction that before six o'clock every morning at least 10 buckets of well-water should be drawn and used to wash down each street and its central channel. The streets were to be swept twice a day and the scavenger was to remove all the garbage collected at least once every two days; water which had been used for boiling puddings and tripe must be emptied directly into the Thames, not poured into the streets. Fear of decaying fruit corrupting the air prompted the requirement that pears, plums, damsons and other soft fruit should be sold in shops, warehouses or at market, and not at stalls in the streets. The corpses of plague victims were to be taken directly to the grave and not to a church; in the following year this was adjusted and a church service could be considered if the deceased was 'some person of honor or Worshipp'.[1]

The disease was thought to have 'utterly ceased' during the winter of 1569-70, but already by mid-February it had reappeared. That was blamed partly on lack of information on the numbers of infected, who were alleged to have continued as though nothing were amiss, stocking their houses with provisions by going to the shops and thereby putting their neighbours at risk. The corporation suspected collusion between the parish officers and the infected families to conceal cases of plague, so that the house would not be closed and the families' lives disrupted, and the parish would not be put to the costs of maintaining them. To ensure that information was as up-to-date as possible anyone who was told about or knew of a plague case, or suspected one, was to inform the alderman of the ward or his deputy in writing within three hours. That should have conveyed the urgency with which the authorities regarded the speed of response to the first signs of the disease. An accurate weekly return of the number of plague deaths was also required and that was made the responsibility of the constables. To ensure that a death was correctly categorised, an order of 1569 required that 'searchers of the dead' were to be appointed by the parishes, to inspect a corpse and its symptoms and decide whether death had been caused by the disease. They were appointed thereafter when plague threatened and typically were women old enough to have witnessed deaths from plague. In 1574 St Margaret Lothbury hired two women to 'view all syck persons suspected to have the plagg'; they were paid 2d for each examination. In 1593 St Bartholomew-by-the-Exchange appointed four women as 'keyppers for the syck', two searchers of the dead and two more who were searchers 'for the syck susspectyyd'. As the orders were developed, so the number of people involved in their implementation was increased.[2]

To reinforce its appeal for the orders to be observed, Common Council stressed that the transfer of the Michaelmas law term from Westminster in 1568 had caused 'greate losse and discommoditie to the whole estate of this Citie and chiefely to the poorer sort of the Inhabitants'. That may have been the case, but household quarantine remained so unpopular that there were bound to be families who would risk punishment rather than report a plague victim in their house, or in that of a neighbour. The parish and ward officers were paid so little for their tasks that they could be enticed to conceal or misreport plague deaths, for a fee. The Privy Council was sceptical of the accuracy of the returns from London, suspecting that 'the number of those that die of the plague is made less than they are by the corruption and indirect dealing of some inferior minister'.[3] With such concealment the counter-measures were ineffective and the disease rumbled on throughout the 1570s, with the Michaelmas law term adjourned from Westminster in

every year between 1574 and 1582, with the sole exception of
1580, and even in that year there were 128 plague deaths. In 1578
some 3,500 deaths from plague were recorded within the City and
liberties, and more than double the average number of burials.
During the epidemic William Fleetwood, the Recorder of London,
conscientiously carried out his duties, even permitting people
with plague sores to come to him daily and going around the
City himself to look for 'lewd persons', but the shock of finding
'dead corses under the table' in some of the houses he entered 'did
greatly amaze him' and so he withdrew to Buckinghamshire for
a respite.[4]

Fleetwood was appointed Recorder in 1571, the same year that
Thomas Norton was appointed Remembrancia, effectively the
Town Clerk. That was also the year in which William Cecil was
ennobled, as Lord Burghley, and both owed their advancement to
his patronage. He needed to have clear lines of communication
with the City's administration so that he could be aware of
how efficiently it was being conducted, on plague matters as on
others. As the lord mayor, aldermen and common councillors
admonished the ward and parish officers for not fully and properly
implementing its orders on plague and cleanliness, so the Privy
Council took them to task for the same reasons. Under Burghley's
oversight the government moved towards a codification of the
orders, to introduce conformity and clarity. Copies of plague
orders were obtained from Milan, but in truth those which
were already in place in London and other English cities and
towns were as good a guide as any, as there was experience of
putting them into practice during epidemics. Eventually, after the
College of Physicians had been consulted, in 1578 regulations to
be observed 'throughout the realm' were issued as a printed set
of orders. They did not apply to London and negotiations took
place between the Privy Council and the aldermen about how
the orders could be adapted for the metropolis. The city wished
to maintain its existing system of aldermen and parish officers,

rather than paid officials, and voluntary contributions rather than a weekly tax, which would in any case be difficult to collect during an epidemic.

The orders for London were eventually issued in 1583, a plague year. They were arranged in 21 paragraphs and were substantially those already in use. The period of household quarantine was set at 28 days and the closed houses were to be marked by the clerk or sexton, in a place 'notorious & plaine for them that passe by to see it', with the inscription 'Lord Have Mercy Upon Us', which was to remain in place for the 28 days of quarantine. The structure of aldermen, ward and parish officials was continued, but with two general overseers appointed monthly in each ward by the aldermen, who were to go through their wards once a week to ensure that the overseers were executing the precepts and punishing the defaulters 'without respect of persons'. The city did plan to build a hospital or pest-house 'where maye be certen officers and orders as in other countries'; a site was chosen and 'skilful men' were to be appointed to prepare a plan and estimate for the building. But it seems unlikely that one was built before 1593.[5] The lord mayor and aldermen approached the College of Physicians and asked three questions: how many physicians did the fellows think would be required to treat just plague cases, who were the physicians in London best suited to the task, and what stipend would the College recommend as appropriate? The replies were that at least four physicians would be required, that all 20 of the fellows were satisfactory and that the College hoped that the city would provide a generous allowance to those who undertook that dangerous task, without mentioning a sum. In fact, the physician who is known to have treated patients during the epidemic was Stephen Bredwell, who was not licensed but was a son-in-law of one of the fellows.[6] In planning for a pest-house and providing a stipend for physicians the City was recognising that it should contribute to the costs of dealing with plague and moving away from its previous policy of drawing solely on charitable collections.

As well as attempting to manage outbreaks in London, the Privy Council was taking more resolute action to prevent the disease from reaching the city. In 1579 it issued orders preventing carriers from Norwich, Salisbury and Great Yarmouth, where the plague was present, from coming to Bartholomew's Fair, and it also prohibited the Great Yarmouth fishermen from bringing their herrings to London. Then, in June 1580, it acted on the lord mayor's suggestion and authorised the detaining of ships from Lisbon, which was suffering from a plague epidemic, Plymouth or anywhere else where the disease was present. Their cargoes had to be aired before they could be unloaded, and the crews and passengers were not to disembark until they had served a period of quarantine. In 1585 similar orders were issued banning traffic from Bordeaux and other ports on the River Garonne because of plague there (that was the epidemic which had driven Montaigne away), anyone from Norwich or other places suffering from the plague was prohibited from coming to London, and the Londoners were forbidden from receiving goods or visitors from those places.[7] Naval quarantine and the prohibition of shipping from infected places was to become a major element in plague prevention in the future.

The playhouses added another dimension to the growing body of orders to prevent plague and its spread. They were patronised by a wide range of people from across the social spectrum, yet it was those who were assumed to go to them for nefarious purposes who attracted the attention of the authorities and became scapegoats for closing them in time of plague. The ban on performances and closure of the playhouses created some controversy, because the players explained that they were required to perform before the queen, notably during the Christmas festivities, and needed to be proficient by then. That required actual performances, not just rehearsals. The Council was prepared to endorse that argument, while at the same time appearing to support the corporation in maintaining its prohibition during plague times, while the church supported prohibition. In 1564 Archbishop Grindal responded to Cecil's request for 'some politic orders to be devised against infection' with the opinion that the epidemic should be blamed on the players, whom he described as 'an idle sort of people ... who now daily, but specially on holy-days, set up bills, whereunto the youth resorteth excessively, and there taketh infection'. His suggested remedy was that plays should be banned in the City and within a three-mile radius for one year, adding grumpily 'and if it were for ever it were not amiss'.[8] Thomas White, rector of St Dunstan-in-the-West, waded into the argument in 1577 during a time of plague, in a sermon delivered at Paul's Cross; those sermons commonly drew large congregations. He preached against luxury and self-indulgence and warned about London's need to repent as it grew: 'London builds apace, beware of blood and iniquity ... God shall reckon with you in his rage and give you a taste of his anger.' He specifically mentioned the playhouses, with the warning:

> Looke but uppon the common playes in London, and see the multitude that flocketh to them and followeth them: beholde the sumptuous Theatre houses, a continuall monument of Londons prodigalitie and folly. But I understande they are nowe forbidden bycause of the plague, I like the pollicye well if it holde still, for a disease is but bodged or patched up that is not cured in the cause, and the cause of plagues is sinne, if you looke to it well: and the cause of sinne are playes: therefore the cause of plagues are playes.[9]

The city's population had begun to grow rapidly after the mid-sixteenth century as its economy expanded, fuelled by the growth in overseas trade. That prompted the first codified building regulations for London, which were issued in 1580, as an attempt to curb its rapid growth, the hasty erection of sub-standard housing, and subdivision and overcrowding of existing buildings.

The proclamation expressed the concern that 'great multitudes' of people, mostly the poor, were 'heaped up together' in small rooms. The policy was so ineffectual that it was reiterated in an Act of Parliament of 1592, which stated that 'Great Infection of Sickness and dearth of Victuals and Fuel hath growen and ensued and many idle vagrant and wicked persons have harboured themselves there [in London] and divers remote places of the Realme have been disappointed of Workmen and dispeopled.'[10] The policy was intermittently enforced until the mid-seventeenth century, but London continued to grow remorselessly.

Fears of the young rakehells and those on the margins of society who disregarded authority extended to concern about the spread of plague. But the regulations were as likely to be flouted by reputable citizens who encountered the disease, at home or at a friend's or a relative's, as by dissolute playgoers or masterless men. Indeed, when epidemics erupted and the orders were implemented, not only did the disease cut swathes through the city's population, but the orders themselves and those who issued them were condemned by those who they were meant to protect. Perceptions of what was necessary and the experience of those living through the crisis were substantially different, so that policy and practicality did not correspond. In 1570 Katherine Welsh, a baker's wife, went almost every day to see a friend who was seriously ill with the plague. On the day before her friend died Katherine was at her bedside from nine o'clock in the evening until two or three o'clock the next morning, comforting the victim, before returning home to see her husband go to work.[11] In that case, a sound person crossed the city to attend a sick friend, in defiance of the regulations. Warders should have been on patrol outside the infected house and although she could have been allowed into it, she should have been confined there until she had served the quarantine period. Perhaps the parish had been unable to act swiftly enough to close and seal the house, lacking the staff and funds to do so, or maybe its officers had acted out of kindness, or for a gratuity, in allowing Katherine and others to go in and out.

Even households which took steps to minimise the risk felt threatened by the irresponsible behaviour of others. In 1575 Lord John Russell and his wife Elizabeth moved from the Blackfriars precinct when she was pregnant, taking lodgings close to Westminster Abbey, as more secluded and so hopefully safer. Yet he remained anxious, not only because of the number of plague deaths in Westminster, but also the way that the servants were constantly 'straying abroad', putting the entire household in danger should they mix with the sick. Of course, they were probably carrying out necessary errands as well as socialising, but that would not have allayed Lord Russell's concerns.[12]

In 1592 the most serious epidemic since 1563 began. Quarantining of shipping was not introduced, presumably because the disease was identified in the city before the danger was recognised. In August four burials of plague victims were registered in the parish of St Botolph-without-Aldgate and in the middle of the month the Privy Council released a prisoner on bail because of 'the contagion of the plaige dailie increasing in London'. Also in August, Francis Bacon and three friends 'abandoned Gray's Inn and went post to Twickenham where he meaneth to continue for some few days, only upon a flying report spread through the town of the sickness'. The rumours were not false ones and by early September the Council accepted that the disease was 'nowe greatly increased' in the city.[13] This it attributed to the failure to implement the orders, especially in not separating the sick from the healthy. One issue which it addressed was the number of prisoners in the city's gaols who were incarcerated on actions of debt or offences of 'mean qualitie'. The lord mayor and aldermen were to investigate those cases and 'to deale with them by way of perswasion to be contented', releasing those charged with petty offences on bail and taking some security from debtors, convincing their creditors that they would lose the whole of their debt due to them if the debtors should die, which was likely when they were imprisoned in a crowded gaol during an epidemic.[14] The unnecessarily large number of prisoners was doubtless a characteristic feature of the laborious workings of the legal system and the Council was using the danger of plague as an opportunity to draw attention to the issue.

Diplomatic exchanges were interrupted by the plague, as the customary restrictions on access were put in place. A French envoy lodging in Hackney had his audience with the queen deferred because a servant of his entourage had died of plague. He wrote to explain that he did not go into London for fear of alarming the court and protested that he had not lent his coach to take the sick man to the city, adding that he would not have risked his own health for one of 'such lowly condition'. The plague victim had never come into the house and was lodged in a building some distance from his own and as soon as his illness was known he was sent to London. Movement of the sick from the homes of the wealthy or prestigious, before those buildings could be closed as being infected, became a feature of epidemics in London. Thomas Phelippes noted in 1593 that the court 'kepeth in out places, a great part of the household being cut of' from London. The queen spent most of the outbreak in Oxfordshire, Buckinghamshire, Middlesex and Surrey, although she twice stayed in London during the winter.[15]

On 1 October the Council again wrote to the lord mayor and aldermen to berate them for their lack of diligence in dealing with the epidemic, so that the infection was 'daily and dangerously' increased. The queen was to spend part of the coming winter at Hampton Court, and so Londoners would be forbidden to go to Kingston-upon-Thames and all other places where there was plague. Greater care was to be given to separate the sick and the mayor and aldermen were to explain why they had not ordered the lighting of fires in the streets, which the Council favoured, as it thought that nothing was more effective in purging and cleansing the air. The celebrations for the swearing-in of the new lord mayor were not to be held and the preacher at the next Sunday sermon at Paul's Cross was to explain to the citizens that this was done not to save money but because of the danger of 'drawinge of assemblie of people togeather'. But money would be saved and that was to be assigned to help those whose houses were infected. Although the intention was safety from infection and to donate assistance to the poor, that cancellation of the festivities did further economic harm to those who supplied the finery, food and drink to the corporation and livery companies, and sold to the many people who came on to the streets in holiday mood. In October the law term was transferred to Hertford, on the queen's wishes, the places in London which the lord mayor and aldermen had suggested as relatively safe having been rejected. The Council scarcely needed to point out to the mayor and aldermen that this was 'to no small inconvenience of the cittie in general and of you in particulare', but it did anyway. They could have responded by commenting that the danger of spreading the plague was not eradicated by the transfer because Londoners moved to the town to sell provisions and to hire rooms, which they would then sublet to the lawyers and others who needed to go there to attend the courts. The topographer John Norden emphasised the economic harm to the inhabitants of Westminster, with the comment that the Michaelmas term was 'the most beneficiall of all the reste' and so its removal was 'to the greate decay of the comen state of the poore inhabitants of Westminster'. He also noted the wider effects of the outbreak, which 'banisheth manie from the Cyties [London and Westminster] that were inhabitants, and preventeth the cominge of others, to the great hindraunce of the people'. He was convinced that the cause of the plague was that 'the ayre was pestilently infected' as God's punishment, because 'all have corrupted their ways, and a more gentle correction the Lorde can not lay upon us; it is in love, to call us to reformation, and without spedy and hartye repentaunce, we shall likewise perish'.[16] While the Privy Council did not miss the opportunity to once again tick off the lord mayor and aldermen for their lack of diligent application in not taking adequate steps to check the outbreak in time, the citizens continued to regard the reasons and remedies for the epidemic in altogether different terms.

Plague had been recorded in some parishes in the late summer of 1592: at St Martin's-in-the-Fields and St Michael, Cornhill (in the 'red lyone Taverne') on 12 September. A letter from London in September mixed reassurance with concern: 'All your friends in London are in health, God be praised ... We have small doings by reason of the sickness. Yet I thank God it is no nearer unto us than the alleys as yet; there died two children more out of the other alleys this week.'[17] The lateness of the season helped to restrict the number of deaths that year, for the winter brought some respite. But a return of the disease was anticipated and on 28 January plays and sports were banned in the city and for a radius of seven miles around. Sure enough, plague deaths increased again in the spring. From August 1592 until February 1593 there were 47 of them in St Botolph-without-Aldgate; the number then increased steadily, to 11 in March, 32 in April, 48 in May and 59 in June. July saw a big jump in the number, to 152 and it more than doubled again in August, when there were 379 plague burials. That was the peak month and the number then fell, to 260 in September, 81 in October, 34 in November and just 13 in December. During 1593, 1,463 corpses were buried in the churchyard, 1,078 of them plague victims. However, the yearly Bill gave the totals for the parish as 1,771 burials, 624 of them from plague.[18]

Londoners dosed themselves with potions from the apothecaries to try to ward off the disease. English authors drew on the works of Italian writers on plague and their prescriptions for medication which were alleged to cure, even to prevent, the disease. Thomas Hill, a collector of books and manuscripts, obtained a copy of Leonardo Fiovaranti's tract on plague remedies and began a translation, which was unfinished at his death, but was taken up by John Hester and published in 1576 as *The newe jewell of health,* with a follow-up volume in 1579 entitled *A joyfull jewel*. This recommended a potion to be taken for three or four successive mornings and suggested that the patient's body should be rubbed with a balsam. For those who had developed buboes, 'You shall open the sores quickly that the matter may come forth, and when they are broken you shall put therein our caustic once only, because it purgeth it divinely.'[19] Further advice and practical remedies were advocated by Hugh Plat, who was both a promoter and practitioner of science and medicine in Elizabethan London, who would try out on patients his prescriptions for various types of fever, including his 'plague cakes', which acquired a considerable reputation. They were large lozenges, containing a mixture of herbs and other substances, and proved to be very popular during the plague outbreak of 1592–3. He dispensed nearly 500 of them in and around London during the summer of 1593, in addition to a 'great number' which went to 'persons whose names are not here recorded'. Those which he did note included Charles Howard, Lord High Admiral, who took 45, the Bishop of Winchester, who acquired 50 for his diocese, and two apothecaries, who purchased 50 each for their customers. A Justice of the Peace who lived in St Mary Abchurch used his parish to try out the efficacy of the cakes, dispensing them to 33 parishioners, all of whom 'were preserved from the plague'; when the Privy Councillors learned of this they sent for more details and then obtained 60 of the lozenges for themselves.[20] Plat was not licensed to practise medicine so he could not charge a fee but was well recompensed with gifts or money from grateful clients who just happened not to succumb to the disease after taking his concoctions.

Simon Forman, doctor and astrologer, having contracted the plague in the summer of 1592 and survived, treated those sick from the disease throughout the epidemic, enhancing his reputation. He was critical of those members of the medical profession, including the fellows of the College, who had left, penning a doggerel verse to express his scorn.

And in the time of Pestilent Plague,
When Doctors all did fly,
And got them into places far
From out the City
The Lord appointed me to stay
To cure the sick and sore,
But not the rich and mighty ones
But the distressed poor.

Forman was flattering himself, because he undoubtedly made money by treating his patients during the epidemic and he also took the opportunity which his enhanced reputation gave him to publish a short book on plague and its treatment.[21] Another author to rush into print during the outbreak was Simon Kellaway, whose *A defensative against the plague* was issued in 1593. He repeated previous notions, stressing the need for cleanliness, both personal and civic, and describing how bad smells could be overlain with good ones by spreading flowers and herbs and burning sweet woods. He recommended a range of nostrums to ward off the plague and suggested that those who feared that they had contracted the disease should get themselves into a sweat to expel it. Henry Holland's *Spirituall Preservatives against the Pestilence*, also published in 1593, emphasised the need for prayer and repentance and warned against the wicked spirits which could poison souls 'suggesting and breathing most pestilent motions into the minds of men'.[22] The Council itself recommended 'a litle booke sett forth in the tyme of the Great Plague and the last yeare printed againe, which doth containe divers goode preceptes and orders, which booke wee wyshe might be recommended by the mynister of everie parishe to be hearde of all house-keepers and the rules sett downe in the same observed'. It evidently favoured using the churches as a way of disseminating recommendations during the plague.[23]

Others could not afford the plague cakes or other potions and had recourse to more traditional treatments. They included Richard Lane, of St Margaret's, New Fish Street, and his wife in 1593. When he felt 'weake and faynte' in the early stages of his sickness from plague, Richard went to see his aunt, who lived in the parish of St Botolph-without-Aldersgate, half a mile away. He needed her help, explaining that 'I am very sicke and my wife also is more sicke and I know and am persuaded my selfe that not any of my friendes or kindred or of hers will venture to come and visit us this time of infection.' He asked his aunt that she would 'take the paynes to come to my house and looke unto us in this tyme of our visitacion and sicknes of the plague.' So that her own affairs would be looked after in her absence, he handed her 6d to give to 'some woman to dispatche her busines in her absence and to go home straighte with hym and helpe to caste hym in a sweate'. The incentive for his aunt was that if Richard and his wife should die, she would inherit everything of theirs, and that is what happened; Richard and his wife died and his aunt claimed their estate.[24] As with the case of Katherine Welsh in 1570, ill and healthy people met together and went across the city without regard for the orders which required the sequestering of the sick and those with whom they had been in contact.

The spread of plague in a neighbourhood was a dismaying experience. News of the outbreak in Southwark had reached Edward Alleyn in Bristol when he was travelling with Lord Strange's acting company. On 1 August 1593 he wrote an anxious letter to his wife, expressing the hope that although the sickness was around their house, she would escape. He told her to 'kepe yor house fayr and clean which I knowe you will and every evening throwe water before yor dore and in yor bakcsid and have in yor windowes good store of rwe [rue] and herbe of grace and with all the grace of god which must be obtayned by prayers and so doinge no dout but the Lord will mercyfully defend you'. During that month Philip Henslow wrote to Alleyn summarising the situation and reassuring him that 'thanckes be unto god we are all at this time in good healthe in our howsse', while presenting a rather alarming picture, for

> Round a bowte us yt hathe bene all moste in every howse about us & whole howsholdes deyed & yt my frend the baylle doth scape but he smealles monstrously for feare & dares staye no wheare for ther hathe deyed this last weacke in general 1603 of the wch number ther hathe died of them of the plage 1135 wch hause bene the greatest that came yet.

Robert Brown's wife in Shoreditch, all her children and her household were dead, and, mixing those sombre tidings with a touch of everyday news, he told Alleyn that the joiner had delivered a court-cupboard which he had been making for him. Fear was uppermost, but daily life went on.[25]

A suggestion that the figures were being manipulated to avoid spreading alarm that would cause people to avoid the city was included in a letter from Alleyne's wife Joan. She wrote in the middle of August that 'as for newes of the sycknes I cane not seand you no Juste note of yt be cause there is commandment to the contrary but as I thincke doth die within the sitteye and withowt of all syckneses to the nomber of seventen or eyghten hundredth in one weacke'.[26] The Bills of Mortality were issued continuously from 21 December 1592 for three years, but some precincts were excluded, and they did not yet cover the whole of the city. Although the procedure was in place to make the numbers for most of London available, it seems that in the face of a full-blown epidemic there was a loss of nerve on the government's part and during the outbreak the figures were not made freely accessible. In any case, as the corporation had previously admitted, the Bills gave the figures for those who had died of plague and they had no information on the numbers of sick who recovered and went around the streets, to their mind carrying the infection about them in their clothing or on their persons. Someone who had been stricken with plague probably would not be overly concerned with their personal hygiene while they were recovering, and so could have carried fleas and lice. The corporation was correct to be concerned about the spread of the disease, without being aware of how that occurred. The numbers of plague dead may also have been falsified because 'sometimes fraud of the searchers may deceive'.[27]

Robert Henslow gave Alleyn a gloomy picture of the prevalence of the plague in Bankside in a letter dated 28 September 1593, in which he wrote 'almoste alle my nebores dead of the plage & not my howsse ffree for my two weanches have had the plage & yet thankes be to god leveth & ar welle & I and my wife & my two dawghters I thancke god ar very well & in good healthe'. Yet he went on to write that the market at Smithfield had been held, although it lasted only three days and prices were low; he could not get an offer of more than £4 for a horse that was worth more and so he had not sold it. Despite having had sickness in his house, he had crossed London to go to the market. Conditions were not back to normal, despite a fall in the numbers of recorded deaths, and he was obliged to tell Alleyn that 'as for your tenenantes we cane geat no Rent'. Just a few weeks later, however, on 21 October, Joan Alleyn could be very hopeful when writing to her husband with the news that 'heare is none now sycke neare us'. Her father was at court, but where that was, she did not know.[28]

It may have been the disruption of normal working patterns and the reduction in employment which followed that prompted a burst of posters and handbills in the city, threatening the immigrants who lived and worked there. On 16 April 1593 the Privy Council was made aware of 'a lewde and vyle ticket or placard set up upon some post in London' which threatened that the apprentices would 'attempt some violence on the strangers'. The lord mayor was ordered to investigate and presumably discovered that the handbill was just one of several, for six days later the Council noted that there were 'certain libelles latelie published by some disordered and factious persons in and about the citie of London, shewing an intente in the artyficers and others who holde themselves prejudiced in theire trades by strangers to use some course of vyolence to remove the saide strangers or by way of tumulte to suppress them'. It authorised an investigation to discover the authors and publishers and in the following month repeated that lately there had been 'divers lewd and malicious libells set up within the citie of London, among the which there is some set upon the wal of the Dutch churchyard that doth excead the rest in lewdnes'. It authorised the committee entrusted with getting to the source of the problem not only to arrest suspects and imprison them in Bridwell, but also to 'put them to the torture' if they did not confess. The episode was later referred to as 'the stur betwixt the prentices of London and the straingers'. Anti-alien sentiments occasionally surfaced in Tudor London, and this outburst of hostility, perhaps prompted by the effects of plague, was thought to be too serious and threatening to ignore.[29]

The Privy Council kept up its pressure on the aldermen, telling them in the middle of January that the queen was unhappy with their efforts in London, 'the capitall cittie of the realme and neere to the which her Majestie maketh her continuall residence'. Not only was she displeased in that respect, but also for the welfare of her subjects 'the poorer and meaner sorte of artificers, who maie justlie ascribe their presente mischief, povertie and miserie to you as to the chiefe causes therof'. They were to inspect the infected or suspected houses themselves, to ensure that they were locked on the outside, or guarded by a watch set on every house, so that the occupants could not emerge until they were free from infection. This did not allow for someone to leave the house to buy provisions, as had been the practice hitherto, and food was to be supplied to them, paid for by those householders themselves if they were 'of ability', or from charitable funds collected by the parish.

Once again, the threat that 'clamour and complaintes of the people' would be directed at the aldermen by the citizens 'in case they shall finde their ruyne to have proceeded from you' was used to motivate the aldermen, six of whom were to appear before the Council five days later to report on their actions. The order that no occupants in the closed houses should be allowed out and that provisions should be supplied to them was repeated on 5 April.[30] That was now a firm aspect of the plague policies.

Meetings were banned, including the livery companies' feasts, and Bartholomew's and Southwark fairs. The lord mayor jibbed at the cancellation of St Bartholomew's fair, only to be told that whether it went ahead would depend on the success of himself and his colleagues in implementing the orders. The Council believed that only painted crosses had been set on the closed houses, which were quickly wiped away, so red crosses should be nailed on the doors and a watch set to guard them. Continued charitable collections would make the occupants more willing to comply with their incarceration. The Council had been encouraged to maintain its opinion of the efficacy of household quarantine by its apparent success at Kingston-upon-Thames, where the plague had begun 'very hotly' but had ceased after the restraint of the infected. They suggested that the City should, like all other great cities in Christendom, provide a place some distance outside the city where the infected would be kept apart from others, in other words, a pest-house. Whatever the members of the Council may have thought, the parishes did carry out their duties in fixing crosses on the doors of infected houses, such as the churchwardens of St Mary Woolnoth, whose accounts include 2d for 'setting a crosse upon one Allen's doore in the sickness time', and 4d for 'setting two red crosses upon Anthony Sound his dore'.[31] The vestries also appointed searchers of the bodies and warders, who were commonly people receiving poor relief, so that in 1592 the vestry of St Margaret, Lothbury asked eight women, who 'have weekly pencion out of the parishe for thare releefe' to choose among themselves two viewers of the dead. The two who were chosen alternated their duties. In May of the following year one of searchers was to be replaced and the three who were nominated could not agree which of them should do her job, despite 'the matter beinge longe debated amonge them'. The churchwardens then had to make the choice. That seems to have been a reasonably fair way of appointing someone to carry out that dangerous task, but it may not have been a practice followed in all parishes. The parish's income for the extra payments was from collections, but some did not pay, presumably because they had died or had gone away.[32]

The number of deaths for the year entered by the clerk of St Peter's, Cornhill in the parish register was 25,886, of which the plague accounted for 15,003.[33] His figure was for the whole of London and suggests a death rate of almost 13 per cent; within the City and the Liberties the number of deaths between 21 December 1592 and 20 December 1593 was 17,844, with 10,662 of them attributed to plague. The number of burials was 4.25 times higher than in a normal year. In 1563 the worst mortality had been in the central parishes, but in 1593 they escaped relatively lightly and it was those around the City which suffered worst. In the crowded north-east parishes of St Botolph-without-Aldgate and St Botolph-without-Bishopsgate the numbers of burials were six times higher than normal. Perhaps more of the wealthy parishioners left during the epidemic in 1593 than had been the case 30 years earlier, and they lived in the City parishes, for the smaller parishes there were able to achieve a lower mortality among the quarantined sick by maintaining them more efficiently than the larger, sprawling parishes around the city's fringe were able to do. The epidemic declined during the winter and although it reappeared in 1594 it was much less destructive, with 421 out of a total of 3,929 deaths attributed to the disease.

According to hostile critics of the plague policy, some deaths were unnecessary because they were caused by neglect.

William Reynolds, a soldier and pamphleteer, peppered the city with letters and petitions during the epidemic. In one of them he made the bitter claim that 'There hath been such ungodly and uncharitable severity used in the time of this your plague, that women and others has perished by your strict course for want of relief and [at]tendance.' He cited the case of a woman known to him who 'being sick and great with child' died, with her child, 'having no help of man or woman'. He took aim at the 'villainous villains that lock up the sick in outrageous manner, not regarding to visit them as their necessity requires'. Yet for others, plague time seems not to have been too disruptive. Richard Stonley, a teller of the Exchequer, bought a clutch of books during 1593, including Shakespeare's poem *Venus and Adonis*, on 12 June, during the height of the plague. Like other playwrights who found themselves temporarily out of work and pocket while the theatres remained closed, Shakespeare had turned his attention to obtaining an aristocratic patron and his poems written at that time, *Venus and Adonis* and *The Rape of Lucrece*, were dedicated to the young Earl of Southampton. Without the plague epidemic, presumably he would not have needed to write those works.[34]

Even when the playhouses re-opened, plague remained a lingering threat, and another major epidemic struck London in 1603, with the disease recurring until 1611. Londoners could hardly fail to be aware of the threat, and the popular notions of its causes. Shakespeare alluded to them in terms which the audiences would have recognised. In *Timon of Athens* he coupled divine punishment with tainted air, with Timon telling Alcibiades, 'Be as a planetary plague, when Jove / Will o'er some high-vic'd city hang his poison / in the sick air'; and in *Henry VI Part II* the king banishes the Duke of Suffolk, allowing him just three days to leave, with the phrase 'He shall not breathe infection in this air / But three days longer'. More simply, in *Hamlet* Shakespeare described the air as 'a foul and pestilent congregation of vapours', and when Hamlet, in a gloomy mood because now satisfied of his uncle's responsibility for his father's death, prepares to confront his mother, he says to himself "Tis now the very witching time of night, / When churchyards yawn, and hell itself breathes out / Contagion to this world.' The churchyards' yawns would be exhalations of fumes from the graves, while hell's breath delivers contagion. Shakespeare expresses a similar idea in *Henry V*, during the Agincourt campaign, with the king commenting that those who die in France and are 'buried in your dunghills' will still aid his cause by 'Leaving their earthly parts to choke your clime, / The smell whereof shall breed a plague in France'.[35] The connection between bad personal hygiene and dangerous air was alluded to by Isabella Whitney in *The Manner of Her Will*. She lived in Abchurch Lane and died in 1573 and in the poem mentioned various aspects of London, which she imagined she could bequeath to the city, including bath-houses near the Thames: 'I houses leave / For people to repair / To bathe themselves, so to prevent / Infection of the air.'[36]

Another writer who turned his hand to different genres was Thomas Nashe, who put forward some uncomfortable insinuations in his *Christ's tears over Jerusalem, whereunto is annexed A comparative admonition to London*, printed in 1593. Like Reynolds, he complained bitterly of the covetousness and lack of charity in London, and how unrepentant its citizens were: 'In this time of infection we purge our houses, our bodies, and our streets, and look to all but our souls.' The city surely deserved its fate, for 'London, thou art the seeded garden of sin, the sea that sucks in all the scummy channels of the realm: the honestest in thee, for the most, are either lawyers or usurers; deceit is that which advanceth the greater sort of the chiefest.' This he saw as a reason for the divine punishment through plague: 'The Lord thinketh it were as good for him to kill with the plague, as to let them kill with oppression.' God saw how charitable funds were diverted from their intended purpose, with 'subtle conveyances and recognizances; he beholdeth how they pervert foundations, and will not bestow the bequeathers free alms, but for bribes, or for friendship. I pray God they take not the like course, in preferring poor men's children into their hospitals, and converting the impotent's money to their private usury.' This was an allegation that the powerful and wealthy men in the city diverted charitable alms to their own ends. Whether there was the least truth in this is not clear, but he was certainly aiming at the City's elite when it was vulnerable because of the failure to prevent the plague from spreading. He also claimed that Londoners were niggardly when it came to charitable donations, and as that was how the City required the parishes to fund the extra expenditure during epidemics, so it was a disparagement of its plague policy.[37]

More chillingly, Nashe alleged that cruel dumping of plague victims had taken place during the epidemic, for there were some

> ...in the heat of the sickness, that thought to purge and cleanse their houses, by conveying their infected servants forth by night into the fields, which there starved and died, for want of relief and warm keeping. Such merciless cannibals, instead of purging their spirits and their houses, have thereby doubled the plague on them and their houses. In Gray's Inn, Clerkenwell, Finsbury, and Moor-fields, with mine own eyes have I seen half a dozen of such lamentable outcasts.

That is, if servants or journeymen exhibited plague symptoms, they were taken out at night and laid away from the property, in an open space, so that the house would not be closed, with all the social and economic drawbacks that would bring. Nor could they get help once they had been abandoned, for their 'brethren and their kinsfolks have offered large sums of money to get them conveyed into any outhouse, and no man would earn it, no man would receive them. Cursing and raving by the highway side, have they expired, and their masters never sent to them, nor succoured them. The fear of God is come amongst us, and the love of God gone from us.' In his criticism of the lack of adequate care for the sick, he shared some views with the Privy Council, with his complaint that in other countries,

> They have hospitals, whither their infected are transported presently after they are stricken. They have one hospital for those that have been in the houses with the infected, and are not yet tainted; another for those that are tainted, and have the sores risen on them but not broken out; a third for those that both have the sores, and have them broken out on them. We have no provision but mixing hand over head, the sick with the whole.

Nashe might have over-stated the facilities that some foreign cities could provide, but he made his point effectively, and that was an aspect of plague policy that had not been developed.[38]

Nashe achieved a steady output during the epidemic and in 1594 his *The Unfortunate Traveller* was issued, dedicated, like Shakespeare's poems, to the Earl of Southampton. It purported to describe the travels of Jack Wilton, who was in Rome during 'a vehement hot summer' during which it experienced a devastating outbreak of plague. Rome was a stand-in for London, for Nashe portrayed conditions which surely were based on what he knew of London's experience. The futility of the physicians' efforts was admitted, for they 'would come to visite those, with whose infirmities their arte had no affinitie: and even as a man with a fee should bee hyred to hang himselfe, so would they quietly goe home and dye presently after they had been with their patients'. Nashe also described the depressing routine of collecting the dead for burial: 'All day and all night long carremen did nothing but goe up and downe the streetes with their carts and crye, Have you anie dead to burie, have you anie dead to burie: and had manie times out of one house their whole loading: one grave was the sepulcher of seuenscore, one bed was the altar whereon whole families were offered.' Two villains took the opportunity to break into rich men's houses where the occupants had died of the plague, to plunder the contents. Nashe did not overlook the spiritual aspect of an epidemic, writing that plague was God's vengeance and asking 'what is the plague, but death playing the provost marshall, to execute all those that wil not be called home by anie other meanes?' His descriptions were strongly drawn, but perhaps were not overly exaggerated in the minds of readers in a city emerging from a disheartening epidemic.[39]

The social and economic divide between plague victims and the wealthy was demonstrated when the cargo of the *Madre de Dios* was brought to England and divided among the investors. The Portuguese vessel from the East Indies had been captured in a naval expedition led by Martin Frobisher and was a rich prize indeed, for it was said to be largest ship afloat and richer than 'any shypp that ever came into England'. Its cargo of spices, diamonds and other precious stones, amber, ivory, porcelain, cloth, carpets, calicoes and quilts was estimated to be worth half a million pounds. Pilfering had begun while the ship was still at sea and continued apace after it had been brought into Dartmouth on 7 September 1592. A syndicate of the City's merchants had put money into the venture and they received twice the value of their investment. Many of those who hoped for a profit set out from London to the west country to secure their gains, so that the Council became afraid that the plague would be spread by them and prohibited the merchants from going there without its warrant. The contrast between the wealthy citizens dividing this fabulously rich cargo among themselves, with the queen taking her share, while the poor were fearful of the growing plague epidemic, exemplified the distinction between wealth and poverty at such a time. But a part of the windfall from the *Madre de Dios* was used towards the cost of building the city's pest-house, on the north side of the city, in a road that became known as Pest-house Lane, and later Bath Street. The Bill for 1593 recorded 208 deaths there, 195 of them from plague.[40]

The Tudor era closed with a coherent plague policy in place for London, which the government and the city's rulers struggled to implement during times of crisis because of its practical and social failings. Plague had become inextricably associated with the poor, and especially beggars, vagrants and others on the fringe of society who were regarded as disreputable and ungovernable, occupying overcrowded, shoddy and dirty premises. The response to the epidemic contributed to the tensions in the city during the 1590s, which were partly caused by very high food prices in its middle years and the increased numbers of those arriving from the Low Countries and France to escape persecution. The government could see no alternative to its policies on plague and overcrowding, which were reiterated, with harsher punishments for those who did not comply. Nonetheless, in little more than two generations the government's attitude to plague had been greatly developed, from being regarded as a problem that should be addressed by reducing sinfulness and self-indulgence, to an issue which was integral in the development of its environmental policies for London.

II

DISARMED OF ALL COMFORT

No great change was made to the regulations regarding plague in the last years of Elizabeth's reign because the disease did not recur during the period. The queen died on 24 March 1603 and the earlier fears concerning the succession proved to have been unnecessary, for Sir Robert Cecil, her chief minister, had arranged matters so that the accession of James VI of Scotland went smoothly and unchallenged, and he took the English throne as James I. There had been no coronation since 1559 and a great event was now planned for the occasion. People arrived in London to show respect for the memory of the late queen, as well as to prepare themselves, socially and sartorially, for the new reign and the benefits which it might bring in terms of offices, grants, pensions or other profitable awards. There must, too, have been a sense of a new beginning, for many of the chief figures of Elizabeth's council and court had died. James tactfully timed his journey south so that he arrived in his new capital after the funeral. No doubt prompted by Cecil, he imitated Elizabeth by going directly to the Howards' house at the Charterhouse on his arrival in London on 7 May; that was what she had done in 1558, entering at the back gate to avoid the muddy roads. That proved to be a popular gesture in the citizens' eyes, for showing that she was not going to stand on her

227

dignity on such occasions. His replication of her conduct then was appreciated when he made his entrance into the city.

Yet all was not well. As the tailors and haberdashers laboured to outfit their customers in suitably lavish suits, gowns and hats, and workmen constructed the six decorative arches which were to stand on the processional route at the coronation, plague began to appear in the city. An epidemic in Amsterdam in the previous year had been noted and in October the Privy Council ordered that ships arriving from there were not to land their cargoes until they could prove that there was no risk of infection from them.[1] Amsterdam and Danzig (now Gdansk) were said to have been the sources for cases of plague at Wapping and Great Yarmouth. Yet no outbreak occurred over the winter and the few cases reported in the spring were in the suburbs and Southwark, remote enough not to be immediately unsettling, but as they began to increase and spread it became apparent that a serious outbreak was likely. Despite the preparations for the inauguration of the new reign, this could not be disregarded and so the accustomed measures were put in place. On 29 May a royal proclamation directed that all gentlemen without specific business at court were to leave, partly because they were neglecting their estates and local administration, and partly because of the risk of plague 'for that we finde the sicknesse already forward within our City of London, which by concourse of people abiding there is very likely to be increased'. On 23 June the legal term was adjourned, also in the hope that 'by dispersing of the multitude of people now being in or about ... [the] Cities [London and Westminster], and by staying the accesse of others to the same about Suits in Law ... the said infection shalbe stayed'.[2] The hearings were transferred to Winchester, where the townsmen were alleged to have charged extortionate prices for those attending the courts.

Giovanni Scaramelli, the Venetian ambassador, estimated that London would have attracted 100,000 people by the time of the coronation, which was fixed for St James's Day, 25 July. The Bills of Mortality recorded just a few plague deaths during May, with 22 and 36 in the last two weeks of the month, in six parishes. But as the Bills did not include the out-parishes around the city until they were added for the weeks after 21 July, the figures were misleading, and the true ones may have been double those included. Furthermore, as the weather was unseasonably warm fears grew and the plague orders were issued, including the rule that plague houses should be marked with a printed paper stating 'Lord, have mercy upon us'.[3] By the end of June plague deaths were reported from 30 parishes, a quarter of the total included in the Bills.

The court was initially at Greenwich and later moved to Windsor, partly to avoid the city and the plague, partly because that was the accepted practice until after the coronation. The six arches were erected by early July and were admired by Scaramelli, but he was aware of growing unease about the event, writing to Venice that there had been 'frequent discussions as to anticipating or postponing the date on account of the plague', although he added, 'The dread of plague need not delay the arrival of the Ambassadors, for the Court always lies at an uninfected place.' A week later he could report that the ambassadors from Brunswick and Lorraine had arrived and 'On account of the plague, they passed straight on to Court at Windsor, where the crowd is so great and the dearth so excessive that the King will be forced to move.' Indeed, the pressure on local supplies was such that he and the court went to Oatlands, in Surrey, and then to Hampton Court. The decision was taken that the coronation would take place as arranged, but 'in very private form', with the usual practices much curtailed, for the king would not process through the city from the Tower to Westminster but cross the Thames directly from Lambeth and return the same way 'without touching London'. That was a disappointment for the London livery companies who had erected the decorations, but the 'arches and trophies will be used on the occasion of his solemn opening of Parliament in

October, if the plague stops'.⁴ On coronation day Westminster was sealed off to prevent the crowds of Londoners from going to watch the spectacle. St James's fair in Westminster had already been deferred 'for eight or ten dayes', so that it did not coincide with the coronation.⁵

A letter to Cecil summarising the situation in Westminster showed that some problems similar to those which had arisen during earlier outbreaks were again becoming an issue. His informant knew the houses and streets where the disease had appeared in St Margaret's, St Martin-in-the-Fields and St Clement Danes. The parish officers were attempting to enforce the regulations, but encountering resistance, especially near St Clement's church and at 'The Fields' where 'the people are very unruly' and the officers were 'constrained to watch their houses and force them into their houses, which are infected, and the bills that are set upon their doors are still pulled off, whereby such houses are not known, but to very few'. That reluctance to endure a period of household quarantine could not be tolerated and his suggested solution was that 'a proclamation be granted, wherein some sharp punishment may be imposed corporally upon such as shall go abroad after their houses are infected or shall deface the mark and papers set upon their doors for that purpose, it is to be feared that this infection will much spread itself'. It was not only those in the infected households who were not complying with the orders, however, for 'We find that many persons of good ability, who are chargeable (in respect of such houses they hold here) to contribute towards the relieving of these poor infected people, refuse to pay any reasonable taxation.' Unless funds could be levied from the parishioners, then it would be difficult to implement the policies.⁶

Cecil's attention was again drawn to conditions in Westminster in early August, when one Timothy Willis 'with many others' requested him 'to supply the defect of authority in these places between Westminster and Temple Bar, for want whereof the grievous contagion of this sickness is carelessly dispersed. There is here no justice of peace, but only Harries, a sickly man, dwelling within the Savoy Liberty, against whose authority other liberties except, himself being faint enough.' There were specific places to be dealt with. One was a bowling alley close to Bedford House 'whither all kind of common people without respect of contagion promiscually resort, not sparing the sabbath day'. They also frequented alehouses, especially one adjoining the bowling alley run by one Bevan 'which, without respect of persons or places infected, makes the very sabbath day an advantage to his drinking gain. By both which concourse no doubt many receive hurt, beside the offence of many better minded neighbours.' Furthermore, in Worcester House many carpenters 'and other kind of labourers' were working, who went to and from their houses in the city 'by which means some of them have died in his house of the pestilence, and been conveyed through the garden unto the Savoy'. Then there were 'the swine which divers in this precinct keep, run without order in every unclean place about the street day and night, dispersing the offals of every house heaped in the street'. Many householders also kept dogs in small houses, so that the neighbourhood contained 'too great a number of dogs, as house curs and water spaniels, which greatly annoy the neighbours, unsweeten their keeper's house, and range dangerously to all places'. A first step would be to increase the number of officers, and half a dozen names were suggested, while the petitioners were respectful enough to acknowledge that it was down to Cecil to decide what should be done. Whether some officers had left because of the plague or had died, or there was an unrelated reason for the shortage of officers, was not made clear.[7]

Similar problems occurred across the city, and they could only worsen as the numbers infected and dying from the disease increased. By the time of the coronation the out-parishes had been included in the Bills and they therefore showed a truer figure for the progress of the plague, which caused 917 deaths that week from a total of 1,186, and in the following week the figures were

1,728 deaths, 1,396 of them from plague. The number of plague deaths in August rose from 1,922 in the first week to 2,539 in the last one, and in September they rose to 3,035 in the first week, before beginning to decline, with 1,732 plague deaths recorded in the week ending 29 September. In nine weeks in August and September there were 21,423 deaths from plague, or 89 per cent of the total of 24,249 deaths. The agonies of the infected produced gruesome scenes, as in previous outbreaks, with 'the botches, blains and spots (called Gods tokens) accompanied with raving and death'. Some victims became so irrational that they 'leape out of the windowes, and some runne into the Thames'.[8] It seemed that nowhere was safe. Sir John Harington wrote a pleading letter to Cecil in which he commented that plague was present in the Gatehouse prison in Westminster, to which prisoners arrested on Parliament's orders were confined. He believed that six were dead and a seventh was sick of the disease, 'and therefore I might think him as much my friend [who] would wish me to the gallows as to the Gatehouse'.[9]

To limit the numbers of social contacts, orders were issued restricting attendance at funerals to six people. There was an attempt to enforce them, with the city marshal himself going to funerals and ordering the arrest and imprisonment of those who flouted it, 'and many were bound over to the sessions for answering the said misdemeanour'. Yet that did not prevent the Londoners from continuing their usual practices and the marshal later complained that 'the sickness being at the highest, the meaner sort of people, for the most part women, continuing still in accompanying the dead, and would not by any means be drawn from it'. And so orders were sent to the parish clergy requesting them to dissuade their parishioners, but that was ineffective, for 'most of the ministers breach the same both in preaching at funeral sermons and accompanying the corpses, alleging that the burial was a spiritual jurisdiction belonging to the bishops'. When the marshal intervened at Moorgate at a funeral going towards the New Churchyard he was attacked and beaten by some of the 'great multitude accompanying the corpse of one dead of the plague'. With such divisions between the church and civic authorities having an influence over the population, and such an obstinate adherence to the traditional practices, policy was difficult to enforce.[10]

Further steps taken to prevent people gathering together were the cancellation of St Bartholomew's fair in Smithfield, and Stourbridge fair at Cambridge. Londoners were also prohibited from attending any fairs across the country while the epidemic continued. Yet they were not at all averse from going into crowds, so that when Sir Walter Raleigh, who had been one of Elizabeth's leading courtiers and the captain of her guard, was taken from the Tower to trial at Winchester on a charge of treason, people lined the streets to mock him as he passed in his coach, protected by an armed escort. The citizens were required to attend church and so gather in a congregation, and they expected the support and solace of the clergy. James Balmford, rector of St Olave's, Southwark, posed the question why the clergy should reprove those who 'for the comfort of their soules' attended church, although he admitted that some of them were 'either with plague sores, or out of infected houses' and that when they were in church they sat 'in a throng and heat'. But others were people who 'of charitie visite such as have the plague, and accompanie the diseased of that disease, unto the grave. In all which duties we thinke (with your favor) that Preachers should rather incourage then discourage us.' In his imagined dialogue the response was that 'Princes and Magistrates (which are called sheapheards) may and ought to be very carefull, to keepe the sound from the infected, and the infected from the sound, especially in assemblies.' Directly addressing the rule that only six people should be permitted at a funeral, his response was that authority should be obeyed, yet 'I could wish the friends of the diseased would respect the preservation of life more than complements of burial ... I utterly mislike that infected persons should thrust into the throng, and it grieveth me to heare how the poorer sort, yea women with yong children, will flocke to burials, and (which is worse) stand (of purpose) over open graves, where sundry are buried together.' He believed that they did this defiantly, so that 'all the world may see that they feare not the Plague'. He discussed, too, the practice of household quarantine, which had again been implemented. This remained most unpopular and even those who could maintain themselves if they were interned 'thinke it an hell to be so long shut up from companie and their businesse: the neglecting whereof is the decay of their state'. He was critical of the way in which the crisis had been managed, expressing the view that 'If authoritie had regarded these things betimes, when there were but few infected houses, they might have bene well shut up and provided for, till they were cleansed, either of their owne, or the common charges.' That was why so many concealed the presence of plague in their household for as long as they could; policy itself was one of the reasons for the spread of the disease. But another was fear, which thwarted the implementation of procedures and even common charity, so that those 'by whose meanes the sick and sound are especially to be provided for, do runne away, viz. Magistrates, Ministers ... Phisitians and rich men'. It also explained why 'so many be thrust out of doores, perish in town and field for want of help, and are so cruelly used by country people'.[11]

Henoch Clapham, another clergyman, was even more forthright and challenging, questioning why people should not go to the customary ceremonies together or attend church, for surely it was God's providence whether someone died or lived and so no policies could prevent that. If that was not the case, then why were services held and prayers offered pleading with the divinity to end the epidemic? He urged, 'We have sinned together, and the hand of God hath come upon us togither: let us therefore humble our selves togither before the Lord in fasting and prayer.' The pestilence did not pick out individuals who had been especially sinful, for 'it seizeth upon old and yong, rich and poore, of all complexions whatsoever, so well as some of all sorts are spared', therefore we should acknowledge that 'all sorts have sinned'. Balmford observed that if death came through the will of God, then 'if I go where the plague is a thousand times, I shall not die of the plague, if God have not appointed me to dy thereof: and if he have, I shall die thereof though I come not neare it by a thousand miles'.[12]

Clapham pressed his views so strongly, from the pulpit, in pamphlets and in person, that he could not be ignored. In November he was arrested and was interrogated by Lancelot Andrewes, rector of St Giles, Cripplegate and Dean of Westminster. His responsibilities extended to Westminster school, which he ordered to leave and go to its buildings in Chiswick, and he joined the boys there. In July he requested a butler, a cook, a carrier and two rowers, described as 'a skull and royer', to be sent to Chiswick with the boys. This raised the question of whether the leaders of the community should withdraw at such a time. Andrewes compounded what some saw as his lapse by delivering a sermon in which he said that the epidemic was 'the very handy-worke of God', but also that the disease was partly caused by natural phenomena and partly was the act of a destroying angel. His retreat to Chiswick laid him open to a blast from Clapham, for he would only have withdrawn had he felt himself to be at risk, as a sinner; a pure and sinless person should, by Andrewes's own reckoning, have been immune in Westminster and when checking the condition of his parishioners in Cripplegate and offering them solace. In casting doubts so publicly on someone of the Dean's rank Clapham had gone too far and he was incarcerated for 18 months when he refused to retract by agreeing to a form of words, written by Andrewes, which stated that 'A faithful Christian man, whether magistrate or minister, may in such times hide or withdraw himself, as well corporeally as spiritually, and use local flight to a more healthful place (taking sufficient order for the discharge of his function).' Eventually, Clapham was prepared to admit that there were two types of plague, one a contagion, which could be guarded against by the plague orders and measures taken by the individual, and the other was the stroke of God's avenging angel. This was acknowledging what Andrewes had preached during the epidemic, although of course this dispute between the two men did nothing to resolve the continuing debate regarding personal responsibility at a time of crisis.[13]

The controversies did not deflect the government from pressing on with attempting to reduce overcrowding. It had renewed the policy of preventing infilling caused by 'building over stables, in gardens, and other od corners'. Its solution was demolition, which John Chamberlain observed 'is far from removing the mischeife'.[14] The epidemic again focused attention on those neighbourhoods where the poorer people lived. Balmford wrote that alleys and houses 'did vomit out their undigested dead, Who by the cartloads are carried to their grave'. His explanation for this was a simple one, that 'all those lanes with folk were overfed' and 'the plague sweepeth where it findeth many together'. He recognised the difference between those householders 'who have spacious houses, so as they come not neere the sicke of their family, and be sound themselves' and those 'betweene whom and the infected there is but a wall'.[15] Thomas Lodge, too, acknowledged that the poor suffered disproportionately, having been 'left without guide or counsaile how to succour themselves in extremitie: For where the infestion most rageth there povertie raigneth among the Commons, which having no supplies to satisfie the greedie desire of those that should attend them, are for the most part left desolate & die without reliefe'. He advised his readers to avoid dirt and company, specifically 'the narrow wayes and streets where are dunghils' and the 'vaine assemblies of feasts'. He also made dietary recommendations and stated that sex should be avoided because it stirred and distempered the bodily humours and so would 'dispose the body to receive infection'. He added a 'finall Proviso, that the houses be kept cleane and well ayred, and be perfumed with water and vinegar in Summer time, and in winter time with perfumes, of Juniper, Rosemarie, Storax, Beniamin, and such like. That the windowes thereof be kept open to the East, towards the shining Sunne and the Northren winde, shutting out all Southerly windes, and such as blow from contagious places'. He recommended that those reaching the city from an infected area should be excluded, although that rule should not be applied to 'men of respect, who have the meanes, and observe the methode to preserve themselves', but 'such as are vagabonds, masterlesse men, and of servile and base condition ... they ought not to be admitted'. He was repeating advice with a long history, yet evidently it was still treated with respect. The printer and playwright Henry Chettle would have agreed and was unequivocal about the spread of plague, writing that there was 'no doubt that the corruption of the ayre together with uncleanly and unwholesome keeping of dwelling, where many are pestered together, as also the not observing to have fiers private & publiquely made as well within houses, as without in the streets, at times when the ayre is infected, are great occasions to increase corrupt and pestilent diseases'.[16]

Their view of overcrowding chimed with government policy and in mid-September, at the height of the crisis, a royal proclamation was issued 'against Inmates and multitudes of dwellers in strait Roomes and places in and about the Citie of London: And for the rasing and pulling downe of certaine new erected buildings'. Stating that 'the great confluence and accesse of excessive numbers of idle, indigent, dissolute and dangerous persons, And the pestering of them in small and strait rooms and habitations in the Citie of London, and in and about the Suburbes of the same, have bene one of the chiefest occasions of the great Plague and mortality', it ordered that no-one should be allowed to occupy any house or place in the City or suburbs which had been infected. That was to apply for up to four miles from the city, so long as the epidemic lasted, and then it would be permitted only when an officer or person of authority permitted it. It also reiterated the instruction in a proclamation issued in June 1602 that new tenements within three miles of London should be pulled down 'as the same shall hereafter become voide', which was an attempt to check the growth of the city and consequent overcrowding.[17]

The proclamation was referred to by Shakespeare in *Measure for Measure*, which is set in Vienna, but that city clearly was meant to evoke London. Mistress Overdone, a bawd, is told by her servant Pompey that a proclamation had been issued that all the houses in the suburbs 'must be plucked down'; they were 'houses of resort', in other words brothels. He adds that those in the city would have 'gone down too, but that a wise burgher put in for them'. Shakespeare was referring to the opinion that the city and the suburbs were not treated equally in such matters and the 'wise burgher' probably was an allusion to an alderman, using the city's influence to obtain a concession. The proclamation had not mentioned brothels and the fact that Shakespeare equated the demolition with them may have been because some of the buildings which had been pulled down on the authority of the earlier proclamation had been used for that purpose. Mistress Overdone is dismayed, because her business is not doing well as she has lost customers, 'what with the war, what with the sweat, what with the gallows and what with poverty'. As the last outbreak of the sweat had hit London more than 50 years earlier, the mention of it here probably was a reference to the plague, with the term sweat a popular usage for the disease, or perhaps because putting oneself into a sweat was one way that people tried to rid themselves of the plague when its early symptoms were suspected.[18] The play had its first recorded performance in December 1604; the playhouses did not open in the spring of 1603 because of the period of mourning following the queen's death and had remained closed after the plague struck.

The pamphlet-writer and playwright Thomas Dekker made critical observations on several aspects of policy and practices during the epidemic. He harshly judged those who left London because of their fear, making their way westwards because the plague was virulent downstream: 'Hacknies, water-men & Wagons, were not so terribly imployed many a yeare; so that within a short time, there was not a good horse in Smith-field, nor a Coach to be set eyes on. For after the world had once run upon the wheeles of the Pest-cart, neither coach nor caroach durst appeare in his likenesse.' Dekker grimly observed that some of those who fled were shunned in the country and died of the plague anyway: 'sickning in the hie way, [they] would have bene glad of a bed in an Hospitall, and dying in the open fieldes, have bene buried like dogs', when they could have remained in the city and received 'both bodily & spiritual comfort' before their death.[19]

For those who stayed, the sorrow caused by the plague deaths made a doleful impact, with 'Servants crying out for maisters: wives for husbands, parents for children, children for their mothers ... Bells heauily tolling in one place, and ringing out in another: The dreadfulnesse of such an houre, is in-utterable.' The plague swept through the city and 'Men, women, & children dropt downe before him', giving the impression that 'Whole housholds, and whole streets are stricken, The sick do die, the sound do sicken.' The reprehensible behaviour which ensued was comparable to that described by Boccaccio in Florence during the Black Death, for 'houses were rifled, streetes ransact ... rich mens Cofers broken open, and shared amongst prodigall heires and unthriftie servants: poore men usde poorely, but not pitifully'. He referred to the practice of body dumping when he mentioned those who were 'fearfully sweating with Coffins, to steale forth dead bodies, least the fatall hand-writing of death should seale up their doores'. He alleged that the City tradesmen dispatched their servants and employees who had contracted plague in sacks to their outworkers who lived in the suburbs; it would then be the outworkers' houses which were quarantined, not theirs. He cited the case of a poor boy who was a chandler's servant in Thames Street who succumbed to the plague and 'was first caryed away by water, to be left any where, but landing being denied by an army of browne bill-men that kept the shore, back againe was he brought, and left in an out-celler, where lying groveling and groning on his face ... there continued all night, and dyed miserably for want of succor'. With so many sick and dying, 'Every house lookt like S. Bartholomewes Hospitall, and every street like Bucklersbury, for poore *Methridatum* and *Dragon-water* (being both of them in all the world, scarce worth three-pence) were bort in every corner, and yet were both drunke every houre at other mens cost.' Bucklesbury was where many apothecaries had their shops and mithridatum and dragon-water were common treatments for plague. The prices of other popular preventatives shot up as demand soared and rosemary, which had been sold for one shilling for an armful, was now sold for six shillings a handful. He lambasted the physicians because their recommendations and treatments, which he listed, had been completely ineffectual and so 'not one of them durst peepe abroad'.[20]

The numbers of deaths were such that a victim would probably be buried with 60 others in a mass grave, having been dealt with by 'dumpish Mourners, merry Sextons, hungry Coffin-sellers, scrubbing Bearers, and nastie Grave-makers'. Dekker did not spare the parish officers, the clerks and the sextons, who insisted on taking their fees for burials and bragged about how wealthy they were becoming, 'for Sextons now had better doings than either Tavernes or bawdy-houses'. He singled out for criticism 'the three bald Sextons' of St Giles-in-the-Fields, St Sepulchre's and Saint Olave's, who 'for tearing money out of their throates, that had not a crosse in their purses. But alas! they must have it, it is their fee.' In summary, 'In this pittifull (or rather pittilesse) perplexitie stood London, forsaken like a Lover, forlorne like a widow, and disarmde of all comfort.' Chettle was censorious of those whose inconsiderate behaviour was assumed to exacerbate the problem, such as 'the over-boldnes of many preasing into infected places, and the lewdness of others with sores upon them, presuming into the open ayre, some of wilfulness, but truly many of necessitie'.[21]

Within this maelstrom of sickness, death and burial, Londoners struggled to cope with the crisis. A member of the Dutch community, Jacob Cool, did what he could to help the victims and he and his family survived. But he found the epidemic a dreadful experience and looking back on it he felt that he would never forget 'the grief that the city was drenched in'. He admitted that his courage had faltered, because 'I have seen so much'. Cool believed that the longer the outbreak lasted, the more the citizens' fear of it diminished and that because of the rising unemployment it became easier to recruit nurses, watchmen and searchers of the dead. He was aware of the practice of body dumping and commented that the balance of recorded deaths between the inner and outer parishes might have been distorted by householders in the central area sending their sick servants to their 'garden- or pleasure-houses' in the suburban parishes, where they died.[22]

Cool gave the number of deaths for the 23 weeks from 14 July to 22 December as 33,681, of which 29,083 were attributed to plague. Just 135 had died in the pest-house.[23] For the whole of 1603 the total deaths in the city, liberties and suburbs was 42,945, of which 33,347 were from plague. That was a far heavier death-toll than in any previous epidemic since the Black Death, but as the population had grown the proportion was, as in 1563, roughly 20 per cent of the whole. The previous pattern of plague deaths had generally been that deaths from the disease continued into the year after an epidemic and then fell away to a low level. That produced a certain confidence in those who had survived the outbreak that they would be safer as the numbers of plague deaths fell away towards the end of the year. Those who had left returned and those who had been drawn into the city for casual work and alms remained. Nicolo Molin, the Venetian envoy, was aware of this and on his return to London in the middle of December he wrote that 'No one ever mentions the plague, no more than if

it had never been. The City is so full of people that it is hard to
believe that about sixty thousand deaths have taken place.' Yet
before the end of January he was anxious, noting that 'The plague
has shown signs of increasing again, owing to the carelessness with
which the bedding and clothes of persons who died of the disease,
are being used by the living.' The trend did not continue and at
the end of February he was more optimistic: 'The last week sixteen
deaths of plague, and this week only twelve. This gives hope that
the scourge will soon cease.'[24] The situation was thought to be safe
enough for the king to make his long-delayed entry to the City on
15 March, and in the second week of April the actors' companies
were permitted to resume their performances. But plague claimed
896 of the 5,219 deaths in London that year.

The number of plague deaths was below 500 in 1605 before
increasing, contrary to expectations, and exceeding 2,000 in each
of the next three years. More than 100 plague deaths were recorded
in the Bills for seven of the nine weeks in September and October
1606, for seven consecutive weeks in those months in 1607 and
for ten consecutive weeks from September until early November
1608. The accepted pattern was that cold winter weather put an
end to an epidemic; the winter of 1608 was indeed so cold that the
Thames froze over, but the plague continued. In 1609 as many as
4,240 were recorded as dying from the disease and in September
that year the weekly plague toll peaked at 210.[25] The intermittent
outbreaks produced similar responses to the earlier full-blown
epidemics. The Privy Council continued to berate the aldermen
for the feebleness of their efforts and they continued to respond.
In 1606 Sir Leonard Halliday replied to one such missive with the
comment that 'you conceive a great fault in me in not taking meet
care in repressing the contagion of the plague within this city'. To
justify his handling of the situation he described in some detail the
procedure that was being followed, enclosing a copy of the printed
orders issued by the aldermen in their wards. To check that those
orders were being enforced the City's Provost Marshal 'in his own

person repairs twice every day to every infected house within this city, to see whether they have been guarded with warders, and papers set over every door according to those printed orders; and myself not therewith satisfied have also sent two of my own officers abroad the city every day as superintendents on the marshal and constable, to understand whether they have done their duties'. The Council had expressed particular concern regarding the crosses, and Halliday assured the members that 'Touching your directions for setting of red crosses over the doors of infected houses, I have given present order to see the same carefully performed, which shall be laid in oil to the intent they may not easily be put out.' He assured them that with all of his many duties he had given priority to 'the stay, if God so please, of this contagion of the plague which principally concerns the lives and states of the citizens'. He took the opportunity to have a swipe at the justices of the peace and other officers in the counties around the city, asking the Council to ensure that they 'be careful to put in execution the like orders as in London, otherwise it will be very dangerous for this city, they having their daily recourse hither for buying and providing of their necessaries'. In other words, in terms of the spreading of the plague, it was not only a case that Londoners leaving the city might carry the disease with them, but also that the country people and those from the suburbs might bring it to London.[26] Halliday was having a difficult period of office, which included the Gunpowder Plot and had begun inauspiciously with bad weather for his inauguration ceremonies, staged by his company, the Merchant Taylors. Its records noted that 'by reason of the great rain and fowle weather hap'ning and falling upon the morrow after Syman and Jude's day, being the day my Lord Mayor went to Westminster, the great costs the Company bestowed upon their pageant and other shows were in manner cast away and defaced'.[27]

The king and queen kept away from the city as much as possible. In October 1607 they made separate visits, the king staying for only a few hours and the queen for just one night. The king broke the tradition that the monarch, Knights of the Garter and all the court should be in the city to celebrate All Saints Day, 1 November. In February 1609 the presence of the disease over the winter caused apprehension that a serious outbreak would follow in the summer, so that, according to the Venetian ambassador, Marc' Antonio Correr, 'Every one is trying to get a house in the country, as they fear a great scourge in this city when the heat begins.' He planned to do the same, but would leave his property well guarded, as there had recently been a break-in at the chapel when 'all the fittings' were stolen. In May things looked so bad that the aldermen made plans to care for the sick and the Earl of Salisbury asked Correr what steps were taken in Venice against the plague. But a proposal that six doctors should be appointed to treat plague victims was not proceeded with because the city would not agree to pay their stipends. St Bartholomew's Fair was held as usual, although Correr noted that this was 'to our considerable surprise, for the plague, fostered by the unripe fruit the poor eat, has been more deadly than at any time in the last three years'. The Earl of Salisbury described the fair as 'memorable for a massacre and continual origin of the plague'. He was referring to the St Bartholomew's Day massacres in France in 1572, which had no connection with plague, other than the fear and horror which they both provoked; although the gathering of people from a wide area at the fair was a recurrent fear of the authorities. Towards the end of September Correr wrote that 'The Court and the Ministers are scattered about the country to escape the fury of the Plague, which has spread to many villages. Little work can be done and the ordinary sittings are put off for three weeks.' In October and November deaths from plague were recorded in the royal households, but by the second week of December Correr could write that the disease 'has almost disappeared in this cold, dry weather'.[28] He was troubled by occasional news of plague during 1610 and the final year of that prolonged outbreak was 1611, when the number of recorded plague deaths was 627. For the eight years from 1604 to

1611, the total number of deaths was 50,242 and 14,752 of them, almost 30 per cent, were from plague.

By the end of that first decade of the seventeenth century Londoners must have wondered if such a high level of plague infections had become the norm. In 1606 Shakespeare closed *King Lear* with the lines: 'The oldest hath borne most, we that are young / Shall never see so much, nor live so long.' Those who did take such a view would have been mistaken, for after 1611 there were very few deaths from the disease in London and across the country. But the continued presence of plague had made it a topic for playwrights to draw upon. In *Romeo and Juliet* Shakespeare used enforced household quarantine as the reason that Friar John was prevented from delivering the crucial message to Romeo. He was suspected by the searchers of coming into contact with plague victims and so was detained in a house and they 'Seal'd up the doors, and would not let us forth'. The message contained the information that Juliet had taken a potion to make her insensible, and she was not dead. Without that knowledge Romeo assumed the worst and returned to Verona, and from that point the story moved on to its tragic climax.

In contrast, Ben Jonson used reactions to plague to comical effect in *The Alchemist* (1610). The premise of the play was that the master of the house had fled because of the danger of plague, leaving it in charge of a servant, who mocked his master's fears with the remark he could be relied on not to return to London 'While there dyes one, a weeke, O' the plague'. With that apparent security the servant invited two rogues to join him there and set about defrauding their fellow-citizens, playing on their greed. When the master appeared unexpectedly, the servant had to explain to his accomplices that he had meant one death a week within the walls, not within the Liberties. Playgoers would have understood that distinction. The servant and his accomplices had indeed shut up the house and had intended to burn rose-vinegar, treacle and tar to purify the air. That provided the perfect cover while they carried out their swindling activities, for who would wish to enter a building marked as closed because of plague, on the suspicion of nefarious activities within? Jonson explained in the Prologue that he set the play in London because nowhere else 'breeds better matter, for your whore, Bawd, squire, impostor, many persons more'. The villains' activities were revealed after the master returned and discovered from the neighbours that the house had been visited regularly, day and night, when it was supposed to be closed. Confronted with this, the servant declared that the house 'has beene visited' with plague, not by himself, he hastened to add, but by 'My fellow, The cat that kept the buttry, [who] had it on her A weeke, before I spied it: but I got her Convay'd away i'the night'. This was an allusion to the practice of surreptitiously moving the dead and dying away from houses in the City. The play would have raised the laughter of recognition from the audience, as well as giving them pause for thought.

John Fletcher also drew on the context of plague in the city in *The Tamer Tamed* (c.1611). Petruchio found himself locked out of his house on his wedding night by his wife Maria, so he feigned illness to arouse her sympathy. But Maria countered that by claiming that 'The plague is i'th' house, sir, My husband has it now; Alas he is infected and raves extremely'; she later added that 'I saw the tokens'. When she was advised to 'lock the doors up, And send him in a woman to attend him' she responded that she had already sent for two women 'and the city Hath set a watch by this time. Meat nor money He shall not want, nor prayers.' Sure enough, two watchmen appear and are told by Maria to 'do your office, seal the doors up, friends'. She continues to play her part by arriving at the house and complaining that she is not allowed to visit her husband, while he objects that while he is shut up 'no man must come near me … my substance [is] bezzl'd, And an old woman watch me.' The situation was resolved after Maria also feigned sickness: the couple were then reconciled. By using the setting of household quarantine, Fletcher was able to draw attention to the way in which the system could be exploited by someone with spiteful intentions. Plague policies were obviously on his mind and he made a brief mention of one of the standard measures in *The Scornful Lady* of 1609, with the comment that 'I would 'twere lawful in the next great sickness to have the dogs spared, those harmless creatures.'[29] Whether they dealt with people or animals, many of the plague controls were unpopular enough for playwrights and writers to take an occasional swipe at them.

After 1611 plague was not an imminent threat and so playwrights rarely referred to it. They had been directly affected during the years of intermittent outbreaks by the closing of the playhouses when the number of plague deaths in the Bills reached a threatening level. In *Ram Alley* Lording Barry gave one of his characters the line 'I dwindle as a new player does at a plague bill certified forty.' The play was registered in 1610 but probably dates from 1608, and in that year Thomas Middleton, in *Your Five Gallants*, gave the figure as 30, with the line ''tis e'en as uncertain as playing, now up, now down, for if the bill rises to above thirty, here's no place for players.' This implies that if those writers were correct with the number, and they should have known, the threshold figure for closing the playhouses was 30 until 1608 but rose either in that year or soon afterwards to 40, which indicates some leniency by the aldermen. But whatever the rule, plague was undoubtedly disruptive for playwrights and players in London during those years.[30]

Earlier epidemics had not been forgotten and although Spitalcroft had not been used for plague burials since the fifteenth century and was now the outer precinct of an aristocratic mansion, its origins were still acknowledged. John Stow noted, 'I have seen and read an inscription fixed on a stone cross, sometime standing in the same churchyard': that was the text which mentioned 50,000 burials. His phrasing suggests that the cross was no longer there when he wrote, in 1598, and only the memory of the space as a burial ground remained. A second edition of Stow's *Survey of*

London was published in 1603, as was Henry Chettle's broadsheet entitled *A true list of the whole number that hath died*, which gave information on previous outbreaks in London and elsewhere. For London in the Black Death Chettle wrote that 'In one yeere, in a little plot of ground of 13 acres compasse, then called Spittle-croft, and now the Charter-house, was buried fifty thousand persons, besides all them that were then buried in the Churchyards, and divers places in the fields.'[31] It may be that Stow was Chettle's source, or perhaps it was tradition, strengthened by the inscription, which provided the basis for Chettle's statement, but it does show that into the seventeenth century the area was still known to have been a plague burial ground. It was transformed when Thomas Sutton established his charity there in 1611, having acquired the Charterhouse from the Howards. Sutton was widely believed to be the wealthiest commoner in the country and since the mid-1590s he had been planning to establish a charity, consisting of an almshouse and school. After acquiring the Charterhouse he began the process of adapting the buildings for his charity, the largest hitherto established in England, supporting 80 resident pensioners and 40 scholars. He died before the end of the year, with the work of adaptation barely under way, but it was completed by the governors and the buildings were brought into use in 1614. To secure his foundation against predators Sutton had sought royal protection by designating it 'The Hospital of King James, founded in Charterhouse within the County of Middlesex'. As governors he appointed some of the most powerful men at the heart of the Jacobean establishment, high-ranking churchmen and lawyers with the knowledge and authority to carry out his intentions and protect his legacy. They included the Archbishop of Canterbury and Bishop of Ely, the Deans of Westminster and St Paul's, the Lord Chancellor, the Lord Treasurer, the Chief Justice and one other Justice of the Court of Common Pleas, the Attorney General, and a Master in Chancery. As part of their improvements the governors carried out work to enhance the appearance of the outer precinct. The chapel built in 1481 was demolished, the causeway leading to it and the ground within the square were levelled, and a footpath was created running diagonally across the square to the hospital's gatehouse. The effect of the improvements was to make the square appear 'more neat and comely' and must have made it look less like an old burial ground.[32]

The immediacy of plague for the citizens declined as the number of cases dwindled. But the Council did not relax its vigilance and maintained the quarantining of shipping, which was seen to be successful, for outbreaks on the near-continent did not spread to south-east England. At Amsterdam, 1616, 1617, 1618, 1623 and 1624 were plague years and an epidemic began in Bremen in 1623, but London was not affected. In 1616 just nine plague burials were included in the Bills and in 1617 the figure was only six, even though the disease had extended across the Low Countries. An order was issued that bedding, feathers and other household goods could not be landed in the Thames and in 1619, when plague was present in Rouen, two ships from there were held at Tilbury for 25 days. That freedom from plague extended across England and Wales, which briefly in the middle of the decade were virtually free from plague. It must have seemed that at last a solution had been found.

12

THE FEARFUL SUMMER, 1625

The pattern of the 1610s continued into the following decade, with care taken to intercept shipping from infected places, which in 1623 included Paris and other French towns and cities. Despite the risk, just 17 plague deaths were identified in London during that year, but in August 1624 the Privy Council again became concerned about the presence of plague in France. The lord mayor pointed out that Bartholomew's Fair was due to be held soon and was 'usually furnished with divers comodities brought out of France, wherby the case appeares soe much the more dangerous'. The Council's response was to warn the officials in the ports on the south coast to be vigilant in keeping the infection away, also pointing out that The Hague and other Dutch towns were enduring 'much contagious and pestilent sicknes', so that care should also be taken with goods brought from the Low Countries.[1]

Despite those instructions, the rising number of deaths in 1624 was such that people began to feel uneasy. The cause was not plague but fevers, the deadliest of which were 'purple' or 'spotted' fevers. The pioneer demographer John Graunt wrote that the diseases other than the plague which 'make years unhealthful in this City, are spotted-Fevers, Small-Pox, Dysentery, called by some The Plague in the Guts, and the unhealthful Season is the Autumn'. He classified both 1623 and 1624 as 'sickly years', when there was high mortality from causes other than plague.[2] Lord Carew attributed the unusual sickliness and numbers of deaths to 'the Aboundance of fruites, whereof there was such a store this last summer as Melons had beene sould every where as ordinarily as Coxcombs'. Others blamed the bumper crop of cucumbers. The purgative effects of soft fruits and cucumbers were thought to produce an imbalance in the humours, making a person susceptible to disease. The fevers struck anyone, regardless of rank. The Duke of Lennox, the Lord Steward, died in February and his brother in July, the Earl of Dorset passed away in April, the Earl of Thomond in September and a few weeks later Lord Wriothesley and then his father, the Earl of Southampton, died within a week of each other. In December the Earl of Nottingham died and two months later so did Lord Chichester, and in March the Marquess of Hamilton succumbed to a fever. John Chamberlain remarked that 1624 'hath ben a dismall yeare to great men', with the loss of two dukes, four earls and 'I know not howe many Lords'.[3] Then, in early March 1625 the king became feverish and did not respond to treatment; he died on 27 March. He was succeeded by his son Charles, whose favourite was George Villiers, Duke of Buckingham, who had made the switch from being James's favourite. Villiers was a member of a Leicestershire gentry family and through his good looks, charm and shrewd awareness of the ways of the court he had risen to be effectively James's first minister before dexterously gaining Charles's favour, which Villiers enjoyed until his assassination in 1628. At the head of the government, therefore, the new reign did not bring a change of favourite, although seven Privy Councillors lost their places in early April. The deaths and displacement of so many senior figures in such a short time could affect continuity in government and regional administration through the loss of their combined experience and knowledge. But policy on plague prevention would not have been affected, or challenged, as the absence of an outbreak while the near-continent had endured an epidemic apparently trumpeted the success of the quarantining of shipping and interception of merchandise from infected ports. The Bills of Mortality showed that from December 1624 until the middle of the following April the average weekly number of plague deaths was 'not above five'. But Graunt, looking over the figures, observed that 'many times other Pestilential Diseases, as Purple Fevers, Small-Pox, &c. do fore-run the Plague a Year, or two or three'. There were roughly 8,000 deaths in London in 1622, but 11,000 in 1623 and 12,000 in 1624; did that presage a plague outbreak?[4] London's population had not only recovered after the epidemic in 1603 and subsequent outbreaks but had continued to grow steadily.

James's funeral took place on 7 May and was an impressive event, described by Chamberlain as 'the greatest indeed that ever was known in England ... all was performed with great magnificence, but the order was very confused and disorderly'. He thought that the hearse was 'the fairest and best-fashioned that hath been seen, wherein Inigo Jones, the Surveyor, did his part'. Mourning dress had been issued to about 9,000 people and because of the numbers attending it was not until five o'clock that the congregation was assembled in Westminster Abbey; the sermon lasted for two hours 'so that it was very late before the offering and all other ceremonies were ended'. In the same letter Chamberlain mentioned the death of one of the aldermen, Sir John Garret, and added that 'The sickness begins to show itself and spread in diverse places, having already infected 13 parishes.' From the Bills he noted that the total number of deaths in the previous week was 332, of which 45 were attributed to plague, and that Parliament's sitting had been deferred.[5] A major epidemic developed from those beginnings during the spring, so that Charles's reign began with a devastating plague outbreak in London, as his father's had done. James's coronation had gone ahead in the year of his accession, but Charles's was delayed until the year after he came to the throne.

The aldermen and privy councillors drew the same conclusions as did Chamberlain and the plague orders were issued, with exhortations that they should be efficiently enforced. The City asked for the advice of the College of Physicians, which was sent on 19 and 21 April. Following complaints by the Privy Council that preventative measures had not been taken by the city soon enough, the aldermen responded with a protest about 'those vagrant persons and multitude of poore coming out of the out partes, by which the cittie is annoyed and pestered'. The Council then instructed the justices of Westminster, Middlesex and Surrey to keep the streets very clean, punish all vagrants and remove inmates.[6] In the last week of April nine parishes recorded plague deaths. In the final week of May the number was 16 and for the corresponding week of June it was 50; the numbers of plague deaths rose from 26 to 78 and then to 390 during those weeks. On 9 June John Williams, the Lord Keeper, wrote to the Secretary, Sir Edward Conway, observing that 'The sickness in London does increase into a remarkable number and is very dangerously scattered,' although at that point Westminster and the Savoy were free from 'the infection or suspicion'. He wrote to him again four days later to remind him to make the king aware of the sickness, 'especially the most dangerous scattering thereof into all parts of the City and now into many of the suburbs. A broker has brought it ... into Westminster'; the searchers had reported that the broker had died of the plague three days earlier, yet none of the six members of his family had developed the symptoms. The king should travel by water and enter the city and parliament as privately as possible, to avoid the crowds. He suggested that Parliament should meet elsewhere, which would have the effect of dispersing the senior figures of the kingdom, for 'how fearful it is that the plague should find the whole kingdom convened and united in one city'. That was indeed a powerful argument for the legal term to be postponed, the court to leave Whitehall, and Parliament to assemble in another city able to accommodate the members, which presumably would be Oxford, so long as it remained free of the disease. But dispersal raised the problem of inter-communication between the various sections of government, at a time when travel was not easy at best and could be restricted even for the privileged.[7]

Williams was right to be concerned. On 12 June Chamberlain wrote that 25 parishes were infected, that the number of deaths was 434, with 92 of them from plague, so that 'this town is likely to suffer much and be half undone. And that which makes us the more afraid is that the sickness increaseth so fast when we have had for a month together the extremest cold weather that ever I knew in this season. What are we then to look for when heats come on and fruits grow ripe?' He concluded his letter with 'The sickness is come into the Lord Mayor's house, so that he is driven to shut up his doors, to forsake the town, and hath left Sir Thomas Bennet his deputy.'[8] The lord mayor was John Gore, whose father and grandfather had both served as aldermen, and whose brother William had served as sheriff in the same year as John did; their brother Richard was an MP for London. So John came from a family with a strong practice of public service in the City, yet was not abashed to leave it when plague reached his house. By the first week of June 'many families' had left for the country. The Bills were closely watched; as John Taylor put it Thursday's Bill 'shows us what thousands Death that week did kill'. But the Bills were not trusted by Londoners and when the return for the first week of July was published and it showed 'but 1222 and of the sickness but 500' it provoked the comment that 'by common opinion there died many more'.[9]

Steven Bradwell, a London physician, told his readers that when the plague struck they should fly with speed 'lest by lingering that infection go along with you' and to travel many miles 'whither there is no probabilitie of common trading, or recourse of people from the place forsaken'.[10] That advice was based on centuries of experience, yet some prevaricated. Chamberlain waited to see the arrival of the queen in London for the first time. Charles had married Henrietta Maria of France by proxy on 1 May and she and her entourage were expected in the middle of June, though Chamberlain acknowledged that 'they come in an ill time, for the sickness increaseth and is spread far and near'. Parliament was due to meet, but Chamberlain expected that the sitting would be delayed again, so that the Members 'complain that they are kept here with so much danger and expense to so little purpose, for there is no likelihood they can sit here long, if at all'. Chamberlain intended to go to Ware Park, yet almost two weeks later he was still in London, explaining, 'We cannot find in our hearts to leave this town as long as here is such doings by reason of the Queen's arrival and the sitting of the Parliament.'[11] Those attractions declined when the king and the court left Whitehall.

The Venetian ambassador, Zuane Pesaro, had commented before the end of June, 'Every one remains here at serious risk owing to the very great increase of the infection.' On 4 July he was still in London and was even more alarmed, reporting that 'I remain in the same quarters in even greater peril, as fifty parishes are infected and 390 deaths are notified, but the number is much greater everywhere.' He explained the removal of the king, queen and court that day, contrary to their previous intentions, by the fact that

...plague has penetrated to Whitehall, the king's residence, although among low officials, causing great confusion and peril to the Court and their Majesties, who immediately, contrary to the last decision, betook themselves to Hampton Court. Report says they will make a tour, though nothing certain is known except that they wish to keep as much apart as possible, and a new proclamation has forbidden commerce with the Court upon pain of death.

Allegedly the court left Whitehall after three people were carried out of the back part of the palace, all of whom subsequently died of plague. It moved on shortly afterwards when a case of plague was identified at Hampton Court: 'a Frenchwoman' was said to have died there of the disease and other cases followed, so that a pest-house was erected in the grounds for members of the household suspected of having the plague. The court's progress was unexpected and so unplanned, and it continued to move from palace to palace to avoid the infection, pursued by tradesmen and petitioners.[12]

A few days after the court had gone Pesaro still had not left London, despite his anxieties, and he explained that he was uncertain where he would move to 'as the danger is everywhere'; although he would try to stay close to the court, but that would be difficult 'as they do not like ambassadors near'. By the middle of the month he was at Windsor and the French diplomats were at Richmond; the Dutch envoys 'ashamed of fearing the plague, and expecting orders for their conferences, have remained practically alone in London'. By 21 July the Dutch 'could not hold out against the dangers of the plague' any longer and moved to Staines, but that kept them away from the court and in mid-August Pesaro reported that they 'have transacted no business'. He faced the same difficulties himself and pointed out that being separated from the court, other diplomats and his friends made it difficult for him to find out how state affairs were going, which was one of most important aspects of his duties. That would have applied to others, such as merchants, whether they left London or remained there, because the small communities in which they operated became dispersed as people moved away.[13]

By 20 July the Privy Councillors had to admit that as well as the king 'wee of his Privy Councell are forced to disperse ourselves more then at any time hath beene usuall'. Nevertheless, they wrote to the lord mayor, 'We praie and require your Lordshipp etc. not to abandon the government of the cittie committed to your charge and to continue and increase the usuall meanes for repressing of the contagion.'[14] They had left, but required him, the aldermen and the officers to stay. Many of the members of both Houses of

London in the fifteenth century, depicting the imprisonment of the Duc d'Orléans in the Tower, with the city beyond. © Stephen Porter

Boccaccio and Petrarch, chroniclers of the Black Death: an illustration of *c*. 1400. © Stephen Porter

St Sebastian, a plague saint, pierced by darts. By Hans Holbein the Elder, 1516. © Stephen Porter

Carved statue of St Roch, fifteenth
century, with a bubo on his thigh
and the dog who succoured him.
© Metropolitan Museum of Art

London in the late fifteenth century, an impression by the painter John Fulleylove,
based upon a contemporary illustration. © Stephen Porter

Thomas Linacre professeur en médecine a son ble Angloise homme certes docte aus deux langues Grecq et Latine lequel ayant, espou plusieurs doctes leures, mourat a Londres l'an de n̄re Seign̄

Above left: Death and the maiden: a young lady in her garden is confronted by Death, *c.* 1500. © Stephen Porter

Above right: Thomas Linacre (*c.* 1460–1524), founder of the College of Physicians and translator of Galen's medical works. © Wellcome Collection

Left: Theophrastus Paracelsus (1493–1541). His alternatives to Galen's theories received support in seventeenth-century London. © Stephen Porter

Cardinal Wolsey, Henry VIII's chief minister and originator of plague regulations in London. © Stephen Porter

Henry VIII by
Hans Holbein.
© Stephen Porter

Sir Thomas More, Lord Chancellor and the author of *Utopia*, by Hans Holbein. © Stephen Porter

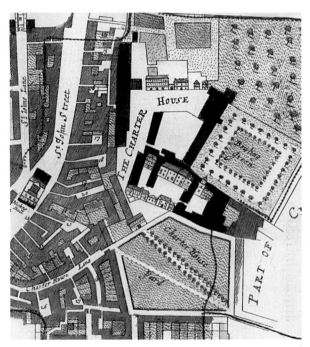

The Charterhouse and Charterhouse Square in the mid-eighteenth century; the site of the Black Death burial ground. © The Charterhouse

Above: The royal fortress of the Tower was not a secure refuge from the plague and the court left London during epidemics. © Stephen Porter

Right: William Cecil, Lord Burghley (1520–98). During his period as Elizabeth's chief minister the plague regulations were codified. © Stephen Porter

Plan-view of London around 1585, when the city was beginning to expand
rapidly, much to the government's alarm. © Stephen Porter

A section of Claus Visscher's view of London in 1616. © Stephen Porter

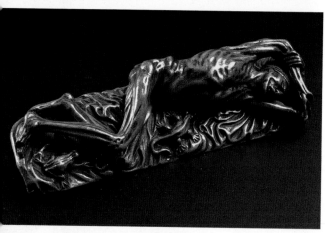

A carving in wood of a plague sufferer, seventeenth century. © Science Museum, London

All-covering apparel for doctors treating plague victims was devised in France in the early seventeenth century and was widely adopted. © Stephen Porter

The closely packed
buildings near the north
end of London Bridge
c. 1632, when the City
was at its period of
densest occupation. Artist
unknown.

Sir Theodore de Mayerne,
author of a report in
1631 on the prevention
and control of the plague.
© Wellcome Collection

A fumigating torch carried as a protection against infected air, seventeenth century. © Science Museum, London

Pieter de Hooch's depiction of a courtyard in Delft in the mid-seventeenth century shows the cleanliness which London's authorities required. © Stephen Porter

Above: Algiers was suspected of being the source of the plague in north-west Europe in the early 1660s. From George Braun and Frans Hogenberg, *Civitatis Orbis Terrarum*, 1572. © Historic Cities Center, via Wikimedia Commons

Below: The harbour of a Dutch town in 1664, painted by Abraham Storck. That year saw a severe plague epidemic in the United Provinces and the Privy Council quarantined shipping from the country. © Stephen Porter

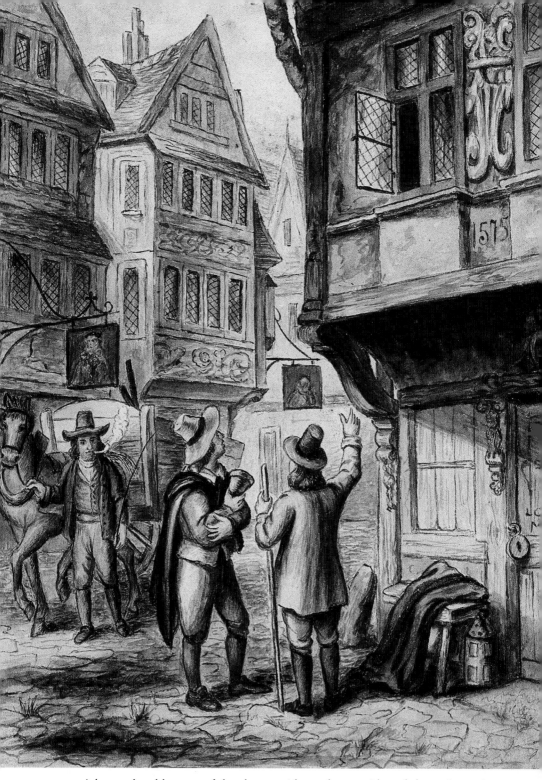

A house closed because of the plague, with warders outside and the notice on its
door 'Lord Have Mercy Upon Us'; the cart is a dead cart. © Wellcome Collection

Humphrey Henchman, Bishop of London, who remained in the city throughout the Great Plague. © Crown copyright, NMR

"BRING OUT YOUR DEAD."

A scene from the Great Plague, with a fire in the street, a dead cart, the bellman calling out 'Bring out your dead' and a homeless family. © Wellcome Collection

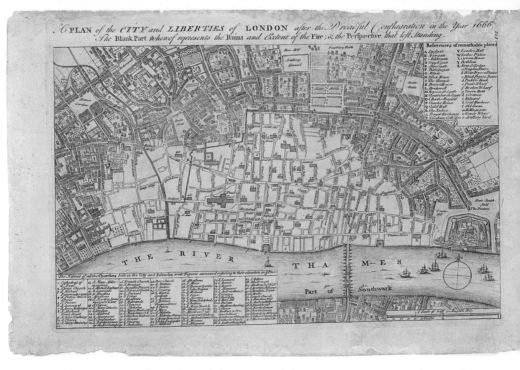

Wenceslaus Hollar's plan of the extent of the Great Fire in 1666: the parishes around the centre were untouched. © Stephen Porter

Johannes Kip's view of Charterhouse Square and the Charterhouse towards the end of the seventeenth century, when all trace of the plague burial ground had been erased. © The Charterhouse

Parliament had gone away already, but Sir Francis Nethersole, the MP for Corfe Castle, stayed on and in mid-July commented that the increase in plague deaths 'doth cause such a distraction and consternation in men's minds that the like was never seen in our age'. He compared the figures with those of the corresponding week of the epidemic in 1603 and on 16 July noted that they were 'now grown the last week near a thousand greater. That makes all men that can, hasten away.' William Lilly later remembered that the 'most able people of the whole city and suburbs were out of town; if any remained, it were such as were engaged by parish-officers to remain; no habit of a gentleman or woman continued'. Pesaro was also shocked at the severity of the epidemic, writing to the Doge and Senate that 'The plague in London is becoming most severe and people are dying by thousands. The air seems infected and many succumb suddenly when walking in the streets. The scourge has spread everywhere.'[15]

Lilly's lasting impression was that 'the woeful calamity of that year was grievous, people dying in the open fields and in open streets.' When the numbers in the Bills rose in August 'very few people had thoughts of surviving the contagion'. As well as the numbers in the Bills, which were treated with a degree of scepticism, anecdotal rumours of the scale of the mortality spread through the city. Nehemiah Wallington, a wood turner in St Leonard's Eastcheap, heard 'that threescore children died out of one alley' and he noted on another occasion that he 'did hear of threescore women with child and in childbed that died in one week in Shoreditch parish and scarce two from that was sick with child that escaped death'.[16] The figures themselves were alarming enough without rumours to stoke the fires of fear. In the last week of July, 3,583 dead were recorded, there were 4,517 in the following week, 4,855 in the next one, which ran to 11 August, and then the next week, ending 18 August, was the 'great bill', with over 5,000 deaths, in fact 5,205, of which 4,463 were from plague. The number declined thereafter, to 4,841, then 3,897 and to 3,157 in the first week of September. The next week showed a significant fall of over 1,000 to 1,994 and in the following week, the last one in September, the figure was back to where it had been in the first week of July, with 1,236 deaths; that was bad enough, but nothing like as frightening as the weeks in late July and throughout August. The number of parishes recording plague deaths did not decline in the same way; during August virtually the whole city was returning plague deaths to the parish clerks and by the end of September that number had fallen from the peak of 114 to 103.

John Evelyn's family took no risks and sent John away. He was born in 1620 and later recalled that in 1625 'I was sent by my Father to Lewes in Sussex, to be with my Grandfather, with whom I pass'd my Child-hood: This was that yeare in which the Pestilence was so Epidemical, that there dy'd in Lond. 5000 a Weeke; & I well remember the strict Watches, and examinations upon the Ways as we pass'd.'[17] The party in which Evelyn travelled would have been regarded as 'genteel' and so was let through after being checked, but others were halted by the country people at their barriers. An addition to the measures taken to prevent plague was the introduction of health certificates which stated that the bearers had come from a plague-free area. This copied the Italian practice of issuing such certificates and was designed to restrict movement during epidemics; in August a writer in Southampton assured Dudley Carleton that 'No man comes into a town without a ticket.'[18] But the practice was flawed, for hand-written ones could be forged and so only printed ones were valid, and some certificates, hand-written or printed, may have been issued in return for a bribe to those who were known to be moving from an infected district.

Those who were halted and questioned at a barrier were sometimes treated in a rough manner by country people armed with pitchforks and other implements, which kept the travellers at a distance while their credentials were checked. The locals manning the road-blocks were implementing the policy of restriction of movement in an attempt to confine the disease, but the way in which they acted was objectionable. The view from London was that the extent of the disaster was being exaggerated; in Henry Petowe's words, 'The rumour in the countrey went currant, that London had not people enough left alive to bury her Dead.' Petowe was indignant at the treatment meted out by the country's 'illiterated Peasants your Hobnayld Clownes' to his fellow citizens, who had been repelled 'with Pitchforkes, Staves, Hookes, browne Bills, and such like rustick Weapons'. When they had demanded passage they received the reply, 'No, for you are Londoners.' Petowe accused the country people of being so uncharitable that when some died 'in the High-wayes and other places ... you would not affoord them Christian buriall'. He put words into the mouth of the city, which asked 'Can this be true that my poore Children should be thus misused, amongst my Neighbours, such as have daily Commerce with me; If they bring me Food, I give them Money, the Land-lord must be paid.' And when they are in need, do not the countryman 'come unto mee thy charitable Neighbour London; and doe not I from time to time, nay, at all times helpe you in the midst of your extremitie?' The city goes on to emphasise the point that it is open to all comers at all times: 'I have no Barrocadoes to keepe you forth; but my Gates all houres of the night are open for the meanest Hynde or Swaine that comes. I, nor none of mine examine what Countriman thou art: from whence thou camest? or whither thou wilt? but come and welcome.' Despite the city's openness and charity, when 'in the time of my Visitation, did my poore fearefull Children, come amongst you into the Countrie for a little refuge or recreation, presuming upon the like welcome there, as you found here, and did you give them Jack Drumes entertainment. Oh uncharitable, inhumaine and ingratefull people: Indeed it argued no Christianitie in you.' The citizens were not so fearful that the country people would bring an ague into their city that they excluded them, so nor should they be so alarmed that the citizens were carrying plague. Petowe asked for a greater degree of charity from those in the country when the citizens sought refuge, to reflect the economic and social interaction which prevailed at all other times.[19] Road-blocks were set up along the highways not far from the city, yet the urge to leave grew stronger as the epidemic developed. John Donne, Dean of St Paul's, described the citizens as fleeing from London as from a house on fire, having 'stuffed their pockets with their best ware ... and were not received so much as into barns and perished so, some of them, with more money about them than would have bought the village where they died. A Justice of the Peace told me of one that died so with £1,400 about him.'[20]

Unlike Petowe, Stephen Bradwell emphasised how deadly plague was: 'We see continuall Burialls, and some die in the very streets ... we finde also that few of those that are stricken doe recover againe.' He acknowledged that some Londoners could not or should not leave 'some through povertie, and want of friends in the Countrey; or by reason of the dependence of their living upon the Towne infected'. He listed those who ought to remain 'whose callings be helpful to the sick and weak'; they were the magistrates and officers, clergy, physicians, surgeons, apothecaries, midwives, keepers and searchers. Bradwell advised those who stayed in the city to restrict the company they kept and avoid crowds and assemblies. If they stood to talk to someone to keep two yards away, and if they suspected that they had the plague then four yards away and upwind of the sick person. Misty, moist and smelly places were to be avoided, as were narrow alleys and lanes, common sewers and ditches. He recommended that they did not go out early in the morning, or at all on moist, cloudy or misty days, because of the damp air, but also noted that they should not stand in the heat of the sun. They should not live in houses which were crowded and confined, they should often change beds and rooms and air them every day and afterwards they should keep windows and doors closed. The house should be fumigated with juniper, pitch, turpentine, frankincense, bay leaves, mint, lavender, wormwood and rue, perhaps steeped in vinegar. In the public places the streets before everyone's door should be cleaned every day and the streets, alleys and courts must be cleaned, swept and washed, leaving no dirty puddles, dunghills, carrion or mud; the channels should be washed down but without using too much water. The aim was cleanliness but keeping the air as dry as possible. To purge the air fires should be lit in the streets and firearms discharged in every street, lane and street-corner to 'forcibly move the air'. Bradwell also had copious advice about diet, but no-one could adapt their accommodation, diet and mode of life quickly enough to improve their chances of survival, especially at a time when so many aspects of daily life were becoming difficult.[21]

For the plague orders to be implemented and the poor cared for, coherent organisation was required. An example of a conscientious local officer who stayed and continued to carry out his duties is provided by John Boston, who had held the post of clerk of St Saviour's, Southwark, since 1604.[22] His responsibilities included keeping the accounts and preparing the monthly bill of baptisms, marriages, churchings and burials. In 1625 the number of burials rose sharply, from 40 in February and 43 in March to 65 in April, 101 in May, 180 in June and 539 named persons 'and many unknowne' in July. It was the increase in deaths recorded in the Bills during July which prompted an exodus from the parish, for 'the Infeccon of the Sicknes and plague' was 'lamentably spread almost through all the said parishe'. The minister was so afraid that he 'withdrewe himself from doeinge his dutie and excersinge his function in celebratinge devyne service within the said parishe as usually before tyme hee had done'. Most of the churchwardens and 'the rest of the most able parishioners … withdrewe themselves likewise from theire howses and habitacons into remote places'. That left Boston, who was a deacon, to celebrate divine service and conduct burials 'exposinge himself to unspeakable wattchinges labour and travell [travail] both daie and night'. For their safety he sent his wife and two of their 'smalle children' into the country.

From the beginning of August until 15 September there were 1,078 burials in the parish, hastening the departure of those who could get away and abandoning 'the poorer sorte', many of them so destitute that they did not leave enough money to pay the burial fees. As many as 30 or 40 bodies a day were left at the burial ground during the worst of the epidemic, without any indication of their identity. Such body dumping was done to avoid payment of the fees and also, presumably, by relatives desperate not to have their houses closed and quarantined. Boston had to try to discover who they were but was unable to collect fees for roughly a third of the burials. The lists include his record of the interment of servants and many poor people, such as the entry for 16 August noting the burial of 'John Bassett, a boy, and divers other poore unknown'. In September Boston was taken ill, but, conscientious to the last, before he died he spoke out of an open window, so as not to pass on the disease, to explain the financial position to Richard Wright, a grocer. He also mentioned it to the two women who nursed him; they survived. Boston was buried on 22 September, as the epidemic began to wane, with 570 burials during the month but just 90 in October.

Boston's widow married Robert White and, although she handed over money which she found in the house, the vestry was not satisfied that all the fees collected had been accounted for and so sued Sarah and Robert for £62 8s in outstanding fees. According to Richard Wright, testifying on behalf of the vestry, the description of a mass departure was exaggerated and 'Riche middle sorte and poore people' had all died in the parish during the outbreak. Two members of the vestry are indeed recorded among the burials in the register, but it is significant that although the vestry met frequently in normal times it did not assemble at all between 28 June and 7 October, even though there were pressing matters to deal with. Wright's contention is not borne out by other evidence, and although St Saviour's did include unsavoury districts containing brothels and alehouses, in other respects it was a stable and bustling area, not greatly different from the rest of the capital, where the absence of so many citizens had a marked effect. The case highlights conditions in a parish during a severe epidemic and the strains placed on parochial administration and a dedicated officer who remained to carry out his duties, which cost him his life.

Another active parishioner of St Saviour's was Robert Harvard, a butcher, who at various times held the posts of vestryman, churchwarden and overseer of the poor, and he was a governor of the parish grammar school. Robert and three of his nine children died in the outbreak; a fourth, John, survived, married in 1636 and in the following year he and his wife emigrated to Massachusetts, where he died in 1638. His bequest to a newly established college in Cambridge nearby brought him enduring fame, as it adopted his surname. John Fletcher, the dramatist, was invited to go into East Anglia to avoid the risk, but he 'stayd but to make himselfe a suite of Cloathes, and while it was making, fell sick of the Plague and dyed'. More than 40 years later his tailor described to John Aubrey how, while treating his arm for an injury, he had 'found the Spotts upon him'. In Fletcher's case vanity outweighed prudence; he, too, was buried in St Saviour's, when he could have been in the relative safety of East Anglia. Others delayed beyond all prudence. Raphael Thorius, a physician and poet, was a member of the Dutch community in London and a friend of Jacob Cool. He had survived the epidemic in 1603 and presumably chose to remain as the outbreak in 1625 developed, when he could have left; he died of the plague during the summer in his house in St Benet Finck.[23]

The Dutch community acted independently once again to ensure that its members were cared for during the outbreak. At a meeting on 10 July Jan Schram, who lived in Southwark, was appointed as a temporary visitor after his wife had been asked if she agreed to his appointment, which she did. He was to be paid an advance of 15s and 9s per week so long as the outbreak continued; when he was discharged in December he was given a bonus of £2. The permanent visitor of the sick had remained in post and he was now paid an extra £10. Both men had survived the disease, as had the church's ministers. Some controversy had arisen when complaints were made about some worshippers attending the church 'with open sores'. If they wished to continue going to the services, they were to be segregated in a section of the building.[24]

William Lilly lived in his master's house in the Strand and found that he had to carry out his master's charitable duties. He later related that his master 'having a great charge of money and plate, some of his own, some other men's, left me and a fellow-servant to keep the house, and himself in June went into Leicestershire. He was in that year feoffee collector for twelve poor alms-people living in Clement-Dane's Church-Yard; whose pensions I in his absence paid weekly, to his and the parish's great satisfaction.' For his solace at such a difficult and lonely time Lilly bought a bass-viol and engaged a tutor to teach him to play it; he also went bowling in Lincoln's Inn Fields 'with Wat the cobler, Dick the blacksmith, and such like companions'. They worked long hours, sometimes without a meal break. He also attended church and listened to funeral sermons 'of which there was then great plenty' and went to St Antholin's in Budge Row daily to hear the early morning sermon. One day he passed only three people between the Strand Bridge and St Antholin's. Admittedly that was at half past six in the morning, but he had to go roughly a mile and his direct route would have taken him through a normally busy quarter of the City, down Fleet Street, up Ludgate Hill, past St Paul's and along Watling Street. Despite going around the city, working, bowling and worshipping, Lilly was 'nothing at any time visited, though my conversation was daily with the infected'. When he was at a communion service at St Clement Dane's church in August three ministers officiated because of the size of the congregation, but one of them

...fell sick as he was giving the sacrament, went home, and was buried of the plague the Thursday following, Mr. James, another of the ministers, fell sick ere he had quite finished, had the plague, and was thirteen weeks ere he recovered. Mr. Whitacre, the last of the three, escaped not only then, but all the contagion following, without any sickness at all; though he officiated at every funeral, and buried all manner of people, whether they died of the plague or not. He was given to drink, seldom could preach more than one quarter of an hour at a time.

It is not clear from Lilly's account whether he thought that Whitacre's survival and his drinking habits were connected.[25] Among the other clergymen who stayed was William Crashaw, rector of St Mary's, Whitechapel, who buried as many as 40 or 60 victims a day, but survived, dying in 1626. Nehemiah Wallington remained at home in Eastcheap with his household and they were in good health through the worst of the outbreak until October, when a servant girl complained of 'a pricking in her neck', a symptom of the plague. On the following morning their daughter, not yet three years old, fell ill with the disease and 'she continued in great agonies (which were very grievous to us, the beholders) till Tuesday morning', when she died. She was buried that night.[26]

Some attributed their continued health to the potions which they took, or their mode of life. Tobacco was brought from North America in increasing quantities in the early seventeenth century and smoking became a popular habit, especially so during the plague of 1625, for the smoke was thought to ward off foul infected air and was cheaper than the expensive contents of nosegays and pomanders. Others went with prostitutes in the hope of contracting syphilis; it was thought that it brought immunity from the plague, although it was itself often fatal. Some sought solace in drink, to ease the tensions and loneliness which came from the breaking up of neighbourhoods and work patterns, and the deaths of friends and relatives. John Donne delivered a plague sermon in which he evinced little sympathy for many of those who had died. He was not impressed by people who declared 'let us eat and drink, and take our pleasure, and make our profits, for tomorrow we shall die, and so were cut off by the hand of God, some, and in their lusts and wantonness in licentious houses'. They were men 'whose lust carried them into the jaws of infection in lewd houses, and seeking one sore [from syphilis] perished with another [from plague]'. Others were men who 'sought no other way to divert sadness, but strong drink in riotous houses, and there drank up ... the cup of condemned men, of death, in the infection of that place'. Nor was he sympathetic to those who had taken the opportunity to rob houses which had been left empty and had thereby brought on their own death. He described them as men who died 'even in their robberies, in half-empty houses' and were those who in their 'rapine and covetousness broke into houses, and seeking the wardrobes of others, found their own winding-sheet, in the infection of that house where they stole their own death'. His conclusion was that those who had died because of what he regarded as transgressions were 'men that died in their sins, that sinned in their dying, that sought and hunted after death so sinfully, we have little comfort of such men'.[27] It seems doubtful whether all of the clergy took such an unsympathetic approach, for those who stayed and continued to minister to their ailing and bereaved parishioners would have been all too aware of the anguish which they were going through. But their efforts were circumscribed to some extent by the intervention of the Privy Council, which acknowledged that usually funeral sermons were 'of most excellent use being applied with zeale and judgment' but objected that during 'these tymes of contagion they augment the danger by reason of the greater concoursse of people'.[28]

In the City commerce slackened as people left, networks were broken up, Londoners were forbidden to attend fairs elsewhere and carriers were restricted from coming into the city. At the end of August Pesaro told the Doge and Senate bluntly that 'the plague has stopped all trading' and that the harvest had been poor; a few days later no members of the Levant Company were in London.[29] The designated days for prayers and fasts were like any festival days, so far as business in London was concerned. The Duke of Buckingham acknowledged that 'many poor people' there were 'imprisoned by reason of the contagion and want of commerce [and] are in a miserable case; that, for want of means, many perish'. In October the Council conceded that the Wiltshire clothiers could take their cloth to London, despite the earlier orders, so long as it was not sold in the open markets but delivered directly to the merchants' warehouses, taking care when they did so that the disease should not be increased and spread further into the country 'wherein there hath already to[o] great neglect and carelessenesse bene used'. Also in October, it received a more personal petition, from Henry Girton, executor of his brother Thomas of Westminster, a vintner, who complained to the Privy Council that he was trying to tie up his brother's affairs and satisfy the creditors, but could not do so because he had been unable to sell the estate to the best advantage 'by reason of the late infeccion and the deadness of the tymes'.[30] Among other groups whose livelihoods were curtailed was the schoolmasters, because schools in the city were closed and as a consequence they could not even pay their rents.[31]

When Parliament reassembled at Oxford it addressed the problem of poverty and the Lords prepared an order 'for relief of the poor at London, Westminster etc'. The preamble referred to 'the lamentable distress of the poor people inhabiting in the cities and suburbs of London and Westminster, and in the out-parishes adjoining, and in the parish of Stepney, who, in this time of plague now reigning in those parts, are less subject to good orders, being left destitute of convenient relief, in respect that the rich and able citizens, and other inhabitants of all sorts, being departed thence for avoiding the infection, have not taken sufficient order for relief of the poor people remaining behind'. The Order directed that those citizens who were assessed for taxes and were 'not so impoverished themselves by this visitation as they shall be forborne to be taxed' should pay at least double the accustomed rate 'and more if it shall be found requisite by the magistrates, justices of the peace, or other officers there abiding for the time'. Parliament did acknowledge the difficulty that in all epidemics collection was difficult, because those who were taxed had gone away and the collectors were afraid to go into some neighbourhoods because of the risk of infection. And so it directed that 'because it is conceived that very many are removed so far from London as that notice cannot be conveniently given with such speed as may presently supply the necessity of the poor' the City Chamber or its Bridge House Estate, which administered money set aside from the city's properties to repair and maintain London Bridge, should advance at least £1,000 for the purpose, to be repaid when the taxes could be collected. A general collection throughout the country on a charitable brief was also ordered and the Lords agreed to contribute to that fund, £1 each by those who held the rank of baron and £2 by the earls; this brought in £80 and the Bishop of London added a further £40. They also commended those livery companies which had cancelled their feasts and paid the money which would have been spent on them to the relief of the poor and recommended that the lord mayor, sheriffs and the other senior officers should do the same. For those who refused to pay the special rate there was the dire warning that they would be punished 'so exemplarily as shall be a terror to others'.[32]

This was both an acknowledgment of the problems of London's poor during the crisis and a considered attempt to address them, backed by the authority of Parliament. Yet the Recorder of London wrote to the Lord Keeper asking that the city's poor should be excluded from the general relief for the kingdom, as the city was able to relieve its own poor. This may have reflected the city's determination to maintain its freedom of action and not act solely on the instructions of the government, or perhaps an awareness that the city genuinely could deal with the crisis without further measures. The account by Sir John Gore and his successor as lord mayor, Allen Cotton, in April 1626 showed that the brief had produced £1,000 and other charitable gifts were £120. From 6 August 1625 some £861 16s 1d had been spent on assisting the poor, distributed by parishes. St Sepulchre, Newgate Street, received the most, £130 10s, almost double the next largest payment, the £70 paid to St Olave, Southwark. In all, just ten parishes received more than £20 each. The city's hospitals were given £333 6s 8d and Bridewell, also the city's responsibility, £400, while the cost of the pest-house in St Giles, Cripplegate, including medicines and provisions for those sent there, was £314 19s. The keeper of the pest-house received £5 per annum and the surgeon there in 1625 was paid a salary of £30. Those physicians, surgeons and apothecaries who were 'wholly employed for the use of the infected poor' were paid £290 6s 8d, which included rent for their accommodation. An extra city marshal was appointed and he and his men were 'employed all the sickness time, day and night, to see to the good government of the sick, and to look into the safety of the city, and to attend upon the lord mayor besides the other marshal and his men newly employed'; their costs were £111 3s 0d. Other outlay included the printed orders and books concerning the epidemic distributed to the parishes.[33]

The impression that the poor were being cared for was not given by contemporary London writers, such as John Taylor, who summarised the situation in *The Fearfull Summer: Or, London's Calamitie*. The year had progressed from a healthful April to a diseased June and dangerous July, so that:

The name of London now both farre and neere
Strikes all the Townes and Villages with feare;
And to be thought a Londoner is worse,
Than one who breakes a house or takes a purse.

Houses shut up, some dying, some dead,
Some (all amazed) flying, some fled.
Streets thinly man'd with wretches every day,
Which have no power to flee, or meanes to stay,
In some whole street (perhaps) a Shop or twaine
Stands open, for small takings, and less gaine.

Nor were landlords any better off, for houses that were 'late exceeding deare' at £50 or even £100 per annum, could now be obtained for a quarter of that. On the other hand, in the country a cottage usually let for a yearly rent of just £3 now was sought by a London citizen prepared to pay £5 per quarter for just two rooms. Petowe stressed the disruptive aspect of the epidemic when he appealed to landlords and creditors not to be 'over-hasty with your poore Tenants, for your Rents', or severe with 'weake and impoverished Debtors: But consider the lamentable misery they have a long time endured: and the extraordinary expences they have beene at, and no meanes to get a penny'. Trading would surely revive and the arrival of the ships expected from the East Indies presaged that return to normality.[34]

Lilly found that food was cheap during the epidemic, which was contrary to the expectations, or rather apprehensions, of the aldermen. The lord mayor wrote to the Privy Council explaining that although it might seem reasonable to restrain 'carriers and men dealing with ware' from entering London, yet to prevent higglers (pedlars) and all other people who were bringing in victuals from doing so was to risk shortages, yet that is was the Essex justices had ordered. As any scarcities would be attributed to official actions he was afraid of a backlash and that it would not be in his power, or that of the few magistrates who remained in the city, 'to restrain the violence hunger might enforce'. Farmers in Middlesex, Surrey and Essex complained that they could not sell their produce in London and so could hardly be expected to pay the special rate for poor relief. According to Thomas Dekker the countrymen took unsold produce away with them from London, which 'cannot for any Gold or Silver be receyved', hence the low prices. In practice, supplies were adequate to meet the falling demand, as the citizens died or left.[35]

Dekker again turned to writing plague pamphlets, stressing how awful was the atmosphere in the city, with the frequent ringing of knells, the many burials, the churchyards rapidly filling up and graves kept open to receive more bodies until they were full, with 40 or 50 bodies in some of them. Many streets were almost deserted, for if 'one Shop be open, sixteene in a row stand shut up together, and those that are open, were as good to be shut; for they take no Money'. In such circumstances 'None thrive but Apothecaries, Butchers, Cookes, and Coffin-makers'. Dekker was aware of and condemned the practice of body-dumping and concealment of deaths. Some citizens 'shift your poore servants away to odde nooks in Gardens', and others who had lost perhaps a child or a servant 'hath hushed all' by paying a 'little bribe' to the searchers of the bodies, or acting with the connivance of the officers, or by a 'private departure' and secret burial. He included anecdotes of sudden deaths and cases of cruelty, such as one involving a countryman who came to London to get work, with 16s or 18s in his purse, and took a lodging in Old Street. He was taken ill and so 'in the night time thrust out of doors, and none else receiving him, he lay upon Straw, under Suttons Hospitall wall, neere the high way, and there miserably dyed'. He was not short of money to pay for accommodation and care, yet received none, and lay against the street wall of an almshouse, yet was not taken in. Perhaps even more harrowing was the tale of a woman who suddenly fell sick as she walked near the Barbican and so she sat down, but 'the gaping multitude perceiving it, stood round about her, afarre off'. She made signs asking for a drink and a bystander gave money to buy her some, but the woman alehouse keeper 'denyed to lend her Pot to any infected companion'. The woman died suddenly and, although everyone had kept their distance while she was alive, when she was dead, 'Some (like Ravens) seized upon her body (having good clothes about her) stripped her and buried her, none knowing what she was, or from whence she came.'[36]

Dekker mixed anecdotes and sweeping generalisations to create a dire and depressing picture of London during the epidemic; he castigated his fellow citizens for their conduct in leaving the city, or in staying yet being cruel to the victims. Many of the deaths he described occurred soon after the victim was taken ill, which made for vivid stories yet are not consistent with cases of bubonic plague, and the pattern was not mentioned by other contemporary writers; perhaps Dekker was using dramatic licence as he created a horrifying picture of life in the stricken city. But support for his anecdotes comes from the case of a man who was reported, at the end of August, to have reached Southampton, but he died 'without the town, in the fields. He came from London. He had good store of money about him, which was taken before he was cold.' That incident supports claims of refusal of hospitality and thefts from the dead, while his assertion that members of the medical professions could make money during the epidemic should be qualified, for example by the claim of Gideon Delaune, a prominent apothecary, that the business in his shop was curtailed by the deaths of his servants there from plague.[37]

The numbers of deaths and plague deaths continued to decline through the autumn and in the first week of November Pesaro could even tell the Doge and Senate that 'the plague shows signs of dying out'.[38] By December the Council was looking at the possibility of a return to Whitehall by the king and court and so wrote to the lord mayor and aldermen instructing them to disinfect all infected houses and their contents, by lighting frequent fires and exposing them to the 'frosty and kindly' weather. They replied, predictably, that they were doing all they could in that regard and were also expelling inmates. During the week ending 22 December the total deaths were 157 and in Westminster in the following week there were just four deaths, which was said to have been the fewest for 30 years. There was no reason for the court to keep away and Charles returned to Whitehall on 7 January.[39] Pesaro had followed the court to Oxford and now returned to London. He anticipated that the coronation would be in February, but noted that because of 'the mourning, the plague and present expenses, they will not prepare all the usual splendour. However the public and private expenses will be very heavy.' The coronation now became the principal focus of his involvement in state affairs, as the plague had almost dwindled away, and his request to be recalled had been granted.[40]

The annual Bill of Mortality gave the number of deaths in London as 54,265, of which 35,417 were designated as plague deaths, adding the figure of 8,736 deaths in Westminster brings the total to 63,000, and plague deaths to 41,313.[41] This was a far greater number than in 1603, but as the population had increased during the intervening years, the proportion was much the same and roughly one-fifth of Londoners had died. Other cities and regions suffered high mortality during the outbreak, continuing into 1626, with 68,596 plague deaths across the country; the areas which suffered most were the ports along the east and south-east coasts of England and their hinterlands.

The mortality in London had been greatest in the poorer parishes fringing the centre, where the inhabitants had no choice and had stayed, while in the smaller central ones, many of whose wealthier citizens had left, there had been a smaller increase in the mortality rate during the crisis. In the 97 parishes within the walls, the death-toll was 14,340, while in the 16 parishes outside the walls, including those in Southwark, the figure was 26,972, and in nine out-parishes, including Clerkenwell, Whitechapel, Shoreditch, the two parishes 'in the fields' (St Giles and St Martin) and Bermondsey, with the Savoy, 12,953 deaths were recorded. The heaviest mortality was in St Giles, Cripplegate, with almost 3,000 deaths, St Olave's, Southwark, with 3,689 and St Sepulchre's, with 3,425. At the pest-house there were 194 deaths and five of them were not from plague.[42] The lord mayor had drawn the Privy Council's attention to the geographical pattern during the epidemic, when he used the evidence of the Bills to point out that 'within the walls of the City and liberties it had not raged so much as in the skirts of the City, where the parishes spread into other Counties and the multitude of inmates was without measure'.[43] He was pointing out that enforcement of the orders was partly the responsibility of the county justices, not just of the city's officers, and that overcrowded accommodation was the problem. The distribution of mortality within the metropolis reflected the varied social impact of plague.

Chamberlain was back in London by 19 January and was in a gloomy mood, not improved by a fire in his house; although 'there was no great loss more than the breaking up of chimneys and floors' he was 'confined to a narrower circuit' until the repairs were carried out. He added, 'Neither indeed do I take any pleasure in going abroad to see the decay and desolation of this town, without hope almost in my time to see it better.' This reaction to the aftermath of a major epidemic was in stark contrast to that of Molin after the outbreak in 1603, and conflicted with information in a letter written as early as mid-October, which mentioned 'the wonderful number of people in the city' and when the writer had passed through the city 'he found the streets full of people, and the highways of passengers – horse and foot'.[44] The implication is that Londoners had begun to return in some numbers during the autumn, as the numbers of deaths recorded in the Bills began to fall significantly. Chamberlain's impression was certainly to prove to have been unnecessarily gloomy, for the population of the city soon began to recover, in terms of numbers and probably in terms of mood, as the trading and other restrictions were lifted. The artist-cum-diplomat Peter Paul Rubens certainly did not detect parsimony or restraint during a mission to London in the summer of 1629. His impression was that 'splendour and liberality are of primary consideration at this Court ... public and private interests are sold here for ready money'.[45] Of course, the court did not equate with London, but the two were closely interrelated economically.

Plague was not a constraint on economic recovery; there were just 134 deaths from the disease in 1626, and the population recovered to its former level after two years. The number of baptisms increased from 6,701 in 1626 to 8,408 in the following year, but the greatest contribution to the replenishment of the population came from migration from within the British Isles, and there was no outbreak of plague or other disease during the three years after the 1625 epidemic to impede the demographic revival. Once again, London had suffered far more than anywhere else in the country and the outbreak came to be designated the 'great plague', but the pattern established during the previous epidemic years was repeated and the city then drew in enough newcomers, undeterred by the risk, not only to replace the losses, but to add to its continually growing population.

13

A TIME OF TROUBLE

The early seventeenth century was a period of prolonged warfare in Europe. The Eighty Years' War saw Spain make a futile attempt to recover the northern Netherlands, which had seized their independence as the United Provinces, while the Thirty Years' War engulfed Germany along confessional lines, with the Habsburgs fighting the Protestant states and their allies. Both wars involved other countries before they came to an end in 1648, and fresh conflicts erupted as part of the rivalry between France and the Habsburg states, and between Protestant and Catholic countries. England's direct military involvement was limited to an unsuccessful expedition under the Protestant commander Count Ernst von Mansfeld to recover the Palatinate for the King's son-in-law in 1625, a raid on Cadiz later that year and the occupation of the Île de Ré in 1627, to support the Huguenots in La Rochelle. Apart from those brief forays England remained outside the European conflicts, partly out of policy and partly financial necessity, as Charles ruled without calling Parliament after 1629, and so was unable to raise enough revenue to engage in a more ambitious foreign policy.

The serious plague outbreaks in Europe during the late 1620s and 1630s were attributed to the movements of armies and the soldiers' disregard for the established practices designed to restrict the spread of the disease. A poor harvest in southern Europe in 1629 was also blamed for the high mortality of those years. France endured plague epidemics from 1628 until 1632, which did not reach Paris and the north yet killed possibly as many as two million people, roughly 10 per cent of the population. Over a half of the citizens of Augsburg died in an epidemic in 1627 and 1628, and with the Swedish involvement in the Thirty Years' War during the 1630s and their campaigns in southern Germany, Nuremberg experienced three plague epidemics; that in 1634 claimed at least 20,000 victims and was the worst demographic disaster in the city's history. The Italian cities suffered outbreaks in 1630–1, after the arrival of German and French troops in Lombardy and Piedmont, with 60,000 deaths in Milan, 46 per cent of the city's population, and 46,000 in Venice, 33 per cent of its inhabitants. The Low Countries experienced an epidemic in 1635-7: in 1636 Amsterdam suffered more than 17,000 deaths and there were 18,000 in Leiden.

London's aldermen were naturally wary during such epidemics, for the city was at risk as a supplier of men and materials for the continental wars as well as through its regular trade. Professional soldiers and gentlemen volunteers served with the Dutch, Danish, Swedish, French, Spanish and Imperial armies, especially during the 1630s. London was both a recruiting ground and the port of arrival for many of those returning from campaign and remained by far the most important port for both imports and exports.

In October 1629 the Privy Council warned the lord mayor that because of plague in and around Amsterdam, in the Breton ports and at La Rochelle, he should ensure that no passengers or goods from those places were landed at London, and that nobody went aboard incoming vessels until it could be ascertained that plague was not present in the ports from which they had come. Goods were to be aired until they were thought to be free from the possibility that they harboured plague.[1] The policy was seen to be successful, for no plague burials were recorded in London in 1629, although it was present elsewhere, including

Cambridge, where the college authorities gave permission for the fellows and scholars to disperse.

Hopes that the city may continue to escape the infection were dashed in the early months of 1630, when plague cases were reported. They included two of the children of Sir Francis Cottington and his wife. Cottington had served intermittently as a diplomat in Spain since 1609 and in 1629 went there again on another ambassadorial mission. During his absence his wife and three children moved to a house in Charing Cross and in the spring of 1630 their two daughters died of the plague, and their son almost died.[2] In March the Privy Council noted that plague deaths had been registered in St Giles-in-the-Fields, on the western edge of the city, and in Shoreditch and Whitechapel. Its response was to order that infected houses should be shut up and guards posted outside them 'as usual', and both those who were confined and the officers attending them should be paid by the parishes. It also required that a book of instructions should be reprinted and distributed as guidance to the authorities. Yet a few days later the Council revoked that part of its instructions that related to the closing of houses and ordered that infected houses should be emptied and sealed, with the occupants sent to the pest-house. This reversal of policy suggests that the numbers suspected of suffering from plague was still small enough for them to be accommodated in the restricted space provided by the pest-houses. The City should also take steps 'for freeing the City and liberties' from 'the multitude of poor Irish, and other vagabond persons with which all parts about the City were pestered', because they must cause great danger of spreading the infection. The Council also complained that the number of ale-houses and inmates was excessive and ordered that the existing measures to reduce the numbers should be implemented. Care was also to be taken to keep the streets clean and ditches scoured. Finally, the king requested that the College of Physicians should meet and recommend steps to be taken to prevent the disease from increasing.[3]

The Council continued to take a close interest in the risk of an epidemic, to the extent that it passed on to the lord mayor an allegation that someone from the city had gone to a poor woman's house in Whitechapel and had died there of the plague, and that the cause of death had been concealed. Further information suggested that a boy in the household of John Taylor, a butcher in that district, had developed symptoms of plague and that Taylor had sent him away 'to find a lodging'. The boy had been taken in by a widow and had died in her house the same night. The Council wanted the lord mayor to make an example of Thomas for his 'ill carriage', by removing him and his family to the pest-house, a case of using incarceration in the pest-house as a punishment, rather than to provide a period of isolation while the staff waited to see if plague symptoms developed. It had also heard of a case in which the occupants of a house where the plague had been identified had 'gone away'. The Council was made aware of another instance of abuse of the rules which echoed complaints of the practice reported in earlier epidemics of removing a plague victim to another building. A sick person was said to have been taken from Lothbury to a garden house in Finsbury Fields and, if that was the case, the occupants of the Lothbury house ought to be taken to the pest-house and their own house sealed up.

Public entertainments were forbidden on 14 April, including 'all extraordinary assemblies of people at taverns and elsewhere'. The Council was giving close attention to the risk of an outbreak at the general level and in specific cases where its regulations were reported to have been flouted.[4]

News of the epidemic in London had prompted the Common Council of Exeter to prohibit anyone who brought goods from there from offering them for sale at its forthcoming fair. But the Privy Council ruled that 'as the sickness in London was decreasing, and was not nearly so bad as was reported at Exeter', that ban should not apply if the sellers carried a health certificate from the lord mayor stating that the house from which the goods were taken was not infected. The councillors' impression that the disease was on the wane was not borne out by their further orders instructing the mayor to see that the designated practices should be followed. In mid-September the livery companies were instructed not to hold their accustomed annual feasts, partly because of the plague and partly because of the current high prices and food shortages. The aldermen responded with a sturdy defence of their actions, which had followed the orders, and pointed out that some people already had been punished for removing the inscriptions on infected houses and others had been bound over to the next sessions.[5] Indeed, the numbers of plague deaths did not rise dramatically during the summer, with the average for the first four Bills issued in July being 40, although the next week produced a figure of 77, the highest of the year, and the weekly return did not fall below 50 until 28 October. From 24 June until 16 December there were 10,545 burials, of which 1,317 were from plague, and the Bill for the week ending 16 December included just five plague deaths.

The year had passed off without a major epidemic and, despite some anxieties in the early months of 1631, this could have been interpreted as confirming the success of both the plague policies and their effective enforcement. Nevertheless, some disquiet lingered and a review of the orders and practices was put in place. The College of Physicians had responded to the king's request with two reports, one in 1630 and the second in March 1631. In its first report it explained that it had drawn on the experience of 'Paris, Venice and Padua and many other cities'.[6] Continental practices were now of great interest and the senior author of a separate report, dated 19 March 1631, was Sir Theodore de Mayerne. He was born in Geneva in 1573, the son of a Calvinist family who had fled from Lyon in the wake of the massacre of St Bartholomew's Day in the previous year. He was trained as a physician and led a varied life as a doctor, diplomat and secret agent, with considerable artistic interests, chiefly at the French and English courts, but also during tours of Europe, including visits to the Italian cities.

The report was submitted by Mayerne and two other senior royal physicians, David Bethune and Sir Martin Lister; it was 38 pages long, in Mayerne's handwriting and clearly was largely his work.[7] It covered both the medical and environmental aspects of plague policies and had an immediacy, because plague 'has lingred & hunge aboute the skirts of this Citty all this last winter & present yeare 1631'. Mayerne did not challenge the theological contention that the underlying cause of the disease was sin; plague was deployed by God to chastise men for their wicked conduct, but that was no reason not to try to combat the infection by using remedies which nature and reason offered. On the administrative side, the most significant proposal was the creation of a permanent College of Health for London, similar to the Italian boards of health. This was to consist of 12 members: the lord mayor, two aldermen, the Recorder, the Bishop of London and one other bishop, two members of the Privy Council, three members of the College of Physicians, one of whom 'hath beene a Traveller' and so had experience of how such a system was operated elsewhere, and a surgeon. The College's powers would apply across a wider area than the city, Westminster and Southwark, with authority from Brentford to Blackwall and Richmond to Greenwich. It would have a regular income with which to finance all expenditure relating to public health, including the employment of food inspectors, with powers to confiscate unwholesome meat, corn, beer and wine. Mayerne also recommended that London should have five divisions for health purposes, each with its medical staff, including doctors, surgeons, apothecaries and women searchers, who were to be regularly paid. The College was also to have the power to make regulations, appoint junior officers and build four or five plague hospitals, one in Southwark and the remainder north of the river. The principal one was to be named King Charles's Godshouse, at Chelsea or Paddington, adjoining the River Westbourne, because running water close by was essential. In London, household quarantine should last for 40 days, but ideally the sick ought to be separated from the healthy, and the relatives and contacts of those who were infected should also serve the period of quarantine. If implemented, this would have ended the practice of incarcerating together those with plague and those who were free from the disease but suspected of being contacts, which was so resented by the citizens.

Awareness of the danger of plague from abroad was to be enhanced by the merchants promptly notifying the College of Health of the danger when they became aware of an outbreak, especially when it was present in the Low Countries 'from whence it is ordinarily brought into England'. Health passes were to be required for those arriving at the ports and they would be quarantined for 40 days 'in commodious houses for that use'. Those who would not accept that 'let them remayne out of the land till the storme be passed', in other words they would not be allowed to land. This was a formalisation of existing and long-standing practice, with the College acting as the central point of information. That was also true of the social measures recommended, with the unemployed, beggars and masterless men to be sent out of the city and poor strangers, especially the Irish, not allowed to land at the ports because their miserable poverty and general nastiness was enough to engender the plague without any former contagion. Crowded alleys were a danger and the rapid growth of London was causing dearth and scarcity elsewhere, so the poor alleys should be demolished or 'dispeopled'; nobody was to be allowed to live in cellars. New houses were to be fit for 'the better sort of persons' to live in. The numbers of taverns, alehouses and tobacco shops should be reduced and odiferous and otherwise offensive premises, such as slaughter-houses, tanners' yards and fishmarkets, ought to be moved to remote places outside the city. Cleanliness was to be maintained, with no rubbish dumped in the streets, and ditches and common sewers were to be cleansed. The usual orders for killing stray dogs and cats and destroying rats, mice, weasels and other vermin were to be issued.

The conventional view that windows should be opened during the day but closed before dusk was repeated.

Mayerne's report was not innovative, except for the establishment of the College of Health and that it was to operate as a permanent body, not only during plague epidemics, the division of the city into administrative areas for health and the erection of purpose-built and adequate pest-houses. The Privy Council sent the City 'Directions for erecting of an Hospital or Workhouse to be set up in London, according as was said to be at Paris', which described in detail the operation of the hospitals of St Louis and St Marcel, erected by Henri IV, and their care of plague victims, which clearly were Mayerne's inspiration.[8] But all of this would require money and the king ruled without calling Parliament until 1640 and so the government could not raise revenue for such schemes, and finance for plague measures had been a point of contention with the city previously. The proposals were allowed to drift away without any action being taken to implement them.

In one respect government policy would have been in accord with Mayerne's proposals. Because of its divided government the Privy Council acted as co-ordinator of the actions of the corporation and the county justices and it attempted to resolve the problem with the incorporation of the suburbs in 1636. But the city resented the creation of a separate and potentially rival authority. Even so, in 1637 the Council still hoped that the aldermen would supervise the area covered by the new Corporation of the Suburbs in a commission of the peace, because of 'the great need for magistrates in those places in the time of plague'. But the arrangements proved to be one of several sources of dispute between the city and Charles's government and were not effective. Yet the city's own evidence suggested that co-ordinated control of new housing was required. In 1639 the mayor produced a list which showed that 1,361 houses had been erected since 1603, only 57 of them within his jurisdiction, but 618 to the west of the City, 404 to the north and 282 to the east.

A petition to the Council in 1632 had complained of newly built tenements around the city on both sides of the river, which brought beggars, pollution, higher prices for food and the danger of plague. An area of Clerkenwell surveyed in 1635 displayed the characteristics regarded as typical of such a district, both in the condition of the buildings and the insalubrious habits of those who lived in them. Some of the houses were close to collapse and most of them were 'pore Raskoly habitations and Inhabited with Such like people for the most part'. They threw their rubbish, including dead cats and dogs, into the alleys 'which in a contagious or infectious Tyme of Sicknes is very dangerous' for those living nearby. The conclusion was that 'unlesse that kind of people be Rowted from that place it wilbe both dangerous and unholsom to com neare them at Any tyme'. They were a health threat to the occupants of the nearby Charterhouse and to those who walked in its gardens, which were open to the public.[9] The logical, albeit brutal, solution which was recommended was the eviction of the occupants and demolition of the buildings. Here, at least, social prejudice dovetailed with plague policy and Mayerne's recommendations. The social divisions of the 1630s could hardly have been more clearly expressed.

In 1635 the Privy Council became alarmed at the epidemics in the Low Countries and asked the corporation for advice, which was rather strange, as the quarantining of shipping was an integral part of its own policy and it, not the lord mayor and aldermen, had the authority to impose the restriction. Nevertheless, it did respond, with the recommendation that vessels should require a licence from the customs officers before they could land passengers or cargoes, that officers should board incoming vessels to prevent anyone or anything being taken off, and that ships from infected places should not be granted permission to discharge people or goods for 'some certain days'. The Council issued a proclamation accordingly 'to restraine the landing of Goods, or comming ashore of Men out of such Shipping, untill due tryall shall bee had, that the same may bee done without perill or danger of Infection'. The Venetian ambassador Anzolo Correr approved the policy but thought that it should have been introduced sooner, and he commented that it was not the habit of merchants to do anything to damage their own commercial interests.[10]

Because the controls were introduced too late, or because they were not thoroughly enforced – or perhaps because they didn't stand a chance of working in the first place – they were ineffective and in 1636 London endured a serious plague epidemic. In April the officers at Gravesend reported that they had detained a ship from Rotterdam, but that the watermen, more concerned with making money than observing the regulations, had boarded the ship and had been hired by the passengers, probably to take them to London. The officers had been powerless to prevent this and indeed could only enforce the regulations with much danger and trouble to themselves.[11] Already the number of plague deaths was beginning to rise, although the figures in the Bills were distorted by the addition of St Margaret's, Westminster and six other parishes from 14 April, and so they are not directly comparable with those for earlier years. Those seven parishes added roughly 3,000 burials to the annual total. It may be that the incipient plague outbreak was the reason for the addition of the extra areas, because it was realised that a truer picture of plague deaths was needed. But the corporation pointed out to the king that the inclusion of the numbers for Stepney gave a false impression, for when they were included, 'it is generally taken abroad that London is more infected than, God be thanked, it is: so it not only breeds a fear in the country-people of coming to London, but of receiving any commodities from the city.'[12] Stepney was a large parish east of the River Lea and although some of its districts were suburbs of London, others were detached from the metropolis. By excluding Stepney a part of London was not included in the figures, but incorporating it in the Bills gave higher figures for the city than was in fact the case.

Whatever the debates about the administrative arrangements, by the spring there was no doubt that an epidemic was under way. The plague orders were issued on 22 April and on 27 May the Trinity law term was adjourned. At the end of April Correr predicted that the court would soon be moved to Hampton Court, so that the king would avoid the plague, 'which grows worse every day'. It had already been identified in some of the aristocrats' houses, which, as he wrote, was unusual, and especially in the early stages of an outbreak. According to Correr: 'People foretell great destruction, the evil being aided by the warmth of the season. Accordingly every one is exceedingly afraid and if it makes much progress the city will not only be abandoned by the Court but deserted by all sorts of the civil population.' In the middle of May he wrote that the court would set out for Hampton Court shortly 'being driven by the violence of the plague, which has spread to almost all the parishes of this city and the surrounding villages, appearing even in more than one house of the nobility. His Majesty had accordingly intimated to all the ambassadors and foreign ministers that if they wish to have communication with the Court they must leave the city and go somewhere which is not suspect.'[13]

The number of plague deaths was given as 62 for the week ending 26 May and 77 for the following one. Correr was not greatly concerned at that stage, despite reporting the queen's fears, but the heat and lack of rain was ominous:

> Upon such occasions the greatest precautions cannot fail to be helpful, but personally I do not think matters are bad enough to require them. In a city like London, which contains hundreds of thousands of souls, there is nothing dreadful in hearing that fifty or sixty persons die of plague in a week, and the number has not exceeded this so far ... [Though] there were indications that it may increase greatly, as the heat, which does not usually trouble this country over much, has become very great, accompanied by so great a drought that

no one remembers the like. This is the third month that not a drop of rain has fallen ... [The drought] will certainly cause a great scarcity of everything, much greater than is experienced at present, owing to the shortage of water last year, but even that was not nearly comparable to this.[14]

The Privy Council was more anxious than Correr and on 22 April issued an order authorising the justices in Middlesex and Surrey to make collections for building pest-houses 'and other places of abode for infected persons'. It also required them to co-operate with the aldermen in issuing additional orders and directed that the parish officers should have copies of the book previously issued by the College of Physicians as 'Certain necessary directions as well for the cure of the Plague as for preventing the infection'. That was reprinted, with amendments, as Mayerne had recommended. In mid-May the Council turned to an aspect of enforcement which had become a regular feature of plague outbreaks when it complained to the lord mayor that the red cross and the inscription 'Lord have mercy upon us' were not being correctly displayed on infected houses. They were 'placed so high, and in such obscure places ... as to be hardly discernible', and the houses themselves were not being guarded, as was required, for 'few or none had watchmen at the doors, and ... persons had been seen sitting at the doors of such houses'. In other words, the houses and their occupants were not properly sequestered as was required, which was the whole purpose of the policy.[15]

By the first week of June, Correr's calm had given way to anxiety. He had moved to Tottenham yet was concerned enough to report that the plague 'makes great progress in London and has even spread to the villages near here'.[16] The Bills for that week showed that almost a quarter of the 339 deaths were attributed to plague, but Viscount Chaworth was still calm; while admitting that 'apprehension of the Plague' was greater than ever, in his opinion the disease was 'not considerable'. He lived in the Strand

and when he checked the Bills he interpreted them as showing plague 'in all Stepney & those parishes'. He was being sanguine rather than realistic and from mid-July the plague deaths in the Bills exceeded 100 per week and continued at that level until mid-December. Correr was trailing after the court as it kept on the move to avoid the disease and wrote in mid-August that in the capital 'more than 800 die per week at present of this scourge, and it increases considerably every day'.[17]

Stourbridge fair at Cambridge and Bartholomew and Southwark fairs were all cancelled and the start of the Michaelmas law term was postponed on 6 September and again on 2 October. A general weekly fast was announced on 18 October and a form of service was issued to the clergy, but with the direction that no minister was to keep the congregation in the church longer than was required to hold the service 'because such detaining of the people so long together, may prove dangerous to the further increase of the Sicknesse'.[18] Public performances of plays, entertainments and sports were prohibited altogether, but this was not fully observed, for despite the ban a bear-baiting, which drew a large crowd said to number many thousands, was held on 18 October at the Paris Garden at Bankside, the principal bear-baiting house in the capital.

The corporation ordered the closure of all schools in the city. The school of Thomas Sutton's charity at the Charterhouse was at risk because 'many Towne Boyes and Outcommers from divers parts of the Citty and Suburbs are received and taught in the hospitall Schoole' and so it, too, was closed. That had been provided for in the charity's statutes, promulgated in 1627, which directed that during an epidemic scholars with parents or friends nearby should be sent to them, and those 'destitute of friends or means, they shall be sent out and maintained by the hospital'. Similar provision was made for the almsmen, but those too infirm or elderly to leave were to remain in the almshouse, where they were to be cared for by 'two elder grooms to make the provisions, and three old women lodged in the house'. The rules evidently were compiled in the belief that the elderly were less likely to succumb to plague, having survived previous outbreaks. A further order relating to the plague was issued in May 1637 and instructed the residents that if they left the almshouse they should visit only 'such persons as they knowe are not common and carelesse goers abroad'.[19]

As the crisis deepened London's minority communities faced the challenge of providing help for their members, while keeping within the plague regulations. The poor Catholics were reluctant to observe the rule that infected houses should be sealed, for they believed it to be 'a matter of conscience to visit their neighbours in any sickness, yea, though they know it to be infection; even the red cross does not keep them out'. Matthew Wilson, Superior of the London Jesuits, and the chapter of the secular clergy each appointed a representative to care for the victims. The clergy chose Fr John Southworth and Wilson's choice was Fr Henry Morse, who since 1633 had been based in St Giles-in-the-Fields. Wearing a 'distinctive mark on his outer garment' and carrying a white rod, throughout the epidemic Morse busied himself in visiting the sick in rooms that were 'oppressive with foul and pestilential air', acquiring medicines for them, providing bedding and clothes to replace those which had been burnt, hearing confessions and laying out the dead. When those guarding the closed houses refused to allow the priests to enter, the money was handed over at the windows. Morse visited Protestant as well as Catholic families and some of those he had helped later testified to his dedication. Margaret Allen of St Giles-in-the-Fields later attested that 'I sent for Mr. Morse when I was visited with the plague and he many times gave alms to me, my husband and my two little children, who all died of the plague, the parish not giving us anything, we being very poor and seven persons in number shut up.' Elizabeth Godwin of the same parish told a similar story, that she was 'a poor labouring woman ... being shut up seven weeks, buried three of my children, which Mr. Morse relieved with her Majesty's and with divers Catholics' alms … six persons of us were shut up for seven weeks and never had of the parish but five shillings'.

In October Morse and Southworth were trying to support around 50 families and they appealed to fellow Catholics to contribute assistance because of 'the extreme necessity which many of the poorer sort are fallen into', and the queen and others responded. The priests' appeal stressed just how bad the disaster was, indeed 'the greatnesse of this calamitie exceedeth all beleife, in so much as wee should never have imagined the least part, of that which really is, had not our owne eyes, and daily experience sufficiently attested the same unto us'. To encourage donations they pointed out how generously the Protestants had responded to the crisis as well as the dire distress of some victims, including those who 'notwithstanding they were well borne, and bred, having beene constrained, through extremity of want, to sell, or pawne all they had, remaine shut up within the bare walls of a poore chamber, having not wherewithall to allay the rage of hunger, nor scarcely to cover nakednesse'. Then there were others who 'for the space of three days togeather have not gotten a morsell of bread to put into their mouths. Wee have just cause to feare, that some doe perish for want of food: others for want of [at]tendance: others for want of ordinary helpes and remedies.' Nor were the poor helped by the arrest of Southworth at the end of October and of Morse in the following February.[20]

To overcome their exclusion from the system of poor relief, the French-Walloon and Dutch congregations, which contained roughly 1,400 and 840 members respectively, appointed 'consolators' to take alms and comfort to the sick or bereaved. They had to visit houses where plague victims lived and then go around the streets and mix with others, and in doing so they disobeyed the quarantine orders for the closing of houses and incarceration of those who visited the infected. The Dutch consistory at Austin Friars appointed a visitor of the sick, but as early as May was aware of the problems which he would face and approached the

French-Walloon community to discover if it had received relevant information from the authorities. That was forthcoming in June, when the Privy Councillors instructed the justices to inform the 'consolators' that infected houses should be closed and that if they continued with their existing pattern, they too would be confined in them. This aroused the consistory's defiance and it agreed that the visitor should continue to act 'in accordance with God', a higher authority than the corporation or the Council. The crisis placed a severe strain on its relief funds, especially as 'the wealthier members have taken up their residences in the countryside'. When an extra collection was required, they were contacted and asked for contributions, even if they would not return in person. The collection raised £803, which did something to restore the poor-relief funds, although the outlay in 1636 was £2,860, compared with £1,530 in 1635.[21]

The economic impact of the epidemic worsened the poor's circumstances whatever their background, because they were unable to get employment, 'all manner of worke fayling them at this time'.[22] On New Years Day 1637 the vicar of St Leonard's, Shoreditch, John Squier, summarised the situation in a sermon delivered at Pauls' Cross: 'When the Able fled ... and the Multitude must tarry, notwithstanding a multitude of Dangers to themselves, to their servants, but especially to their poor Children, then was a Time of Trouble, when Tradesmen became poor; when the poor became Beggars; and when the Beggars were ready to starve.'[23] In October one John Eliot wrote from his house near the Savoy to Sir John Coke, one of the Secretaries of State, complaining that the plague orders were being disobeyed and he feared the lawlessness that had followed the departure of all those in authority, with 'many thousands' of dubious characters in the suburbs who lived 'by the spoil' of others. Apprentices and servants were in want because their masters had gone and the absence of the justices had contributed to the increase in the numbers of beggars, rogues and vagabonds. Among those who had suffered from the downturn in business during the epidemic were the watermen, porters, coachmen, tailors, shoemakers, glovers, silkweavers and 'discarded Irish footmen'. He recommended the appointment of a city marshal to tackle the problems, with power to go through the suburbs to root out the vagrants; he was bold enough to enclose a draft warrant for his own appointment to the post.[24] Problems produced by plague brought opportunities as well as disruption, although they did have considerable risks attached.

The poor could raise some money by selling clothes to the dealers in rags, who supplied the paper-makers. The dealers stored the clothes in cellars on their premises in the suburbs around the northern fringes of the city. Textiles were thought to be one of the ways in which plague was disseminated and so the trade attracted the attention of the justices. They had the power to arrest and punish the dealers as 'rogues' but needed authority to seize and destroy the stocks of rags. This could be done most easily and quickly by burning them, but with the risk of spreading the plague by infecting the air with the burning debris. Burying the rags was safer, yet, perhaps surprisingly, the Privy Council preferred that they should be burnt. It attempted to halt the trade in rags and old clothes by cutting demand when it ordered that the paper mills should stop operating during the epidemic.[25] When enforced, with the good intention of limiting the spread of the disease, it closed down one way in which the poor could raise a little money; the ramifications of an outbreak of plague were far-reaching.

The deadliest months were September and October, with 6,582 deaths from the disease in nine weeks. The worst weeks were the last one in September and the first one in October, with 928 and 921 plague deaths; the figure never exceeded a thousand, although it was accepted that 'more die than are certified'. Archbishop William Laud's secretary, William Dell, thought that in the large parish of St Botolph-without-Bishopsgate there had been 22 deaths in one week, 12 of them plague victims, yet only four had been entered in that category, so that the number of deaths was accurately returned, but the figure for plague deaths had been falsified.[26] Yet a case in the central parish of St Anne and St Agnes suggests considerable care in the diagnosis of the cause of death, for the churchwardens paid the surgeon of the pest-house to inspect the corpse of a parishioner 'after our searchers had been there, for better satisfaction'. Those churchwardens also paid for provisions for the occupants of five houses shut up in one alley. In St John Zachary parish the Goldsmiths' Company paid towards the costs of a widow's house that was closed, and the churchwardens contributed to that and to the charges for other houses shut up. They also paid the wages of the warders who guarded them and the searchers of the bodies and keepers of the pest-house. That does suggest that they conscientiously carried out their duties during the crisis, as did the churchwardens in the much larger parish of St Sepulchre-without-Newgate, where they spent more than £10 to maintain two families in two closed houses in St John Street. Maintaining sequestered householders was an expensive operation and bore heavily on the resources of the large, sprawling parishes around the City.[27] In those parishes the overseers of the poor and churchwardens were so hard pressed that, according to John Graunt, 'Many of the poorer Parishioners through neglect do perish, and many vicious persons get liberty to live as they please, for want of some heedful Eye to overlook them.'[28] Graunt was born in Birchin Lane in 1620 and was apprenticed to his father, a 'haberdasher of small wares', so that his observations were based not only on his analysis of the records, especially the Bills, but also personal knowledge of his city.

The more populous parishes not only bore the brunt of the charitable effort required but also took a share of the blame for the scale of the outbreak. When the reasons for the epidemic came to be considered the owners of houses in Southwark were blamed, for dividing their houses among so many families 'for the lure of the rents'. Some owners of poor tenements in Southwark, Newington and Lambeth where 'these miserable people are lodged' were unknown. The parishes south of the river had suffered terribly and their expenses in maintaining the poor were way beyond the sums due to be collected on the special rate which had been approved.[29]

In mid-October Correr noted that there was 'very little sign' that the number of plague victims in London was diminishing, although two months later he was able to write that the plague 'being confined by the very sharp cold, is beginning to lose the malignity with which for nine months on end it has troubled a great part of this kingdom. It is hoped that the country is entirely free, and in the city of London the deaths from it do not exceed some 200 a week. If this improvement continues the Court will make no further scruples about admitting intercourse with the city.' The improvement continued and on 20 January he provided the summary that 'The plague keeps diminishing rapidly. The kingdom is entirely free and only a few cases still remain in the city of London.' Despite his impression, the governors of the Charterhouse still felt the need to prohibit everyone who lived in the buildings from going along Charterhouse Lane, which led to Smithfield, 'during such tyme as the sicknesse or plague shall there continue or at any tyme whiles any house in the Lane or in any court or ally in that Lane is or shall be or continue shut upp for or by reason of the plague'. They took this so seriously that they imposed the penalty of expulsion for anyone who broke the order. They also forbade any resident from 'sitting standing walking or talking without the home gate of the hospitall'; that was to prevent chatter with people passing by the gate, some of whom would have been from Charterhouse Lane. The porter was to see that they did not disobey this rule. Not consorting with others or getting close to them was a logical extension of the orders aimed at protecting the healthy from the sick and was advocated by some writers on plague. The Charterhouse gave senior figures the opportunity to implement such a policy because the porter could enforce it; it would have been impractical to try to apply it generally. Given the rank of its governors, the Charterhouse could

act as a test-bed for such plague strategies. The experience of the
epidemic in 1636 and of the plague deaths recorded thereafter
did not cause them to change another policy, established in
1627, of not retaining a surgeon for the almshouse. Instead, they
authorised the Master to engage one as the need arose 'in the
best and cheapest way he can; But wee will not have any settled
Chirurgeon in fee with the hospitall'.[30]

The Bills recorded 23,359 deaths during 1636, 10,400 of which
were attributed to plague. This was a less destructive outbreak
than those in 1563, 1603 and 1625, in terms of the proportion of
the inhabitants who died, and it was also a much smaller one than
those which some continental cities endured during the decade.
The increased mortality in the City parishes was relatively small,
but St Giles Cripplegate, St Botolph-without-Bishopsgate and
St Botolph-without-Aldgate experienced an almost fourfold rise
in deaths. Those were the areas where members of the foreign
communities were concentrated and their burials were not recorded
in the parish registers, and so the true numbers of deaths there
would have been higher than the figures indicate. St Martin-in-the-
Fields also suffered severely, with an increase from 13 burials in
March to 72 in July, 75 in August and 101 in September, when the
registers break off. The epidemic showed a similar geographical
pattern to those in 1603 and 1625, with a relatively low incidence
of plague deaths in the centre and a high impact on the suburbs,
especially those on the north and north-east sides of the City.

The plague continued into the new year, despite hopes that
the cold winter weather would put an end to it. In April Correr
reported that there had been three plague deaths in the Spanish
ambassador's household and that 'this curse creeps into every part
of the city' and at the end of June that the disease was 'making
considerable progress not only in London, but in the neighbouring
villages'. Not until the middle of October could he state that it had
almost entirely disappeared.[31] The epidemic of 1636 resembled
that of 1603 in that plague continued to be a significant cause

of death in the following years. Graunt noted that 'as it was not so fierce' as in the other years with plague epidemics 'so it was of longer continuance' and described it as lasting 12 years, in eight of which the death-toll from the disease averaged 2,000 per annum and was never fewer than 300. His conclusion was that 'the Contagion of the Plague depends more upon the disposition of the Air, than upon the effluvia from the bodies of men'.[32]

The epidemic in 1636 had a potentially depressing effect, if only because it came so soon after a comprehensive attempt to identify the best practices to be followed in such an emergency. The recommendations of 1631 had not been put in place; neither the principal plague hospital nor enough smaller pest-houses had been built to accommodate the sick, nor had houses to accommodate those who had been in contact with plague sufferers but had not themselves developed the symptoms. That was ideally what the system should have provided, with stages of segregation, rather than space for a comparatively few victims in pest-houses and the remainder of those displaying symptoms incarcerated with others who were not sick. But household quarantine had become the lynchpin of the system and the Privy Council's orders and urgings were aimed at ensuring that it should be enforced, with the symbols of the sickness displayed and the houses guarded, with no-one allowed in or out and the occupants reliably provided with supplies. The need for regular payment for dedicated plague officers and servants was recognised, but no finance was put in place for that to be done, and the burden continued to fall on the parishes, which required more income at a time when any tax collection was hazardous and difficult and was likely to produce less than anticipated. When Parliament next met, perhaps it would give some further attention to providing adequate and dependable finance for plague prevention, if indeed it did meet again.

14

CIVIL WAR AND PEACE

Government by the Privy Council proved to be unpopular and ultimately impracticable, yet a successful legal challenge to the most significant financial innovation of the decade, known as Ship Money, did not bring about a change in policy. Only when the king and the Archbishop of Canterbury, William Laud, chose to impose the use of the Book of Common Prayer in Scottish churches by force did the system begin to fall apart. The royal army met its match in the two Bishops' Wars, in 1639 and 1640, and to add to the indignity Newcastle-upon-Tyne was occupied by the Scots, who levied a sum from the English government to maintain their army. No financial expedient could raise the amounts needed to pay for the wars and the Scottish levy and so the king had no choice but to recall Parliament, which he did in February 1640. It sat for only three weeks before being dismissed, but the king's situation had not improved and in September writs were issued for the summoning of another Parliament, which was more tenacious and was to be designated the Long Parliament. From those inauspicious beginnings and with a rebellion in Ireland in the autumn of 1641, relations between king and Parliament deteriorated to the extent that the English Civil War broke out in the summer of 1642. Several other wars ensued within the British Isles over the rest of the decade and into the early 1650s.

The king left London in January 1642 and it became Parliament's headquarters and indeed one of its principal assets throughout those conflicts.

The examples of continental cities might have suggested that with the movement of troops, displaced civilians and military supplies plague would be a significant threat to the citizens so long as the conflicts lasted. Plague deaths had fallen to 363 in 1638 and 314 in the following year, but in 1640 they increased to 1,450, within a total of 10,850. In 1641 the disease threatened to disrupt Parliament's business, as it strove to restore what its members saw as their constitutional rights, as well as addressing many other issues that had arisen during the Eleven Years' Tyranny. Following its familiar chronology, plague began to increase in the city from May, so that some MPs' relatives pressed them to leave, and there was even talk of moving the sitting to Oxford, away from Parliament's many and vociferous supporters and into a potentially hostile atmosphere. The idea was not seriously entertained, but anxieties grew when plague deaths were reported in Chancery Lane and Holborn in mid-July and at Westminster itself in mid-August. To increase Parliament's security, on 16 August the House of Lords ordered the closure of the water-gate on the river and designated New Palace Yard as the only dropping-off point for members arriving by coach.[1]

Giovanni Giustinian was now the Venetian ambassador and towards the end of August he gave a somewhat alarming account of the disease's progress. He wrote that the plague 'keeps increasing in this city. Many districts are already shut up and 200,000 persons have gone away from here. All the ambassadors have gone. I shall do the same so soon as I have secured a dwelling that will hold my household and where I can discharge my duties with the least difficulty.'[2] His figure for the number of people who had left was clearly a wild exaggeration but did reflect the feeling of unease. The MP Sir Simonds D'Ewes was so unsettled that he began to search for new lodgings that were 'sweet and in a good air'.

Sir Richard Shuckburgh was said to have lodged in a house in the Strand where plague was present and he was promptly given leave to go out of town. As the numbers attending both Houses fell during the summer, so the risk that the sitting would be suspended increased.[3] On 26 August the House of Commons gave directions that houses where infected people had been quarantined should be marked, 'safely locked up' and guarded.

The justices for Middlesex and Westminster were anxious about the extent of their own authority while Parliament was in session and so they asked for a conference with the Commons to decide how to deal with the plague cases. The plague orders were agreed by both Houses on 8 September, the day before Parliament was adjourned. Smallpox was also a concern and figures reported on 26 August for the preceding week showed 131 deaths from plague, 118 from smallpox and 610 in all. September was the peak months for plague deaths and, aware that the highest incidence of plague was commonly recorded in the autumn, D'Ewes suggested that it would be as well if Parliament did not have to meet during September and October.[4] Giustinian was clear that plague was a reason for Parliament to be suspended and commented that 'the perils of the plague have at last persuaded the most daring of the parliamentarians to agree to some pause in the sitting of parliament'.[5]

The fear of plague and smallpox was just one of the matters which had to be dealt with by the consummate parliamentary manager John Pym, who had swiftly emerged as the most prominent of the king's opponents in the House of Commons. He was a potential target for assassination and the ingenious method which was said to have been devised was to infect him with the plague. On 15 October a letter was entrusted to a porter at the Parliament House with the instructions that it must be delivered to him in Parliament, and if he was not there it should be left with the door-keeper with orders that he should deliver it to Pym with his own hands. The intention was that Pym would open the letter in the chamber, which he did. With the letter was 'a filthy clout' with a plague plaster on it, and the letter stated 'Mr Pym, Do not think that a guard of men can protect you, if you persist in your traitorous courses and wicked designs.' If the plague plaster enclosed did not touch him, then a dagger would. A suspect was arrested after having been identified by a boy as the man who had handed over the letter, but he was released the next day. This was valuable propaganda for the parliamentarian writers, who ascribed the attempt to the Catholics, and the author of a pamphlet which told the tale, described as 'a Divellish, and Unchristian Plot against the High Court of Parliament', was forthright in stating that the 'filthiest puddle of Hellish Corruption, cannot be more detestable'. He asked rhetorically 'what rationall man in the world will not say, that such Popish Inventions come from the Divell?' Pym was not taken ill.[6]

Nor did the full-blown epidemic feared by many develop, although Giustinian did remark in the middle of October that plague 'troubles London and the country alike'.[7] It caused 3,210 deaths during the year, including those in the 'distant parishes', which was the highest figure since 1637. The proposal to transfer Parliament's sitting to Oxford probably was what prompted the paper on plague prepared for the House of Commons by Louis du Moulin; a comprehensive set of policies implemented in the capital would provide a strong argument that the move was unnecessary. The son of a French Protestant minister, du Moulin had been educated at Leiden, had come to England in 1630 and was licensed by the College of Physicians in 1640. His main point was that adequate plague prevention measures would contain outbreaks, forestalling the 'huge and fearfull increase' in the number of deaths, removing the need for Parliament to sit elsewhere and avoiding 'the great decay of trading' in London.[8]

Du Moulin favoured the creation of a permanent health board, as proposed earlier by the College of Physicians and Mayerne. Nothing had been done, so the Commons should now take the initiative and order that the plans be put in place, with doctors, surgeons and apothecaries appointed and approved by the College for treating plague victims. They would be sworn to visit anyone, attending the poor 'for God's sake' and the 'abler sort' for the usual fees. This should be done before an epidemic began; once one had erupted it was too late to implement such arrangements. Having dedicated plague doctors would free the other members of the medical professions from attending its victims and reduce the risk of them spreading the disease by visiting both plague sufferers and those who were free from it. To compensate the members of the plague board for the loss of their usual practice and for the risks which they ran, he suggested generous rates of remuneration and pensions for their widows, equivalent to a third of the salaries. He was also aware of the need for spiritual comfort for victims and commented that it was 'to be expected and wished that the Bishopp of the dioces should during the Infection appoint Ministers to visitt the Infected'.

The scheme required funding of at least £1,100 annually for salaries alone, which could be raised by contributions from the city and surrounding districts that produced £2,500 per annum, the equivalent of 3d per house, based on an estimate of 50,000 houses. That would overcome the difficulty of trying to collect rates during an epidemic, which had again been obvious during the epidemic in 1636. Unspent sums could be used to build new pest-houses and enlarge the existing ones.

Du Moulin's proposals were a cogent summary of current thinking and similar to those put forward by the College and Mayerne. But, like the earlier ones, they were not implemented. The physicians' relations with the other two branches of the medical profession were still unsettled and the city continued to oppose perpetual levies for plague care. In 1636 the Privy Council had been concerned that the numbers of poor had increased so much that the wealthy were unable to provide relief for them during normal years and 'much less' during an epidemic, with the consequence that those who were unwell had to mix with the healthy because they could not be maintained if they were sequestered. A constant tax of the kind proposed would be a serious burden on those citizens who were well enough off to have to pay it.

Plague deaths in 1642 were not much lower than the previous year, at 1,274; that was the year when the war of words degenerated into a shooting war. In November the Earl of Essex's army, including the citizen militia of London known as the Trained Bands, repulsed a royalist advance on the city at Turnham Green and it became apparent that the war would not be over quickly. With royalist military successes in the spring of 1643 London was enclosed by a ring of earthwork fortifications roughly 11 miles long, designated the Lines of Communication. Professionally laid out, they were constructed by London's citizens, in a notable communal effort. They not only provided a defensive circuit which enabled Parliament's armies to campaign away from London, without fear of a royalist army slipping past them to threaten and even capture the city, but also allowed the control of movement both in and out of the metropolis and the enforcement of a night-time curfew. With just a few points of access, travellers and their merchandise could be checked. Common Council kept an eye on the effectiveness of the controls and in July 1643 requested that the searches at the guard posts should be carried out more carefully.[9] While those searches were not primarily aimed at the scrutiny of health certificates and the exclusion of the undesirables so often mentioned in anti-plague advice and controls, that now became a possibility, as it had not been before. It would have been admitted, however, that continental cities and towns ringed by permanent circuits of such defences were no less subject to plague outbreaks than open ones.

The classification of people who might have been considered undesirables in normal circumstances had to be redefined during the war, as London received many who needed refuge or assistance.

Jane Beck and her husband had lived in a house in Birmingham with their three children, but when the war began he joined the parliamentarian army and became a junior officer in the cavalry; he was killed at York. Things got worse when their house in Birmingham was burnt by the royalists after they captured the town in May 1643, one of more than 80 houses burnt down there, and Jane then took the children to London. By February 1645 she was lodging in a house in Whitecross Street and she narrowly avoided eviction, but she and the children had to move to a 'low room in the inner garden' and a little cellar. The house was overcrowded, for many others were lodged in it, including people from Bristol 'driven from their habitation', a family 'driven by the king's forces from Salisbury', two brothers 'plundered and driven away from Staffordshire', a man from Wells in Somerset 'driven away by the enemy', others from Berkshire, Lyme Regis, Tetbury in Gloucestershire, and from Ireland. In the summer of 1645 there were 12 families lodging in this one house and its outbuildings. The house belonged to Sir Robert Foster, a senior lawyer who was a justice of the common pleas; he spent the war years at Oxford and so his house was commandeered for those who needed a refuge in London. And that happened across the capital, with the empty mansions of other royalist supporters providing accommodation for destitute incomers. Mary Searle had come from Exeter because, as she put it, she 'could not be quiet there' among the king's party, having looked after sick and wounded parliamentarian soldiers; Dorothy Salway had come from Worcestershire, where her house had been plundered and she had lost all her goods; William Taylor was rector of Cirencester but moved to London after that town was sacked by the royalists in 1643; John Tombes, the vicar of Leominster, and Walter Cradock and members of his church at Llanvaches in Monmouthshire, first went to Bristol and then, following its capture by the royalists in July 1643, moved to London. Another clergyman, Nicholas Staughton, had come only from Surrey, but had fled to London when the royalists were busy plundering in Surrey in November 1642. William Walter had arrived from Pembrokeshire, where the royalists had pillaged and then fired his castle and his tenants' houses and, in his own words, his 'disloyal and malignant wife' had betrayed him so that his estate was sequestrated by them.[10]

Other categories of those who were in need also arrived; those soldiers and the widows of soldiers who were in London hoping to collect their pay arrears or to get work, and those who had been wounded. Deserters from the parliamentarian armies skulked in the city hoping to escape detection and make a living in the anonymity that London always seemed to offer. Royalist prisoners and those who were detained because their loyalties were uncertain were also brought to the capital, some of them well-to-do and able to pay for their keep, but others penniless and dependent on charity and on allowances being made by Parliament for their upkeep.

London always had a high turnover of population, with incomers drawn in by the economic opportunities it offered. But the inflow during the Civil War of many thousands of indigenous displaced persons produced overcrowding such as that which was evident in Sir Robert Foster's house. The Scots writer William Lithgow commented in 1643 that 'I never saw London, these fourtie years past, so populous as now it is.'[11] That created just the conditions which, for many decades, had been condemned by the Privy Council, the aldermen and justices, and various writers as helping the spread of the plague.

The hospitals came under increasing pressure at a time when their income was reduced by the effects of the war. In November 1644 Parliament recognised that 'great numbers of sick, wounded, and other Soldiers have for the time of above Twenty monthes past, been constantly kept' in St Bartholomew's, St Thomas's, Bethlehem and Bridewell hospitals. They were exempted from taxation to help them cover their costs in 'these dead and troublesome Times'. The Savoy Hospital was taken over as a military hospital and was so full by 1645 that an overflow of 1,500 soldiers and widows had to be accommodated elsewhere.[12]

The Bills of Mortality which have survived for the war years show that the proportion of deaths caused by plague was rising and was between 14 and 17 per cent of recorded deaths in 1644, 1645 and 1646. That was enough to cause alarm in the summer months, for in August and September 1645 one-third of deaths were from plague and a year later the proportion reached almost 37 per cent.[13] John Greene was a lawyer at Lincoln's Inn and lived in Old Jewry during the legal terms. In May 1644 he noted in his diary that the plague was present in three or four houses in his parish and that two or three people had died in each infected house. That was too close for comfort, but he found no reason to comment on the disease again until October, when the numbers in the Bills showed a decline. He was again unsettled by the figures in August and September 1645, when plague deaths were more than 30 per cent of the total, as they were again in August 1646, and he was surprised that Bartholomew's fair was held in 1646.[14]

The London plague orders were re-issued in August 1646. They reiterated the regulations included in the earlier ones, acknowledging that 'there hath beene heretofore great abuse in misreporting the disease' and specifying that the women searchers in every parish should be 'of honest reputation'. Anyone who was seen to be sick of the disease was to be kept in their house overnight and the victim should then be transferred to the pest-house; the house was then to be closed for a month. The sick could be moved to another of their houses with their household if that was done at night, but they would be sequestered for a week even then. Burials were to take place only between sunrise and sunset; no friends or neighbours were to accompany the corpse to church or enter the deceased's house, with the stiff penalty of having their own house closed or even serving a prison sentence for breaking that rule. Some of the proposals made by Mayerne and du Moulin were incorporated in the new orders, such as the division of the city into districts, although six rather than five were now set out, each to have a surgeon assigned to it to join the searchers in identifying the cause of death. Cleanliness of public places and the prohibition of pigs, dogs, cats, pigeons and rabbits were repeated. As was usual, public entertainments were banned; the playhouses had been closed four years earlier. No beggars were to be allowed on the streets and it was noted that nothing had been complained of so much as the 'multitudes' of wandering beggars 'that swarm in every place about the City, being a great cause of the spreading of the Infection'. Drinking houses were another familiar target and it was ordered that 'disorderly Tipling in Tavernes Ale houses and Cellers, be severly looked unto, as the common sinne of this time, and greatest occasion of dispersing the Plague'.[15]

Careful attention to the orders was required, for plague remained a concern and in 1647 the relatively high number of 3,597 plague deaths was recorded in the Bills, but only 611 were included in 1648 and just 67 in 1649. The first Civil War petered out in the late summer of 1646 and the political machinations of the various factions replaced the military campaigns as the principal focus of attention. London had escaped relatively lightly from the war years in terms of mortality from plague, perhaps because of its cordon, but more probably because its administrative structure was not disrupted by the conflict and it remained under the control of one side. Other English cities did not fare so well from military occupation, the ravages of sieges and the disruption caused by the soldiers, and some endured severe epidemics of plague and typhus: Bristol's population may have fallen by 25 per cent during the war years.

For those who sought advice from books on how to avoid or treat the plague, there was no shortage of material available to them during the 1640s, on that disease and health prescriptions in general. The Bohemian intellectual Jan Comenius arrived in London in 1641 and he was impressed by the number of bookshops in the city. With the lifting of censorship as the authority of the church courts collapsed, there was a veritable explosion of printing after 1640. The bookseller George Thomason collected a copy of every publication that he came across. That amounted to 24 items in 1640, 721 in 1641 and a staggering 2,134 in 1642. Parliament's attempt at pulling back from such freedom of publication because of the openings it provided for royalist propaganda, through a new system of regulation introduced in July 1643, did reduce the number somewhat; but Thomason still collected an average of 1,413 items each year from 1643 to 1647, and the number then rose again, to 2,036 in 1648.[16]

Medical tracts and recipes for plague nostrums were readily available and from the 1640s they could be read in English as well as Latin, but they were largely derivative or cases of downright plagiarism, for there was no new medical evidence to discuss. Microscopic optics were greatly improved during the seventeenth century and they enabled careful observations to be made, such as those of Robert Hooke, who produced fine detailed drawings of what he saw. Athanasius Kircher was born in 1601 and held posts at Würzburg, Avignon and Rome, and he was probably the first physician to employ the microscope in the study of disease. The bacteria of *Yersinia pestis* were too small for him to see with the microscopes available, but he may have observed larger bacilli.

The Galenic orthodoxy in medicine was challenged in the mid-century by the so-called Chemical Physicians who promoted their theories and medical system, based on the writings of the early sixteenth-century Swiss physician Paracelsus and the Flemish chemist Jean Baptiste van Helmont. They met with stiff resistance from the College of Physicians, which also sought to maintain its own position against encroachment by the apothecaries, who were prone to prescribing medicines and treatments rather than just dispensing those prescribed by the physicians. The apothecaries scored a significant success with the publication by Nicholas Culpeper in 1649 of a translation of the College's *Pharmacopoeia Londinensis*, which had been issued in 1618, with a second, enlarged, edition following soon afterwards, both in Latin and so of little use to lay people. Culpeper's *A Physical Directory* was not only a translation into English of the *Pharmacopoeia* but included 'many hundred additions' that it had not approved. Three years later he followed this with *The English Physitian*, which, as *Culpeper's Complete Herbal*, was to become a best-seller. His printer was Peter Cole, who lived and had his printing house at a building near Leadenhall but sold the books at the Sign of the Printing Press close to the Royal Exchange. He found works on medicine and disease profitable, for he issued 17 of Culpeper's titles before the latter's death in 1654 and 79 more for his widow thereafter, including the *Art of Chirugery*. The age of the work from which a translation was made was no bar to publication. In 1644 *The Workes of that famous Chirurgion Ambrose Parey* was issued, with comments on the nature of plague and a section on the English sweating sickness. Ambroise Paré was a Frenchman who was born in 1510 and died in 1590. He spent much of his career as a military surgeon and was well-regarded; his book *Les Oeuvres* had appeared in 1575.

Prescriptions for preventing or curing the plague were also repetitive; as no-one had come up with an effective remedy. Despite the extravagant claims for some treatments, the field remained open for those eyeing the potential riches which surely would come the way of anyone who did succeed. Gervase Markham's *The English Housewives' Household Physic* of 1638 recommended warming a quart of old ale on the fire and when it had risen skimming off the surface layer. That should then be mixed with birthwort, widely recommended in herbal medicine, angelica, a common preventative against plague, and celandine, a woodland herbaceous plant of the buttercup family, and the mixture well boiled. When the drink had been strained through a cloth a dram of mithridate should be added, with ivory that had been finely powdered and sifted, and dragon-water, which was also a popular medicine. Five spoonfuls of the potion should be taken every morning and afterwards 'bite and chew in your mouth the dried root of angelica, or smell a nosegay made of the raffled end of a ship-rope, and they will surely preserve you from infection'. Sniffing the end of a ship's rope does not seem to be an appealing or even relevant treatment, but other concoctions make even more unpleasant reading.

In Edward Fountaine's *A Brief Collection of Many rare Secrets* of 1650, his readers were instructed to 'Take of a healthy male young child's water, fine treacle and aniseed water, of each a like quantity, mingle them, and give about a quarter of a pint or a little more at a time to the patient in the morning fasting, for three mornings altogether; this hath cured many.' Fountaine recommended this as 'An assured remedy for the plague, approved of throughout Venice in 1504'. Drinking a boy's urine may not have appealed as much as the recipe 'Against all manner of pestilence and plague' included by Salvator Winter and Francisco Dickinson in their *A Pretious Treasury, Or a New Dispensary*, published in 1649. Their instruction was to divide an onion into two and make a small hole in each piece which was then filled with treacle. The two halves should be re-united and wrapped in wet brown paper, then roasted in hot embers. When they had been 'roasted enough' the juice was to be squeezed out and a spoonful given to the patient 'and suddenly he shall feel himself better'. This repeated a remedy published by William Langham in 1578. For someone with a plague sore, Elizabeth Grey, in 1653, recommended laying on it a poultice formed of a roasted onion and a white lily root soaked in milk. But she was not certain of the efficacy of her poultice and added 'if these fail, lance the sore and so draw it, and heal it with salves for botches or boils'. That was sound advice, but it reads as an almost casual mention of a very hazardous procedure, to lance a bubo and keep the wound clean.[17] Those were representative of such plague concoctions, which typically were a mixture of herbs familiar to the readers from their common use in medicine and homespun remedies, a more exotic ingredient or two, and at least one element to make the mixture at least mildly palatable.

It may be that from the late 1640s such recommendations were read in London with a detached interest rather than an assumption that the reader would need to use them. The numbers of plague deaths fell to a low level, with just 145 plague deaths recorded for the ten years 1650–9, in a city which then contained roughly 400,000 inhabitants. The system that was arranged for plague could be adapted and the Westminster pest-house at Tothill Fields and its adjoining burial ground were used in the autumn of 1651 for Scottish prisoners captured after the battle of Worcester. Of the 4,000 kept there, 1,200 died and they, not the victims of an outbreak of epidemic disease, formed the largest group of 'excess deaths' in London that year. After the prisoners had gone the churchwardens asked for repayment of £30 spent 'for repairing the pest house and churchyard where the Scotch prisoners were kept'.[18] Despite a decade with so few plague deaths traditionalists anticipated a major eruption of the disease in 1660 when Charles II returned from abroad and claimed his throne. The epidemics in 1603 and 1625 had both occurred immediately after the accession of a new monarch, which was explained as being a process to purge the sins of the previous reign. Charles I had been executed in January 1649 and royalists acknowledged his son as the new king, but he was in exile and it was his attempt to defeat Parliament and gain the throne which had resulted in the campaign that ended at Worcester. As no epidemic had occurred in 1649, because he had not become the *de facto* monarch, perhaps one would erupt in 1660; but in fact there were only 13 deaths from plague that year, followed by 13 in 1660, 20 in 1661, 12 in 1662 and only nine in 1663.

A generation grew up without experience of a major outbreak. Older people would have recalled the plague in 1636, even the epidemic in 1625, but they were becoming increasingly remote events. The habit of checking the weekly Bill during the summer and early autumn probably lapsed and almost everyone born in London after the mid-1640s would not have had a direct knowledge of an outbreak and everything which it entailed. Those cases which did occur were in the poorer districts, 'for it pleases God that the plague most commonly inflicts and visits the poorer sort of people such as live in Close Allyes, and out places of the City'.[19] Samuel Pepys was born in 1633 in Salisbury Court, off the south side of Fleet Street, the son of a tailor he was educated at St Paul's school and Magdalene College, Cambridge. After he graduated in 1654 he took a post with a distant relative, Edward Montagu, created Earl of Sandwich in 1660, who proved to be a first-rate patron. Most of the remainder of Samuel's life was spent in London and until 1688 he held senior posts responsible for the Navy's administration. He began his diary on 1 January 1660 and during the first three years did not mention plague at all and the earliest entries which comment on the disease related to an outbreak in Holland, not cases in London. The Dutch artist William Schellinks was in England from July 1661 until April 1663 and did not mention plague in the journal which he kept of his visit.

England's freedom from a plague epidemic came at a time when much of continental Europe was ravaged by outbreaks of the disease. The Mediterranean world fell victim to plague from the late 1640s, when there were devastating outbreaks in Spain from 1647, including a major epidemic at Seville, and another in Barcelona in 1651. The disease took a heavy toll in Sardinia in 1652–6 and then reached the Italian port cities: in 1656–7 Naples lost roughly a half of its 300,000 inhabitants, Rome's loss was 23,000, or roughly 19 per cent of the total, but Genoa's proportional loss was higher even than in Naples, with 45,000 of its 75,000 inhabitants succumbing to the disease in an epidemic in 1657. Of course, those outbreaks were known in London and John Graunt noted some details. In the disaster at Naples, he wrote, by the first week of June 1656 80,000 were sick and unable to help treat the others 'or bury the dead'. At Genoa in 1657 in the week of midsummer 1,200 died and the death rate then increased to 1,600 per day 'insomuch that in the beginning of August they burnt the dead Corps for want of hands to bury them'. Northern Europe did not escape, with epidemics in Krakow in 1652, Danzig in 1653, and Copenhagen and Moscow in 1654; the period also saw plague epidemics in Bremen and Hamburg. Closer to home, plague again swept Holland in 1655, when there were 13,287 deaths in Amsterdam between July and November, the worst week being that ending 25 September with 896 deaths. The figure for the whole year was 16,727, from a population of roughly 175,000. Leiden suffered severely from plague in 1654 and 1655, with more than 22,000 deaths in a population of perhaps 60,000, its worst outbreak of the century. Haarlem, Deventer, Rotterdam and Leeuwarden also experienced severe outbreaks in 1656.[20]

Merchants, diplomats and a miscellany of travellers would have been aware of the outbreaks in Europe and sought to circumvent them. They could not always be avoided and Lady Anne Bendish, wife of Sir Thomas Bendish, English ambassador in Istanbul, died of plague there in 1649; her body was taken back to England. Those journeying overland needed advance notice of potential problems so that they could plan their route accordingly, as well as holding valid health certificates. The certificates were also required by those travelling by ship, for a ship's crew and passengers needed them to obtain pratique, the licence permitting a ship to trade at a port after its authorities were assured that the vessel had come from a place free from plague, or they and their merchandise would have to serve a period of quarantine. That could last for a variable length of time. A few weeks after the artists Anthony van Dyck and Jan Brueghel arrived in Palermo from Genoa in 1635 an outbreak of plague erupted, which was soon claiming more than 100 victims a day and by mid-June the city was isolated, with its inhabitants forbidden to travel and even local movements restricted. Among the scapegoats condemned by the city's fearful citizens was a woman who was accused of being a witch, who was sketched by van Dyck, wearing a tall conical hat and carrying a wand, regarded as the tool of her trade. Van Dyck began a portrait of the Viceroy, a grandson of Philip II of Spain, who bravely remained at his post until he contracted the disease, which killed him. Without his patron and in the awful conditions which the epidemic produced in the city, van Dyck resolved to get away, breaking the quarantine, perhaps with a health certificate. That could have been a forgery or obtained for a bribe, or it may have been legitimate, if he had not been in a district where plague was present. By whatever means, he managed to get away and returned to Genoa, where he was held in quarantine in the lazaretto for 17 days, as was Brueghel, who arrived later.[21]

Robert Bargrave was a London merchant trading with the Levant and in 1647 he undertook a voyage to Istanbul. Soon after his arrival there was 'a violent & Generall Pestilence'. When he summarised his experiences he included 'the terrour of horrid Plagues, when the Streets were filld with infected bodies as well alive as dead; the living seeking remedies either from the Phisitians or at the Bathes, the Dead lying in open Beers, or elce quite naked at theyr dores to be washed before theyr buryalls'. In November 1652 Bargrave was travelling across a part of eastern Europe on his way back to London from Istanbul and encountered the plague during the journey, notably at a small village near Lublin, from which he and his companions could hear 'the lamentable Cries of Men, women & Children; who being infected with the Plague, were thrown out into litle Hovells; and Dying miserably there, sang theyr own deplorable Dirges: we searched diverse houses, whose late inhabitants the Plague had engrossd ere we could find a person alive; & those, when found, (alas) not enough to bury the dead'. The travellers certainly showed considerable courage and curiosity in entering the village and searching its houses; convention and self-preservation would have counselled them to give the place a wide berth. Moreover, if they were known to have investigated a plague village so closely they could well have been refused entry at their intended destination, and even beyond. Such an experience would no doubt have long remained with them and been passed on by them as an example of the awful effects of plague.[22]

Bargrave continued to trade with the eastern Mediterranean and in 1656 his ship anchored within the Venetian lagoon, about 10 miles from the city. 'I went to the Sanità (or Health-house) where I was soon dismissd with my Sentence from the Lords della Sanità that in regard we came from Turky (which is always taken for an infectious Shoar) we must attend our full Quarantine for Prattick.' He had hoped that they could serve a shorter term but explained that a Venetian sailor in the ship had sent into the city a package of wool, 'which Commoditie being esteemd highly infectious, we were all severely examined (with our lives at Stake) who had a hand therein: and Divers infallibly had [would have] suffrd, but what with bribes to some powerfull Officers they were perswaded to countenance a framd Excuse'. So the only penalty was to serve the full quarantine period of 43 days. That was at the height of the plague epidemics in the central Mediterranean and the Venetians did have the reputation of strictly enforcing their quarantine regulations.[23]

James Yonge also recorded some bizarre experiences in obtaining pratique. He was an apprentice surgeon from Plymouth on the *Robert Bonadventure*, a ship of 150 tons that in 1664 sailed firstly to the Cape Verde Islands and then across the North Atlantic to Newfoundland. On returning to Europe during the autumn the ship was sailed directly to Genoa, where the merchants who wished to trade with her could not go abroad 'till we had prattick; we had no bill of health to certify the place not having the pest whence we came'. So Yonge forged one, purporting to come from the Governor of Newfoundland, signing himself as Secretary, and something resembling a seal was contrived and added to the certificate. This was accepted and pratique was granted. Clearly, the authorities were not as rigorous as those encountered by Bargrave at Venice.

That did not end Yonge's experiences regarding pratique. After a stay at Genoa the *Robert Bonadventure* sailed along the Italian coastline to Messina, carrying a new and legitimate certificate issued in Genoa. After they had waited outside the port for some time, with no-one allowed to go ashore, they were all 'called out of the ship and directed to a small quadrangle, where an old fellow, perusing the bill of health we had from Genoa, puts on a great pair of spectacles as big as saucers and, making each man expose his groins and armpits, he looks into them and with a stick thrusts in them, where, finding nothing, we are allowed prattick, and then we went into the town'. The inspector was of course looking for evidence of bubos, but he found none.[24]

Tales of both routine and peculiar experiences such as theirs would have been told and re-told in the City's coffee-houses and the taverns and alehouses along the Thames. The stories and deaths such as that of Lady Anne Bendish helped to maintain an awareness of the presence of plague abroad and its impact, while England was virtually free from the disease. That was not to last. In the spring of 1665 Yonge's ship put into Plymouth on its way up the Channel and he disembarked and was discharged before it sailed on to London. Yonge later acknowledged his great good fortune 'for a most dreadful plague broke out while they were in London that ever yet happened, which killed by computation near 100,000 people'.[25]

15

GUILTY AS CHARGED?

By the early 1660s the government and the City had a clear policy which could be put in place when plague threatened London. A naval blockade would prevent the disease reaching the city and if that failed what had become standard regulations would be implemented. No large pest-house had been built and so the accommodation for the sick was limited, hence the reliance would be on household quarantine, with the means to enforce it, compelling those who were confined in their houses to stay indoors and with the funds to keep them supplied. The posts of the senior and junior officers who were to oversee the operation, supervise the sick and deal with the victims were specified, even though some appointments were left until an emergency occurred. Those arrangements were based on experience gained during plague epidemics over a long period, and the absence of the disease despite the epidemic in Holland in the 1650s may have engendered some confidence that the city would be spared again should another outbreak erupt in north-west Europe.

When the disease appeared at Amsterdam and Hamburg in 1663 the Privy Council acted promptly and again put the quarantining of shipping in place. Dutch physicians believed that the infection had reached Amsterdam from Algiers, not directly from Turkey. On the other hand, Nathaniel Hodges, a physician, thought that the plague had spread to Holland from Smyrna, on Turkey's Aegean coast. The Privy Council was aware of the danger and in the autumn of 1663 received advice from the lord mayor and aldermen. Rather surprisingly, that was based not on experience of previous practice but 'after the example of other countries'. They recommended that all vessels from the infected areas should be stopped from reaching London, with Gravesend the furthest point upstream that suspect ships, both English and foreign, were to be allowed. There lazarettos should be provided into which the cargoes would be unloaded and aired for 40 days, but with all members of the crew and passengers kept on board for the same period. At a meeting on 23 October the Council accepted the recommendations, although two weeks later it referred the matter to a committee of its own members for further consideration. Pepys was at a coffee-house in Cornhill on 19 October 'where much talk about the Turkes proceedings and that the plague is got to Amsterdam, brought by a ship from Argier [Algiers] – and it is also carried to Hambrough'. The Duke of York had said that the king intended 'to forbid any of their ships coming into the River [Thames]'.[1]

The committee's report developed the policy of naval quarantine by suggesting that two Royal Navy ships should anchor as far down the Thames estuary as they could do in safety, to intercept shipping. Any vessels from places that were free from plague were to be issued with health certificates, but those from Amsterdam, Hamburg or any infected place would be asked to turn back. If they chose to continue their voyage, they had to serve a quarantine of 30 days. They would not be allowed so far up the river as Gravesend, which was easily reached by the London watermen, but a further ten miles downstream, at Hole Haven on Canvey Island. The island had been reclaimed around 1620 by Dutch engineers and had then been settled by Dutch labourers. Its remoteness made it a suitably secure place for a quarantine station. A Royal Navy ketch, manned by six men, would cruise off the island when any vessels were in quarantine to prevent anyone slipping away from them prematurely in small boats. Any ships which evaded the naval cordon would be stopped by the garrisons at Tilbury fort on the north bank and the blockhouse at Gravesend on the opposite shore. This system of a double cordon should have been difficult to breach.[2]

The arrangements were in place by the middle of November, when three merchantmen and one warship were being held at Hole Haven. They had come from Holland and although no one on board had developed any plague symptoms the Council ordered that they should be detained for a further two weeks before being boarded and inspected. On 11 November the Council extended 'the Method observed here in the River of Thames' to all English ports, with the order that the period of isolation should be 30 days. In January it received a request for advice from Great Yarmouth, where the Bailiffs were concerned about the risk from vessels arriving there from Amsterdam, and it repeated its earlier advice.[3] Pepys noted on 26 November that the plague

> ...grows more and more at Amsterdam. And we are going upon making of all ships coming from thence and Hambrough, or any other infected places, to perform their Quarantine (for 30 days as Sir Rd. Browne expressed it in the order of the Council, contrary to the import of the word; though in the general acceptation, it signifies now the thing, not the time spent in doing it) in Holehaven – a thing never done by us before.[4]

Pepys's fussy accuracy about the use of the term quarantine summarised the change in meaning, from a period of time to a process.

The Council displayed some flexibility by releasing perishable cargoes. In February 1664 it was informed that five vessels from Rotterdam carrying 'considerable quantities' of cod and peas for London for the Lent season were held at Hole Haven. Sir George Downing, in Holland, had provided a health certificate and the magistrates in Rotterdam had also given an assurance that the place where the cargoes were loaded was free from plague. The Council ordered that the merchandise could be transferred to other vessels, but that the passengers in the ships must continue at Hole Haven until they had served the full term. A London merchant appealed to the Council that he had a cargo of Rhenish wines that had been loaded at Dordrecht; the vessel was stopped at Hole Haven and because the paperwork was in order it was permitted to sail to London. But the customs officers would not allow the cargo to be unloaded and the ship was so defective that it took five or six men working the pumps to keep it afloat. The Council ordered that if that were found to be true, then the wine could be unloaded. Another ship was ordered back to Hole Haven, however, as the account of its itinerary was suspect. In a rather different case a merchant bound for Persia in an East India Company ship was being delayed because one of his servants had paid a visit to Rotterdam and was detained at Hole Haven on his return; the Council permitted him to leave so long as he boarded the outward-bound vessel and did not land at any English port. Other exceptions were allowed, but some appeals were rejected and the persons and cargoes were ordered to be held for the full period of the quarantine.[5]

The epidemic in Holland worsened during the spring of 1664 and the Council reviewed its policy, widening the restrictions to ships from all Dutch ports, and in May it ordered that the quarantine period should be extended to 40 days. If anyone had come ashore from a vessel from the United Provinces without serving the whole quarantine, the justices were to close the house where they were living for 40 days, as if it contained someone with the plague. Such tightening of the restrictions was prompted by the growing epidemic on the continent and 'the heat of weather approaching, which renders the contagion more dangerous'. In July the orders were extended to shipping from Hamburg, where the disease had broken out again.[6]

The regulations 'to prevent the bringing in the Pest from the parts beyond the sea' were enforced so effectively that at the end of July the Dutch ambassador protested that the trade of both countries was being adversely affected, to which the Council responded that the king was sympathetic to his appeal, but he had to protect his people from plague, 'which cannot be done without such restraints'. Rather than ease the restrictions, the Council tightened them further on 31 August with an order that no people or goods were to be permitted to land at any port for the following three months, excepting only those ships which were already at sea.[7] That drastic widening of the policy may have been designed to prevent any vessels gaining exemption by claiming to have come from a plague-free port, as well as an awareness that the epidemic in Holland had worsened. In May 1664 the number of deaths registered in Amsterdam was 338 in one week and the figure had doubled by the end of July, when Sir George Downing reported to the Earl of Clarendon, the Lord Chancellor, that 'the plague is scattered generally over the whole country even in the little dorps and villages, and it is gott to Antwerp and Brussels'.[8] The peak was 1,050 in a week and the weekly figure was 800 even at the end of September. In London there were only nine plague deaths in 1663 and just five in 1664 and the risk of infection from Holland apparently declined, as diplomatic relations worsened and both countries kept their merchant shipping in port in preparation for war, which was declared in February 1665. Pepys's only mentions of the plague in 1664 were to note that it had broken out in the Dutch fleet and that a Dutch ship had been cast ashore at Gothenburg on which 'all the men were dead of the plague', which may have been a tale that had grown in the telling.[9]

Despite the efficient naval blockade, plague deaths were reported in London in the autumn of 1664, but no epidemic had ever erupted during the winter, and that season in 1664–5 was a cold one. Perhaps the source of the outbreak was not infection transferred by ship from the outbreak in Holland and north Germany, but developed from incipient contamination by the plague bacillus in London. William Boghurst was an apothecary who lived in White Hart Yard at the junction of Drury Lane and the High Street of St Giles-in-the-Fields. In his account of the epidemic he wrote that the most common disease in the parish in 1664 was smallpox, with about 40 families between the church and the pound contracting the disease, although he did observe that: 'The plague hath put itself forth in St. Giles's, St. Clement's, St. Paul's, Covent Garden, and St. Martin's this 3 or 4 yeares, as I have been certainly informed by the people themselves that had it in their houses in those Parishes.' He also wrote that in the summer of 1664 'there was such a multitude of flyes that they lined the insides of houses, and if any threads or stringes did hang downe in any place, it was presently thicke sett with flyes like a rope of oniones, and swarms of Ants covered the highways'. That suggests warm, muggy weather, which, although he does not say so, from the context of his statement he thought was connected with the development of plague in the following year. As an apothecary who was prepared to go into the houses of the sick to administer medicines he was well placed to know what diseases were afflicting the inhabitants, so his account is more dependable than the figures in the Bills of Mortality, because of the concealment of plague deaths. He also wrote that 'the Plague began first at the West end of the City, as at St. Giles's and St. Martin's, Westminster'.[10] It appeared again in the spring of 1665 which, at that time of the year, was a more worrying development. Those who could remember the epidemic in 1625 thought that the pattern showed some similarities. On 26 April the Privy Council noted that 'the Plague is broken out, or vehemently suspected to bee, in some houses within the parish of St Giles in the fields, and other out parishes'.[11] Those other parishes were not named, and St Giles's was to shoulder the blame for the epidemic that was to spread remorselessly across the city. Sir Thomas Peyton had no doubt about where the responsibility lay. Early in August 1665 he wrote from Knowlton, in east Kent, to Joseph Williamson, Under-Secretary of State: 'That one parish of St. Giles at London hath done us all this mischief.'[12] By that time the parish had suffered more deaths than any other district of London, with 58 per cent of the plague deaths in the city during June.

Did the parish's officers deserve to be censured for their negligence, especially in not enforcing household quarantine? On 23 December 1664 the churchwardens paid the 'searchers of the body' of the parish 'for veiwing the Corps of Goodwife Phillips who dyed of the Plague' and they shut up the other members of the household and paid for their maintenance. Another plague death was recorded in the parish in the first week of February and in that month the churchwardens and the overseers of the poor met with the Lord Chief Justice and the Justices of the Peace 'about the vissited houses'. Towards the end of March Silla Lewis was confined as a plague suspect in her house in Three Crane Alley off the north side of the High Street, a court of just five houses, their occupants so poor that they could not 'pay to church or poor'.[13] She died of the disease. Towards the end of April two houses were closed in the Drury Lane area. It seems on this evidence that the parish cannot be accused of complacency and the officers acted properly in closing infected houses and keeping the justices informed. As the epidemic developed the Privy Council continued to be involved and ordered the parish to build a pest-house where the victims could be isolated, and the churchwardens complied with that instruction, despite having to spend £315 on the building, roughly the equivalent of one year's revenue, at a time when the maintenance of the quarantined families was becoming expensive.

The parish's reputation was badly damaged by an incident towards the end of April, which showed that the efforts of its officers were not completely effective. The Privy Council noted that 'the house, the Signe of the Ship in the New buildings, in St Giles in the fields, was shutt up as suspected to bee Infected with the Plague, & a Crosse and paper fixed, on the doore; And That the said Cross & paper were taken off, & the doore opened, in a rioutous manner, & the people of the house permitted to goe abroad into the street promiscuously, with others.' The Council ordered the

Lord Chief Justice and the justices to discover 'the offendors in the said Ryott, And inflict ... the severest punishments, the Rigor of the Law, will allow, against offendors in accons of soe dangerous a Consequence; And soe much to the contempt of his Ma[jes]ties orders as theese'.[14] As well as that rather damning incident, the parish's cause was not helped by another case which attracted the attention of the justices and led to the indictment of Rebecca Wilts 'to aunswere the opening and entring a house infected'.

Despite the growing scale of the problem, the churchwardens at St Giles's conscientiously continued to maintain those who were incarcerated. During May the Bills of Mortality recorded 20 plague deaths in the parish and the entries in the burial register were broken off on 13 May and were not resumed until 22 June. On 17 June the diarist Samuel Pepys went to visit the Lord Treasurer, the Earl of Southampton, on business, only to find that he had left Southampton House in Bloomsbury because of the danger, so Pepys took a coach to return to the city, but going along Holborn he noticed that the coachman was driving slower and slower and 'at last stood still, and came down hardly able to stand; and told me that he was suddenly stroke very sick and almost blind, he could not see'. Pepys thought that this had been his first contact with the disease, which 'stroke me very deep'. The death toll in the parish continued to rise inexorably until it peaked in the third week of July, when there were 370 deaths, 329 of them attributed to plague. The bellman who went around the streets with the dead cart stopped ringing his bell because 'there die so many that the bell would hardly ever leave ringing'.[15]

During 1664 the average weekly number of deaths had been just 15, but in 1665 from the first week of June until the beginning of September the average was 219, fourteen-and-a-half times the figure for the previous year. On 1 July there were 38 burials and three weeks later, on 21 July, as many as 53 were carried out on just that one day. Because of the maintenance of quarantined families the churchwardens' expenditure during 1665 was almost seven times higher than it had been in the preceding years. Nevertheless, they tried to maintain the designated practices in the face of appalling difficulties and could scarcely be blamed in that respect. But the policy failed. During the year 4,457 deaths were recorded in the parish, at least 3,216 from the plague. Estimating the population from the Hearth Tax returns suggests that more than 40 per cent, perhaps even more than 50 per cent, of the parishioners died. The scale of the mortality presented the large and immediate problem of disposing of the dead. The church had an unusually large churchyard for a London parish, but traditional burials in single graves would be too slow and difficult and use too much space. And so the sexton, John Geere, supervised the excavation of five large pits in the churchyard and in them were placed almost 1,400 corpses.[16]

The parish contained 'multitudes of poor' and its normal revenues were hopelessly inadequate in such a crisis; the cost of maintaining the poor people in their houses or the pest-house had to be paid from rates levied especially for the purpose and charitable donations. St Giles's did well in both respects, managing to collect almost all of the £600 which the vestry ordered to be levied by a special rate and receiving more than £1,000 from charitable donors, including large sums from such prominent people as Lord Craven and the Duchess of York, but most in smaller sums of £5 or less. It seems that the parish was well served by its prosperous neighbourhoods and it attracted the sympathy of members of the elite, at the same time as it felt the wrath of the Privy Council. Even so, there was a deficit on the year's account of £200, but part of this was recouped in the following year by selling the new pest-house for £70.[17]

During the summer plague dispersed across the whole city and the numbers of deaths continued to rise until the middle week of September and subsided only with the coming of cold winter weather. St Giles's was fortunate, because its rector, Robert Boreman, remained in the parish. He had been rector only since November 1663 and may not yet have fallen out with the members of the vestry (within five years he had gone to the Exchequer Court over a dispute with them about the appointment of churchwardens). He had links with the court through his brother Sir William Boreman, Clerk Comptroller of the Household. Boghurst also stayed on, dispensing medicines, and he visited and nursed the sick in their homes – up to 60 a day by his own account – and, at the last, laid out the bodies of the victims. He was not afraid that the disease was said to be contagious, and he survived. As well as medicines, the parishioners of St Giles's were subject to fumigation as a possible preventative, for the justices encouraged the experiments of James Angier, who burned a fumigant in houses in Newton Street, off High Holborn. This seemed to be a success, for there were no further deaths in the houses that had been fumigated, although in one of them four people had died of the plague already and two more were infected. The justices were impressed and sent a favourable report to the Privy Council, and he was paid £86 'for fumes in the late sickness time'. But he charged £10 for treating Mrs Southall's house in St Giles's, making it a prohibitively expensive treatment to apply at all infected houses in the parish. The justices continued to keep an eye on St Giles's and indicted two women of the parish for theft: Eleanor Unckles 'to aunswere the imbezilling the goods of Doctor Parker late dead of the plague' and Elizabeth Ellis 'to aunswere the suspition of having feloniously imbezilled the goods of Sir John Underhill'.[18]

As the number of victims continued to rise the Council again intervened, on 21 June, when it ordered that the parishes that shared a boundary with St Giles's should guard the streets to stop any 'vagrant loose persons', or anyone coming from a house where plague was suspected, from leaving the parish. The quarantining of whole districts was not a new idea, probably was unenforceable, and failed in this case. There was no need to prevent movement in the opposite direction and restrain outsiders from entering the parish, because by now it was shunned: in the middle of July, 'Nobody that is in London feares to goe anywhere but in st giles's.'[19]

That was a rather weak attempt at reassurance; Londoners were already greatly alarmed at the spread of the disease and those who could were beginning to move away. During June plague cases became more common in Westminster, even close to Whitehall Palace, where several people died in just one alley.[20] In the early part of the month attention was focused on the fleet's successful engagement with the Dutch at the battle of Lowestoft on 3 June, and then the return of the Duke of York and the other naval commanders. It would not have been tactful to have withdrawn from court before having offered congratulations to the proud victors, who did not arrive at Whitehall until 16 June. But thereafter the threat of the plague produced a stream of departures, including the Earl of Southampton, the Lord Treasurer, who had left by 17 June. The Spanish ambassador was formally received by the king and queen in the Banqueting House of Whitehall Palace on 23 June, but the whole court moved away at the end of the month, going first to Syon House and then, on 9 July, to Hampton Court. The king accompanied his mother, Henrietta Maria, to Dover on her way to France. By the end of June Pepys found that the Duke of Albemarle, the Earl of Clarendon and Sir Henry Bennet were the only ones among the 'great statesmen' left in the capital, although other leading figures were also to remain during the epidemic, including the Earl of Craven, the Archbishop of Canterbury, the Bishop of London and Sir John Lawrence, the lord mayor. According to the Venetian ambassador, Lawrence 'being very fearful about the plague has caused a cabinet to be made, entirely of glass, in which he gives audience and determines the affairs of the city'.[21]

John Allin was studying medicine in London and in 1665 was living in Horsleydown. During April he heard of deaths in the pest-house and of two houses in Drury Lane which had been closed. On 26 May he wrote that the Bill had recorded three plague deaths in the previous week and 14 in the current one 'but its rather believed to bee treble the number. At the upper end of the towne persons high and low are very fearfull of it, and many removed'.[22] The nonconformist minister Thomas Vincent saw the increase in plague deaths from three to fourteen to forty-three in successive weeks as arousing the citizens' alarm:

> Now secure sinners begin to be startled, and those who would have slept at quiet still in their nests, are unwillingly awakened. Now a great consternation seizeth upon most persons, and fearful bodings of a desolating judgment ... The great orbs begin first to move; the lords and gentry retire into their countries; their remote houses are prepared, goods removed, and London is quickly upon their backs: few ruffling gallants walk the streets; few spotted ladies [prostitutes] to be seen at windows: a great forsaking there was of the adjacent places where the plague did first rage [St Giles's and the adjoining parishes]. [23]

On 5 June the theatres were closed on the orders of the Lord Chamberlain, yet during May the plays had been 'thronged with people of all sorts and sizes'. The Inns of Court broke up around the middle of the month. At Lincoln's Inn rules were put in place for the regulation of the inn during the epidemic, which involved control of visitors and a strict overnight curfew on everyone from ten o'clock until morning. In early July the lord mayor ordered that all schools in the City were to close until the end of September. The scholars of Westminster School also departed; Dr Busby, the headmaster, took them to Chiswick, but, when that proved to be unsafe, told them that they were free to return to their own homes.[24]

In the middle of June the Venetian ambassador reported that the plague continued to spread: '112 having died of it this week according to the bulletins and as the bulletins admit such a number it is feared that the numbers are double, more than fourteen parishes being affected.' By the end of the month he had moved to Tunbridge Wells.[25] While the plague had caused much disruption around Westminster, the City was still relatively free

from the disease, with just 18 plague deaths recorded within the
walls in the four weeks to 27 June. Yet on the 21st, at Cripplegate
Pepys found 'all the town almost going out of town, the coaches
and waggons being all full of people going into the country'.[26]
A Mr Radcliffe wrote on 13 June that the plague 'increaseth so
much that all the gentry are eather gon or agoeing out of Towne ...
This day a house in Queen Street, opositt to us is shut up so that
we are resolved for Northumberland next weeke.'[27] But this was a
gradual process and on 18 July Samuel Herne wrote to his tutor at
Clare Hall, Cambridge, that 'there is but very little notice tooke of
the sicknesse here in London'. Elsewhere in his letter, however, he
contradicted himself with 'the citizens begin to shut up apace' and
observing that there were few houses still open even in the Strand
and little business at the Royal Exchange.[28] Herne's account mixed
an attempt at reassurance with an awareness of the growing crisis.

The Bills for the week in which Herne wrote show that plague
deaths in the parishes within the walls had doubled to 56 since
the previous set of figures and were increasing steadily elsewhere.
The City parishes outside the walls saw a rise from 166 plague
deaths in the first week of July to 755 in the last week. The
Westminster parishes, meanwhile, experienced an increase from
105 to 322 over that period. In the 130 parishes recorded by the
Bills the weekly number of deaths from the disease rose from 470
to 2,010 during the month, and total deaths from 1,006 to 3,014.
By the end of July the mortality rate was almost ten times that of
the preceding ten years and even in the area within the walls it
was four times that level. With 8,828 deaths during July, 5,667
of them from plague, there was no disguising the scale of the
unfolding disaster. Nor was there any indication of the beginning
of a decline, for recorded deaths at the end of July were three times
the number noted for the last week of June, and those attributed
to plague had increased more than fourfold, while the number of
parishes in which deaths from the disease had occurred rose from
33 to 73. The Bills gave no cause for hope of an imminent end to

the epidemic and previous outbreaks had shown that the summer months were likely to be the worst of all.

Pepys packed his mother off home to Huntingdonshire on 22 June. But she was reluctant to go and evidently had no great fear of the growing menace; she prevaricated for so long that 'she lost her place in the coach and was fain to ride in the waggon part', which was the open section at the rear, neither comfortable nor dignified.[29] Four days after his mother had left, Pepys noted in his diary: 'The plague encreases mightily – I this day seeing a house, at a bittmakers over against St. Clements church in the open street, shut up; which is a sad sight.' Most people going about their business would not have been aware of houses in the alleys which were closed, hence Pepys's discomfort at seeing one fronting a thoroughfare. Two days later he saw 'several plague-houses' in King Street in Westminster and close to Whitehall Palace, which was equally unsettling, so that he 'was fearful of going into any house'. Vincent's comment was that Londoners began 'to fear whom they converse withal, and deal withal, lest they should have come out of infected places'. In Pepys's summary of the month he noted that he was considering moving his wife to Woolwich, 'the plague growing on'. Even so, he was mostly aware of the disease when he was in Westminster and not at home in St Olave's. His growing anxiety prompted him to put his own paperwork in order, 'the season growing so sickly that it is much to be feared how a man can scape having a share with others in it'. On 5 July he sent his wife and her maids to Woolwich, which he regretted doing as he realised how much he was going to miss her, while admitting that 'some trouble there is in having the care of a family at home in this plague time'.[30]

Three weeks after Pepys's wife had left he began to fear for the safety of his cousin Kate Joyce and her husband Anthony, who kept a tallow-chandler's shop, because of 'the sad news of the death of so many in the parish of the plague, 40 last night – the bell always going'. He was also disturbed by the fact that the disease 'is got into our parish this week; and is got endeed everywhere'.

That week the number of dead in the Bills had increased by 1,000 and most of them were plague-deaths. He visited Kate Joyce for a second time 'and there used all the vehemence and Rhetorique I could to get her husband to let her go down to Brampton [Huntingdonshire], but I could not prevail with him – he urging some simple reasons, but most that of profit, minding the house – and the distance, if either of them should be ill'. After much ado Anthony agreed that Kate could go to Windsor and stay with friends there.[31] Like Anthony Joyce, Pepys remained in London for the time being, but from early September he spent his nights at Woolwich, although he continued to go regularly to his house and office in Seething Lane. In contrast, the Presbyterian minister Richard Baxter made a complete break, although he lived at Acton, well outside the city and so in comparative safety. He left when plague appeared in the parish at the end of July and moved to Great Hampden in Buckinghamshire.[32] Thomas Rugg was based in Covent Garden and, according to his account, in July 1,800 families left London; some of them met with such hostile receptions that they were forced to 'abide in the fields in tents or hedges or the like'. As some citizens left and many of those who remained were reluctant to go to public places if they did not need to, the city began to exude a growing air of desertion. Before the end of July the Dutch ambassador wrote that many Dutchmen were requesting passes to return to Holland as there was no trade left or conversation, at court or at the Exchange.[33]

Those who were unable or unwilling to leave could try to avoid infection by taking sensible precautions and limiting their contact with others as much as possible. In the last week of July John Allin wrote that 'I goe about my buisines without any slavish feare ... many whole families of 7, 8, 9, 10, 18 in a family totally swept away'. His explanation was not a medical or administrative one but rather that the epidemic was 'more a judgment than any thing else, and true repentance is the best antidote, and pardon of sin the best cordiall'. Two weeks later he had modified his views somewhat: yes, sin needed to be suppressed, but at a practical level 'I am troubled at the approach of the sicknesse neerer every weeke, and at a new burying place which they have made neere us, and with some piece of indiscretion used in not shutting up, but rather makeing great funeralls for such as dye of the distemper.'[34] Henry Oldenburg, the Secretary of the Royal Society, lived in Pall Mall and had considered that if plague 'should come into this row, where I am, I think, I should then change my thoughts, and retire into the Country', but at the end of July he told one of his correspondents that he intended to remain at his house anyway, endeavouring 'to banish both fear and overconfidence, leading a regular life and avoiding infected places as much as I can'. A month later he reported that very few houses where the occupants lived 'orderly and comfortably' and had healthy constitutions had been infected, whereas those 'wanting necessaries and comfortable relief' suffered most.[35]

A degree of selfishness was acceptable. As Edward Wood wrote to his agent John Pack, who lived in Thames Street, 'Every man is bound to use the meanes for his preservation in this sad visitation.' He had earlier offered Pack the simple advice to 'Lock upp the Dores, & shun the danger what you can & to goe abroad as litle as may be', while he chose to remain at Littleton, near Staines: 'In these Contagious times [I] am loath to stay in London.' Communication between the two men was interrupted when the boatman who plied between London and Laleham did not make the journey. Sir Robert Long also stayed out of London, telling his clerk to keep his house in New Palace Yard as insulated as possible, not letting anyone out, or permitting visitors to come to either the house or the office. Such isolation was seen to be the safest course. At the end of the following January Edward Swan, one of the pensioners at the Charterhouse, wrote that he had not been out of the almshouse once in the previous seven months. That had not been entirely of his own choosing. On 3 July the governors had issued an order that no pensioner or scholar could leave the buildings without having leave to do so from the Master or one of the senior officers 'And that not to be given upon any slight or triviall, but only upon some weighty & urgent occasion'. They would have felt that they had been correct in imposing such stringent rules, for the occupants experienced 'hardly a head aking of above forty left in the house in the great sicknesse year 1665'.[36] The Brothers of Charterhouse can readily be equated with the citizens of Florence described by Boccaccio, who shut themselves away during the Black Death.

It was early August when Peyton made his allegation that the officers of St Giles's were responsible for the growing epidemic, and from that perspective they did look culpable, for the disease had made most inroads in the west of the city and had forced the court to withdraw. That was Pepys's impression from his observations as he went around London and it was borne out by the figures in the Bills; the greatest numbers of deaths had, until then, been in the parishes near to St Giles's and in Westminster. From the evidence of its own records St Giles's appears to have been a well-run parish that faced up to the crisis, liaising with the justices, building a pest-house, employing nurses, warders, examiners and a surgeon, and disposing of the bodies. Yet it had to shoulder the blame for those early months, the reluctance of the parishioners suspected of having the plague to be quarantined and the suspicion that infected households were not closed quickly enough. Perhaps it was 'guilty as charged', but the charge was a harsh one and, as the epidemic across the country began to decline, in October 1666 the Earl of Clarendon took stock and blamed the metropolis in general: 'It is indeede a sadd season that wee are chased from one place to another to save our lyves. Wee have reason to complayne of the ill government of the citty of London, which, for want of shuttinge up infected houses, hath skattered the contagion over the kingdom.'[37] With the scale of the disaster the blame had been widened from one parish to the whole of the city.

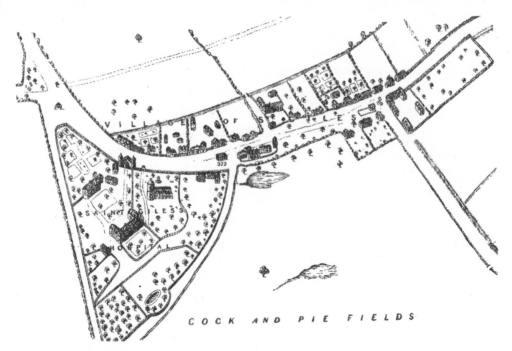

The Great Plague began in St Giles-in-the-Field on the western fringe of the city, and the parish was blamed for the disaster. © Stephen Porter

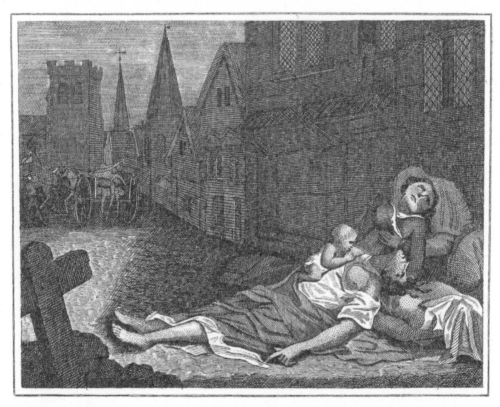

A mother and her children dying in a London street during the Great Plague. © Stephen Porter

Left: An eighteenth-century impression of burials at Holywell during the Great Plague. © Wellcome Collection

Below: Scenes depicting the Great Plague, including deaths in a well-to-do home and in the street, burials, funerals and Londoners fleeing by land and on the river. © Wellcome Collection

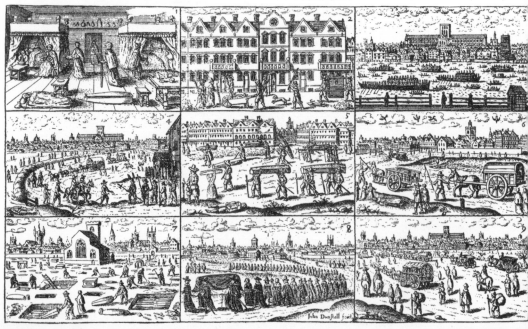

Above left: Samuel Pepys sent his reluctant mother out of London when the plague threatened. The scene was depicted by E.H. Shepard in 1925. © Stephen Porter

Above right: A dead cart collecting victims of the plague in 1665. © Wellcome Collection

A street scene during the Great Plague; the citizens cover their faces to avoid inhaling the miasmic air. A woman in the foreground has already died. © Stephen Porter

By Tнo. D.

Lord, haue mercy

on London.

I follow.

We fly.

Wee dye.

Keepe out.

Printed at London for *Iohn Trundle*, and are to be fold at his Shop in Smithfield. 1625

Above: The triumphant figure representing death stands on the citizens' coffins, while those attempting to flee are repelled by countrymen with pitchforks. © Stephen Porter

Right: Pepys described an incident when a girl was passed out of a window of a house in Gracechurch Street to save her from the plague. Drawn by E.H. Shepard in 1925. © Stephen Porter

A merchant's dilemma about whether to flee the Great Plague is resolved by a ship's captain, who offers him places aboard for himself and his family. © Stephen Porter

The Manner of Dissecting the

PESTILENTIALL BODY.

Printed for Nath: Crouch at the Rose and Crowne in Exchang Ally.

Dissection of a plague victim by George Thomson and a colleague. © Wellcome Collection

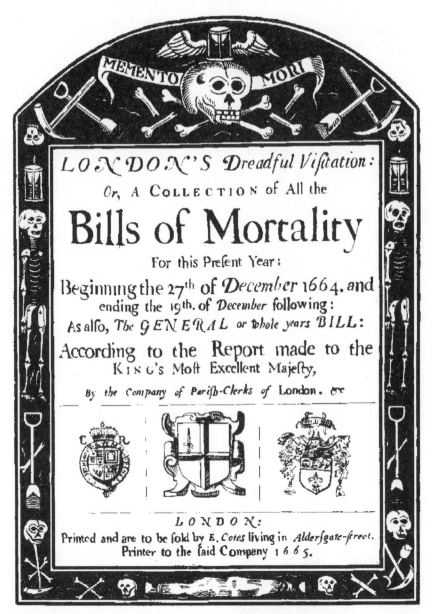

The Bills of Mortality title page for 1665. © Stephen Porter

The pest-house in Tothill Fields, Westminster, looking forlorn in this lithograph from around 1840. © Wellcome Collection

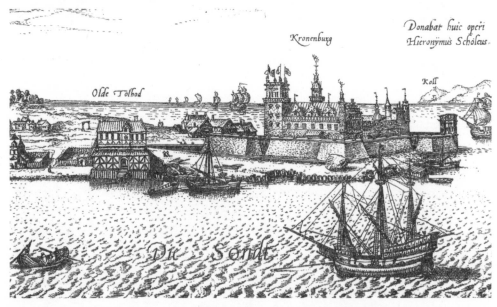

Elsinore was the port where tolls were collected from passing ships for the Danish crown and it suffered terribly from plague in 1709–10. © Stephen Porter

M: Daniel De Foe
Author of the True born Englishman

Right: Portrait of
Daniel Defoe, novelist
of the Great Plague, by
Michiel Van der Gucht.
© Wellcome Collection

Below: The Plague
at Marseilles in 1720
depicted by Michel
Serre (1658–1733).
© Wellcome Collection

A
JOURNAL
OF THE
𝔓𝔩𝔞𝔤𝔲𝔢 𝔜𝔢𝔞𝔯:
BEING
Obſervations or Memorials,
Of the moſt Remarkable
OCCURRENCES,
As well
PUBLICK *as* PRIVATE,
Which happened in
L O N D O N
During the laſt
GREAT VISITATION
In 1665.

Written by a CITIZEN who continued all the
while in *London*. Never made publick before

L O N D O N:
Printed for *E. Nutt* at the *Royal-Exchange*; *J. Roberts*
in *Warwick-Lane*; *A. Dodd* without *Temple-Bar*;
and *J. Graves* in St. *James's-ſtreet*. 1722.

Above: A stow-away rat on a cart,
carrying the plague. Drawing by Albert
Lloyd Tarter (1913-88). © Wellcome
Collection

Left: The title-page of Defoe's
ever-popular novel *A Journal of the
Plague Year* of 1722.

The beginnings of plague in a desolate town, depicted by Albert Lloyd Tarter
(1913-88). © Wellcome Collection

16

THE GREAT PLAGUE OF 1665

Throughout the epidemic attention was focused on the effectiveness of the officers and behaviour of the citizens, for the enforcement of the regulations was difficult and hazardous. Not only did the officers have to run the risk of contracting the disease, but also to suffer being violently confronted by those who resented being delayed or prevented from carrying on with their normal routines. One man was charged with 'assaulting and striking' a parish constable who had questioned him, suspecting that he was bringing goods into the parish from a house in St Giles-in-the-Fields without a health certificate.[1] Most challenges to authority were passive – people simply continued with their regular behaviour despite the regulations.

Clarendon was particularly exasperated by attendance at funerals, in defiance of orders to the contrary that should have been read in every church, fearing that 'goinge to publique buryalls must infecte the whole kingdome'.[2] The officers' tasks were not made easier when those ultimately responsible for their enforcement decamped. Sir Theodore de Mayerne had envisaged the justices taking control and exercising 'absolute power' when an epidemic struck. In practice, they often appear to have been more active in directing the setting up of quarantine arrangements when plague threatened than supervising the collection of rates when it had broken out. Their absence from a stricken community not only left a void in the direction of measures to contain the disease, but also provoked resentment. This fuelled one of the government's major concerns during the epidemic, which was fear of disorder, more than likely whipped up by the nonconformists. In practice, the small number of officers appointed to enforce the orders were faced not with unrest borne of political or religious discontent, but agitation resulting from the effects of the plague policies. They could not hope to deal with a recalcitrant population who were unwilling, out of economic necessity, to observe restrictive regulations. Their efforts required co-operation and perhaps, too, perceptible evidence that the policies were effective. By the summer of 1665 it was all too obvious in London, and indeed elsewhere, that this was not the case.

Some physicians left, apparently to avoid the epidemic, although Nathaniel Hodges justified their action on the basis that it was due 'not so much for their own preservation as the service of those whom they attend'; the patients they were treating had gone away from London and so the physicians followed them to continue with their treatment.[3] Members of the parish clergy also departed. Early in August the physician Peter Barwick wrote to William Sancroft, Dean of St Paul's, who had retired to Tunbridge Wells to take the waters, telling him that the 'mouths of a slanderous generation' were criticising 'those that are with drawn both of your profession and ours'. Some clergymen did stay in London throughout the epidemic, including Simon Patrick at St Paul's, Covent Garden, Richard Peirson at St Bride's, Fleet Street, who signed every page of the burial register, and Robert Breton, vicar of St Nicholas's, Deptford. But the problem was serious enough for the Bishop of London, Humphrey Henchman, to try to stem the tide by warning those clergy who had left that they would be replaced if they did not return. His anxiety was caused partly by a concern that nonconformist ministers would step in to conduct services where the Anglican clergy failed to meet the population's spiritual needs and maintain routines. These included conducting funerals and so observing the proper forms at a time when there were so many deaths. Not all of the parish clergy heeded Henchman's threats, and those who had moved away were censured in a pamphlet with the expressive title of *A Pulpit To Let*, which achieved high circulation.[4] Indeed, Henchman's fears were realised to a certain extent, for ministers who had lost their livings after the Restoration returned to the London pulpits and attracted large congregations. According to Gilbert Burnet, who was to become Bishop of Salisbury, 'Many ministers were driven from town, and several churches were shut up, when people were in a more than ordinary disposition to profit by good sermons; whereupon some of the Nonconformists went into the empty pulpits, and preached with great freedom, reflecting on the vices of the Court and the severities that they themselves had been made to suffer.' While their sermons were welcome to many citizens who remained in London, the size of the congregations was a cause for concern to those who believed that crowds were likely to increase the spread of the disease. The clergy themselves were scarcely less at risk than the physicians and apothecaries in carrying out their duties: conducting services, officiating at funerals, receiving visitors from houses where the plague was present, and having to go to the poor who were ill to distribute alms. Of the Anglican clergy, at least eleven died of the plague, and some nonconformist preachers also died, with six ministers recorded in the burial register of St Giles, Cripplegate.[5]

By the end of July most of those who were able to leave London had probably gone; they escaped the worst months of the epidemic. During the four weeks of August the numbers of deaths attributed to the disease had been 2,817, 3,880, 4,237 and 6,102, with 22,413 deaths from all causes in this period, and the number of parishes in which plague victims had died had risen from 86 to 113. The peak of the epidemic in 1603 had been the last week of August and in that of 1625 the third week, but those dates were passed without any sign of a slackening in the rising death toll. Indeed, the first week of September saw a further increase, to 6,988, which Pepys regarded as 'a most dreadfull Number' and caused Clarendon to lose hope of an improvement in the figures, writing that if those for the following week also showed an increase he would 'despayre of the whole winter'.[6]

By far the majority of Londoners remained in the city and necessarily adapted their lives so that they could continue to work and maintain their daily habits, so far as was possible. Samuel Pepys and Simon Patrick probably were typical in continuing to go about their business, while being cautious. Pepys followed the progress of the disease, noting the figures in the Bills and the districts where it was present. He scrupulously put his affairs in order, sorting his papers, making up his accounts, packing his books into chests, and getting 'all things in the best and speediest order I can'. He also re-drafted his will because he was now aware that 'a man cannot depend on living two days to an end'. In some ways he was fastidious, not wishing to visit a house two doors away from one which had been shut up, avoiding unnecessary conversations in public places, not attending his parish church for almost five months, and even not wearing his new periwig for a while, because the plague had been in Westminster when he had bought it there. Diet was a consideration, for the safety of daily provisions was questionable, with 'the butcheries being everywhere visited'. Pepys's own baker died of the plague, together with his entire family, and his brewer's house was shut up. He noted those occasions when he may have been exposed to the disease, such as when he 'met a dead Corpse, of the plague' in a narrow alley, or passed 'close by the bearers with a dead corpse of the plague', and when he had news of those who lived near to him, or that he may have been in contact with, who had been taken ill or died. Yet he quite consciously took unnecessary risks, such as going to Deptford for an amorous encounter in a house where 'round about and next door on every side is the plague', enjoying oysters out of a barrel sent from Colchester, knowing that the town was suffering badly from the disease, and even setting out to Moorfields to try to see a corpse being carried to burial in the plague-pits there.[7]

Despite his awareness of the extent and impact of the disease on both personal and general levels, which engendered gloomy comments from time to time, Pepys was by no means an unhappy man during the outbreak. He occasionally referred to being 'very merry' and one night he had the best dream that he could remember, in which he had Lady Castlemaine in his arms and she allowed him 'all the dalliance I desired'. These were more than occasional moods, for he noted that he ended July 'with the greatest glut of content that ever I had' and as September drew to a close he summarised the previous three months in much the same terms, as having been 'much the greatest' that he had ever experienced 'for joy, health and profit'. Nor had his impression changed when he came to look back over the whole year, commenting, 'I have never lived so merrily ... as I have done this plague-time.'[8]

As a clergyman Simon Patrick could not be as selective in choosing his company as Pepys. He had to conduct services and deliver sermons, administer alms to his parishioners and meet others who may be carrying the disease. The wife and one of the children of his parish clerk died of plague, and a visit to a friend also put him at risk, for the friend was entertaining another clergyman, who died just a few days later. Yet Patrick, too, was essentially cautious, without being too restricted in his movements, going out from time to time and walking to Battersea and back to visit his brother. He was careful not to be too bold and confident on the one hand, or too timorous on the other, noting that some were struck by the plague 'that stir not half so much abroad as I'. When he bought a pair of stockings he was sure that the friend from whom he purchased them was clear of the plague and that the stockings had been in his shop for a long time. Other risks had to be run. He realised that the containers of wine and beer might carry the disease, and bread was thought to be a possible means by which it was transmitted, but he had to buy those items. Yet he did alter his habits to some extent, admitting that 'I have quite changed my Diet. I eat boiled Meats & Broths more than I used: something at Supper also.'[9]

For all his care and the changes in his regime, Patrick did have some scares. His brother was taken ill on one occasion, his servant's face swelled up, and Patrick himself began to suffer with 'a sore pain in my leg … which made me suspect some touch of the plague'.[10] As sores or buboes on the leg were indeed symptoms of the disease, Patrick's anxiety was understandable, but in the circumstances the reaction to almost any illness was that it could be the beginnings of the plague. Evelyn's family responded with alarm when he had a fainting fit after having recently been in places containing plague victims. Some took quite drastic action if they suspected an acquaintance or colleague of being ill. Pepys was so appalled when his clerk Will Hewer came in one day and complained of a headache, one of the early signs of the onset of plague, that he told the servants to 'get him out of the house … without discouraging him'. Hewer went to his lodgings, but the following day was back at work, perfectly recovered from what had been just that, a headache. William Outram, rector of St Mary Woolnoth in the City, was visited by a fellow clergyman, but suspecting from his appearance that he was unwell, he instructed his servant that if he returned, he should not let him in. Pepys noted how the epidemic had produced a cruelty in the way that people treated each other.[11]

Those who were taken ill with another disease were likely to be dealt with as though they were plague victims, or to be left without proper nursing in case their illness was plague. William Taswell wrote that his household was afflicted with the plague and two maidservants were sent to the pest-house. Both of his parents were taken ill and his brother had 'a tumour in his thigh'. None of the family died, however, and Taswell does not specify if their ailments had been plague or not, but nor does he relate whether the servants did indeed have the disease, or their fate.

The mortality rate at any pest-house was very high, although some victims did survive. Early in September Patrick saw a group of about 30 people making their way along the Strand carrying white sticks. They were the patients of the doctor at one of the pest-houses who had recovered from the plague and were on their way to the justices to obtain official certification of their recovery.[12]

In such a climate of anxiety and fear many put their faith in quack medicines and homespun remedies. Sir Walter Raleigh's cordial was very popular and Lady Giffard felt that its use had saved her family from plague during the epidemic. Thomas Vincent noted that 'rue and wormwood are taken into the hand: myrrh and zedoary [white turmeric] into the mouth; and without some antidote few stir abroad in the morning.' He explained that roses and other flowers were left unsold in the markets and withered in the gardens because people did not dare smell them 'lest with their sweet savour, that which is infectious should be attracted'. Pepys, in contrast, seemed to take a sceptical view of what was on offer, observing that some suppliers said one thing and some another, but after noticing houses that were shut up and marked as plague-houses he had recourse to a plug of tobacco to smell and chew. A later tradition held that no London tobacconist died of plague during the epidemic.[13]

The suppliers of nostrums placed advertisements in the newspapers from the middle of May, often citing the success of their potion in previous outbreaks, especially that of 1625. Their cures were priced according to the means of their customers, Henry Eversden offering Sir Theodore de Medde's Anti-pharmocan for just 3d yet charging 2s 6d for a glass containing five ounces of the Universal Elixir. For the apothecaries who stayed in London this was potentially a very profitable time. Boghurst saw 50 or 60 patients a day, and the Charterhouse's apothecary, William Rawlins, presented a bill for £10 4s 5d for physic supplied there during the epidemic, even though many of the residents had left when the plague began to threaten.[14] Rawlins survived to present his bill for payment, but although supplying medicines was a lucrative business it was also an exceptionally dangerous one for those apothecaries who were prepared to visit the sufferers. Boghurst nursed his patients in their homes, remaining until they died and even staying to help place them in their coffins, while another apothecary described to Simon Patrick, with whom he shared a coach, the plague victims he had visited, detailing 'the nature of their swellings and sores'. According to Pepys, by the middle of October only one apothecary was still alive in Westminster.[15]

As a physician, Nathaniel Hodges took some satisfaction from the fact that 'these blowers of the pestilential flame' were themselves victims of the epidemic, thus in some way excusing the neglect of the magistrates who had allowed them to continue to peddle their useless medicines. He was severe in his condemnation of those 'chymists and quacks' who were 'equal strangers to all learning as well as physic' and yet 'thrust into every hand some trash or other under the disguise of a pompous title'. Hodges believed that those 'wicked impostors' supplied medicines that were 'more fatal than the plague' and added to the numbers who had died, for 'hardly a person escaped that trusted to their delusions'. Yet a member of his own profession, Dr Tristran Inard, advertised a 'Grand Preservative, or Antidote Epidemical' and, although Hodges regarded the wine known as sack as the best antidote, he acknowledged that it could be impregnated with wormwood or angelica.[16]

Hodges's uncompromising reaction partly reflected the tension between the physicians and the apothecaries, which produced a pamphlet war that continued for the remainder of the century. The physicians particularly resented those apothecaries who acted independently of them by attending patients and prescribing treatments. Boghurst justified this with the comment that the apothecaries were 'bound by their undertakings to stay and help' the victims of plague, as they would with those suffering from another disease, and that members of any profession were committed to 'the good and the evill, the pleasure and the pain, the profit and the inconvenience altogether'. In any case, the distinction which the College of Physicians sought to maintain between the three branches of the medical profession – the physicians, surgeons and apothecaries – was difficult to achieve in practice and many apothecaries acted more or less as general practitioners during the crisis.[17]

Hodges's comments reflected a common mistrust of the efficacy of the apothecaries' remedies and their cost, which led many to prepare their own concoctions. John Conyers remained at his shop in Fleet Street throughout the epidemic and was aware of such criticism, judging from the title of his pamphlet, *Direction for the prevention and cure of the plague, fitted for the poorer sort*. This was just one of 46 publications concerned with plague that appeared in 1665 and 1666, and books issued during earlier outbreaks were also consulted. Robert Boyle wrote from Oxford that he had a copy of a book published in 1605 containing remedies and suggested that it could be reprinted, with the addition of those approved in the plague of 1625.[18] Sir Robert Long advocated taking a small dose of a compound known as London treacle every morning, or the kernel of a walnut with five leaves of rue and a grain of salt, beaten together and roasted in a fig. Treacle was recommended in a broadsheet distributed by the parish churchwardens and by the College of Physicians. Simon Patrick told a friend that 'now and then I take a little Treacle' and Pepys took some Venice treacle before he went to bed one evening in July, when he felt 'out of order'.[19] John Allin's favoured protection was to keep a piece of gold in the mouth, preferably a coin of Elizabeth's reign, when walking out or being visited by the sick. He was scornful of the faith which many placed in amulets made of toad poison, considering that a preparation of his own would prove to be an effective remedy. As mentioned earlier, others took the more drastic and dangerous step of trying to contract syphilis, believing that it conferred immunity from plague. In 1665 the Bills noted 86 deaths from the 'French pox', compared with fewer than

20 in an average year, although Graunt warned that the disease was always under-recorded, with its victims entered in the category of 'consumption'.[20]

The control of livestock and domestic animals and the extermination of strays was again tried in 1665, as in previous epidemics. The dog-catcher for St Margaret's, Westminster was paid for burying 353 dog corpses and the corporation's dog-catcher claimed payment for the 4,380 dogs he had slaughtered. Sir Robert Long was concerned about the danger posed by rodents and cats, for he told his clerk to 'take all course you can agaynst the ratts, and take care of the catts; the little ones that will not stirre out may be kept, the great ones must be kiled or sent away'.[21] The regulations also extended to the sale of produce, with an order that no 'stinking fish or unwholesome flesh, musty corne or other corrupt fruites' should be sold and brewers' premises and tippling houses should be inspected for 'musty and unwholesome casks'. Bread should not be taken from bakehouses while it was still hot. The danger of the disease being spread in fabrics prompted a ban on street-sellers hawking old clothes and shopkeepers displaying them for sale.[22]

Fumigation of houses was practised once again, with the guidance of the College of Physicians, which advocated the lighting of fires and frequent discharging of guns, despite the obvious fire risks that they presented during such a dry period. The advice was followed by both the magistrates and individual householders, prompted by the government.[23] The post office in Cloak Lane, Dowgate, was fumigated morning and evening, to such an extent that those working there could hardly see each other across the room; letters were aired over vinegar before being dispatched. Householders, too, regarded fumigation as a preventive measure. Sir Robert Long told his clerk that combustible materials should be gathered and burnt daily and Dr John Worthington commended the burning of brimstone twice each day to fumigate a house. William Sancroft was assured that his London residence was fumigated twice a week, with an exotic mixture of brimstone, hops, pepper and frankincense.[24] .

The lighting of fires in the streets was not carried out in 1665 until early September, perhaps because of doubts about the effectiveness of such a strategy, not least among the physicians. Hodges regarded it as a 'showy and expensive' policy that was 'of no effect' because the air in itself was not infected. But by the beginning of September it was thought that anything should be tried that might check the remorseless increase of plague deaths. It was against this background that the street fires were tried, one to every twelve houses with the watchmen checking that they were kept alight. The bonfires required a considerable expenditure on fuel, including tar barrels, which cost the City parishes between £3 10s and £5 6s. They burned for three days and nights until doused by heavy rain on 9 September, ending a dry spell that had lasted since the middle of August. The drought of the previous winter and spring and the hot spell early in June had not been followed by a particularly warm summer, with both July and August somewhat cooler than the average for the previous six years.[25]

Hodges found justification for his scepticism in the continuing high numbers of plague deaths in the week after the fires, with 6,544 recorded. In fact, that was a decrease of 444, the first since the epidemic had begun, and it engendered a burst of optimism, but in the following week, beginning 12 September, the numbers rose again to 7,165. That was to prove the peak and the next week saw a fall to 5,533 deaths from plague. Clarendon was at Oxford with the court and his relief at the news was obvious, especially as he had received a gloomy forecast from the Archbishop of Canterbury, who was still at Lambeth Palace. When he was given the actual figures, Clarendon replied in a lightly teasing tone:

I do thanke your Lordship with all my hearte for keepinge us wakinge all this night with the dismall newes of the continuance of the Bill, to the same number as the last week, with only an abatement of three of the plague.[26]

In fact the decrease was 1,632 of plague deaths and 1,837 in all. Here at last was a sign that the worst may have passed and that the epidemic in London was on the decline. The Bills recorded 30,899 deaths during September, the highest monthly figure of the year. The parishes within the walls suffered 15 per cent of plague deaths in the metropolis during the month, compared with fewer than 6 per cent during July, and far more were dying there of plague than in the Westminster parishes. But the worst affected areas were still those parishes around the walls, where between 40 and 50 per cent of all plague deaths were recorded during the summer months.

Despite the absence of some members of the medical professions, the corporation was able to put in place a team of 10 or 11 physicians headed by Nathaniel Hodges and Thomas Witherley. They not only attended the sick and advised the authorities on treatment, but also were curious to establish what they could about the nature of the disease. This led George Thomson and others to perform an autopsy on the body of a youth who had died of plague and later to publish the results. Thomson and other advocates of Paracelsianism established a Society of Chemical Physicians in 1665, in a direct challenge to the College of Physicians, but it was short-lived. Some of its members succumbed to the disease, demonstrating that their methods were no more effective in the face of a plague epidemic than were those of the medical establishment. Even with the results of the autopsy the debate regarding plague could not come close to identifying the cause of the disease and means of transmission, and therefore produce effective treatment. But medical staff had been appointed at the pest-houses: a surgeon at that built by the parish of St Giles-in-the-Fields, and a physician at the one erected by St-Martin-in-the-Fields.

As the members of the medical and spiritual professions came under a tremendous strain so did the parish officers, with poor relief a growing and unavoidable expense. Some officers tried to move suspected plague victims out of their parish, to reduce the cost as well as to contain the outbreak, but the numbers involved must have made that impractical in many cases. The purchase by one parish of a sedan chair with restraining straps suggests that attempts were made to move the reluctant ones elsewhere, perhaps to a pest-house. In social terms the epidemic in 1665 followed the pattern of earlier plagues, with the poor particularly badly hit, while the wealthier citizens had moved away and so were not available to pay the rates levied to help the victims. Put succinctly, 'the rich hast away that should supply the pores want'.[27] Edmund Berry Godfrey, a Justice of the Peace in Westminster, complained that those who had gone away paid nothing. He regretted that the collectors of the plague and poor rates did not have the powers granted by Parliament to those gathering national taxation, which permitted them to force an entry and distrain goods for unpaid taxes.[28] By December less than half the sums due on the poor and plague rates had been received in some parishes. In such circumstances the levying of extra rates was unlikely to produce money on the scale required, especially so in the less wealthy outer areas, where the crisis was far greater than in the City.

The shortfall in revenue from the rates was partly made up by voluntary donations from individuals such as Sancroft, who sent money that was divided among the officers of several parishes for them to distribute to those in need. Simon Patrick was given £50 by just one benefactor for the sufferers in his parish and £10 by the Earl of Bedford, who donated a further £10 to help the victims in Westminster. Edward Wood instructed John Pack to give the needy poor in his parish up to 2s 6d each, but when he discovered that in four weeks only 4s 6d had been paid in all he told him to donate £5 to the churchwardens for them to distribute. The authorities at St Margaret's, Westminster received £1,652 for plague victims during the year, £1,117 of which was from such contributions by 'honourable persons'.[29] In addition, charitable collections across the country were added to those taken on the fast days to provide a relief fund from which £7,664 was distributed between July and December. In addition, the lord mayor requested the livery companies to give to the poor relief effort one-third of the sums saved by the cancellation of their feasts and other entertainments. The aldermen authorised the levying of two extra years' poor rates and the chamberlain paid £600 per week during the summer to support parishes where the plague was present. The vestry of St Alphage's, London Wall, collected £53 4s from its plague rate, but received £70 from the City. In those circumstances it was agreed that money raised outside the City should be directed to the outer parishes.[30]

The problems of providing for the poor and the growing numbers of orphans were greatly increased by the policy of shutting up houses when plague was suspected, for those confined had to be supplied with provisions. That became a major worry to the authorities, who were aware of the threat to the poor in London 'whose Calamity is farr to be pityed than any elswhere, Not only by the raging of the Infection but even for the very want of Necessaries for life'.[31] Neighbours who could have provided help to those held in quarantine were likely to move away in alarm, afraid both of contracting the disease and of finding themselves confined within their own houses. The more houses that were shut up and the greater the mortality, the fewer were the numbers able to help those restrained in their houses. In an alley off Fleet Street almost half the households were closed at some stage during the epidemic, and there were 36 deaths among the 20 houses.[32] Concern was aroused both in terms of the difficulties of providing aid on the large and increasing scale required and because of the fear that it could lead to disorder, with those who were immured being compelled to break out to search for food. In practice, the policy of sequestration seems to have been gradually abandoned for economic reasons and the shortage of people available and willing to undertake the duties of watching and nursing in the growing number of infected houses, rather than because of anxieties about disorder. By the middle of August the numbers infected in St Giles, Cripplegate, were so great that the parish could not deal with the problem and so stopped confining plague suspects to their houses 'least the sick and poore should be famished within dores'. A month later Pepys spoke to as few people as possible when he visited the Exchange, 'there being now no observation of shutting up houses of infected'. Thomas Vincent, too, noted that the shutting up of plague houses came to an end, 'there being so many'.[33]

Added to the fear of hunger and neglect felt by those who were quarantined was anxiety about the behaviour of the nurses who attended them. A harsh critic of the system of confinement described them as 'the off scouring of the city' who were 'possessed with rooking avarice', watching for an opportunity to ransack the houses of their patients. Nathaniel Hodges was no less severe on the conduct of such nurses than on that of the apothecaries, asserting that they were 'barbarous wretches' who stole from those in their care. He also believed that they wilfully spread the disease, to increase the number of victims from whom they could steal, and even alleged that some had strangled their patients. The searchers who examined the bodies to establish the cause of death were also accused of pilfering from the houses of the plague victims.[34] Contemporaries regarded such thieving as especially reprehensible because the circulation of goods stolen from those with plague was thought to be a means by which the disease was spread.

Attendance at funerals was also considered to show disregard for the common good. In mid-July the lord mayor directed the aldermen to take greater care to prevent public funerals within the City, but they were not successful. A few weeks later Clarendon wrote to the lord mayor to demand greater efforts. As the numbers of deaths continued to rise, at the end of August Roger L'Estrange pointed to 'the incorrigible license of the multitudes that resort to publick funerals' as one of the causes. Pepys commented on the numbers going to burials, with 40 or 50 mourners at funerals that he saw in Southwark early in September. While such behaviour may have reflected a desire to continue to observe the normal rituals, he attributed it to sheer perversity, a defiance of the ban on funeral processions and assemblies, and he agreed with members of the parish vestry at Greenwich that measures should be taken to prevent it. The lutenist and composer William Smegergill remained in Westminster throughout the year and he thought that attendance at funerals was done 'in sport' by those taking risks out of sheer bravado.[35]

Pepys was also aware of the beggars in the streets. In October in Kent Street, which was 'a miserable, wretched, poor place' leading out of Southwark, he saw people begging 'sitting sick and muffled up with plasters'.[36] A rise in the number of beggars was a consequence of the increasing inability to provide for the poor indoors and effectively assist the plague victims. Evelyn went through the city on business during October, and whenever he got out of his coach he found himself 'invironed with multitudes of poore pestiferous creatures, begging almes'. In the previous month, while William Taswell's parents and his elder brother were lying ill at their house in Greenwich, he was ordered by his father to take some letters to London. Protected by angelica and 'some aromatics', the reluctant Taswell made his way to the city, where he encountered 'distressed objects … some under the direct influence of the plague, others lame through swellings, others again beckoning to me, and some carrying away upon biers to be buried'.[37]

Burials of victims should have been inconspicuous, as the plague orders directed that they should be conducted only during the hours of darkness. That system gradually broke down as the numbers increased, with too many dying each day for all the corpses to be interred during the short summer nights. At St Bride's there were more than 30 burials a day at the height of the epidemic. Furthermore, parish officers were faced with the problem of finding space in their churchyards and burial grounds, many of which were crowded already. In St Dunstan-in-the-West individual interments were replaced by burials in common graves from mid-August and St Bride's adopted the same practice shortly afterwards. Those two parishes had to dispose of 958 and 2,111 corpses respectively during the year, but the problem was even greater at St Botolph, Aldgate where 4,926 deaths were recorded, almost seven times the average annual number. There the parish had to resort to a 'great pit', into which 1,114 bodies were placed. As the parishes began to fill their burial grounds they arranged for interments in the available space in the New Churchyard at Bethlem. Pepys was shocked to see how the graves lay 'so high upon the churchyard' of St Olave, Hart Street at the end of the epidemic, yet more than 48 of the 194 burials from the parish during the year were in the New Churchyard, which was where at least 150 of the 355 whose deaths were recorded at St Benet, Paul's Wharf were buried. But even the capacity of the New Churchyard was not enough and so the city acquired another new burial place at Bunhill Fields, which was walled around by the middle of October. A burial ground was also provided at the pest-house in Soho Fields. At the height of the plague, the bodies were placed in pits, with up to 40 in a pit, but as the number of deaths decreased individual graves were dug.[38]

The use of mass graves was dictated not only by the lack of space, but also by the need to bury the corpses as quickly as possible and so reduce the risk of the infection spreading. This was made more urgent by a shortage of coffins. The officers at St Bride's stopped placing bodies in them from the last week of July, suggesting that only shrouds were used. Many families could not pay the burial fees, which were received for only 17 per cent of interments during August, September and October. The organisation necessary for rapid burials was made more difficult by the high mortality among the parish officers. Both churchwardens at St Bride's and three churchwardens and the clerk of St Giles, Cripplegate died during the epidemic. Yet in the intramural parish of St Thomas-the-Apostle rapid disposal of the dead was achieved. There were 152 burials in the second half of 1665, eleven times the average for the previous 20 years. Although this must have placed considerable pressure on the parish administration, all the burials recorded after the end of June took place either on the day of death or during the following one. In non-plague years more than a third of interments there were on the second day after death or later.[39] Nevertheless, across the city so many coffins had to be dealt with that some were left in the streets awaiting collection. Evelyn was shocked to see 'so many Cofines exposd in the streetes'.[40]

Londoners were also made aware of the high mortality from hearing the frequent passing of the carts collecting the corpses and the mournful tolling of the church bells. The carts were all the more intrusive because of the behaviour of their crews, which offended Thomas Rugg. He noted that many of them were 'very idle base liveing men and very rude' who drew attention to their task by 'swearing and cursing'. To John Allin the 'dolefull and almost universall and continuall ringing and tolling of bells' was a sign of just how bad the epidemic was. Even those who, like Oldenburg, had sealed themselves away and so avoided much unpleasantness, could not escape the sound of the bells. Yet he seems to have succeeded in being somewhat detached from the disaster. By the third week in August the only person known to him who had died was an under-postmaster, who 'lived closely and nastily' and, perhaps more significantly, had 'all sorts of people' calling on him to bring him letters.[41] Others, less secluded, knew of far more cases. Thomas Vincent later thought that he had heard of the death of someone known to him on almost every day for at least a month, and that perhaps as many as three-quarters of those he was used to seeing regularly had died during the epidemic. At the end of September Simon Patrick could think of ten clergymen who had died. A tenant of Dean Sancroft's was reported to be well on 18 August but died five days later and within three more weeks his entire family was said to have been 'swept away', except for one maid. Pepys heard that Will Griffith, an alehouse-keeper, his wife and three children, had died, 'all I think in a day'. Taswell visited a house where the mother was the sole survivor in the family, all seven of her children having died of the plague.[42] Those may have been unusual cases which attracted attention because they were abnormal, for a sample of six parishes shows that in almost two-thirds of affected households there was only one death, and that in only one-twentieth were there more than three deaths. The pattern suggests that many households were infected, but typically lost only one or two members. The example of St Dunstan-in-the-West shows that at a more local level there was a contrast between the main streets, where single deaths were typical, and the alleys and courts, such as Cock and Key Alley, where there was an average of three deaths in each of the 12 infected houses.[43] This may well have been because the wealthier citizens living in the principal thoroughfares were those who had gone away, leaving much-reduced households consisting of just one or two servants to take care of the property. That is what Taswell's family did, entrusting the house to a 'good old faithful servant'; she contracted the plague, but recovered, and the only death in the house was that of a man-servant.[44]

As the high mortality continued, conversations naturally included exchanges of information about who had died or been taken ill. Pepys found this a depressing aspect of going around London, noting at the end of August that 'everybody's looks and discourse in the street is of death and nothing else', and again later that he overheard 'so many sad stories ... everybody talking of this dead, and that man sick, and so many in this place, and so many in that'. Lady Giffard, too, was dismayed by the almost constant reports of victims, with 'people coming in like Job's messengers all day, with one sad story before another was ended'. Given the disruption of social intercourse there was much uncertainty, leading to false reports. Patrick had to correct his list of deceased clergymen, one minister reported dead was still alive, although his curate was not; and the rector of St Andrew's, Holborn, had not died but gone away.[45]

At times of uncertainty, sudden death and high anxiety, suspicions were quickly aroused. The Fenchurch Street house of Alexander Burnet, a physician, was one of the first in the city to be infected with plague when his servant William Passon died from the disease. Although Burnet was respected by his neighbours for reacting swiftly and causing the house to be shut up, a rumour spread that he had killed Passon, and this became so widely reported that the doctor felt compelled to place a denial in *The Intelligencer*. He also showed Pepys the note from the master of the pest-house certifying that Passon had a bubo on his groin and two spots on his thigh, providing clear evidence, as Pepys agreed, that he had died of the plague.[46]

Such swellings of the lymph nodes, commonly in the groin but perhaps in the armpit or on the neck, made the cause of death evident, and were accepted by the searchers as proof of a plague death. John Allin's close friend Peter Smith died within four days of being taken ill, first having a fever and then developing a swelling under his ear. The fever and neurological and psychological disturbances that the victim suffered often produced delirium accompanied by erratic and uncontrollable behaviour and loud shrieking. The fear that the disease engendered was succinctly expressed by Allin: 'It is a greate mercy now counted to dye of another disease.'[47]

Unusually high numbers of deaths from other diseases were recorded in the Bills throughout the period of the epidemic. This may have been due partly to a lack of nursing because of a fear of going near anyone who was ill, in case plague was the cause. The disruption resulting from the conditions is likely to have increased the number of deaths among those who were vulnerable through age or illness, but it is improbable that it produced a thirty-fold increase in deaths from 'surfeit'. Specific cases also cast doubt on the reliability of some attributions. For example, it seems unlikely that 'dropsy' caused the death of the parish clerk of St Giles, Cripplegate and his wife, who died on the same day. Deliberate misidentification of the cause of death to reduce the number entered as attributable to plague must partly account for the apparent increase in non-plague deaths. The pattern of such deaths was similar to those from plague, with the weekly numbers steadily increasing until the end of August and beginning of September, when they were three times the level recorded in June and more than four times the average for that time of year. Fever and spotted fever accounted for 36 per cent of the 13,741 non-plague deaths entered in July, August and September, and consumption for a further 12 per cent. Those attributed to spotted fever during the summer months were twenty times higher than the average of recent years. The numbers for all three categories declined thereafter as plague deaths fell, but those succumbing to fevers fell to 21 per cent of non-plague deaths, while the proportion of consumption victims remained at the same level.[48]

From 4,327 deaths from plague in the week ending 10 October there was a steady decrease to just 1,031 four weeks later. However, the growing optimism was checked by the returns for the next week, 1–7 November, when there was a sharp rise to 1,414 plague deaths, which Pepys noted 'makes us all sad'. He had expected an increase during the previous week, which in fact had seen a fall of 390 plague deaths, although without giving a reason for his pessimism. The increase was attributed to a premature return by some of those who had left earlier, increasing the size of the population at risk from infection. Those who returned to London doubtless wished to get back to normal as soon as possible, with economic necessity overriding their caution, and they may also have been concerned by the vulnerability of their empty premises to burglary. Rugg noted that 'many thieves rob houses' and described how burglars had broken into a stocking cellar to steal silk stockings and fine linen, putting their booty into two coffins, hoping to get away unnoticed. They thought that carrying coffins was likely to go unchallenged. Despite their resourcefulness, those would-be robbers were caught, but the circulation of such stories were likely to alarm those who were away from home.[49]

The rise in plague deaths was also blamed on the unseasonably mild weather, but it proved to be short-lived, for the following week produced figures similar to those at the end of October, while the next return, ending 21 November, showed a sharp fall, from 1,050 deaths from plague to 652. Even so, the disease remained widespread, with 82 of the 130 parishes recording plague deaths during that week. It had been anticipated that cold winter weather would reduce the incidence of the disease and Pepys hoped that the frosty spell towards the end of November would bring 'a perfect cure of the plague'.[50] But that did not happen, for although the numbers of deaths from the disease continued to fall at the end of November and into December, they rose again in the second and third weeks of December. The four weeks following 22 November produced a combined total of 987 victims. During that period deaths from other diseases were below the normal level, but the plague deaths kept the total numbers of dead at more than 50 per cent above the decennial average.

The decline in the numbers of plague victims was not greeted with universal relief, for clergymen who regarded the epidemic as a divine punishment felt that the burden was being lifted before the full lesson of the need to repent had been learned. According to Simon Patrick the increase at the beginning of November was due to His wise goodness and should be interpreted as a warning, showing that 'wee are not yet so safe', as complacent sinners might imagine. Already there had been a falling off in the numbers in his congregation and so the effect of the increase in the number of plague deaths after several weeks of decline might be to 'rouse up dull Souls'.[51] The view of the Anglican hierarchy that plague should be seen as a punishment for sin and demonstrated the need for repentance was expressed in the Form of Common Prayer issued for use on the fast days, which also reflected the fear of widespread disorder, perhaps even rebellion.[52] Among other texts, it drew attention to the passage in the book of Numbers, which describes how a rebellion among the Israelites against Moses and Aaron was punished by God with a visitation of the plague. The connection between resistance to authority and the pestilence was clear. To emphasise the point a parallel was drawn between the defiance of Moses and Aaron and those in England 'that strive both with their Princes and their Priests'. Traitors had dared to lift up their hands against the Lord's anointed and so 'what wonder that there is wrath gone out from the Lord, and the Plague is begun?' That could be interpreted as a reference to the events of the 1640s and 1650s, as well as a warning not to countenance rebellion against the Restoration regime, reflecting the government's apprehension of political disorder at a time of suspected plots and conspiracies.

The threat posed by religious dissent could be lessened by the enforcement of the Conventicle Act, which provided for the imprisonment and transportation of those who attended nonconformists' religious meetings. Of the Quakers who were rounded up, 52 died of the plague in Newgate gaol and 27 more while they were being held on a ship awaiting transportation. They were on board for seven months, by which time the vessel had got no further than Plymouth, where permission to land was refused, and she was captured by the Dutch as she finally set sail for the West Indies. To hold in check the more threatening elements in the capital, Albemarle had at his disposal a detachment of soldiers quartered in Hyde Park and the garrison of the Tower. Neither force escaped the plague, with 58 of the soldiers from the Tower removed to a pest-house and a third of those in Hyde Park falling victim to the disease. Many of their officers fled to avoid the infection.[53]

Evelyn noted 26 sermons that he heard between 23 July and the end of the year. Both the texts and the explications reflected the Anglican clergy's interpretations of the epidemic. In his sermon on the fast day in October, Thomas Plume, vicar of Greenwich, drew on the Form of Common Prayer and preached on the plague sent among the Israelites for disobeying Moses and Aaron. Evelyn described the subject as 'the sinn of rebellion against Magistrates and Ministers'. Another of Plume's sermons addressed personal rather than political sinfulness, using a text from Colossians which explicitly mentioned 'fornication, uncleanness, inordinate affection, evil concupiscence, and covetousness, which is idolatry' as bringing the wrath of God on the children of disobedience. It was not entirely a wrathful God who was portrayed from the pulpit, however, especially as the numbers of victims declined. John Higham, rector of Wotton, liked the analogy of the story of the Prodigal Son, which showed that those who repented would be forgiven, using it on 8 October and 19 November. The need for repentance had to be recognised from the warning of the plague, as did God's mercy and forgiveness in limiting his anger by ending the plague and thereby reducing the number of victims. But some of the population may not have realised that they should be penitent, being reassured of their own worthiness by their survival when so many others had died. The clergy were aware of the danger of smugness and false pride among those who escaped the plague, based on the assumption that the sinners had been taken and the worthy citizens had been left. Evelyn particularly commended as 'a seasonable discourse' a sermon at Greenwich in December when the preacher drew on a text from St Luke's gospel which showed that those who died a sudden death were not 'sinners above all men', to make the point that those who had survived the epidemic should not condemn those who had not. Evelyn's own reaction to having lived through the year was to echo the words of Psalm 91, noting his thankfulness for His mercy when 'thousands and ten thousands perish'd and were swept away on each side of me'. He believed he had 'gon through so much danger, & lost so many of my poore officers, escaping still my selfe, that I might live to recount & magnifie' God's goodness in allowing him to live.[54]

Edward Wood also praised God for 'his mercyfull preservation of us in the midst of soe great contagion'. But he was aware that

God's mercy should not be taken for granted, writing to John Pack that 'as tis not goode to distract gods power in protecting you soe tis not goode to tempt god too far'. Wood regarded the outbreak as God's punishment and a means to attempt to 'teach us righteousnes', using the image of a destroying angel controlled by the Almighty and praying that God would 'stay his hand and send health amongst us'. There is no reason to doubt Wood's sincerity or his faith, yet his letters to Pack moved seamlessly from such sentiments to the practicalities of their trade in commodities.[55] Pepys's survey of the plague months was even more secular, for he noted that the epidemic had cost him money in having to maintain separate households at Woolwich and London as well as his clerks at Greenwich. That was alleviated on 6 January when his wife returned to Seething Lane. By then there was a general movement back to the metropolis, Pepys noticing that by the end of December 'the town fills apace'. Even Daniel Milles, the rector of St Olave, Hart Street, had returned by the first Sunday in February, being castigated by Pepys for leaving the parish before anyone else 'and now staying till all are come home'. Pepys's irritation was more than matched by those who had provided hospitality for apprentices who had been left behind, but who were unable to recover the costs from their masters when they had returned. Simon Romney's apprentice William Law had lived with Francis Taylor, a cook, during Romney's absence in the country and had died in Taylor's house. Yet Romney refused to pay not only the costs of Law's board and lodging but also those of his funeral, and had to be sued by Taylor for payment.[56]

There was a scare in December when the Bills showed a steady increase in deaths from plague. However, when the weather turned cold enough for ice to form on the Thames, it was assumed that the numbers would fall again. Pepys was concerned that if that did not happen the disease would continue into 1666. Evelyn, too, was cautious and even in the middle of January he was unwilling to bring his wife and family back to Deptford. They eventually moved there early in February. Richard Baxter returned to Acton a month later. The most significant return was the king's to Whitehall on 1 February, bringing a restoration of something close to normality for those who were economically dependent on the court.

Pepys's apprehensions for the coming year were realised, for although the numbers of plague victims declined, a few dozen burials were returned each week. During March and April the weekly average was only 30 plague burials, but the first three weeks of May brought a steady rise. Yet this increase did not cause the alarm that a similar rise had produced in the previous year, and the numbers decreased again. Throughout June, July and August the average weekly return was 36, with a high point of 51 in mid-July, and the number of parishes with plague deaths peaked at 21 in the second week in August. Almost 1,800 plague burials were recorded during 1666, making it the worst year for the disease in London since 1647, with the spectacular exception of 1665.

The annual Bill for 1665 covered the period 27 December 1664 to 19 December 1665, during which there had been 97,306 deaths, 68,596 of them attributed to plague. Contemporaries were sceptical of the numbers of plague deaths recorded, Clarendon speculating that the true figure had been 160,000. His estimate is implausibly high but is indicative of the lack of confidence in the figures presented in the Bill. The average number of burials over the previous ten years had been 16,600 per year. Graunt and Sir William Petty made estimates of the death rate in London that ranged between 31.2 and 34.1 per 1,000, excluding plague victims; in 1665, by contrast, the death rate was 195 per thousand. The figures are not entirely comparable as the population of London was somewhat smaller during the second half of 1665 because of those who had left to avoid the epidemic and the number of deaths. In addition, the problems of maintaining an accurate record were much greater during the plague, because of disrupted parochial administration and the sheer scale of the operation in some parishes during the worst weeks.

The actual number of plague deaths is difficult to estimate. The 'expected' number of burials of 16,600 should be adjusted to take account of the shrunken population from July to December. A rate assessment for Westminster in September suggests that 12 per cent of the inhabitants had left. Applying this proportion to the whole city for the second half of the year, but with a 'normal' mortality rate for the first six months, reduces the 'expected' number of burials for the year to 15,600. Subtracting that from the total in the Bill produces a figure of 81,700 for the 'excess' deaths, the majority of which were caused by plague and were either entered as such or concealed under other categories. But it cannot be assumed that all the 'excess' deaths attributed to such categories were in fact concealed plague deaths, for the patterns of burials within the parishes suggest upsurges of other diseases during the summer. The proportion of 'false' and 'true' attributions cannot be recovered.

Further deaths went unrecorded because some victims may have left London after contracting plague and died elsewhere, and not all of the population came within the jurisdiction of the parishes. The Jewish community was so reduced in numbers by departures and deaths that in the spring of 1666 attendance at the synagogue was 'much diminished'. The Quakers recorded 1,177 deaths during the year and according to contemporaries burials of members of other nonconformist sects took place 'whereof no churchwarden or other officer had notice'.[57] Parish registers record the reading of the burial service, not the names of all those who had died, and so some of those outside the Anglican church may not have been enumerated in the Bills. That is suggested by a comparison of the numbers entered in the registers of eight City parishes with their returns in the Bills, which in seven cases shows little variation between the two sets of figures. In other words, the numbers in the Bills were a record of those buried according to the Anglican rites. The only exception in the sample is Allhallows, London Wall, where 333 burials are listed in the register, but the

Bills have the much higher, and suspiciously round, figure of 500. The discrepancy between the two figures suggests that the system of registration may have broken down during the epidemic and that the number of deaths in the Bills is an estimate. Furthermore, deaths within the seven liberties outside the parish system were not included in the Bills.

Despite its imperfections, the evidence suggests an estimate of more than 70,000, and perhaps as many as 75,000, deaths from plague. This represented roughly 15 per cent of the population, and 17 per cent of those citizens remaining in London in the second half of 1665. Allowing for those deaths which went unrecorded in the Bills, it is possible that the total number exceeded 100,000, or perhaps 20 per cent of the inhabitants and a six-fold increase on the annual average.

The overall total conceals variations in the chronology and distribution of the epidemic. The peak in the number of burials in St Giles-in-the-Fields came in late July 1665, but in St Andrew, Holborn and St James, Clerkenwell, the high point was towards the end of August. In St Giles, Cripplegate, the worst week came in mid-August, and by the third week in September the numbers had fallen to only a little over a half of those buried at the peak, while in St Botolph, Bishopsgate, the greatest number of deaths was in the week ending 5 September. In Stepney the first three weeks of September produced the highest mortality of the epidemic. But the pattern cannot be interpreted simply in terms of the disease moving steadily eastwards from a source in the west of the city, for burials in Westminster also peaked in September.

The intensity of the epidemic varied. The worst affected areas lay around the edge of the city: to the west, in St Andrew, Holborn and St Giles-in-the-Fields; to its north, in St Giles, Cripplegate, St Leonard, Shoreditch and St Botolph, Bishopsgate; to the east, in St Botolph, Aldgate, Whitechapel and Stepney; and, across the Thames, in Southwark. By the 1660s the suburbs south of the Thames, including Southwark, had a population of approximately

50,000 and 15,533 deaths were recorded there in 1665, or roughly 30 per cent of the inhabitants. Dividing the number of deaths by the annual average over the previous decade produces a multiple of 6.4 for this area. By contrast, the 97 parishes within the city walls escaped relatively lightly, for although there were 15,207 deaths, the crisis mortality ratio was only 4.6. Indeed, those parishes which experienced the smallest increases in the numbers of burials in 1665 were generally clustered in the wealthiest part of the metropolis around Cheapside.

Not all of the badly stricken areas were outside the walls, for a group of four parishes just inside them, in the north-east of the City, had levels of mortality that were almost eight times the average, amongst the highest in the capital. Adjoining them, but beyond the walls, there were 8,390 deaths in St Botolph, Aldgate and St Botolph, Bishopsgate, compared with the annual average of 1,231, a multiple of 6.8 times the annual average, slightly higher than the 6.5 in the outer East End parishes of Whitechapel and Stepney, which had 13,364 deaths. Whitechapel and Stepney were large and relatively poor, with an average of 2.7 hearths per household as assessed for the hearth tax, and a high proportion of householders who were exempt from paying the tax because of their poverty, with as many as 70 per cent in Whitechapel falling into that category. The comparable figure in St Andrew, Holborn, and St Giles-in-the-Fields, to the west of the City, was approximately 25 per cent, and those parishes experienced 8,415 deaths, 5.7 times the annual average.

Generally, there was an inverse relationship between wealth and mortality, with the richest parishes suffering the least impact during the year. The 12 parishes with the lowest crisis mortality ratios had 5.9 hearths per household, while the average household in the 12 parishes with the highest such ratios had 2.8 hearths. The parishes in these samples were also markedly different in their population size, however, for the wealthier ones were small, while the 12 worst-affected ones were on average 15 times more populous and so contained a much greater range of household types. A similar contrast in wealth and death rates is apparent between the extensive parishes of St Giles, Cripplegate and St Leonard, Shoreditch, north of the City, where the mean number of hearths per household was 2.9, and Westminster, where the comparable figure was 5.0 hearths. The 10,738 deaths in St Giles and St Leonard produced a crisis mortality ratio of 7.2, compared with 4.7 in Westminster, where 12,194 deaths were recorded. The effects of the plague broadly reflected the distribution of wealth within the metropolis.

According to Clarendon's assessment of the Great Plague in London: 'The greatest number of those who died consisted of women and children, and the lowest and poorest sort of the people,' to which he added, 'not many of wealth or quality or of much conversation' had been killed. John Gadbury wrote in similar terms, that the plague destroyed the 'dregs' of society, but that the more 'noble' part of the population survived.[58] Despite the crudeness of their summaries, in social terms they seem to have been broadly correct. The ability to move away from London in time undoubtedly reduced the number of deaths among the well-to-do; to that extent the Bills served their purpose by providing a warning of the onset and escalation of the epidemic. In the wealthy areas, therefore, a high proportion of those who died during the epidemic were poor, their better-off neighbours having left. But even within a relatively poor parish such as St Giles, Cripplegate, where the economy was dominated by small craftsmen, 30 per cent of the burials between June and December 1665 in which the occupational category was recorded were those of servants and labourers.[59] Nevertheless, the plague had claimed victims from all sections of society. They included Sir Thomas Noell, a prominent merchant and former MP, Peter Llewellyn, who had been under-clerk of the Council of State, John Bide, an alderman for four years in the 1650s, and two of the members of Westminster Abbey choir. Among the artistic community there had been the death in 1665 of the sculptor John Colt the younger, in St Bartholomew the Great, which was probably attributable to plague, and Wenceslaus Hollar's only son was certainly a victim, and a sad loss, for he was described as 'an ingeniose youth [who] drew delicately'.[60]

Clarendon's reference to the deaths of women and children also needs to be modified, although it was not without some truth, so far as the impact on the female population was concerned. London contained more males than females and so in normal years male deaths exceeded those of females. In contrast, the pattern for 1665 shows slightly more female than male deaths over the whole year, and during the months of the epidemic the mortality rate among females increased more than it did among males. Before the outbreak there were 130 male burials for every 100 female ones in the parish of St Thomas the Apostle and 88 male burials for every 100 female burials in St Olave, Old Jewry. During the epidemic those ratios were markedly different, with just 104 male burials per 100 female burials in St Thomas's and 55 in St Olave's. The two parishes clearly had a different population structure, with males in the majority in St Thomas's and females in St Olave's, and in both the proportion of female deaths was much higher during the plague, a pattern which occurred in both rich and poor parishes. It may be that the composition of the population changed during the epidemic, at least in the wealthier parishes, where women housekeepers remained behind in houses left almost empty. The vulnerability of domestic servants may also account for the death rate among females, through their having to go to public places to buy provisions and to run other errands. The evidence for the impact on children is much less certain because of the inconsistencies in recording them, although it seems unlikely that there was a disproportionate upsurge in deaths among the young during the plague.

The Great Plague in London was undoubtedly a shocking experience that touched all the city's inhabitants in differing degrees. Pepys saw a great deal of the consequences of the epidemic yet could write at the end of the year that none of his immediate family or friends had died, perhaps forgetting that his aunt, Edith Bell, of the parish of St Bartholomew-the-Less, and his physician, had been among the victims. Thomas Rugg was even more detached, making entries in his journal regarding the progress of the disease and its effects, but no reference to the death of anyone known to him. Anselm Herford had come much closer to death and looked back with relief and gratitude that he had survived, when the entire family he had been lodging with had not.[61] To the Earl of Clarendon, who spent the second half of the year away from London, it meant a frustrating separation from friends, prompting him to ask, 'Are wee always to be separated and never meete agayne?' The disruption of which he wrote was a consequence of dispersal; to many families it was brought by death. In St Giles, Cripplegate Felix Bragg, his wife and daughter were buried on the same day; four children from one family were interred within six days; and in the space of four days the parish clerk recorded the burials of Thomas Crawley, his wife, son, two daughters and a journeyman who worked for him.[62] Experiences such as those made up a complex pattern of death and upheaval, concentrated into seven months, varying between households and from one part of the capital to another. Other diseases may have contributed, but plague was the predominant killer in an epidemic that produced more deaths in London in a single year than ever before.

17

THE PLAGUE DISSECTED

The government's preventive policies were put in place only when plague threatened and others dealing with the effects of the disease once it had erupted. While Graunt's pioneering analysis drew attention to some of the characteristics of an outbreak of plague, there was no reason to reconsider the regulations in the intervals between the major epidemics. Only when they were put to the test could their effectiveness be assessed and, if found wanting, modified strategies could be devised. Thus, during the mid-1660s the government first ordered the implementation of the measures previously employed, and then was forced to reappraise them, as the epidemic produced both large numbers of deaths and economic dislocation, affecting its own revenues and ability to carry on the war with the Dutch.

All had failed: the naval blockade, household quarantine, guarding infected houses, taking victims to the pest-houses, issuing and checking health passes, demolishing buildings, cleaning streets, filling potholes and repairing pavements, moving rubbish heaps, fumigating houses, expelling beggars and evicting poor tenants, burning bonfires in the streets, killing animals, sniffing pomanders, taking potions prescribed by doctors and dispensed by apothecaries, prayer, fasting and berating congregations for their sins. State, church, city and justices had not protected those whom they governed from the foulest of diseases, which had been afflicting London for more than 300 years. Not surprisingly, the failure of the measures taken to contain the outbreak in the capital led to questioning of their value; the policy of isolating suspects in their houses especially was criticised. Its social unfairness was one aspect that aroused hostility, with the few who gave the 'Cruel Direction' to shut up houses able to retire to their 'Country-Gardens', leaving 'many thousand poor Innocents' to be incarcerated, with only such allowance for subsistence as the parish could afford. Why could the procedure not be applied uniformly? Thus, if someone died who had attended a meeting of the parish vestry, then surely 'the doors should be shut upon the Assembly', or the others who had been there ought to be quarantined in their houses. This was presumably the logic behind an attempt to shut up the lord mayor's own house in St Helen's, Bishopsgate, for which several men were bound over to appear at the sessions.[1]

Those who were likely to be condemned to a 'miserable, noisome, melancholy, close imprisonment' in their houses were motivated by the same sense of self-preservation as those who imposed the policy and then withdrew to safety. The author of *The Shutting up Infected Houses as it is practised in England Soberly Debated* pointed out that they, too, had recourse to flight, thereby 'scattering the infection along the streets' as they went and leaving their families to the support of the parish. Shutting up a house had to be done quickly once the plague had been identified, if the action was to be effective. Allowing the occupants to continue to circulate and buy provisions risked spreading the disease. But swift action would mean that those who were confined to their houses would be unprepared and reliant on what could be supplied to them. This was one of the reasons for a reluctance to admit to a suspicious illness and so it often happened that a house was not closed until an occupant had died, probably after the infection had been spread. Such lack of confidence in the arrangements for feeding and nursing the sick made enforcement of the policy difficult.

But this could be overcome, it was argued in one report, by the provision of medical assistance and payments to compensate those who were incarcerated for the loss of their earnings. These could be drawn from a fund administered by commissioners approved by the king.[2]

Even if such practicalities could be managed efficiently, the basis of the practice was still open to question, especially the confinement of those who were healthy with those who were sick. With such a virulent disease, to sequester the occupants in their houses was to put their lives at risk and almost inevitably to increase the death toll. This was partly because to seal up a house for the statutory 40 days created the conditions which were thought to facilitate the spread of plague. The 'unquenchable stench, and fest' produced would invariably be dispersed through the windows, or when the doors were unsealed to admit the searchers and bearers. This exposed a major contradiction in the measures taken against the disease, enjoining cleanliness wherever possible and yet creating an insanitary environment by compelling people to remain together in a confined space. The conditions thought to favour plague were to be found in the very houses that were sealed in order to prevent its transmission, so that the 'Infection may have killed its thousands, but shutting up hath killed its ten thousands.'[3] As low down the list as the 'Fifth Reason against shutting Men in infected Houses' was the following:

> ...imagine Infection it self penned into a rage and fury ready upon the least passage through a door or window to break out and choak a whole street, as that will in a while a City, and that a Kingdome; and this infection growing stronger by the Leaveless despair of the poor Inhabitants, the Rooms hung with Cobweb, the Flowre having dust and rubbish enough to bury the Infected, the Meat stinking in the Pantry, and the Beer soweing in the Cellar, while the people rot in their several Chambers; the Cloaths when clean infected by

the owners, and now being foul infecting them ... the Air they breath subtly conveying death that way it did formerly life, the water stinking and readier to provoke the flame within, then to quench it.

Not only were the environmental conditions conducive to the spread of plague, but so too were the psychological ones. Nathaniel Hodges wrote that 'the consternation of those who were separated from all society, unless with the infected, was inexpressible' and he believed that this 'made them but an easier prey to the devouring enemy'. Their gloom could not but be intensified when their incarceration was prolonged if, for example, a new case was suspected in a house just before the period of quarantine was due to end, requiring all the occupants to endure a further term. Hodges poured out his righteous indignation against the practice, which he regarded as 'abhorrent to religion and humanity'. William Boghurst drew similar conclusions, noting that being shut up 'bred a sad apprehension and consternation' among those who were confined, and that 'one friend growing melancholy for another' in those circumstances was a reason for the plague spreading through a family.[4]

The views of senior churchmen were expressed in the 'Exhortation Fit for the Time' that accompanied the *Form of Common Prayer* for the fast days. Sinfulness was still to be blamed for the epidemic; there was too much scandal, fornication, swearing, blasphemy, licentiousness and profaneness, which were all part of the causes of plague. The Exhortation enjoined sensible behaviour and condemned those who acted in a careless and fatalistic way by going 'desperately and disorderly into all places, and amongst all persons, and pretend our faith and Trust in Gods providence', for that smacked of Satan tempting Christ to throw himself from the highest point of the temple. Lessons could be learned from the way that leprosy had been dealt with and those who had the plague should act charitably towards their fellow citizens, not disobey authority by thrusting themselves into others' company 'whereby the mortality daily so increaseth'. Such behaviour was all the more reprehensible because those who were infected were 'the meanest among the people' and yet 'think scorn to keep their houses, though but for a short time; and break abroad they will, whatsoever come of it, no Authority, Orders, Laws, or Proclamations can restrain them.' While this was condemned as being a wilful defiance and disobedience of authority, the authors of the Exhortation also recognised that it was often necessary; for those who were incarcerated could be deprived of an adequate supply of provisions. Their conclusion was that care had to be taken to keep those who were ill separate from those who were well, but that close confinement was self-defeating, for those within the houses that were shut up 'will break forth for the succour of their lives' and no authority or orders could restrain them. The solution was for the wealthy to play their part in the process by making generous contributions towards maintaining the poor who were confined.[5]

Dissatisfaction with the policy appears to have been widespread, but what were the alternatives to the isolation of households, which was one of the fundamental components of the government's strategy? Sir William Petty's imaginative solution was a large-scale evacuation of London's population to the surrounding area where, he calculated, there were as many houses as in the city. Within a 35-mile radius of the capital 'large wide roomey' detached houses could be prepared, each having a water supply and a garden, and the inhabitants, who would be given seven days' notice of moving, could be transported to them in 'Convenient wagons or coaches'. According to his calculations this would be cost-effective. Whilst the expense of moving and lodging the evacuees would be £50,000, the value of each individual killed in the epidemic he calculated to be £7, producing a total of £840,000 if, as he anticipated, the next great plague of London claimed 120,000 victims. Although his solution may have seemed an impractical one, similar schemes of mass evacuation had been implemented by some Italian cities in the 1570s, albeit using less salubrious accommodation than that envisaged by Petty. The government of Venice had moved those citizens most at risk to 1,200 huts on an island in the lagoon, and some of the Milanese poor were transferred to huts made of wood or straw. Petty was evidently dissatisfied with the effectiveness of the policy of shutting up some suspected of having plague in their houses and moving others to pest-houses close to the city. He was also aware that the remedies of killing dogs, lighting fires in the streets and taking medicines were not 'considered sure'. He argued against the complacent, and chilling, opinion that the death toll in an epidemic was 'but a seasonable discharge of its Pestilent humour'. If the plague distinguished between those who supported and those who opposed peace and obedience, or between the bees and the drones, then 'the Fact would determine the Question', but if it destroyed without distinction then the country lost the productive contribution of the victims.[6]

Such doubts about the existing policies were not so strongly expressed by the Earl of Craven when, in February 1666, he reported to the Privy Council the measures that had been taken since the previous spring, and the difficulties encountered.[7] He was well placed to assess the effectiveness of the policy set out by the Council during the previous spring and summer, having supervised its implementation under the authority of the Duke of Albemarle. Writing four days after attending a meeting of the Middlesex justices, Craven first drew attention to the problems of disposing of the dead. The opening of new burial grounds had been limited by the Bishop of London's unwillingness to consecrate them unless the title to the site had been obtained. Practical problems had also arisen with interments in churchyards, for the price and scarcity of lime had restricted its use. Nevertheless, fresh earth and lime had been spread in many of them, and bodies buried at such a depth 'that we hope no inconvenience can from thence arise', especially as the graves were not to be reopened. Craven then considered the implementation of the orders concerning cleanliness. Those instructions regarding the removal of garbage from the streets had been observed, with the carts passing along every morning, also giving householders the chance to dispose of their domestic rubbish. On the other hand, he had to admit to 'many difficulties' in trying to get laystalls moved away from thoroughfares. Evidently that had not been too successful, but he was hopeful that the justices would be able to clear those that remained.

The success of the policies concerning beggars and inmates had also been mixed. While beggars had been removed and punished, the justices' instructions to eject inmates could not be implemented quite so easily, for although beggars could be dealt with 'according to law', many inmates held 'particular leases and contracts' granted by the householders with whom they were lodged. As with laystalls, tenurial rights circumscribed the ability of the justices to implement the Privy Council's orders. They were, in any case, aware of the consequences of enforcing a policy which would have the effect of making 'poor necessitous persons' dependent on the relief that could be dispensed by the parishes at a time when they were least able to provide it. Despite such reservations, at their meeting in February the justices had reissued the regulations directed at the removal of inmates, with an order stipulating that houses which had been divided should be reconverted into single dwellings and inmates expelled from all buildings, with the aim that only one family should live in each house.[8] In the same month the Privy Council directed the corporation to clear inmates from houses 'as a thing of very great Moment'. Just three months later the MP William Prynne pointed out that the implementation of the policy had caused discontent, with complaints that its effects would be worse than those of the plague. He also challenged the wisdom of the measure, pointing out that the expulsion of inmates would remove those who were too poor to rent an entire house, or who required only small and temporary lodgings, thereby depriving employers of their labour and reducing landlords' rental incomes.[9]

In his report Craven drew attention to the role of the pest-houses, which he regarded as 'the most probable means of hindering the spreading of the contagion', and the inadequate accommodation provided in them. He had taken the initiative during the epidemic to help to remedy the shortage of space in the pest-houses by acquiring first a lease and later the freehold of a plot of ground in St James's, Westminster. There he erected a pest-house, described in 1739 as 'thirty-six small Houses, for the Reception of poor and miserable Objects ... afflicted with a direful Pestilence, Anno 1665'.[10] Even with this addition, there were few places in the pest-houses compared to the numbers of victims. The one in Soho could hold just 90 people and the one in St Giles-in-the-Fields had space for only 60 in a parish with 'multitudes of poor'. Indeed, the five pest-houses around London in 1665 could hold fewer than 600 people. Given the burden of taxes and parish rates, the financial problems of the 'middling people' because of the plague, and the absence of the wealthy, simply maintaining the existing pest-houses was likely to be a problem, let alone further resources being required for their enlargement. This was a matter which Craven referred to the Privy Council, asking for aid, having described the role of the pest-houses during the epidemic as receiving those infected 'who were removable'. When appointed to the Council's committee for the plague in May, Craven repeated his belief that plague was spread not by the air, but by the failure 'in the beginning' to remove from their houses those suspected of having the disease. From his experience of the plague in London he concluded that the key to limiting an outbreak was to have adequate and well-provided pest-houses.[11]

While Craven's analysis of the role of pest-houses was sensible, his summary of the way in which the policy of household isolation was carried out was highly questionable, for he reported that there had been 'no complaints brought to the justices of any neglect therein' and that they believed that 'due execution hath been generally made of this order, having themselves made a particular observation in several places'. This contradicts both the general impression, expressed by Pepys and Vincent among others, that the system had not only been challenged but had actually broken down, and also the evidence of cases that had come to the justices' attention. They included an incident in which a weaver had torn the lock off the door of a house in St Stephen, Coleman Street, where a friend was quarantined; another involved a woman of St Giles-in-the-Fields 'opening and entring a house infected'; and examples of goods being moved from houses containing plague victims. Despite Craven's account, the Privy Council could hardly have failed to be aware of both the shortcomings of the system and the opposition which it had aroused. Nevertheless, its directions to magistrates in the early months of 1666 showed no change in its policy, although they did stress the importance of the pest-houses.[12]

The Council's procedures regarding plague were codified in its Rules and Orders, issued in May 1666 and directed to all justices, mayors and bailiffs.[13] They contained many regulations already in force, such as those regarding certificates of health for visitors and goods, a ban on travelling vagabonds and beggars, and the prohibition of public gatherings, including funerals and wakes, in any place where plague was suspected. Fire was to be provided 'in movable Pans, or otherwise' where 'necessary publique Meetings' were held, for instance in churches. The need for cleanliness both in public places and houses was reiterated, and it was ordered that pigs, dogs, cats and tame pigeons were not to be permitted to wander around the streets or go from house to house, but there was no requirement that they should be killed. Previous regulations regarding burials of plague victims were extended with an order that prohibited them in churches and churchyards altogether, unless the churchyard was so large that a space could be set aside for such interments and was surrounded by a fence 10 feet high. Despite objections to the practice of expelling inmates, the Rules and Orders included a directive that the law against them should be enforced.

A significant modification in policy was made regarding isolation, supporting Craven's conclusions by giving prominence to the role of pest-houses. It was ordered that a pest-house, huts or sheds be provided in every town, and that those who were sick should be removed there 'forthwith ... for the preservation of the rest of the family'. A house from which the sick had been taken should then be closed and guarded for a 40-day period, with warders appointed to provide supplies for the occupants, as well as to 'keep them from conversing with the sound'. When the house was opened, strangers could not be lodged there for a further 40 days, and no clothing or household goods removed within three months. By ordering the segregation of those who were ill, this measure did meet the objections of those who condemned the shutting up of the sick with the healthy. Of course, for the system to be effective the pest-houses had to be large enough to accommodate all plague victims, and in a major epidemic they were likely to be deluged. The policy also depended on adequate preparations and the prompt removal of those who showed the symptoms of the disease. If that were done, then such an eruption could be prevented, although recent experience showed that even cities which had large-scale quarantining facilities nevertheless suffered devastating outbreaks of plague, most recently Genoa in 1656–7 and Amsterdam in 1663–4.

A major stumbling block to the operation of the policy of household quarantine in the past had been the reluctance of those with plague symptoms to co-operate by volunteering themselves for internment. To meet the objections that those who were quarantined faced deprivation because of the inability of the authorities to maintain them, the Rules and Orders made provision for financial relief for those communities unable to support their sick. The justices were given authority to levy a rate on the nearby parishes without delay, to be confirmed at the next quarter sessions. Adequate support would not only reassure those who faced isolation, but also prevent the conditions which were perceived to be among the reasons for the spread of the plague: 'want and nastiness being great occasions of the Infection'. Here was a major reason for tying in the action against inmates to plague control, for they were regarded as being 'poore indigent and idle and loose persons' who placed such a strain on poor relief that 'the wealthy are not able to relieve the poore in times of health', and even less so during an epidemic. Without the burden which they imposed on the system, more resources could be directed to the poor who were sick.[14]

The justices' powers to set an emergency rate in such circumstances were not new but were a restatement of a measure that had been given parliamentary sanction in an Act of 1604. That Act was designed to overcome the problem of providing charity for the poor plague victims by giving the justices authority to levy rates within the affected community and, if the sums raised were insufficient, to extend the collection to the area within a radius of five miles. With that provision in place, those who were confined to their houses had no justification for attempting to go out, and so the watchmen were empowered 'with violence to inforce them to keep their houses' and given immunity 'if any hurt come by such inforcement'.[15]

The measures for financial assistance had not worked well under the strain of the epidemic in London in 1665, and the Oxford Parliament, meeting in October, set about dealing with the imperfections of the legislation. A committee of the House of Commons was appointed to consider the Act of 1604 and bring in a Bill that would remedy its shortcomings. The proposals were amended to some extent when they had been considered by the Lords, who queried clauses regarding pest-houses and churchyards and sought exemption for their own houses from shutting up. But on the day that the two Houses debated the Bill, the king prorogued parliament. Another Bill was introduced into the Commons a year later, reaching the committee stage by December, and the Lords at the end of January 1667, but it, too, was lost.

When it was debated by the two Houses, the Commons pointed out that experience had shown that the Act of 1604 should be modified. Yet the Lords again attempted to exempt their houses from shutting up, a measure not included in that Act, and were opposed by the Commons, who argued that it would weaken the legislation rather than strengthen it. So many houses came within the peers' jurisdiction that to leave them unsealed when plague had been identified was to endanger the public. The Commons held it to be unreasonable that 'the People's Safety should depend upon their Lordships Pleasure to shut up themselves', making the obvious point that 'No dignity can exempt from Infection.' While they had no intention of reducing their lordships' privileges in this case, what was to be gained from insisting on such privileges when 'Death equals all'?[16]

The failure to get the Bill through all of the stages in October 1665, and the subsequent delays in recalling parliament – which was first scheduled to meet in the following February and then in April – may account for the timing of the Rules and Orders. Although the seasonal pattern of the disease was known, they were not issued until May, when the numbers of plague victims were already rising steeply in such towns as Colchester. Only if they had been produced and distributed during the winter months could they have been effective, giving the justices time to implement such arrangements as the provision of pest-houses before the upsurge of cases during the spring. Furthermore, the Privy Council had little choice but to adopt the financial provisions of the 1604 Act if it were not to infringe Parliament's rights. The legislation did not allow for the provision of an adequate fund from which those sequestered could be supplied, so that they were not dependent on such money as could be raised on the rates, nor did it grant enough powers to those collecting the rates. The problems therefore remained unresolved, especially of how to raise funds when the wealthy citizens had left and the economy was disrupted; the rate-collectors feared for their lives in some streets where plague was present. Hence the reaction to the plague policies reported in London in 1665 was repeated in the worst affected towns in the following year, and the spectre of widespread popular discontent remained.

In contrast to the Oxford Parliament's failure to tackle the issue of raising money for plague victims, it did respond to the problem created by the dispossessed clergy and the crown's need for funds to pursue the war with the Dutch. The ease with which nonconformist ministers, who had been ejected from their livings since the Restoration, had been able to move into the pulpits vacated by the clergy during the plague (especially in London) alarmed the senior churchmen. Their concern coincided with the government's fear of sedition, the danger of which had been increased by the withdrawal from the towns of many of the wealthier citizens and magistrates. Parliament, however, reacted not by strengthening the powers of the crown, but with a further measure designed to curb the influence of the nonconformists. The Five Mile Act required the ejected ministers to take an oath not to take up arms against the King or to attempt to try to alter the government of Church or state. Those who refused were forbidden to live within five miles of a corporate town or their former parishes, or to teach as a schoolmaster. There was an assumption behind the legislation that the nonconformist preachers had the potential to foment discontent or even disorder, and that this was likely to occur in towns. A greater priority for the Oxford Parliament was to meet the government's needs for money to finance the war with the Dutch. It swiftly approved the levying of a further £1.25 million, to be raised by monthly assessments. Yet collection of the new tax and the receipt of income from the regular revenues were both circumscribed by the economic dislocation caused by the plague. According to Clarendon, 'Monies could neither be collected nor borrowed where the plague had prevailed, which was over all the city and over a great part of the country; the collectors durst not go to require it or receive it.'[17]

Reluctance on the part of tax collectors to venture into areas where plague was present was both understandable and difficult to overcome. Furthermore, interruptions to inland and overseas trade, the quarantining of goods, cancellation of fairs, closure of workshops, the absence of groups of prosperous consumers, fear of plague and the high death toll, all contributed to the economic disruption. Health certificates were designed to prevent the breakdown of trade, by providing an assurance that goods had been brought from a place that was free of plague. Yet from the summer of 1665 and throughout 1666 the disease was so widespread across southern and much of eastern England that the system could not prevent a reduction in internal trade, and of normal travel. Inns were best avoided even in places which apparently were free from plague, making long-distance journeys difficult. Carriers stopped serving towns where the disease was present, perhaps for their own safety, but also because of the regulations imposed by the communities which they served, involving at least a period of quarantine and possibly the risk of confiscation. Farmers faced a similar difficulty in reaching their markets because of the health cordons around infected towns, and a longer-term one with the reduction in the number of urban consumers because of the high mortality.

The health regulations were bound to disrupt normal business. The Scottish Privy Council introduced strict measures prohibiting traffic with Holland in 1664 and in July 1665 banning all trade with London and other infected places in England, both by sea and overland, subsequently extending the order until June 1666. The ports on the east coast of England also felt at risk and imposed controls on shipping coming from London and other infected ports, as well as from the United Provinces. While this kept some of them free from the disease, such as Whitby, Hull and Lowestoft, trade through them with their hinterlands was disrupted. With overland trade also subjected to restrictions, many places could not obtain those goods which they usually received from London.

The humblest items were in short supply, such as the wax candles for services in Gloucester cathedral, for when the existing stock ran out they could not be brought from the capital 'by reason of that calamitie which of late hath hindered commerce with that place'. Postal services, too, were affected, as carriers ceased to travel. In the issue of its *Philosophical Transactions* dated 3 July 1665, the Royal Society anticipated that the printing of the journal would be suspended, because the epidemic 'may unhappily cause an interruption aswel of Correspondences, as of Publick Meetings'. The government itself found it difficult to overcome the problem of delays in the postal service. As late as mid-October, mail from the north and west of England was still being sent to Oxford through London, producing delays.[18] The conduct of government business was made even more complex by the dispersal of its offices. The Exchequer and Tally Office were established at Nonsuch Palace near Ewell in mid-August 1665 and did not return until the following January, and the Navy Office was moved to Greenwich, the Court of Admiralty transferred to Winchester.

The interruption of trade with London caused disruption over a large part of the country, but that was not of course confined to domestic production, for the capital handled roughly three-quarters of English overseas trade. Cloth formed a significant element. Not only did it account for about three-quarters of the capital's exports by value, but many of the finishing processes were carried out there. Conduct of business and the capital's foreign trade was hindered by the absence of many of the merchants. Most members of the East India Company's Committee left, and so could not meet 'to consider and directe affaires'.[19] Trade was also curtailed as foreign governments prohibited vessels coming from London. The ban introduced by the French authorities on all shipping going to the British Isles was especially damaging, for France accounted for one-sixth of London's trade.[20] Furthermore, in January 1666 France entered the war as allies of the Dutch. Both coastal and overseas trade became more hazardous as Dutch privateers made inroads into English merchant shipping, capturing perhaps as many as 500 vessels. The policy of the privateer captains was to seize all vessels trading to or from England, regardless of nationality. The coal trade between the Tyne and Wear and London was seriously disrupted as the east coast was especially vulnerable to their depredations, but losses were not confined to vessels in the North Sea, for by June 1666 Bristol's merchants had lost 'the greatest part' of their ships.[21] Thus, the producing areas were cut off from their markets so long as the plague continued in London, and even when it had subsided there, cloth brought from those towns in East Anglia where the disease was still prevalent was held in quarantine for 40 days before it could be taken into the city. As trade declined, foreign merchants saw no reason to remain.[22]

Further dislocation was caused by the absence from London of the court, which was arguably the single richest market in the country. Those traders and merchants who supplied it with both routine provisions and luxury goods were separated from their clients for the second half of 1665 and were unable simply to send their wares to Oxford because of the regulations imposed there. Nor could they find alternative customers among the gentry, the lawyers or the City's affluent elite, for many of them had also left. They may, in any case, have had difficulty in obtaining supplies, for not enough produce reached the markets to allow buyers to be selective. The absence of the court and other wealthy elements brought unemployment and increased the pressure on the system of poor relief, especially in Westminster and the West End. In Edmund Berry Godfrey's opinion, some of the nobility forgot their debts as well as their charity.[23]

As trade and markets were disrupted and the plague threatened, so workshops were closed because of the danger of the disease, the absence of the proprietors and the difficulties in moving the finished goods. Such closures were carried out swiftly, almost literally overnight. When plague was identified among the inhabitants of the houses in Old Gravel Lane off Houndsditch, Edward Wood wrote to John Pack early in August and recommended him to close their hemp-spinning workshop there and discharge the workmen. Some weeks later he discovered that Pack was still taking sugar into their warehouse in Thames Street, and so directed him 'to keepe the shopp dores shutt ... 'tis better to loose the warehouse rent than to hazard your health'.[24] During an epidemic the risk to life took precedence over the drive for profit.

The economic impact of the plague was especially apparent in London. On 31 July 1665 the Archbishop of Canterbury wrote to the Bishop of London in support of collections for the poor 'in and about London and Westminster whose Calamity is farr more to be pityed than any elswhere' and he stressed that they included 'many thowsands of poore Artisans being ready to starve for want of meanes to be imployed in their callings, all trading being become dangerous and layed aside by reason of the spreading of the Contagion'.[25] In August Pepys estimated that at least two-thirds of the shops in his neighbourhood were shut. By late September only 'poor wretches' were to be seen in the streets; he would encounter fewer than 20 people while walking the length of Lombard Street, and grass was growing in Whitehall Court. The City had become 'like a place distressed – and forsaken'. Pepys noted, too, that there were 'no boats upon the River' and when he met Sir George Carteret in November he watched with interest Sir George's reaction when he saw 'the river so empty of boats'. The Royal Exchange was at the heart of the mercantile community in London, but before the end of July the numbers who were appearing there were 'very thin' and when Pepys was there at the end of August he thought that there were no more than 50 people in all. Thus, he was surprised a few weeks later to find as many as 200, but he noted another factor, which was that the crowd did not include 'a man or merchant of any fashion, but plain men all', and again in October it was being frequented by 'but mean people'.[26]

The absence of the wealthier merchants and goldsmiths was significant so far as the government was concerned because it hampered its attempts to raise money to finance the war with the Dutch. Few men who were left had the resources to provide loans or advance sums in anticipation of tax revenues. Pepys discussed the problem with the wealthy goldsmith Sir Robert Viner, and they came to the depressing conclusion that there was 'no money got by trade' and that those in the City who had money could not 'be come at'. Viner protested his own shortage of funds and told Pepys that the yield from the hearth tax in London 'comes almost to nothing'.[27] This was bad news for the City corporation, which was assigned the receipts from both collections in 1665 and that at Lady Day 1666 as repayment of loans to the crown of £200,000. As London provided roughly 18 per cent of the yield from the tax, the difficulties there were not in themselves catastrophic, but as the plague spread, so the problems of collecting the tax increased. By the end of 1666 approximately £100,000 had been received for the three collections, representing less than 60 per cent of the anticipated yield.

The impact of the plague and the war on customs and excise revenues was equally severe. London accounted for 65 to 75 per cent of customs revenues and 30 to 40 per cent of those from the excise. The sharp fall-off in trade from the Thames was therefore bound to reduce the receipts from the customs, as were the problems faced by the other ports, both from the decline in traffic with the capital and the activities of the privateers. Indeed, the estimated shortfall was admitted by a government auditor to be more than £320,000, while the farmers responsible for collection claimed that the figure was nearer £400,000. Their estimates indicate that the loss was not far short of the anticipated yield for one year. The deficit for the excise was not as heavy, but nevertheless the figure of £88,000 that was allowed for the effect of the plague was one-third of the average annual yield in the preceding three years. The loss of potential revenue was divided between that which should have been drawn from London, which was valued at £70,000, and the provinces, with £18,000.

The plague also interfered with the collection of the two assessments known as the Royal Aid, voted in 1664, and the Additional Aid, voted by the Oxford Parliament in October 1665. Revenue from the Additional Aid was particularly slow to come in, with only 59 per cent of the anticipated yield having been received by September 1667, its collection having been hampered by the effects of the plague. Given such losses, the net income of £281,000 from Dutch and French prizes was a comparatively small gain, although it had been hoped that such revenue would make an important contribution to the cost of the war.

With such financial problems the autumn of 1665 was a particularly difficult one for those struggling with the administration of the Navy. The Navy Board received no revenue for two months at the end of the campaigning season and the fleet was powerless to respond when the Dutch reappeared in the North Sea, so that they were able to cruise off the mouth of the Thames with impunity. Without money, the fleet could not be refitted and the crews retained, but nor could the seamen be paid when they were discharged. Most of them who were paid off were given tickets, which they had to redeem for cash at the best rate that they could find. Some were reduced to squatting outside the Navy Office, where Pepys was disconcerted by the 'lamentable moan of the poor seamen that lie starving in the streets for lack of money'.[28] Evelyn, too, was almost at his wit's end, as he wrestled with the problem of trying to provide for nearly 10,000 wounded seamen and prisoners. When the two men and Evelyn's fellow Commissioners for the Sick and Wounded talked things over in September, they were pessimistic about the prospect of raising money during the epidemic. Things were so bad by the end of the month that Evelyn wrote, 'Our prisoners ... beg us, as a mercy, to knock them on the head; for we have no bread to relieve the dying Creatures.'[29]

The plague impinged on the war effort not only through its contribution to the government's financial problems, but also by creating difficulties in provisioning and manning. Barrels were in short supply because of the number of coopers who had died in the plague or had moved away from London, leading to problems in victualling the fleet. The impact on manning came both from the number of deaths, reducing the potential numbers of sailors, and the risk of taking on board someone who was already infected. Isolation was virtually impossible to achieve on board a ship and so there was a danger of plague spreading through an entire crew. Both merchant and naval captains were understandably cautious when manning their vessels, not accepting those who had been discharged as sick and wounded and had since recovered, nor those from infected areas. The rejection of men from places known to have plague victims was a serious restriction, given the prevalence of the disease in the riverside parishes of London in the second half of 1665 and in many towns on the lower Thames and the Medway in both 1665 and 1666. Manning the fleet remained a major problem throughout the war.

The obstacles faced in the autumn of 1665 were tackled during the winter, as the plague in London diminished; the government could operate more normally and the wealthy goldsmith-bankers returned to the City. Loans were advanced to cover the immediate difficulties and the fleet was fitted out for sea in the spring of 1666. The summer campaigns saw a major engagement in early June, known as the Four Days Fight, and the St James's Day Battle in July. Then in early September came the Great Fire of London, which destroyed 13,200 houses and 87 churches in the space of four days. In addition to the value of the buildings and goods that were destroyed, which were worth perhaps £8 million, trade through London was again disrupted and tax revenues were lost. During the following winter the problems of finance and the provisioning of the Navy once more became acute. In the spring of 1667 the Navy Board realised that it could not send out the fleet but would have to rely upon patrols by guard ships. The folly of the decision was brutally exposed by the Dutch, who raided the Medway, captured Sheerness, burnt three warships and towed away the flagship, *The Royal Charles*. The war came to an end in July with the Dutch fleet cruising off the mouth of the Thames, paralysing the capital's trade.

Contemporaries ascribed the depression of the years 1665–7 to the plague, the Great Fire and the war with the Dutch, but without apportioning the effects of each. In fact, the coincidence of the plague and the fire with the war worsened the problems of financing the campaigns but did not cause them. An indication of the extent to which the plague disrupted the economy, and hence contributed to the difficulties encountered in maintaining the war, may be judged from the loss of tax revenue attributed to the epidemic. The combined shortfall in the customs, excise and hearth tax was approximately £525,000, while the total cost of the war was ten times that sum, at approximately £5.25 million.[30] The outbreak also delayed the collection of other taxes and caused problems with provisioning and manning the fleet that could not be completely overcome.

The impact of the epidemic was felt over much of the country, not just in London, and at many levels. Individuals suffered the loss of relatives and friends, household economies were disrupted by the enforcement of isolation and the loss of employment, many communities were affected by the dislocation of trade, and the government's efforts to maintain the fleet and wage war were impeded. The need for effective regulations was obvious, but the issue of the Rules and Orders in May 1666 came too late for those places which were already experiencing an upsurge of the disease. Preventive controls had also apparently been unsuccessful. Although effective in 1664, the regulation of incoming shipping failed to avert the outbreaks of the following years. Yet the experience did lead to an examination of the policies employed, which could be drawn upon in the future, should plague threaten again.

London experienced a remarkable recovery from the Great Plague in demographic terms. The collectors of the hearth tax reported that the capital quickly filled up after the epidemic, and Nathaniel Hodges's impression was that the high mortality was 'after a few months … hardly discernable'.[31] Those reactions are supported by the burial figures. The numbers in the Bills record a low of 12,697 in 1666 in the aftermath of the plague, which had carried off many of the most vulnerable, such as the elderly and the sick. The figure may also have been affected by the temporary displacement beyond the area of the Bills of some made homeless by the Great Fire. The number of burials in 1667 shows a marked rise, however, and was no lower than in 1663, and the mean annual return of burials in 1668–72 was 18,176, compared with 17,017 in 1660–4, a rise of almost 7 per cent. These were the years during which the houses destroyed in the Great Fire were replaced, with 8,000 erected by the end of 1672. The post-fire reconstruction brought in building workers and craftsmen from beyond London. Indeed, steps were taken to remove possible obstacles to their arrival by suspending the regulations restricting trading in the City to the citizens. Even so, this influx does not explain immigration on the scale necessary to replace so quickly the numbers killed in the epidemic.

Urban areas tended to attract young unmarried people, including many females who worked in domestic service, one of the groups which suffered high levels of mortality during the plague. It may be that much of the migration into London was accounted for by an acceleration of a continual process, with the replacement of domestic servants and apprentices who had died, and the re-establishment of households, as those who had temporarily moved away from the capital returned, bringing staff with them. Although most such incomers would have been in the age group that experienced low mortality in normal conditions, and so would not be well represented in the burial record, those who remained, married and had children would have been recorded when their deaths, or those of their infants, were registered. Thus, the numbers of burials may provide a reliable guide to the size of the population, and an indicator that, despite the scale of the mortality, the plague produced only a short-term loss of numbers in London. Such a swift recovery supports John Graunt's conclusion that the population attained its former size by the second year after a major epidemic.[32]

It may be that those who moved to London thought that they would be safer from the pestilence there than in their own region. The plague struck many towns and villages in South East England, East Anglia and eastern England, as far north as Northumberland, in 1665 and again in 1666 after a lull over the winter. The west country, Wales and the Marches, the West Midlands and northern England west of the Pennines largely escaped. From experience, it would have been thought that London's devastating epidemic would not recur in the following year, at least not with the same vehemence, while the places which had not yet suffered badly probably anticipated a return of the disease. Southampton, Colchester, Norwich, Cambridge, Yarmouth and Deal were all to suffer a high proportion of deaths during the two-year outbreak. The regions worst affected were those from which London drew the largest part of its incomers; it seems likely that they were leaving a dangerous situation for a relatively safe one. That seems to have been the expectation of the Londoners themselves, for Thomas Sprat, historian of the Royal Society, wrote:

> Upon our return after the abating of the Plague, what else could we expect, but to see the streets unfrequented, the River forsaken, the fields deform'd with the Graves of the Dead, and the Terrors of Death still abiding on the faces of the living? But instead of such dismal sights, there appear'd almost the same throngs in all publick places, the same noise of business, the same freedom of convers, and with the return of the King, the same cheerfulness returning on the minds of the people as before.[33]

Sir William Petty, writing in 1682, still believed that it was plague epidemics in London, occurring on a 20-year cycle and each killing one-fifth of the inhabitants, that checked the growth of the national population.[34] Whatever the effects of the Great Plague, the disease could not have had an impact during the late seventeenth century because, unrecognized by Petty, it had already ceased to be a killer, with the last deaths from plague recorded in the Bills of Mortality occurring in 1679, at Rotherhithe. The column in which plague deaths were entered was removed from the Bills of Mortality in 1703.

18

AFTER THE PLAGUE

After the unparalleled mortality during the Black Death, the worst epidemics carried off roughly a fifth of London's population. The eventual response to those occasional but virulent attacks had been the plague orders. They had evolved gradually, were applied intermittently, reiterated in plague years and scarcely mentioned in the plague-free ones. Creating a policy was a first step; the application of those orders during a time of crisis was more challenging. The sweating sickness appeared and acted so rapidly that counter-measures could scarcely have been implemented quickly enough to have any effect. But the absence of the sweat as the years went by could have encouraged the view that plague, too, might disappear, as indeed it did, in the late seventeenth century.

Household quarantine became the core of the policy to contain the disease once an outbreak had been identified, with the confinement of the sick and those who had been in contact with them, and the closed houses marked and guarded by warders in the streets. There is anecdotal evidence that the sequestration set out in the orders was ignored by some citizens and neither the manpower nor the money was available to allow them to be universally enforced. The policy became increasingly contentious, as harsh punishments of fines and imprisonment were imposed on those breaching the orders on household quarantine. Such penalties were impossible to inflict on the poor and sick, and reflected the desperation of the Privy Council and the corporation that their orders should be implemented. Writers condemned it as cruel, disruptive and counter-productive, even alleging that incarcerated inmates starved because of the failure to keep them supplied, and that the disease was spread by confining the healthy with the sufferers in increasingly foul and polluted air. But the same could be said of pest-houses. The Italian writer Giovanni P. Marana spent many years in Paris and in his – largely ironic – observations on the European world in the seventeenth century he expressed the opinion that 'great and populous cities ... are like hospitals and pest-houses, where people crowd, infect and stink one another to death with a thousand pollutions.' On that topic his comments may have been perceptive and not wholly ironic.[1]

In the early seventeenth century it became the practice to issue the Bills of Mortality weekly, regardless of whether there was an epidemic, and they included many causes of death, not only plague. The disruptive impact of household quarantine on households and neighbourhoods encouraged falsification of the returns from the parishes to the clerks who compiled the Bills, with the number of deaths from plague deliberately under-stated. Health certificates, too, could be forged or copied. Killing dogs and cats and lighting fires in the streets were established aspects of the measures imposed during an outbreak that may have been less contentious, although they were criticised for being ineffective. Certainly, as the regulations were developed, they were socially divisive; the poor took the blame when the disease spread, for their mode of life as well as their reluctance to observe the instructions.

A mixture of frustration and co-operation in the Privy Council's relations with the city's rulers was a recurrent feature of plague epidemics. It cajoled the aldermen into being stricter in enforcing the measures, and they in turn badgered the junior officers in the parishes and precincts, who were faced with dealing harshly with their fellow citizens, including their neighbours, during the most difficult circumstances. From the Londoners' point of view the measures taken to prevent or limit the impact of plague were iniquitous and had failed, and the behaviour of those in authority who left the city was reprehensible, while the attribution of catastrophes to divine punishment for sin was irksome – to say the least – to the victims. The Privy Council and the corporation were exasperated because they felt that the execution of the plague orders and environmental measures by the citizens was not thorough enough. They were convinced that if only more effort was put into cleaning and washing the streets and carrying away rubbish dumped in them, then plague in turn would become 'decayed and unkempt', which was only being prevented by negligence.

Such reactions and tensions were not peculiar to London, or to metropolises. Disgruntlement with the failure of the medical profession to offer a cure was a common response. A plague tract related that at Parma in 1468, after a plague epidemic had abated, 'The medical men and physicians who had attended the patients were arrested by the authorities and thrown into the prisons, being accused of all kinds of murders and manslaughter, and frequently the money which the medical men had acquired with great exertion and work and with extreme danger to their lives was taken from them by force.' A private response was that of a Tuscan peasant who, around 1570, penned a poem which described an ideal society in which all the knowledge of physicians should be judged as vanities and society should 'do without doctors'.[2] The opinions of the poor people, who proportionately suffered the most from the disease, were rarely recorded and it was indignant writers such as Nashe and Dekker who expressed views on their behalf, although the recalcitrant behaviour of those who would not comply with the rules which the authorities set down for them conveyed their reaction equally well.

Contemporaries could speculate that perhaps the naval controls were effective and despite the experience of 1665, which appeared to contradict that, it seemed that only with an early and rigorous application of the naval cordon could an epidemic be avoided. The issue remained a live one, as plague outbreaks continued to ravage parts of continental Europe. They moved across Flanders and northern France between 1666 and 1668, with epidemics at Dunkirk, Lille, Laon, Beauvais and Rouen. Among the worst affected places were Dieppe and Amiens, which lost between 10 and 20 per cent of their populations. The authorities imposed strict quarantine measures, and the plague did not reach Paris.[3] A more severe epidemic devastated parts of central Europe in 1679–82, with Buda, Prague and Belgrade badly affected, Graz losing almost a quarter of its inhabitants, and Vienna suffering its highest mortality of the century, with at least 76,000 deaths.[4] Plague also struck Malta in 1675 and southern Spain between 1676 and 1682, prompting the Privy Council to put in place quarantine restrictions on shipping from Malaga.[5] But it was outbreaks in the early eighteenth century in northern Europe and the western Mediterranean that once more raised the spectre of an epidemic in Britain and led to the adoption of further counter-measures.

The disease spread northwards as the Swedish army retreated from the battle of Poltava and reached Poland in 1708–9, the Baltic in 1710, and Sweden and Denmark before the end of that year. Riga, Tallinn and Königsberg all lost a quarter or more of their inhabitants. A contemporary estimate put the number of deaths in Copenhagen at 25,000 in the space of six months in 1711, although that was only an approximate figure. At Stockholm up to 22,000 people died in a population of 55,000 and in Tallinn only roughly 10 per cent of the population remained in the city after the ravages of plague and the flight of many of the survivors. The Danish port of Elsinore suffered equally badly, with 235 houses described as 'deserted and closed' after the epidemic; almost two-thirds of the population may have succumbed to the plague. The disease also spread to the countryside and the rural population of Estonia and Livonia suffered high rates of mortality.

The epidemic reached the North Sea ports in 1712 and 1713, at Hamburg, Bremen and Stade.[6] As 10 per cent of imports into England came from Scandinavia and the Baltic lands, the epidemic caused considerable alarm, which is understandable. In December 1710 Jonathan Swift wrote, 'We are terribly afraid of the plague,' admitting that he had been fearful for the past two years. He had accosted Robert Harley, who was then Chancellor of the Exchequer, and begged him 'for the love of God to take some care about it, or we are all ruined'. Swift's concern reflected the fear that the prospect of a plague epidemic could still arouse more than 40 years after the last outbreak in Britain. In fact, action had already been taken, with orders in 1709 compelling ships from the Baltic to perform quarantine, but Swift thought that vessels were evading it. Anxieties were heightened by a report that the disease had broken out at Newcastle-upon-Tyne, although that proved to be false. Fears were aroused once more in 1712 when some London physicians became concerned that a fever that was then present was the precursor of the plague, and again in the following year, with the return of soldiers from the continent who were suspected of carrying the disease.[7]

Daniel Defoe referred to the fever as the 'new and unaccountable distemper' in an issue of his periodical *The Review* in August 1712, where he noted that it would 'be mortal, and … contagious'. In the following issues he felt the need to defend himself against criticism that he was being alarmist, worrying his readers 'with melancholy notions of the plague'. His defence was that he was countering complacency, for a similar fever had preceded the Great Plague, and plague had been spreading across eastern Europe in recent years; he expected that it would reach Britain in 1713. He also printed the Bill of Mortality for London for 12–19 September 1665, the worst week of the epidemic, because 'I think the thing a little too much forgotten amongst us.' In an essay in *The Spectator* in March 1712 the poet, playwright, essayist and politician Joseph Addison touched on those anxieties. Addison went to Charterhouse School in 1686, where one of his fellow-scholars was Richard Steele; the two forged a strong friendship and they collaborated on several literary projects, but especially the publication of periodicals. For *The Spectator* Addison created a country gentleman, Sir Roger de Coverly of Worcestershire, as a foil for the urbane metropolitan narrator of the essays in which he featured. When the narrator called upon Sir Roger before they visited Westminster Abbey, Sir Roger 'called for a Glass of the Widow Trueby's Water, which he told me he always drank before he went Abroad'. He said that the widow was 'one who did more Good than all the Doctors and Apothecaries in the County: That she distilled every Poppy that grew within five Miles of her, that she distributed her Water gratis among all sorts of People'. As for his own consumption of it, Sir Roger explained that 'he looked upon it to be very good for a Man whilst he staid in Town to keep off Infection, and that he got together a quantity of it upon the first News of the Sickness being at Dantzick'. Despite the fears expressed by Defoe and satirised by Addison, the outbreak did not spread to western Europe.[8]

Perhaps as alarming as the plague and fever in 1712 was the epidemic that brought death to the towns of southern France in 1720 and 1721. It began at the end of July 1720 at Marseille, reputedly when two dockers unloading wool from a ship that had come from Sidon were taken ill with bubonic plague. A cordon was quickly put in place around the city, but it had to be moved further away as the disease spread. By the end of the outbreak roughly 40,000 of the city's 90,000 inhabitants had died, and similarly high levels of mortality were experienced at Toulon, Aix-en-Provence, Apt, Arles and other towns. In response, in August 1720 the Privy Council directed that no goods or persons from ships coming from the Mediterranean were to be allowed to land, and that the quarantine orders employed in 1710–11 should be renewed. In the Thames estuary, quarantine stations were set up at Standgate Creek on the Medway, Sharpfleet Creek and the lower end of The Hope. The order ruled that some goods, including a wide range of textiles, feathers, wool and hair, could not be landed even on the completion of the 40-day quarantine. Because of trade connections, the regulations were soon extended to vessels from ports in the Bay of Biscay, the Channel Islands and the Isle of Man, and from September 1721 anyone coming from France north of the Bay of Biscay was required to produce a bill of health before landing, or to serve the period of quarantine.[9]

The government's powers respecting quarantine were reinforced by a further Act of Parliament, and the closure of a possible loophole by which crews of vessels suspected of smuggling could escape inspection. The ship which carried Luigi Marsigli from Livorno reached the Thames in October 1721 and had to perform quarantine, together with 40 other vessels. Indeed, the numerous requests for the release of ships and cargoes from quarantine that came before the Privy Council during the next two years indicate both that the procedures were enforced, and the extent of disruption that was caused. Partly to set an example and partly to discourage trade with Turkey, in February 1721 two ships that had been loaded at Cyprus and Scanderoon were burnt, together with their cargoes.[10]

In the autumn of 1721 the Privy Council turned its attention to the steps that should be taken if the plague reached London, although by then the epidemic in Provence was on the wane. Sir Hans Sloane, President of the College of Physicians, and his colleagues Richard Mead and John Arbuthnot were directed to investigate how the information recorded in the Bills of Mortality could be improved in order to obtain 'the earliest and truest Intelligence of the plague, in case it should break out'. The ministers of several of the largest London parishes were questioned regarding the condition of their burial vaults and churchyards, and the parish officers were instructed to make improvements to them. An estimate was obtained of the cost of erecting lazarettos, the corporation of London was consulted about earlier plague regulations, and the Privy Council also received a summary of the steps which had been taken in 1625 and 1665. The quarantine restrictions were published in the *Daily Courant* in October and orders regarding the keeping of pigs within the metropolis, and the state of several 'stinking Ditches about the Skirts of the Town', provided parallels with the precautions taken during the plague outbreaks in the sixteenth and seventeenth centuries. So did the proclamation of a general fast 'in order to put up prayers to Almighty God to avert that dreadful calamity ... from us'.[11]

Quarantining of shipping continued to be the major element in plague prevention, while overland cordons in continental Europe were also proving to be effective, in France and Castile, for example. If the behaviour of country people in repelling health refugees from London during an epidemic was repeated elsewhere, then such informal restrictions of movement were likely to add to the official ones in limiting the dispersal of people and their possessions. When naval controls were applied at other ports around the coasts of north-west Europe the source of the disease would be pushed further away and cities such as London, Dublin, Bristol, Southampton and Amsterdam could be kept free of the disease, for the infected fleas could not survive the long voyages from beyond the cordon. The absence of plague after 1679 did follow the pattern experienced in other cities of north-west Europe.

As in London, the last epidemic in Amsterdam, in 1663–4, was the most destructive. It had taken over from Antwerp as the hub of trade in northern Europe and when it and the other ports which traded with London succeeded in preventing outbreaks the risk was much diminished. Voyages from more distant ports, including those handling the growing Atlantic trade, were fewer and so easier to control, acting upon intelligence from the places of origin of the potential danger of plague. Likewise, as controls were adopted more widely and restrictions were also imposed along land frontiers, they created an effective barrier against the disease. When the Austrian empire enforced the strict closure of its borders with the Ottoman empire at times of risk, the danger from the overland route across Europe was greatly reduced. After the plague had retreated from western Europe, interest in its ravages was maintained through reports of travellers who encountered it elsewhere, and publications, which chiefly related to the seventeenth-century epidemics, especially the Great Plague of 1665. No such accounts existed for the eruptions of plague in Medieval and Tudor London. Yet alarm verging on panic did spread through the city from time to time. In the summer of 1741 Horace Walpole wrote to Sir Horace Mann, 'The City is outrageous, for you know, to merchants there is no plague so dreadful as a stoppage of their trade ... I am in great apprehensions of our having the plague: an island, so many ports, no power absolute or active enough to establish the necessary precautions, and all are necessary! 'Tis terrible!'[12]

Despite such anxieties, the plague outbreaks in England had come to an end. A popular explanation for the abrupt ending of the disease was that the foulness from which it was supposed to have emanated had been destroyed in the Great Fire, which was thereby seen as a purifying force. This ignored the obvious fact that the fire had gutted most of the City, but only a fifth of the built-up area, that the suburbs which had suffered the highest levels of mortality in 1665 had not been touched, and in any case how could a fire in London end plague outbreaks in other towns and cities? Despite such logical and apparently obvious factors, the notion gained ground and has persisted as an explanation for the fact that the Great Plague was the last one in England. Daniel Defoe was so irritated by the opinion that he felt the need to refute it. In his brilliant novel *A Journal of the Plague Year*, published in 1722, he wrote of the supposition that through the fire, 'as some of our Quacking Philosophers pretend, the Seeds of the Plague were entirely destroy'd and not before [is] a Notion too ridiculous to speak of here, since, had the Seeds of the Plague remain'd in the Houses, not to be destroyed but by fire, how has it been, that they have not since broken out?' Those buildings in the suburbs, especially in Stepney, Whitechapel, Aldgate, Bishopsgate, Shoreditch, Cripplegate and St Giles, which the fire did not reach 'and where the Plague rag'd with the greatest Violence, remain still in the same Condition they were in before'.[13] The explanation for the ending of plague outbreaks could be found in the government's policies on naval quarantine and similar measures taken further afield, but until that was fully appreciated there was every reason to feel insecure when plague epidemics erupted elsewhere in western and northern Europe, and such fears persisted even after they had come to an end.

In the early 1850s the scholar Rawdon Brown was transcribing and translating the correspondence of Sebastian Giustinian, the Venetian ambassador in early Tudor England, when he came across the following passage in a letter written at the end of May 1516: 'I had betaken myself to this village of Putney, owing to the case of plague that occurred in my house, in consequence of which, I was not admitted to the right reverend Cardinal, for the purpose of communicating your Excellency's letters ... until yesterday.' When Brown edited the papers for publication he added a note to the reader explaining that the letter was followed by a blank page, 'apparently owing to the confusion caused in the ambassador's household by the catastrophe alluded to' and he speculated that the secretary had omitted to copy letters which Giustinian had written to Venice for a period of three weeks. He then admitted that 'On coming to the blank page, I felt that there was something very wrong; and on reading what followed I closed the MSS. with a shudder, from fear of *contagion*.' That Brown, an experienced researcher in the Venetian archives, should have been so alarmed when he read the letter almost 250 years after the events which it described, and more than 100 years after the plague had receded from western Europe, is a measure of the fear the disease had continued to generate.[14]

Like Addison and Steele, Brown had been a pupil at Charterhouse School, on the site of the Black Death burial ground, and that association, with an awareness of Venice's sufferings during severe epidemics, may have contributed to his reaction to Giustinian's letter. The Carthusian house was closed in 1538 and in 1545 was sold to Sir Edward North, who demolished the chapel erected in 1349 and much of the priory, to make space for a new courtyard house. The outer precinct was not built upon and the two Carthusian buildings standing in it were demolished. Of the other plague cemeteries, St Mary Graces was dissolved in 1539 and was then 'clean pulled down' and replaced by 'divers fair and large storehouses for armour and habiliments of war, with divers workhouses, serving to the same purpose' and there was no remembrance of the role of its site as a plague burial ground. Pardon chapel was converted into a house by 1565 and by Stow's time the burial ground had 'become a fair garden, retaining the old name of Pardon churchyard'. But the building was reconstructed during the seventeenth century and the garden built over, so that the last tangible evidence of the Black Death in London had been removed before the eighteenth century.[15] The ending of a plague epidemic was not celebrated by the building of churches, as was the case in Catholic Europe, such as the five built in Venice (the best-known of which are the Redentore and Santa Maria della Salute), or the erection of plague pillars, which was done in the Austrian empire after 1680.

Curiosity about that aspect of the city's history gradually waned, but it revived during the twentieth century. The school at the Charterhouse was moved to Godalming in 1872 and its part of the site was sold. The almshouse remained and in 1941 a fire-bomb that lodged in the roof began a blaze which spread and burned most of the historic core of the buildings. Because of the charity's modest finances and the constraints imposed by the regulation of building materials after the Second World War, there was a delay before the restoration could begin. John Seely and Paul Paget were appointed as architects in 1944 and during preliminary work in the spring of 1947 they discovered an unexplained feature in the wall of the tower at the west end of the chapel. By the end of the nineteenth century it had become accepted that the almshouse's chapel was that of the priory, which in turn was that built on the Black Death burial ground in 1349. That was not supported by the evidence, particularly a mid-fifteenth century plan of the water supply to the priory from Islington, which included a detailed depiction of the priory. Nevertheless, that had been set aside. Seely and Paget realised that the feature which had been uncovered was a squint in what had been an internal wall, but was now an external one, which would enable the sacrist to take part in services in the chapel without leaving the priory's valuables and documents unattended in the first-floor room of the tower, which was indeed still designated the Treasury. They therefore deduced that the alignment of the squint should indicate the site of the high altar in the chapel, and that was duly confirmed by an excavation. The chapel's wall-lines were then uncovered. Sir Walter de Mauny had requested that he should be buried 'in the centre of the choir of the church at the foot of the high altar steps' and, with the knowledge which they now had, the architects ordered the digging of a trial trench. As Paget later wrote, this 'quickly confirmed our highest expectations, for there, sure enough, was a brick and stone built tomb with inside it a leaden coffin shaped in the rough effigy of a man'. When the coffin was opened it was found to contain the remains of a body and a *bulla* or seal of Pope Clement VI, granted to de Mauny in 1351, confirming that the body was that of Sir Walter, who had acquired the land for the cemetery and built the chapel. From that initial excavation, further work recovered the plan of the Carthusian priory in that area, corrected the assumption that the almshouse's chapel had been that of the priory – it was in fact the chapter-house – and provided the location and arrangement of the fourteenth-century chapel and later additions to it.[16]

The site of St Mary Graces also became available for investigation. Because of the difficulty of access to the river, after 1742 the Royal

Navy's victualling yard was moved to Deptford and the site was occupied by a government-owned tobacco warehouse. The Royal Mint was relocated there from the Tower of London in 1811–12 and accommodated in new buildings designed by James Johnson and, after his death, by Robert Smirke. The Mint was moved to Llantrisant in South Wales from the late 1960s and the buildings on the site were closed in 1975 and then demolished. The archaeological dig which was then carried out remains the largest excavation of a Black Death burial ground in Europe.

The discovery in the Charterhouse of the chapel of 1349 and Sir Walter de Mauny's body, the later excavations in Charterhouse Square and the investigation of the East Smithfield burial ground have provided a direct connection with the Black Death in London. Coupled with more informed research on the archival sources, they have helped to generate a new awareness of its onslaught in the mid-fourteenth century and the intermittent plague outbreaks which followed.

During the generation following the first attack of the Black Death the feudal system came to an end, freeing up the movement of people. After an epidemic, London's population could be renewed quite quickly by inward migration. Its revival was dependent on the city maintaining its growth and position in domestic and international trade, which it not only achieved but greatly strengthened from roughly the third quarter of the fifteenth century. The demographic catastrophe which hit London in the mid-fourteenth century was undoubtedly a major shock to society, but thereafter the disease, in all its horror, became an unpredictable but relatively rare visitor. Plague took its periodic toll of lives, but Londoners adjusted to it as best they could. That adaptability probably contributed to the hostile response to the regulations designed to cope with the epidemics, for the citizens could face those crises and resented restrictions being imposed upon them. The complex issues raised by a plague epidemic were not resolved before the outbreaks came to an end after 1665.

Despite London's dominance within England and growing prosperity, roughly 200 years elapsed after the Black Death before its population recovered to its pre-plague level and it began a period of sustained growth. London's economy was so resilient that it suffered no more than temporary setbacks during the various intermittent epidemics and it continued to gain ground over England's provincial cities. Each of the major epidemics killed more citizens than its predecessor, but the population had time to recover between the outbreaks as the city drew incomers from south and east England to replenish its own numbers. Even so, the long period between the Black Death and the last recorded plague death in the London area in 1679 may well be described as 'the age of plague'.

NOTES

Abbreviations:

APC	*Acts of the Privy Council*
BL	British Library
CSPD	*Calendar of State Papers, Domestic*
CSPVen	*Calendar of State Papers Relating to English Affairs in the Archives of Venice*
HMC	Historical Manuscripts Commission
LMA	London Metropolitan Archives
ODNB	*Oxford Dictionary of National Biography*
TNA	The National Archives

Chapter One

1. *Procopius with an English Translation by H.B. Dewing,* I, London, William Heinemann, 1914, pp. 455-65. Arno Karlen, *Plague's Progress: A social history of man and disease,* London, Gollancz, 1995, pp. 74-5.
2. *Procopius,* pp. 453, 455.
3. A.M. Sellar, ed., *Bede's Ecclesiastical History of England,* London, George Bell, 1907, pp. 204, 233, 248.
4. Edward Gibbon, *The Decline and Fall of the Roman Empire,* IV, London, Everyman, 1994, p. 419.

5. *Procopius*, pp. 457, 459, 461.

6. J.R. Maddicott, 'Plague in seventh-century England', *Past & Present*, 156, 1997, p. 9.

7. Giovanni Boccaccio, *The Decameron*, trans. Guido Waldman, Oxford, OUP, 1993, p. 7.

8. John Kelly, *The Great Mortality: An Intimate History of the Black Death*, London, Harper Collins, 2013, p. 160.

9. Leona C. Gabel, ed., *Secret Memoirs of a Renaissance Pope: The Commentaries of Aneas Sylvius Piccolomini*, London, Folio Soc., 1988, pp. 34-5. Girolamo Cardano, *The Book of my Life*, New York, The New York Review of Books, 2002, p. 10.

10. Benvenuto Cellini, *The Life of Benvenuto Cellini*, ed. John Addington Symonds, London, Heron Books, undated, pp. 47-51.

11. Judith Cook, *Dr Simon Forman: A Most Notorious Physician*, London, Chatto & Windus, 2001, p. 58.

12. W.H.D. Longstaffe, ed., *Memoirs of the Life of Mr. Ambrose Barnes*, Surtees Soc., L, 1867, p. 38.

13. Mervyn Horder, ed., *Memoirs of a Mercenary*, London, Folio Soc., 1987, p. 18.

14. Steven Ozment, *Flesh and Spirit: Private Life in Early Modern Germany*, London, Penguin, 2001, pp. 159, 163-7.

15. John Mole, *The Sultan's Organ*, London, Fortune Books, 2012, p. 89. Nicolas de Nicholay, *The navigations, peregrinations and voyages, made into Turkie by Nicholas Nicholay*, trans. Thomas Washington, London, 1585, II, p. 41.

16. George Bull, ed., *The Journeys of Pietro della Valle*, London, Folio Soc., 1989, p. 43.

17. Robert Halsband, ed., *The Complete Letters of Lady Mary Wortley Montagu*, I, Oxford, Clarendon Press, 1965, p. 432.

18. H. Edmund Poole, ed., *Music, Men, and Manners in France and Italy 1770*, London, Folio Soc., 1969, p. 184. Henry Matthews, *Diary of an Invalid: Journal of a Tour in Pursuit*

of Health 1817-1819, 1820, new edn Stroud, Nonsuch, 2005, pp. 37-9. Charles Dickens, *Little Dorrit*, Oxford, OUP, 1953, p. 15.

19. John Edward Fletcher, *A Study of the Life and Works of Athanasius Kircher, Germanus Incredibilis*, Brill, Koninklijke, 2011, pp. 117-23.

20. Rosemary Mitchell, 'Penrose [née Cartwright], Elizabeth [pseud. Mrs Markham] (c.1779–1837), writer', ODNB. Rosemary Mitchell, *Picturing the Past: English History in Text and Image, 1830-1870*, Oxford, Clarendon Press, 2000, p. 56.

21. S. Haensch, R. Bianucci, M. Signoli, M. Rajerison, M. Schultz, et al., 'Distinct Clones of *Yersinia pestis* Caused the Black Death', *PLOS Pathogens*, 6 (10), 2010.

22. L. Fabian Hirst, *The Conquest of Plague*, Oxford, Clarendon Press, 1953, p. 240. Katharine R. Dean et al, 'Human ectoparasites and the spread of plague in Europe during the Second Pandemic', *Proceedings of the National Academy of Sciences*, early edition, January, 2018.

23. Michel Drancourt et al, 'Detection of 400-year-old *Yersinia pestis* DNA in human dental pulp: An approach to the diagnosis of ancient septicemia', *Proceedings of the National Academy of Sciences*, 95, 1998, pp. 12637-40.

24. Haensch et al., 'Distinct Clones of *Yersinia pestis*'.

25. H.C. Dick et al. 'Detection and characterisation of Black Death burials by multi-proxy geophysical methods', *Journal of Archaeological Science*, 29, 2015, pp. 132-41.

Chapter Two

1. *Bede's Ecclesiastical History of England*, trans A.M. Sellar, London, George Bell, 1907, p. 89.

2. *Bede's Ecclesiastical History*, pp. 233-5.

3. J.R. Maddicott, 'Plague in seventh-century England', *Past & Present*, 156, 1997, pp. 13-14.

4. 'Fitzstephen's Description of London' in John Stow, *The Survey of London*, ed. H.B. Wheatley, Dent, London, 1987, p. 501.

5. *Chronicle of London from 1089 to 1483*, London, 1827, reprinted Felinfach, Llanerch, 1995, pp. 45-6.

6. James A. Galloway, ed., *Trade, Urban Hinterlands and Market Integration c.1300-1600*, Centre for Metropolitan History Working Papers Series No. 3, London, 2000, p. 31. Barbara A. Hanawalt, *Growing up in medieval London*, Oxford, OUP, 1993, p. 18.

7. Stephen Inwood, *A History of London*, London, Macmillan, 1998, p. 99.

8. W. Mark Ormrod, *Edward III*, New Haven & London, Yale UP, 2011, p. 111.

9. Reginald R. Sharpe, ed., *Calendar of Letter-Books of the City of London: F, 1337-1352*, London, HMSO, 1904, f. 158b.

10. Derek Keene, *Cheapside before the Great Fire*, London, Economic and Social Research Council, 1985, pp. 12-13, 20.

11. Helena M. Chew and William Kellaway, eds, *London Assize of Nuisance, 1301-1431: A Calendar*, London Record Soc., vol. 10, 1973, items 382, 383.

12. H.T. Riley, ed., *Memorials of London and London Life in the 13th, 14th and 15th Centuries*, London, Longmans, Green, 1868, p. 478.

13. Reginald R. Sharpe, ed., *Calendar of Letter-Books of the City of London: G, 1352-1374*, London, 1905, f. xxviii.

14. Chew and Kellaway, eds, *London Assize*, items 357, 364, 395.

15. Frank Rexroth, *Deviance and Power in Late Medieval London*, Cambridge, CUP, 2007, pp.333-5. A.H. Thomas, ed., *Calendar of Plea and Memoranda Rolls ... of the City of London, 1323-1364*, Cambridge, CUP, 1926, p. 223.

16. Walter George Bell, *Unknown London*, ed. E.R. Wethersett, London, Spring Books, 1966, pp. 143-6.

17. Chew and Kellaway, eds, *London Assize*, items 325, 365, 394, 396. Sharpe, *Calendar of Letter-Books*, F, f. 157.

Chapter Three

1. Ole J. Benedictow, *The Black Death 1346-1353: The Complete History*, Woodbridge, Boydell, 2004, pp. 49-52. Joseph P. Byrne, *Encyclopedia of the Black Death*, I, Santa Barbara, ABC-CLIO, 2012, p. 49.

2. S. Davis et al, 'Predictive Thresholds for Plague in Kazakhstan', *Science*, 304, 2004, pp. 736-8.

3. H.A.R. Gibb, ed., *The Travels of Ibn Battuta*, II, Cambridge, CUP for the Hakluyt Soc., 1962, pp. 472-3.

4. Gibb, ed., *Travels of Ibn Battuta*, pp. 470-1.

5. Benedictow, *Black Death*, pp. 49, 52, 60-7.

6. Benedictow, *Black Death*, p. 71.

7. Rosemary Horrox, *The Black Death*, Manchester, Manchester UP, 1994, p. 49.

8. Horrox, *Black Death*, pp. 43, 44, 47, 49, 64, 66, 70, 75.

9. William Naphy and Andrew Spicer, *The Black Death and the history of plagues 1345-1730*, Stroud, Tempus, 2000, p. 34.

10. Giovanni Boccaccio, *The Decameron*, trans. Guido Waldman, Oxford, OUP, 1993, pp. 9, 17.

11. Boccaccio, *Decameron*, pp. 9-10.

12. Boccaccio, *Decameron*, pp. 9, 14.

13. Boccaccio, *Decameron*, p. 9.

14. Boccaccio, *Decameron*, pp. 10-12.

15. Boccaccio, *Decameron*, pp. 12-13.

16. Boccaccio, *Decameron*, p. 13.

17. Horrox, *Black Death*, p. 61.

18. Horrox, *Black Death*, p. 58.

19. Johannes Nohl, *The Black Death: A chronicle of the plague compiled from contemporary sources*, trans G.H. Clarke, London, Unwin, 1961, p. 45.

20. Horrox, *Black Death*, pp. 19, 21, 22, 23.

21. Horrox, *Black Death*, pp. 35, 43, 53.

22. Horrox, *Black Death*, pp. 57, 61.

23. Horrox, *Black Death*, pp. 35, 43, 61. Mark Harrison, *Contagion: How Commerce has Spread Disease*, New Haven & London, Yale UP, 2012, p. 8.

24. W. Mark Ormrod, *Edward III*, London & New Haven, Yale UP, 2011, p. 305.

25. Jonathan Sumption, *The Hundred Years War: Volume II Trial by Fire*, London, Faber & Faber, 1999, pp. 19-23, 597 n. 27.

26. Horrox, *Black Death*, p. 131.

27. Michael Packe, *King Edward III*, ed. L.C.B. Seaman, London, Routledge & Kegan Paul, 1983, p. 182.

28. Ormrod, *Edward III*, pp. 142, 299, 303.

29. Horrox, *Black Death*, p. 130.

30. Horrox, *Black Death*, pp. 111-14.

Chapter Four

1. Michael Packe, *King Edward III*, ed. L.C.B. Seaman, London, Routledge & Kegan Paul, 1983, p. 185.

2. Rosemary Horrox, *The Black Death*, Manchester, Manchester UP, 1994, p. 63.

3. Horrox, *Black Death*, pp. 65, 114.

4. Barney Sloane, *The Black Death in London*, Stroud, History Press, 2011, p. 34.

5. Horrox, *Black Death*, p. 81.

6. Sloane, *Black Death in London*, pp. 34-6.

7. Sir William St.John Hope, *The History of the London Charterhouse*, London, SPCK, 1925, pp. 7-8.

8. Ormrod, *Edward III*, p. 358. Gerald A.J. Hodgett, ed., *The Cartulary of Holy Trinity Aldgate*, London Record Soc., vol. 7, 1971, p. 186.

9. Horrox, *Black Death*, p. 81. John Stow, *The Survey of London*, ed. H.B. Wheatley, Dent, London, 1987, p. 384.

10. Hope, *History of the London Charterhouse*, pp. 7-8.

11. Sloane, *Black Death in London*, pp. 47, 54.

12. Sloane, *Black Death in London*, pp. 34-5, 43.

13. Reginald R. Sharpe, ed., *Calendar of Letter-Books of the City of London: F, 1337-1352*, London, HMSO, 1904, f. 173.

14. Caroline M. Barron, *London in the Later Middle Ages: Government and People 1200-1500*, Oxford, OUP, 2004, p. 240. Anne F. Sutton, *The Mercery of London: Trade, Goods and People, 1130-1578*, London, Ashgate, 2005, pp. 96-7.

15. Alan Borg, *The History of the Worshipful Company of Painters* otherwise *Painter-Stainers*, London, Company of Painter-Stainers, 2005, pp. 7, 9. Sloane, *Black Death in London*, pp. 57-8.

16. Horrox, *Black Death*, pp. 65, 69, 74.

17. Horrox, *Black Death*, pp. 153-4.

18. Geoffrey Brereton, ed., *Froissart: Chronicles*, London, Penguin, 1978, p. 111.

19. Sloane, *Black Death in London*, pp. 36, 44, 49, 50, 57, 61, 63, 67, 70, 73-5. Frank Rexroth, *Deviance and Power in Late Medieval London*, Cambridge, CUP, 2007, p. 74 n. 17. Samuel K. Cohn, *The Black Death Transformed: Disease and Culture in Early Renaissance Europe*, London, Arnold, 2002, pp. 183-5. *A Chronicle of London from 1089 to 1483*, London, 1827, reprinted Felinfach, Llanerch Publishers, 1995, p. 60.

20. A.H. Thomas, ed., *Calendar of Plea and Memoranda Rolls ... of the City of London, 1323-1364*, Cambridge, CUP, 1926, pp. 224-5. Helena M. Chew and William Kellaway, eds, *London Assize of Nuisance, 1301-1431: A Calendar*, London Record Soc., vol. 10, 1973, item 418. Sharpe, *Calendar of Letter-Books, F*, ff. 164, 165v. Barron, *London in the Later Middle Ages*, p. 240.

21. George Holmes, 'Chiriton, Walter (fl.1340–1358)', ODNB. T.H. Lloyd, *The English Wool Trade in the Middle Ages*, Cambridge, CUP, 1977, pp. 203-4.

22. Sloane, *Black Death in London*, pp. 44-5, 105-6.

23. Christopher Thomas, *The Archaeology of Medieval London*, Stroud, Sutton, 2002, p. 101.
24. Michael Camille, *Master of Death. The Lifeless Art of Pierre Remiet*, New Haven & London, Yale UP, 1996, p. 155.
25. Sloane, *Black Death in London*, pp. 93, 95, 99.
26. Sam Pfizenmaier, *Charterhouse Square: Black Death Cemetery and Carthusian Monastery, Meat Market and Suburb*, London, MOLA, 2016, pp. 23-5, 30-40, 46, 117-22.
27. Pfizenmaier, *Charterhouse Square*, pp. 23, 47.
28. Sloane, *Black Death in London*, pp. 104-5, reworking the figure against a pre-plague population of 75,000.
29. Frances Stonor Saunders, *Hawkwood: Diabolical Englishman*, London, Faber & Faber, 2004, p. 88.
30. Sloane, *Black Death in London*, pp. 106-8. Horrox, *Black Death*, pp. 64-5.
31. Sloane, *Black Death in London*, p. 107.
32. Sloane, *Black Death in London*, pp. 104-5.
33. Barron, *London in the Later Middle Ages*, p. 239.
34. *Chronicle of London*, p. 60. Brereton, ed., *Froissart: Chronicles*, p. 111.

Chapter Five

1. Rosemary Horrox, *The Black Death*, Manchester, Manchester UP, 1994, p. 80.
2. Horrox, *Black Death*, pp. 287-9.
3. Horrox, *Black Death*, p. 289.
4. Reginald R. Sharpe, ed., *Calendar of Letter-Books of the City of London: F, 1337-1352*, London, 1904, f. 163.
5. Frank Rexroth, *Deviance and Power in Late Medieval London*, Cambridge, CUP, 2007, pp. 75-6.
6. Sharpe, ed., *Calendar of Letter-Books, F*, ff. clxviii, clxxx-clxxxii.
7. Rexroth, *Deviance and Power*, p. 77.

8. Sharpe, ed., *Calendar of Letter-Books, F*, f. clxxvi. H.T. Riley, ed., *Memorials of London and London Life in the 13th, 14th and 15th Centuries*, London, 1868, p. 250.

9. Sharpe, ed., *Calendar of Letter-Books, F*, ff. clxxix, clxviii, clxxi b, clxxxiv b, cxci b.

10. A.H. Thomas, ed., *Calendar of Plea and Memoranda Rolls ... of the City of London, 1323-1364*, Cambridge, CUP, 1926, pp. 228-30, 233-4, 238-40.

11. Riley, ed., *Memorials*, pp. 253-8.

12. Sharpe, ed., *Calendar of Letter-Books, F*, f. clxxvii b. Thomas, ed., *Calendar of Plea and Memoranda Rolls*, pp. 225, 232-3, 235, 236.

13. Sharpe, ed., *Calendar of Letter-Books, F*, f. cxcvii b; ccvii b; ccviii b. Rexroth, *Deviance and Power*, p. 82.

14. Sharpe, ed., *Calendar of Letter-Books, F*, ff. ccxiv, clxxvii b; *Letter-Book G*, ff. i, I b, ii b.

15. Sharpe, ed., *Calendar of Letter-Books, G*, ff. xi, xxix.

16. Robert S. Gottfried, *The Black Death. Natural and Human Disaster in Medieval Europe*, London, Robert Hale, 1983, p. 86.

17. W. Mark Ormrod, *Edward III*, New Haven & London, Yale UP, 2011, pp. 374-5.

18. Ormrod, *Edward III*, p. 387.

19. James Tait, ed., *Chronica Johannis de Reading et Anonymi Cantuariensis 1346—1367*, Manchester, Manchester UP, 1914, p. 41.

20. Horrox, *Black Death*, pp. 133-4. Ruth Mazo Karras, *Common Women: Prostitution and Sexuality in Medieval England*, Oxford, OUP, 1996, p. 109.

21. Richard West, *Chaucer 1340-1400*, London, Constable, 2000, pp. 83-4.

22. Horrox, *Black Death*, pp. 127, 139. Hannah Skoda, 'The 14th century . . .when things weren't what they used to be', *BBC History Magazine*, Christmas 2016, pp. 40-1.

23. Horrox, *Black Death*, p. 134.

24. Horrox, *Black Death*, pp. 127, 310-11.

25. Anna Montgomery Campbell, *The Black Death and Men of Learning*, New York, AMS Press, 1966, pp. 39-41.

26. Campbell, *Black Death and Men of Learning*, pp. 44-56, 65-7.

27. Campbell, *Black Death and Men of Learning*, pp. 56-60.

28. Campbell, *Black Death and Men of Learning*, pp. 67-70.

29. *A Chronicle of London from 1089 to 1483*, London, 1827, reprinted Felinfach, Llanerch Publishers, 1995, p. 65.

30. Horrox, *Black Death*, p. 85.

31. Barney Sloane, *The Black Death in London*, Stroud, History Press, 2011, pp. 123-36.

32. Sloane, *Black Death in London*, pp. 128-32, 141-2.

33. Sloane, *Black Death in London*, pp. 139-40. Samuel Rudder, *A New History of Gloucestershire*, 1779, new edn, Stroud, Nonsuch, 2006, p. 737.

34. Marjan de Smet and Paul Trio, eds, *The Use and Abuse of Sacred Places in Late Medieval Towns*, Leuven, Leuven UP, 2006, pp. 156-63. Christopher Thomas, *The Archaeology of Medieval London*, Stroud, Sutton, 2002, pp. 144-6.

35. Sir William St.John Hope, *The History of the London Charterhouse*, London, SPCK, 1925, pp. 6, 8, 44.

36. TNA, E362/2315. Hope, *Charterhouse*, pp. 9-10.

37. *Calendar of Patent Rolls, 1370-74*, p.44. LMA, acc/1876/D1/1.

38. Bruno Barber and Christopher Thomas, *The London Charterhouse*, London, MOLAS Monograph 10, 2002, pp. 28, 70.

39. Sloane, *Black Death in London*, pp. 142-52. Horrox, *Black Death*, pp. 88-92.

40. Edward Maunde Thompson, ed., *Chronicon Adae de Usk, A.D. 1377-1421*, London, Royal Soc. of Literature, 2nd edn, 1904, pp. 206-7.

41. Jonathan Sumption, *The Hundred Years War: IV Cursed Kings*, London, Faber, 2015, pp. 5, 27-8, 44, 62.

Chapter Six

1. Linda Clark and Carole Rawcliffe, *The Fifteenth Century XII: Society in an Age of Plague*, Woodbridge, Boydell, 2013, p. 1. Robert S. Gottfried, *Epidemic Disease in Fifteenth Century England*, Leicester, Leicester UP, 1978, p. 42.

2. Norman Davis, ed., *The Paston Letters*, Oxford, OUP, 1983, pp. 41, 201. Gottfried, *Epidemic Disease*, pp. 36-43, 47-50, 99, 140. J.M.W. Bean, 'Plague, Population and Economic Decline in England in the Later Middle Ages', *Economic History Review*, 2nd series, XV, 1963, pp. 427-31.

3. Henry Elliot Malden, ed., *The Cely papers: selections from the correspondence and memoranda of the Cely family, merchants of the staple, A.D. 1475-1488*, London, Longmans, Green, for the Royal Historical Soc., 1900, p.16. J.G. Nichols, ed., *Chronicle of the Grey Friars of London*, Camden Soc., vol. 53, 1852, p. 22. Sylvia M. Thrupp, *The Merchant Class of Medieval London*, Ann Arbor, University of Michigan Press, 1989 edn, p. 201.

4. Richard Barber, ed., *The Pastons: a family in the Wars of the Roses*, London, Folio Soc., 1981, pp. 201-2. Davis, ed., *Paston Letters*, p. 251.

5. Richard Grafton, *Grafton's Chronicle; or, History of England*, II, London, 1809, p. 68.

6. Francis Bacon, *The History of the Reign of King Henry VII*, London, Hesperus, 2007, p. 9.

7. Polydore Vergil, *The Anglica Historia 1485-1537*, ed. Denys Hay, Camden Soc., vol. 74, 1950, pp. 7-9. John Caius, *A boke or counseill against the disease commonly called the sweate or sweatyng sicknesse*, London, 1552, pp. 9-10.

8. C.L. Kingsford, ed., *Chronicles of London*, Oxford, Clarendon Press, 1905, p. 193.

9. Jon Arrizabalaga, John Henderson and Roger French, *The Great Pox: The French Disease in Renaissance Europe*, New Haven & London, Yale UP, 1997, pp. 30-1, 265.

10. Reginald R. Sharpe, ed., *Calendar of Letter-Books of the City of London: L, Edward IV-Henry VII*, London, HMSO, 1912, ff. 82b, 83.

11. John Stow, *Annales, or a general Chronicle of England*, 1631, p. 481.

12. Gottfried, *Epidemic Disease*, pp. 36-7.

13. Sam Pfizenmaier, *Charterhouse Square: Black Death Cemetery and Carthusian Monastery, Meat Market and Suburb*, London, MOLA, 2016, p. 44.

14. TNA, SC12/25/55, m. 55.

15. Arthur Burrell, ed., *Chaucer's Canterbury Tales*, London, Dent, 1908, p. 445.

16. J. Huizinga, *The Waning of the Middle Ages*, Harmondsworth, Penguin, 1965, p. 32.

17. Derek Keene, *Cheapside before the Great Fire*, London, ESRC, 1985, p. 20.

18. Thrupp, *Merchant Class*, p. 200.

19. Bean, 'Plague, Population and Economic Decline', p. 434.

20. Eileen Power, *Medieval Women*, ed. M.M. Postan, Cambridge, CUP, 1997, pp. 49, 51-3.

21. A.R. Myers, *Chaucer's London: Everyday Life in London 1342-1400*, Stroud, Amberley, 2009, pp. 51-2. Sharpe, ed., *Calendar of Letter-Books: L*, pp. 11, 37, 67-8, 104, 149, 180. Philip E. Jones, ed., *Calendar of Plea and Memoranda Rolls ... 1458-1482*, Cambridge, CUP, 1961, pp. 65, 73.

22. Clark and Rawcliffe, eds, *The Fifteenth Century XII*, pp. 6, 141-59.

23. Samuel K. Cohn, *The Black Death Transformed*, London, Arnold, 2002, pp. 66-8.

24. Joseph P. Byrne, *Encyclopedia of the Black Death*, Santa Barbara & Oxford, ABC-CLIO, 2012, pp. 67, 86. Charles Creighton, *A History of Epidemics in Britain from A.D. 664 to the extinction of plague*, Cambridge, CUP, 1891; Cass, 1965, p. 302.

25. Thrupp, *Merchant Class*, pp. 104, 111, 158.
26. Thomas Paynell, *Much Profitable Treatise*, unpaged.
27. Gottfried, *Epidemic Disease*, p. 74.
28. Carole Rawcliffe, *Medicine & Society in Later Medieval England*, Stroud, Sutton, 1995, p. 152.
29. John Fenn, *Paston Letters*, London, Charles Knight, 1840, vol.I, pp. 181-2; vol.II, p. 133.
30. Penelope Hunting, *A History of the Society of Apothecaries*, London, The Society of Apothecaries, 1998, p. 23.
31. Sharpe, ed., *Calendar of Letter-Books of the City of London: L*, p. 103.
32. Malcolm Letts, *The Travels of Leo of Rozmital through Germany, Flanders, England, France, Spain, Portugal and Italy 1465-1467*, Hakluyt Society, 2nd series, CVIII, 1955, pp. 110, 142.
33. Gottfried, *Epidemic Disease*, p. 40. Malden, ed., *The Cely Papers*, p. 16. Joan Kirby, ed., *The Plumpton Letters and Papers*, Camden Soc., 5th series, 8, 1996, p. 95.
34. Walter F. Sturmer, *John Lydgate: A Study in the Culture of the XVth Century*, Berkeley & Los Angeles, University of California Press, 1961, pp. 177-8. Alain Renoir, *The Poetry of John Lydgate*, London, Routledge & Kegan Paul, 1967, p. 80.
35. Kirby, ed., *Plumpton Letters and Papers*, p. 131.
36. Caroline M. Barron, *London in the Later Middle Ages*, Oxford, OUP, 2004, pp. 18-22.
37. Matthew Davies, 'Carpenter, John, (d. 1442), common clerk of London', ODNB.
38. Derek Keene, Arthur Burns and Andrew Saint, eds, *St Paul's: The Cathedral Church of London 604-2004*, New Haven & London, Yale UP, 2004, p. 36. John Aberth, *From the Brink of the Apocalypse: Confronting Famine, War, Plague and Death in the Later Middle Ages*, London, Routledge, 2013, p. 234.

39. Louis Lebeer, *De Geest van de Graveerkunst in de XVe eeuw*, Diest, Pro Arte, 1945, pp. pp. 52-3, 61. Klaus Wolbert, *Memento Mori*, Darmstadt, Hessisches Landesmuseum, 1984, p.69.

40. Christine M. Boeckl, *Images of Plague and Pestilence*, Kirksville, Truman State University Press, 2000, pp. 21, 40, 55-8.

41. Nigel B. Saul, ed., *The Age of Chivalry: Art and Society in Late Medieval England*, London, Brockhampton Press, 1995, pp. 45, 47.

42. Mark Ford, ed., *London: A History in Verse*, Cambridge, Mass, & London, Harvard UP, 2012, pp. 49-53.

43. Letts, *Travels of Leo of Rozmital*, p. 45. C.A.J. Armstrong, *The Usurpation of Richard III*, Gloucester, Sutton, 1984, p. 103.

Chapter Seven

1. J.R. Hale, ed., *The Travel Journal of Antonio de Beatis*, London, Hakluyt Soc., 1979, pp. 140-2.

2. Philip Ziegler, *The Black Death*, London, Collins, 1969, pp. 38-9.

3. Samuel K. Cohn, *The Black Death Transformed*, London, Arnold, 2002, pp. 62, 133, 226-7. Paula Suttner Fichtner, *Emperor Maximilian II*, London and New Haven, Yale UP, 2001, p. 101.

4. Frederick J. and Percy Furnivall, eds, *The Anatomie of The Bodie of Man by Thomas Vicary*, London, Early English Text Soc., 1888, pp. 147, 149.

5. Ann G. Carmichael, *Plague and the Poor in Renaissance Florence*, Cambridge, CUP, 1986, p. 121.

6. Jon Arrizabalaga, John Henderson and Roger French, *The Great Pox: The French Disease in Renaissance Europe*, New Haven & London, Yale UP, 1997, p. 36.

7. Furnivall and Furnivall, eds, *Anatomie of the Bodie of Man*, p. 206.

8. Paul Slack, *The Impact of Plague in Tudor and Stuart England*, London, Routledge & Kegan Paul, 1985, p. 214.

9. Sandra Cavallo, *Charity and power in early modern Italy: Benefactors and their motives in Turin, 1541-1789*, Cambridge, CUP, 1995, p. 45.

10. F.A. Inderwick, ed., *A Calendar of the Inner Temple Records, I, 1505-1603*, London, Inner Temple, 1896, p. 27.

11. Janette Dillon, *Performance and Spectacle in Hall's Chronicle*, London, Soc. for Theatre Research, 2002, p. 31.

12. Charles Whibley, ed., *The Lives of the Kings: Henry VIII by Edward Hall*, London, T.C. & E.C. Jack, 1904, I, p. 118. *CSPVen*, II, *1509-1511*, pp. 142, 151. Inderwick, ed., *Inner Temple*, pp. 28-9.

13. R.A.B. Mynors and D.F.S. Thomson, eds, *The Correspondence of Erasmus*, II, Toronto and Buffalo, University of Toronto Press, 1975, pp. 175, 182, 189, 206; V, 1979, p. 306; IV, 1977, p. 405.

14. John Hale, *The Civilization of Europe in the Renaissance*, London, Harper Collins, 1993, pp. 52-63. Mynors and Thomson, eds, *Correspondence of Erasmus*, II, p. 45.

15. Hale, ed., *Journal of Antonio de Beatis*, p. 51.

16. C.H. Williams, *English Historical Documents 1485-1558*, London, Eyre & Spottiswood, 1967, p. 189. R.A.B. Mynors, A. Dalzell and J.M. Estes, eds, *The Correspondence of Erasmus: Letters 1356 to 1534, 1523 to 1524*, vol. 10, Toronto, University of Toronto Press, 1992, p. 471.

17. Hale, ed., *Journal of Antonio de Beatis*, p. 100.

18. Mynors and Thomson, eds, *Correspondence of Erasmus*, II, pp. 283, 290.

19. Rawdon Brown, ed., *Four Years at the Court of Henry VIII*, London, Smith, Elder, 1854, I, p. 224.

20. Hale, ed., *Journal of Antonio de Beatis*, pp. 9-11, 104. *Letters and Papers, Foreign and Domestic, Henry VIII*, II, pp. 1133, 1160, 1166, 1188.

21. *Letters and Papers, Foreign and Domestic, Henry VIII*, II, p. 1476.

22. 'Roper's Life of More', in Mildred Campbell, ed., *The Utopia of Thomas More*, Princeton, Van Nostrand, 1947, pp. 228-9. Mynors and Thomson, eds, *Correspondence of Erasmus*, V, pp. 68, 89.

23. *CSPVen, II, 1509-1511*, pp. 426, 429.

24. *Letters and Papers, Foreign and Domestic, Henry VIII*, II, pp. 1237, 1242.

25. George Clark, *A History of the Royal College of Physicians of London*, Oxford, Clarendon Press, 1964, p. 54.

26. Brown, *Four Years at the Court of Henry VIII*, I, p. 68. Mynors and Thomson, eds, *Correspondence of Erasmus*, IV, pp. 391-2.

27. Paul L. Hughes and James F. Larkin, eds, *Tudor Royal Proclamations, Volume I: The Early Tudors, 1485-1553*, London and New Haven, Yale UP, 1964, no. 81. Peter Gwyn, *The King's Cardinal: The Rise and Fall of Thomas Wolsey*, London, Barrie & Jenkins, 1990, p. 441.

28. Eric Bennett, *The Worshipful Company of Carmen of London*, London, Company of Carmen, 1952, p. 14.

29. Gwyn, *King's Cardinal*, p. 450.

30. R.W. Heinze, *Proclamations of the Tudor Kings*, Cambridge, CUP, 1976, p. 104.

31. *Letters and Papers, Foreign and Domestic, Henry VIII*, II, p. 1276.

32. Susan Bruce, ed., *Three Early Modern Utopias*, Oxford, OUP, 1999, pp. 63-4.

33. Reginald H. Adams, *The Parish Clerks of London*, London and Chichester, Phillimore, 1971, p. 48.

34. Whibley, ed., *Henry VIII by Edward Hall*, I, pp. 234, 140; II, p. 56.

35. *Letters and Papers, Foreign and Domestic, Henry VIII*, IV pt II, pp. 1935, 1957, 2011, 4206, 4332.

36. *Letters and Papers of Henry VIII*, IV, pp. 4391, 4403, 4409, 4440, 4477.

37. *State Papers: Volume I, King Henry the Eighth, Parts 1. and 2.*, London, 1830, pp. 385-6. Adams, *Parish Clerks*, p. 48.
38. Adams, *Parish Clerks*, p. 49.
39. *Letters and Papers of Henry VIII*, IX, items 106, 259, 341, 413.
40. *State Papers, Volume I, King Henry the Eighth: Correspondence between the King and his Ministers, 1530-1547*, London, John Murray, 1831, pp. 438, 443-4, 448. *Letters and Papers of Henry VIII*, IX, items 178, 484.

Chapter Eight
1. Frederick J. and Percy Furnivall, eds, *The Anatomie of The Bodie of Man by Thomas Vicary*, London, Early English Text Soc., 1888, p. 109.
2. Paul Slack, *The Impact of Plague in Tudor and Stuart England*, London, Routledge & Kegan Paul, 1985, pp. 147-8.
3. J.F.D. Shrewsbury, *A History of Bubonic Plague in the British Isles*, Cambridge, CUP, 1970, pp. 175, 178.
4. LMA, Corporation records, Common Council Journal XV, ff. 48r-49r.
5. LMA, Corporation records, Common Council Journal XV, ff. 48r-49r.
6. LMA, Corporation records, Common Council Journal XV, ff. 55r-v.
7. Furnivall and Furnivall, eds, *Anatomie of The Bodie of Man*, p. 161. John Stow, *Annales, or a general Chronicle of England*, 1631, p. 596.
8. *APC*, I, London, HMSO, 1890, p. 202.
9. George S. Dugdale, *Whitehall through the centuries*, London, Phoenix House, 1950, p. 20. *Survey of London*, 13, 1930, p. 261.
10. Slack, *Impact of Plague*, pp. 61, 111.
11. *CSP Ven, vol.5, 1534-1554*, no.934.
12. *CSP Ven, vol.5, 1534-1554*, pp. 541-2. J.G. Nichols, ed., *Chronicle of the Grey Friars of London*, Camden Soc., vol. 53, 1852, p. 70.

13. W.K. Jordan, ed., *The Chronicle and Political Papers of King Edward VI*, London, Allen & Unwin, 1966, pp. 71-2.

14. J.G. Nichols, ed., *The Diary of Henry Machyn Citizen and Merchant-Taylor of London (1550-1563)*, Camden Soc., 1848, pp. 8, 319. W.D. Hamilton, ed., *A Chronicle of England during the reigns of the Tudors, from A.D. 1485 to 1559, by Charles Wriothesley*, Camden Soc., 2nd series, vol.11, 1875, pp. 49-50.

15. John Caius, *A boke or counseill against the disease commonly called the sweate or sweatyng sicknesse*, 1552, pp. 11, 19, 34-5.

16. Francis Bacon, *The History of the Reign of King Henry VII*, London, Hesperus Press, 2007, pp. 9-10.

17. Thomas Paynell, *Moche profitable treatise against the pestilence*, 1534, unpaged.

18. Jean Goeurot, *The regiment of life, whereunto is added a treatise of the pestilence, with the boke of children, newly corrected and enlarged by T. Phayre*, 1545.

19. Susan Brigden, *London and the Reformation*, London, Faber, 1989, pp. 470-1.

20. Daniel Defoe, *A Journal of the Plague Year*, ed. Cynthia Wall, London, Penguin, 2003, pp. 14-15.

21. Charles Nevinson, ed., *Later Writings of Bishop Hooper*, Parker Soc., 1852, pp. 163-5, 167-8, 175.

22. William Bullein, *A Dialogue both pleasaunte and pietifull wherein is a goodly regiment against the fever Pestilence with a Consolacion and Comfort against death*, London, 1564.

23. Elizabeth Lane Furdell, 'Boorde, Andrew (c.1490–1549)', ODNB.

24. H. Edmund Poole, *The Wisdome of Andrew Boorde*, Leicester, Falconer Scott, 1936, pp. 51-2.

25. Poole, *Wisdome of Andrew Boorde*, pp. 21-2, 35.

26. Michel de Montaigne, *The Essays: A Selection*, trans M.A. Screech, London, Penguin, 1993, pp. 208-9. Stefan Zweig, *Montaigne*, London, Pushkin Press, 2015, pp. 142-3.

27. Hans Holbein, *The Dance of Death*, ed. Ulinka Rublack, London, Penguin, 2016, pp. 123, 130.

28. Elizabeth Lamond, ed., *A Discourse of the Common Weal of this Realm of England*, Cambridge, CUP, 1954, p. 28.

29. Victor Cornelius Medvei and John L. Thornton, *The Royal Hospital of Saint Bartholomew 1123-1973*, London, St Bartholomew's Hospital, 1974, pp. 22-5.

30. Lamond, ed., *A Discourse of the Common Weal*, p. 16.

31. J.A. Cramer, ed., *The Second Book of the Travels of Nicander Nucius, of Corcyra*, Camden Soc., 1841, pp. 9-12. *CSP Ven*, vol.5, *1534-1554*, item 934.

Chapter Nine

1. F.J. Fisher, *London and the English Economy 1500-1700*, ed. P.J. Corfield and N.B. Harte, London, Hambledon Press, 1990, pp. 168-9.

2. J.G. Nichols, ed., *The Diary of Henry Machyn, citizen and merchant-taylor of London, from A.D. 1550 to A.D. 1563*, Camden Soc., 42, 1848, p. 163.

3. Nicholas Crane, *Mercator: The Man Who Mapped the Planet*, London, Weidenfeld & Nicolson, 2002, p. 196.

4. Conyers Read, *Mr Secretary Cecil and Queen Elizabeth*, London, Jonathan Cape, 1965 edn, p. 115.

5. LMA, Common Council Journal, XVIII, ff. 123v, 136v, 139r-v. G.D. Ramsay, *The City of London in international politics at the accession of Elizabeth Tudor*, Manchester, Manchester UP, 1975, p. 192.

6. LMA, Common Council Journal, XVIII, ff. 123v, 136r-v. Nichols, ed., *Diary of Henry Machyn*, pp. 310, 312.

7. HMC, *Eighth Report*, Manuscripts of the College of Physicians, 1881, p. 227a.

8. LMA, Common Council Journal, XVIII, ff. 139r, 142r, 204.

9. Joseph Lemuel Chester, ed., *The Reister Booke of Saynte D'enis, Backchurch*, London, 1878, p. 189.

10. Paul Slack, *The Impact of Plague in Tudor and Stuart England*, London, Routledge & Kegan Paul, 1985, p. 152.

11. LMA, Common Council Journal, XVIII, f. 140v. William Nicholson, ed., *The Remains of Edmund Grindal*, Parker Soc., 1843, p. 78.

12. Ole Peter Grell, 'Plague in Elizabethan and Stuart London: The Dutch Response', *Medical History*, 34, 1990, pp. 426-7.

13. HMC, *Sixth Report*, Manuscripts of F.B. Frank, esquire, 1877, p. 455a.

14. LMA, Common Council Journal, XVIII, ff. 142r, 145v. Stow, *Annales*, pp. 656-7. Percy Furnivall, 'The Plague of 1563', *Notes and Queries*, 7th series, vol.5, 12 May 1888, p. 361.

15. LMA, Common Council Journal, XVIII, f. 153.

16. Furnivall, 'Plague of 1563', p. 362. LMA, Common Council Journal, XVIII, ff. 152v, 156r-v, 184r.

17. J.F.D. Shrewsbury, *A History of Bubonic Plague in the British Isles*, Cambridge, CUP, 1970, pp. 190-3. Joseph Lemuel Chester, ed., *The Parish Registers of St Mary Aldermary, 1558-1754*, Harleian Soc., 1880, pp. 133-8; *Reister Booke of Saynte D'enis, Backchurch*, pp. 4-6.

18. Mary Hill Cole, *The Portable Queen: Elizabeth I and the Politics of Ceremony*, Amherst, University of Massachusetts Press, 1999, p. 20.

19. John William Burgon, *The Life and Times of Sir Thomas Gresham*, II, London, Jennings, 1839, pp. 25-6.

20. Ramsay, *City of London*, pp. 179-96.

21. Ramsay, *City of London*, pp. 196-8.

22. John Stow, *Annales of England to 1603*, p. 1112.

23. Stow, *Annales*, p. 1110. Margaret Pelling and Frances White, *Physicians and Irregular Medical Practitioners in London 1550-1640*, British History Online Database, London, 2004, sub Geynes, John.

24. John Jones, *A Dial for all Agues*, London, 1566, cap. 8.

Chapter Ten

1. LMA, Common Council Journal, XIX, ff. 186r-v, 187, 191r-v, 213r.

2. LMA, Common Council Journal, XIX, ff. 213r, 214v, 217r-v, 218r, 228v-230. Richelle Munkhoff, "Searchers of the Dead': Authority, Marginality, and the Interpretation of Plague in England, 1574-1665', *Gender & History*, 11, 1999, pp. 2-3.

3. Paul L. Hughes and James F. Larkin, eds, *Tudor Royal Proclamations, II The Later Tudors, 1553-1587*, London and New Haven, Yale UP, 1969, p. 432.

4. LMA, Common Council Journal, XIX, f. 217v. HMC, *Manuscripts of the Marquess of Salisbury*, vol.II, p. 222.

5. LMA, Common Council Journal, XXI, ff. 283v, 285r-286v.

6. George Clark, *A History of the Royal College of Physicians*, vol. 1, Oxford, Clarendon Press, 1964, pp. 138-9.

7. APC, vol. 11, pp. 211, 249-50; vol 12, p. 61. Hughes and Larkin, eds, *Tudor Royal Proclamations, II*, pp. 514-16.

8. William Nicholson, ed., *The Remains of Edmund Grindal*, Parker Soc., 1843, p. 269.

9. *A sermo[n] preached at Pawles Crosse on Sunday the thirde of November 1577. in the time of the plague, by T.W.*, p. 46.

10. Hughes and Larkin, eds, *Tudor Royal Proclamations, II*, p. 466. Steen Eiler Rasmussen, *London: The Unique City*, Cambridge, Mass., MIT Press, 1982, pp. 73-4. C.C. Knowles and P.H. Pitt, *The History of Building Regulation in London 1189-1972*, London, Architectural Press, 1972, p. 14.

11. Bernard Capp, *When Gossips Meet: Women, Family, and Neighbourhood in Early Modern England*, Oxford, OUP, 2003, p. 57, citing Guildhall Library, MS 9065A/1, f. 108v.

12. Chris Laoutaris, *Shakespeare and the Countess*, London, Penguin, 2014, pp. 105-6.

13. J.F.D. Shrewsbury, *A History of Bubonic Plague in the British Isles*, Cambridge, CUP, 1970, p. 225. R.A. Foakes, *Henslowe's Diary*, Cambridge, CUP, 2nd edn, 2002, p. 276.

APC, vol.23, pp. 118, 182. Lisa Jardine and Alan Stewart, *Hostage to Fortune: The Troubled Life of Francis Bacon 1561-1626*, London, Gollancz, 1998, p. 137.

14. *APC*, vol.23, p. 183.

15. *List and Analysis of State Papers Foreign Series, Elizabeth I*, vol.IV, p.321. Mary Hill Cole, *The Portable Queen: Elizabeth I and the Politics of Ceremony*, Amherst, University of Massachusetts Press, 1999, pp. 21, 198.

16. *APC*, vol.23, pp. 221, 233, 274-6. William Brenchley Rye, *England as seen by foreigners in the days of Elizabeth and James the First*, London, John Russell Smith, 1865, reprinted 2005, p. 96.

17. Herbert Berry, 'A London Plague Bill for 1592, Crick, and Goodwyffe Hurde', *English Literary Renaissance*, 25, 1995, pp. 17-19.

18. Thomas Rogers Forbes, *Chronicle from Aldgate: Life and Death in Shakespeare's London*, New Haven & London, Yale UP, 1971, pp. 126-30.

19. Deborah E. Harkness, *The Jewel House: Elizabethan London and the Scientific Revolution*, London & New Haven, Yale UP, 2007, pp. 88-9. Julian Walker, *How to Cure the Plague & Other Curious Remedies*, London, British Library, 2013, p. 133.

20. Harkness, *Jewel House*, pp. 230-2.

21. Judith Cook, *Dr Simon Forman: A Most Notorious Physician*, London, Chatto & Windus, 2001, p. 61.

22. Margaret Healey, *Fictions of Disease in Early Modern England*, London, Palgrave, 2001, pp. 42, 94.

23. *APC*, vol.24, p. 401.

24. Arthur J. Jewers, 'The will of a plague-stricken Londoner', *The Home Counties Magazine*, III, 1901, pp. 109-10.

25. Foakes, ed., *Henslowe's Diary*, pp. 276-8.

26. Foakes, ed., *Henslowe's Diary*, p. 279.

27. Leeds Barroll, *Politics, Plague, and Shakespeare's Theater*, Ithaca & London, Cornell UP, 1991, p. 98.

28. Foakes, ed., *Henslowe's Diary*, pp. 280-1, 297.

29. *APC*, vol. 24, pp. 187, 200-1, 222, 488.

30. *APC*, vol.24, pp. 21-3, 164.

31. *APC*, vol.24, 1592-3, pp. 347, 374, 401. Shrewsbury, *Bubonic Plague*, pp. 228, 230.

32. Munkhoff, "Searchers of the Dead', p. 17. Edwin Freshfield, ed., *The Vestry Minute Book of the Parish of St Margaret Lothbury in the City of London 1571-1677*, London, 1887, pp. 27-30.

33. Shrewsbury, *Bubonic Plague*, p. 226.

34. Katherine Duncan-Jones, *Shakespeare: An Ungentle Life*, London, Methuen Drama, 2010, pp. 63, 72.

35. William Shakespeare, *Timon of Athens*, act IV sc 3; *Henry VI part 2*, act III sc 2; *Hamlet*, act II sc2; act III, sc 2. *Henry V*, act IV sc 3.

36. Mark Ford, *London: A History in Verse*, Cambridge, Mass., and London, Harvard UP, 2012, p. 69.

37. Thomas Nashe, *Christ's tears over Jerusalem, whereunto is annexed A comparative admonition to London*, London, Longman, Hurst, Rees, Orme and Brown, 1815, pp. 151-2.

38. Nashe, *Christ's tears*, p. 153.

39. Thomas Nashe, *The Unfortunate Traveller*, 1594, pp. 46-7.

40. James McDermott, *Martin Frobisher: Elizabethan Privateer*, New Haven & London, Yale UP, 2001, pp. 394-9.

Chapter Eleven

1. *APC, 1601-4*, p. 490.

2. *Calendar of State Papers, Domestic, 1603-10*, pp. 11, 16. James F. Larkin and Paul L. Hughes, eds, *Stuart Royal Proclamations Volume I Royal Proclamations of King James I 1603-1625*, Oxford, Clarendon Press, 1973, pp. 21-2, 32-5.

3. *CSPVen*, 10, 1603-1607, pp. 33, 42, 45.

4. *CSPVen*, 10, pp. 66, 67.

5. Larkin and Hughes, eds, *Royal Proclamations*, pp. 40-1.

6. M.S. Giuseppi, ed., *Calendar of the Cecil Papers in Hatfield House*, vol. 15, London, HMC, 1930, pp. 189-90.

7. Giuseppi, ed., *Cecil Papers*, pp. 227-8.

8. James Balmford, *A Short Dialogue concerning the Plagues infection*, 1603, pp. 33, 39.

9. Giuseppi, ed., *Cecil Papers*, p. 267.

10. Giuseppi, ed., *Cecil Papers*, p. 266.

11. Balmford, *Short Dialogue*, pp. 2, 8-12, 32, 41.

12. Henoch Clapham, *An epistle discoursing vpon the present pestilence*, London, 1604, unpaged. Balmford, *Short Dialogue*, p. 59.

13. Adam Nicolson, *Power and Glory: Jacobean England and the Making of the King James Bible*, London, Harper Collins, 2003, pp. 26-32.

14. Norman Egbert McClure, ed., *Letters, by John Chamberlain*, London, Greenwood Press, 1979 edn, I, p. 142.

15. Balmford, *Short Dialogue*, pp. 12, 26. Neil MacGregor, *Shakespeare's Restless World*, London, Penguin, 2013, p. 232.

16. Thomas Lodge, *A Treatise of the Plague*, 1603, dedication, Chap. XVII. MacGregor, *Shakespeare's Restless World*, p. 232.

17. Larkin and Hughes, eds, *Royal Proclamations*, pp. 47-8.

18. William Shakespeare, *Measure for Measure*, ed. Jonathan Bate and Eric Rasmussen, London, Macmillan, 2010, act 1 sc 2, pp. 6, 27.

19. F.P. Wilson, ed., *The Plague Pamphlets of Thomas Dekker*, Oxford, OUP, 1925, pp. 28, 32.

20. Wilson, ed., *Plague Pamphlets*, pp. 28, 33, 36, 61, 94.

21. Wilson, ed., *Plague Pamphlets*, pp. 28-9, 35.

22. Jacob Cool, *Den Staet van London in Hare Groote Peste*, ed. J.A. van Dorsten and K. Schaap, Leiden, E.J. Brill, 1962, p. 23. Ole Peter Grell, 'Plague in Elizabethan and Stuart London: The Dutch Response', *Medical History*, 34, 1990, pp. 429-30.

23. Cool, *Den Staet van London*, pp. 30, 58.
24. *CSPVen*, 10, items 175, 186, 192.
25. Leeds Barroll, *Politics, Plague and Shakespeare's Theater: The Stuart Years*, Ithaca, Cornell UP, 1991, pp. 223-6.
26. HMC, *Calendar of the Cecil Papers in Hatfield House*, XVIII, London, HMC, 1940, p. 273.
27. Valerie Hope, *My Lord Mayor*, London, Weidenfeld & Nicolson, 1989, p. 70.
28. *CSPVen*, 11, nos 86, 109, 439, 444, 503, 599, 658, 738. HMC, *Calendar of the Cecil Papers in Hatfield House*, XXI, London, HMC, 1970, p. 230.
29. James Shapiro, *1606: Shakespeare and the Year of Lear*, London, Faber & Faber, 2015, p. 321.
30. Leeds Barroll, *Politics, Plague, and Shakespeare's Theater*, p. 100.
31. John Stow, *The Survey of London*, ed. H.B. Wheatley, Dent, London, 1987, pp. 384-5. MacGregor, *Shakespeare's Restless World*, p. 232.
32. LMA, acc/1876/AR/1/5/1; AR/3/6A; AR/1/22. James Howell, *Londinopolis*, London, 1657, p. 343.

Chapter Twelve
1. *APC*, 1625-26, pp. 78, 302.
2. Charles Henry Hull, ed., *The Economic Writings of Sir William Petty*, Cambridge, CUP, 1899, II, p. 369.
3. Alastair Bellany and Thomas Cogswell, *The Murder of King James I*, New Haven & London, Yale UP, 2015, p. 69.
4. Hull, ed., *Sir William Petty*, II, pp. 366-7.
5. Elizabeth McClure Thomson, ed., *The Chamberlain Letters*, London, John Murray, 1966, pp. 349-50.
6. F.P. Wilson, *The Plague in Shakespeare's London*, Oxford, OUP, 1927, pp. 131-3. *APC*, 1625-26, 1934, pp. 17-18.
7. Maija Jansson and William B. Bidwell, eds, *Proceedings in Parliament 1625*, London & New Haven, Yale UP, 1987, pp. 641-2.

8. Thomson, ed., *Chamberlain Letters*, pp. 352-3.

9. Jansson and Bidwell, eds, *Proceedings in Parliament*, pp. 669, 707. John Taylor, *The Fearfull Summer, Or, Londons Calamitie*, 1625.

10. Steven Bradwell, *A Watch-Man for the Pest*, London, 1625, pp. 6-7.

11. Thomson, ed., *Chamberlain Letters*, pp. 352-4.

12. Simon Thurley, *Hampton Court: A Social and Architectural History*, London & New Haven, Yale UP, 2003, pp. 111-12.

13. *CSPVen*, 19, 1625-6, items 139, 150, 163, 164, 175, 188, 210. Jansson and Bidwell, eds, *Proceedings in Parliament*, p. 707.

14. *APC, 1625-26*, p. 123.

15. Jansson and Bidwell, eds, *Proceedings in Parliament*, p.709. *William Lilly's History of His Life and Times, from the year 1602 to 1681. Written by Himself*, London, 1822, p. 48. CSPVen, 19, 1625-6, item 188.

16. Paul S. Seaver, *Wallington's World: A Puritan Artisan in Seventeenth-Century London*, London, Methuen, 1985, p. 86.

17. E.S. de Beer, ed., *The Diary of John Evelyn*, Oxford, OUP, 1959, p. 5.

18. *CSPD, 1625-26*, p. 90.

19. Henry Petowe, *The countrie ague. Or, London her welcome home to her retired children*, London, 1625.

20. *CSPD, 1625-26*, p. 158.

21. Bradwell, *Watch-Man for the Pest*, pp. 9, 10-15, 43.

22. Winefride Caldin and Helen Raine, 'The plague of 1625 and the story of John Boston, parish clerk of St Saviour's, Southwark', *Trans London and Middlesex Archaeological Soc.*, 23, 1971-2, pp. 90-9.

23. Oliver Lawson Dick, ed., *Aubrey's Brief Lives*, London, Penguin, 1972, p. 185. Conrad Edick Wright, 'Harvard,

John (1607-38)', ODNB. Ole Peter Grell, 'Thorius, Raphael (d.1625)', ODNB.

24. Ole Peter Grell, 'Plague in Elizabethan and Stuart London: The Dutch Response', *Medical History*, 34, 1990, pp. 431-2.
25. *William Lilly's History of His Life and Times*, pp. 47-9.
26. Seaver, *Wallington's World*, p. 87.
27. John Donne, *After Our Disposition by the Sickness*, 1625.
28. *APC, 1625-26*, p. 209.
29. *CSPVen*, 19, item 230. CSPD, 1625-26, p. 96.
30. *APC, 1625-26*, pp. 211, 253.
31. *CSPD, 1625-26*, p. 114.
32. Jansson and Bidwell, eds, *Proceedings in Parliament*, pp. 143-4.
33. Wilson, *Plague in Shakespeare's London*, pp. 167-8.
34. Petowe, The *countrie ague*, pp. 23-4.
35. *Analytical Index to the Series of Records known as the Remembrancia ... A.D. 1579-1664*, London, 1878, p.339. F.P. Wilson, ed., *The Plague Pamphlets of Thomas Dekker*, Oxford, OUP, 1925, p. 157.
36. Wilson, ed., *Plague Pamphlets of Thomas Dekker*, pp. 138-9, 147, 151-2, 158-61.
37. *CSPD, 1625-26*, pp. 90, 136.
38. *CSPVen*, 19, item 310.
39. Wilson, *Plague in Shakespeare's London*, p. 169. CSPD, 1625-26, p. 191.
40. *CSPVen*, 19, items 404, 413.
41. Hull, ed., *Sir William Petty*, II, p. 427.
42. Hull, ed., *Sir William Petty*, II, pp. 339-41.
43. *Analytical Index to ... the Remembrancia*, p. 339.
44. Thomson, ed., *Chamberlain Letters*, p. 356. R.F. Williams, ed., *The Court and Times of Charles the First*, London, 1848, I, p. 54.
45. Ruth Saunders Magurn, ed., *The Letters of Peter Paul Rubens*, Cambridge, Mass., Harvard UP, 1955, p. 314.

Chapter Thirteen

1. *Analytical Index to the Series of Records known as the Remembrancia ... A.D. 1579-1664,* London, 1878, pp. 339-40.
2. Martin J. Havran, *Caroline Courtier: The Life of Lord Cottington,* London, Macmillan, 1973, p. 98.
3. *Analytical Index to ... the Remembrancia,* p. 340.
4. *Analytical Index to ... the Remembrancia,* pp. 341-2.
5. APC, *1630-1631,* pp. 24, 71, 91-2. *Analytical Index to ... the Remembrancia,* pp. 344-5.
6. Hugh Trevor-Roper, *Europe's Physician: The Varied Life of Sir Theodore de Mayerne,* New Haven & London, Yale UP, 2006, p. 306.
7. TNA, SP16/533/17. Trevor-Roper, *Europe's Physician,* pp, 307-10.
8. *Analytical Index to ... the Remembrancia,* p. 340.
9. LMA, acc.1876/D1/A1, f. 4.
10. *CSPVen,* 23, item 560.
11. *CSPD, 1635-1636,* pp. 374-5.
12. R.F. Williams, ed., *The Court and Times of Charles the First,* London, 1848, II, pp. 244-5.
13. *CSPVen,* 23, item 654, 663.
14. *CSPVen,* 23, item 667.
15. *Analytical Index to ... the Remembrancia,* pp. 346-7.
16. *CSPVen,* 24, item 6.
17. *CSPVen,* 24, item 54.
18. J.F. Larkin, ed., *Stuart Royal Proclamations Volume II: Royal Proclamations of King Charles I 1625-1646,* Oxford, OUP, 1983, p. 539.
19. Charterhouse Muniments, G/2/1, pp. 358-9.
20. Philip Caraman, *Henry Morse Priest of the Plague,* London, Longmans, Green, 1957, pp. 79, 86-97, 108.
21. *CSPD, 1635-1636,* pp. 540-1. Ole Peter Grell, 'Plague in Elizabethan and Stuart London: the Dutch response', *Medical History,* 34, 1990, pp. 433-5.

22. Caraman, *Morse*, p. 80.
23. Andrew Cunningham and Ole Peter Grell, *The Four Horsemen of the Apocalypse: Religion, War, Famine and Death in Reformation Europe*, Cambridge, CUP, 2000, p. 292.
24. *CSPD, 1636-1637*, pp. 170-1.
25. *CSPD, 1636-1637*, pp. 119-20, 122, 126.
26. *CSPD, 1636-1637*, p. 37.
27. William McMurray, ed., *The Records of Two City Parishes*, London, 1925, pp. 336, 385. *CSPD, 1636-1637*, pp. 316-17.
28. Charles Henry Hull, ed., *The Economic Writings of Sir William Petty*, Cambridge, CUP, 1899, II, p. 383.
29. *CSPD, 1636-1637*, pp. 347, 353.
30. *CSPVen*, 24, items 93, 127, 147. Charterhouse Muniments, G/2/1, pp. 335-6; G/2/2, p. 18.
31. *CSPVen*, 24, items 188, 256, 311.
32. Hull, ed., *Sir William Petty*, II, pp. 366, 405.

Chapter Fourteen

1. Anthony Fletcher, *The Outbreak of the English Civil War*, London, Arnold, 1981, p. 68.
2. *CSPVen*, 25, item 250.
3. Fletcher, *Outbreak*, pp. 68-71.
4. *Commons Journals, II, 1640-1642*, pp. 273, 275, 280, 195. Fletcher, *Outbreak*, pp. 71-2.
5. *CSPVen*, 25, item 260.
6. BL, Thomason Tracts, E173/23 *A Damnable Treason, By a Contagious Plaster of a Plague Sore*, 1641. *Commons Journals, II, 1640-1642*, p. 295.
7. *CSPVen*, 25, item 271.
8. Paul Slack, *The Impact of Plague in Tudor and Stuart England*, London, Routledge & Kegan Paul, 1983, pp. 220-1. F.N.L. Poynter and W.R. LeFanu, 'A Seventeenth-Century London Plague Document in the Wellcome Historical Medical Library: Dr. Louis Du Moulin's Proposals to Parliament for

a corps of salaried plague-doctors', *Bulletin of the History of Medicine*, 34, 1960, pp. 365-72.

9. LMA, Corporation of London, Common Council Journals, 40, ff.67v-8.

10. *Calendar, Committee for the Advance of Money*, pp. 350, 383, 361, 715, 781.

11. William Lithgow, *The Present Surveigh of London and Englands State*, 1643, p. 537.

12. C.H. Firth and R.S. Rait, eds, *Acts and Ordinances of the Interregnum*, London, HMSO, 1911, I, p. 570. *Commons Journals*, IV, p. 185.

13. Roger Finlay, *Population and Metropolis. The Demography of London 1580-1650*, Cambridge, CUP, 1981, pp. 156-7. John Bell, *London's Remembrancer*, 1665, unpag., tables for 1644-5, 1645-6.

14. E.M. Symonds, 'The Diary of John Greene (1635-57)', *English Historical Review*, XLIV, 1928, pp. 599, 601, 604; 1929, p. 107.

15. BL, Thomason Tracts, E352/2 *Orders formerly Conceived and Agreed . . .*, 1646.

16. *Catalogue of the Pamphlets, Books, Newspapers, and Manuscripts ... collected by George Thomason, 1640-1661*, I, London, 1908, p. xxi.

17. Julian Walker, *How to Cure the Plague & Other Curious Remedies*, London, British Library, 2013, pp. 129-31.

18. *CSPD, 1651-1652*, p. 584.

19. BL, Thomason Tracts, E415, John Cooke, *Unum Necessarium: or, The Poore Mans Case*, 1648, p. 64.

20. Charles Henry Hull, ed., *The Economic Writings of Sir William Petty*, Cambridge, CUP, 1899, II, pp. 402-3.

21. Robin Blake, *Anthony Van Dyck: A Life 1599-1641*, Chicago, Ian R. Dee, 2000, pp. 193-5, 197-8.

22. Michael G. Brennan, ed., *The Travel Diary of Robert Bargrave Levant Merchant (1647-1656)*, London, Hakluyt Soc., 1999, pp. 80, 87, 147.

23. Brennan, ed., *Diary of Robert Bargrave*, p. 236.

24. F.N.L. Poynter, ed., *The Journal of James Yonge [1647-1721]*, London, Longmans, 1963, pp. 70, 75.

25. Poynter, ed., *Journal of James Yonge*, p. 83.

Chapter Fifteen

1. TNA, PC2/56, pp. 592, 607. R.C. Latham and W. Matthews, eds, *The Diary of Samuel Pepys,* 11 vols, London, Bell & Hyman, 1970-83, IV, p. 340.

2. TNA, PC2/56, p. 612.

3. TNA, PC2/56, pp. 624, 676, 683.

4. Latham and Matthews, eds, *Diary of Pepys*, IV, p. 399.

5. TNA, PC2/57, pp. 23, 35A, 45, 89, 93.

6. TNA, PC2/57, pp. 93, 126, 164.

7. TNA, PC2/57, pp. 199-200.

8. Jonathan Israel, *The Dutch Republic: Its Rise, Greatness, and Fall, 1477-1806*, Oxford, Clarendon Press, 1995, p. 625.

9. Latham and Matthews, eds, *Diary of Pepys*, V, pp. 231, 279.

10. William Boghurst, *Loimographia: an account of the Great Plague of London in the year 1665*, ed. J.F. Payne, London, Shaw & Sons, 1894, p. 26.

11. TNA, PC2/58, p. 114.

12. TNA, SP29/128/47.

13. Camden Local Studies Centre, St Giles-in-the-Fields P/GF/ CW/1/1. TNA, E179/252/32.

14. TNA, PC2/58, p. 118.

15. Latham and Matthews, eds, *Diary of Pepys*, VI, pp. 130-1.

16. Camden Local Studies Centre, St Giles-in-the-Fields P/GF/ CW/1/1.

17. Camden Local Studies Centre, St Giles-in-the-Fields P/GF/ CW/1/1.

18. Walter George Bell, *The Great Plague in London*, London, Bodley Head, 1924, reprinted London, Bracken Books, 1994, pp. 35-6.

19. Bell, *Great Plague*, p. 80.
20. Latham and Matthews, eds, *Diary of Pepys*, VI, p. 132.
21. Latham and Matthews, eds, *Diary of Pepys*, VI, pp. 128-30, 142. *CSPVen*, 35, p. 182.
22. William Durrant Cooper, 'Notices of the last Great Plague, 1665-6; from the Letters of John Allin to Philip Fryth and Samuel Jeake', *Archaeologia*, 37, 1857, p. 5.
23. Thomas Vincent, *God's Terrible Voice in the City*, London, 1667; James Nisbet, 1831, pp. 30-1.
24. Bell, *Great Plague*, p. 60. G.T. Elliot, ed., Autobiography and Anecdotes by William Taswell, D.D., *Camden Miscellany*, Vol. 2, 1853, p. 9. BL, Add MS 10,117, f. 139.
25. *CSPVen*, 34, items 211, 221.
26. Latham and Matthews, eds, *Diary of Pepys*, VI, p. 133.
27. HMC, *Tenth report app.IV, Captain Stewart's Manuscripts*, p. 111.
28. Bell, *Great Plague*, pp. 80-1.
29. Latham and Matthews, eds, *Diary of Pepys*, VI, p. 134.
30. Latham and Matthews, eds, *Diary of Pepys*, IV, pp. 140-1, 143, 145, 149. Vincent, *God's Terrible Voice*, p. 32.
31. Latham and Matthews, eds, *Diary of Pepys*, VI, pp. 171, 173, 174.
32. N.H. Keble and G.F. Nuttall, eds, *Calendar of the Correspondence of Richard Baxter*, II 1660-1696, Oxford, OUP, 1991, p. 47.
33. BL, Add MS 10,117, f. 143. *CSPD*, 1664-1665, p. 488.
34. Cooper, 'Notices of the last Great Plague', pp. 7, 8.
35. A.R. and M.B. Hall, eds, *The Correspondence of Henry Oldenburg*, 13 vols, Madison, University of Wisconsin Press, 1965-86, II, pp. 430, 449, 479.
36. LMA, acc.262/43/51, 63; acc.1876/G/3/3, 3 July 1665. Cooper, 'Notices of the last Great Plague', p. 6. Dorothy Gardiner, ed., *The Oxinden and Peyton Letters 1642-1670*,

London, Sheldon Press, 1937, p. 306. BL, Lansdowne MS 1198, f. 23.

37. HMC, *Manuscripts of the Earl of Verulam*, London, HMSO, 1906, p. 67.

Chapter Sixteen

1. J.C. Jeaffreson, ed., *Middlesex County Records*, III, London, Middlesex County Records Soc., 1888, p. 375.

2. Bodleian Lib., Add. MS c.303, f. 112.

3. Watson Nicholson, *The Historical Sources of Defoe's Journal of the Plague Year*, Boston, Mass., Stratford, 1919, p. 112.

4. Nicholson, *Historical Sources*, p. 143. W.H. Godfrey, *The Church of Saint Bride, Fleet Street*, London, Survey of London, Monograph No. 15, 1944, p. 29.

5. Nicholson, *Historical Sources*, pp. 122, 143, 154. W.G. Bell, *The Great Plague in London*, London, Bodley Head, 1924, reprinted London, Bracken Books, 1994, pp. 150-1, 225. Gilbert Burnet, *History of His Own Time*, London, Dent, 1991, p. 79.

6. R.C. Latham and W. Matthews, eds, *The Diary of Samuel Pepys*, 11 vols, London, Bell & Hyman, 1970-83, VI, p. 214. Bodleian Lib., MS Add. c.303, ff. 104, 110.

7. Latham and Matthews, eds, *Diary of Pepys*, VI, pp. 145, 150, 164, 187-8, 192, 207, 210, 225, 253. R.G. Howarth, ed., *Letters and the Second Diary of Samuel Pepys*, London, Dent, 1933, pp. 24-5.

8. Latham and Matthews, eds, *Diary of Pepys*, VI, pp. 145, 164, 177-8, 187-8, 191, 246, 342.

9. Nicholson, *Historical Sources*, pp. 154, 156-64.

10. Nicholson, *Historical Sources*, p. 154.

11. Latham and Matthews, eds, *Diary of Pepys*, VI, pp. 174-5, 201. E.S. de Beer, ed., *The Diary of John Evelyn*, London, OUP, 1959, p. 480. Nicholson, *Historical Sources*, pp. 158-9.

12. G.P. Elliott, ed., 'Autobiography and Anecdotes by William Taswell, D.D.', *Camden Miscellany*, vol. II, 1853, p. 9. Nicholson, *Historical Sources*, p. 157.

13. J.E.D. Shrewsbury, *A History of Bubonic Plague in the British Isles*, Cambridge, CUP, 1970, pp. 479-80. Thomas Vincent, *God's Terrible Voice in the City*, London, 1667; James Nisbet, 1831, p. 32. Latham and Matthews, eds, *Diary of Pepys*, VI, p. 120.

14. Bell, *Great Plague*, pp. 96-7. Charterhouse Muniments, G/2/3, f. 67.

15. Nicholson, *Historical Sources*, pp. 126-7, 154. Latham and Matthews, eds, *Diary of Pepys*, VI, p. 268.

16. Nicholson, *Historical Sources*, p. 111. Bell, *Great Plague*, pp. 38-9, 161.

17. J.G.L. Burnby, *A Study of the English Apothecary from 1660 to 1760*, London, Medical History, Supplement No. 3, 1983, pp. 3-4, 7-8, 17-18.

18. Burnby, *English Apothecary*, p. 99. Paul Slack, *The Impact of Plague in Tudor and Stuart England*, London, Routledge & Kegan Paul, 1985, p. 244. A.R. and M.B. Hall, eds, *The Correspondence of Henry Oldenburg*, 13 vols, Madison, University of Wisconsin Press, 1965-86, II, pp. 483-4.

19. William Durrant Cooper, 'Notices of the last Great Plague, 1665-6; from the Letters of John Allin to Philip Fryth and Samuel Jeake', *Archaeologia*, 37, 1857, p. 6. Slack, *Impact of Plague*, p. 245. Nicholson, *Historical Sources*, p. 157. Latham and Matthews, eds, *Diary of Pepys*, VI, p. 155.

20. Bell, *Great Plague*, pp. 99, 259. C.H. Hull, ed., *The Economic Writings of Sir William Petty*, 2 vols, Cambridge, CUP, 1899, II, pp. 356-7.

21. Bell, *Great Plague*, pp. 51, 102. Cooper, 'Notices of the last Great Plague', p. 6.

22. LMA, WC/R/1, pp. 2-7.

23. C.F. Mullett, *The Bubonic Plague and England*, Lexington, University of Kentucky Press, 1956, pp. 197-8, 219. Slack, *Impact of Plague*, p. 245. Bell, *Great Plague*, p. 35.

24. Cooper, 'Notices of the last Great Plague', p. 6. Nicholson, *Historical Sources*, pp. 146, 149. *CSPD, 1664-1665*, p. 517.

25. Bell, *Great Plague*, pp. 237-8. Latham and Matthews, eds, *Diary of Pepys*, VI, pp. 189, 213, 217. Shrewsbury, *History of Bubonic Plague*, pp. 461, 466.

26. Bodleian Lib., MS. Add. c. 303, f. 126.

27. Nicholson, *Historical Sources*, p. 142.

28. Bell, *Great Plague*, p. 197. *CSPD, 1665-1666*, p. 107.

29. Nicholson, *Historical Sources*, pp. 146, 154. Gladys Scott Thomson, *Life in a Noble Household*, London, Cape, 1937, p. 361. LMA, acc.262/43/60,66. Slack, *Impact of Plague*, p. 282.

30. Bell, *Great Plague*, pp. 130, 196-7, 288-9.

31. Lambeth Palace Lib., Sheldon's Register, f. 207.

32. Justin Champion, 'Epidemics and the built environment in 1665', in J.A.I. Champion, ed., *Epidemic Disease in London*, London, Centre for Metropolitan History, Working Paper Series no. 1, 1993, p. 48.

33. Latham and Matthews, eds, *Diary of Pepys*, VI, p. 224. Nicholson, *Historical Sources*, pp. 120, 132-3, 146, 162.

34. Nicholson, *Historical Sources*, pp. 35, 104-5, 135.

35. Bell, *Great Plague*, p. 131. Bodleian Lib., MS Add. c.303, f. 112. Nicholson, *Historical Sources*, pp. 37-8. Latham and Matthews, eds, *Diary of Pepys*, VI, pp. 207, 211, 213-14; VII, pp. 40-1.

36. Latham and Matthews, eds, *Diary of Pepys*, VI, pp. 279, 297.

37. De Beer, ed., *Diary of Evelyn*, p. 481. 'Autobiography and Anecdotes by William Taswell', p. 9.

38. Vanessa Harding, 'Burial of the plague dead in early modern London' in Champion, ed., *Epidemic Disease*, pp. 55-61.

Latham and Matthews, eds, *Diary of Pepys*, VII, p. 30. BL, Add. MS 10,117, f. 147.

39. Godfrey, *Church of St Bride*, p. 29. Alfred Plummer, *The London Weavers' Company, 1600-1970*, London, Routledge & Kegan Paul, 1972, p. 189. Joseph Lemuel Chester, ed., *The Parish Registers of St. Thomas the apostle. London ... 1558 to 1754*, London, Harleian Soc.; Parish Registers, vol. VI, 1881, pp. 125-38.

40. De Beer, ed., *Diary of Evelyn*, p. 480.

41. BL, Add. MS 10,117, f. 147. Cooper, 'Notices of the last Great Plague', p. 9. Hall and Hall, eds, *Correspondence of Henry Oldenburg*, II, p. 479.

42. Nicholson, *Historical Sources*, pp. 121, 146-7, 149, 158-9. Latham and Matthews, eds, *Diary of Pepys*, VI, p. 186. 'Autobiography and Anecdotes by William Taswell', p. 10.

43. Champion, *London's Dreaded Visitation*, pp. 82-4.

44. 'Autobiography and Anecdotes by William Taswell', p. 10.

45. Latham and Matthews, eds, *Diary of Pepys*, VI, pp. 207, 268. Shrewsbury, *History of Bubonic Plague*, pp. 479-80.

46. Latham and Matthews, eds, *Diary of Pepys*, VI, p. 165.

47. Cooper, 'Notices of the last Great Plague', p. 9.

48. Shrewsbury, *History of Bubonic Plague*, p. 476. Champion, *London's Dreaded Visitation*, pp. 108-9.

49. Latham and Matthews, eds, *Diary of Pepys*, VI, pp. 284, 296.

50. Latham and Matthews, eds, *Diary of Pepys*, VI, p. 306.

51. Nicholson, *Historical Sources*, pp. 163-4.

52. TNA, SP29/126/44.

53. Bell, *Great Plague*, pp. 165, 217-18.

54. De Beer, ed., *Diary of Evelyn*, pp. 479-85.

55. LMA, acc.262/43/48, 49, 51, 55, 58, 60, 63, 71, 79.

56. Latham and Matthews, eds, *Diary of Pepys*, VII, p. 35. LMA, Corporation of London, Lord Mayor's Waiting Book, 2, 2 March 1666.

57. Bell, *Great Plague*, pp. 179-81. LMA, Corporation of London, Lord Mayor's Waiting Book, 2, 29 March 1666.

58. Edward Hyde, Earl of Clarendon, *Selections from The History of the Rebellion and The Life by Himself*, ed. Gordon Huehns, Oxford, OUP, 1978, p. 413. Bernard Capp, *Astrology and the Popular Press: English Almanacs 1500-1800*, London, Faber & Faber, 1979, p. 135.

59. Plummer, *London Weavers' Company*, p. 188.

60. Oliver Lawson Dick, ed., *Aubrey's Brief Lives*, Harmondsworth, Penguin, 1972, p. 324.

61. Latham and Matthews, eds, *Diary of Pepys*, VI, p. 342. BL, Add. MS 10, 117, ff. 139-74. Nicholson, *Historical Sources*, pp. 150-1.

62. HMC, *Sixteenth Report, appendix: Manuscripts of the Earl of Verulam*, London, HMSO, 1906, p. 59. Plummer, *London Weavers' Company*, p. 188.

Chapter Seventeen

1. Watson Nicholson, *The Historical Sources of Defoe's Journal of the Plague Year*, Boston, Mass., Stratford, 1919, p. 130. LMA, Corporation of London, Lord Mayor's waiting book, vol.2, 2 September 1665.

2. Nicholson, *Historical Sources*, pp. 131, 134. *CSPD, 1664-1665*, p. 401.

3. Nicholson, *Historical Sources*, pp. 132, 134-5.

4. Nicholson, *Historical Sources*, pp. 104, 106. Paul Slack, *The Impact of Plague in Tudor and Stuart England*, London, Routledge & Kegan Paul, 1985, pp. 250-1.

5. TNA, SP29/126/65.

6. Charles Henry Hull, ed., *The Economic Writings of Sir William Petty*, Cambridge, CUP, 1899, II pp. 108-10. Brian Pullan, 'Plague and perceptions of the poor in early modern Italy', in Terence Ranger and Paul Slack, eds, *Epidemics and Ideas:*

Essays on the historical perceptions of pestilence, Cambridge, CUP, 1992, pp. 120-1.

7. Walter George Bell, *The Great Plague in London*, London, Bodley Head, 1924, reprinted London, Bracken Books, 1994, pp. 315-16.

8. J.C. Jeaffreson, ed., *Middlesex County Records*, III, London, Middlesex County Records Soc., 1888, pp. 373-5.

9. TNA, PC2/58, p. 347. *CSPD, 1665-1666*, p. 351.

10. F.H.W. Sheppard, ed., *Survey of London, vol. 31, The Parish of St James, Westminster*, London, Athlone, 1963, p. 196.

11. Bell, *Great Plague*, p. 316.

12. Bell, *Great Plague*, pp. 315-16.

13. TNA, PC2/58, pp. 118, 345-7, 390-1.

14. Bell, Great Plague, pp. 334-5. Jeaffreson, ed., *Middlesex County Records*, III, pp. 373-4.

15. D. Pickering, *The Statutes at Large*, VII, London, 1763, pp. 141-4.

16. *Commons' Journals*, VIII, 1660-1667, p. 624.

17. Hyde, Edward, Earl of Clarendon, *Selections from The History of the Rebellion and The Life by Himself*, ed. Gordon Huehns, Oxford, OUP, 1978, p. 455.

18. HMC, *Seventeenth Report, Appendix, Diocese of Gloucester*, London, HMSO, 1914, p. 64. R.V. Lennard, 'English Agriculture under Charles II', in W.E. Minchinton, ed., *Essays in Agrarian History*, Vol. 1, Newton Abbot, David & Charles, 1968, p. 167. LMA, acc.262/43/47. *CSPD, 1665-1666*, pp. 14, 17.

19. Bell, *Great Plague*, p. 188.

20. *CSPD, 1664-1665*, p. 571; *1665-1666*, pp. 56-7.

21. *CSPD, 1665-1666*, pp. 56-7. *The London Gazette*, 26-30 April and 3-7 May 1666. TNA, PC2/59, p. 70.

22. TNA, PC2/58, p. 394. *CSPD, 1664-1665*, p. 488.

23. *CSPD, 1664-1665*, p. 571; *1665-1666*, p. 107.

24. LMA, acc.262/43/63.

25. Lambeth Palace Lib., Sheldon's Register, f. 207v.

26. Latham and Matthews, eds, *Diary of Pepys*, VI, pp. 165, 168, 186, 192, 205, 207, 224, 233, 268, 278, 293. R.G. Howarth, ed., *Letters and the Second Diary of Samuel Pepys*, London, Dent, 1933, pp. 24-5.

27. Latham and Matthews, eds, *Diary of Pepys*, VI, pp. 266-7.

28. Latham and Matthews, eds, *Diary of Pepys*, VI, p. 255.

29. Latham and Matthews, eds, *Diary of Pepys*, VI, p. 218. Guy de la Bédoyère, ed., *Particular Friends: The Correspondence of Samuel Pepys and John Evelyn*, Woodbridge, Boydell Press, 1997, p. 36 n.4.

30. C.D. Chandaman, *The English Public Revenue 1660-1688*, Oxford, OUP, 1975, pp. 210-13.

31. J.E.D. Shrewsbury, *A History of Bubonic Plague in the British Isles*, Cambridge, CUP, 1970, p. 478.

32. Hull, ed., *Economic Writings*, II, pp. 367, 376.

33. Thomas Sprat, *The History of the Royal Society of London*, 1667, p. 121.

34. Hull, ed., *Economic Writings*, II, pp. 475-6.

Chapter Eighteen

1. Giovanni P. Marana, *Letters Writ by a Turkish Spy*, ed. Arthur J. Weitzman, London, Routledge & Kegan Paul, 1970, p. 174.

2. Johannes Nohl, *The Black Death: A chronicle of the plague compiled from contemporary sources*, trans G.H. Clarke, London, Unwin, 1961, p. 49. Carlo Ginzburg, *The Cheese and the Worms: The Cosmos of a Sixteenth-Century Miller*, Baltimore, John Hopkins UP, 1980, p. 115.

3. J. Meuvret, 'Demographic Crisis in France from the Sixteenth to the Eighteenth Century', in D.V. Glass and D.E.C. Eversley, eds, *Population in History*, London, Arnold, 1965, p. 515.

4. John Stoye, *Europe Unfolding, 1648-1688*, London, Collins, 1969, p. 319; *Marsigli's Europe 1680-1730. The Life and Times of Luigi Ferdinando Marsigli, Soldier and Virtuoso*, New Haven and London, Yale UP, 1994, p 19.

5. Henry Kamen, *Spain 1469-1714: A society in conflict*, London, Longman, 1991, p. 270. Paul Slack, *The Impact of Plague in Tudor and Stuart England*, London, Routledge & Kegan Paul, 1983, p. 324.

6. Karl-Erik Frandsen, *The Last Plague in the Baltic Region, 1709-1713*, Copenhagen, Museum Tusculanum Press, 2010, pp. 62, 68, 72-3, 209-10, 411, 415, 480.

7. Jonathan Swift, *Journal to Stella*, ed. H. Williams, 2 vols, Oxford, Clarendon Press, 1948, I, pp. 115-16, 118, II, p. 564. Slack, *Impact of Plague*, p. 324.

8. Richard West, *The Life and Strange Surprising Adventures of Daniel Defoe*, London, HarperCollins, 1997, pp. 266-70. John Hampden, ed., *Sir Roger de Coverly by Joseph Addison, Sir Richard Steele & Eustace Budgell*, London, Folio Soc., 1967, p. 111.

9. TNA, PC2/86, pp. 472, 475, 476-80; PC2/87, pp. 15-17, 27-35, 122-31, 313-17.

10. Stoye, *Marsigli's Europe*, p. 292. TNA, PC2/87, *passim*.

11. TNA, PC2/87, pp. 323-4, 327, 341-3, 351. *The London Gazette*, 25-29 April 1721.

12. W.S. Lewis, Warren Hunting Smith and George L. Lam, eds, *Horace Walpole's Correspondence with Sir Horace Mann*, London, OUP, 1955, II, p. 282.

13. Daniel Defoe, *A Journal of the Plague Year*, ed. Cynthia Wall, London, Penguin, 2003, p. 233.

14. Rawdon Brown, ed., *Four Years at the Court of Henry VIII*, London, Smith, Elder, 1854, I, pp. 224, 228 n. 1.

15. John Stow, *The Survey of London*, ed. H.B. Wheatley, Dent, London, 1987, pp. 114, 384-5.

16. David Knowles and W.F. Grimes, *Charterhouse: The Medieval Foundation in the light of recent discoveries*, London, Longman, Green, 1954, pp. 43-9. Charterhouse Muniments, Paul Paget, 'The London Charterhouse', typescript, 17 March 1970.

BIBLIOGRAPHY

Anon, *Analytical Index to the Series of Records known as the Remembrancia … A.D. 1579-1664*, London, 1878

Anon, *Chronicle of London from 1089 to 1483*, London, 1827, reprinted Felinfach, Llanerch, 1995

Aberth, John, *From the Brink of the Apocalypse: Confronting Famine, War, Plague and Death in the Later Middle Ages*, London, Routledge, 2013

Adams, Reginald H., *The Parish Clerks of London*, London and Chichester, Phillimore, 1971

Armstrong, C.A.J., *The Usurpation of Richard III*, Gloucester, Sutton, 1984

Arrizabalaga, Jon, Henderson, John, and French, Roger, *The Great Pox: The French Disease in Renaissance Europe*, New Haven & London, Yale UP, 1997

Bacon, Francis, *The History of the Reign of King Henry VII*, London, Hesperus, 2007

Balmford, James, *A Short Dialogue concerning the Plagues infection*, 1603

Barber, Bruno, and Thomas, Christopher, *The London Charterhouse*, London, MOLAS Monograph 10, 2002

Barber, Richard, ed., *The Pastons: a family in the Wars of the Roses*, London, Folio Soc., 1981

Barroll, Leeds, *Politics, Plague, and Shakespeare's Theater: The Stuart Years*, Ithaca, Cornell UP, 1991

Barron, Caroline M., *London in the Later Middle Ages: Government and People 1200-1500*, Oxford, OUP, 2004

Bean, J.M.W., 'Plague, Population and Economic Decline in England in the Later Middle Ages', *Economic History Review*, 2nd series, XV, 1963

Bédoyère, Guy de la, ed., *Particular Friends: The Correspondence of Samuel Pepys and John Evelyn*, Woodbridge, Boydell Press, 1997

Bell, John, *London's Remembrancer*, 1665

Bell, Walter George, *The Great Plague in London*, London, Bodley Head, 1924, reprinted London, Bracken Books, 1994

Bell, Walter George, *Unknown London*, ed. E.R. Wethersett, London, Spring Books, 1966

Bellany, Alastair, and Cogswell, Thomas, *The Murder of King James I*, New Haven & London, Yale UP, 2015

Benedictow, Ole J., *The Black Death 1346-1353: The Complete History*, Woodbridge, Boydell, 2004

Bennett, Eric, *The Worshipful Company of Carmen of London*, London, Company of Carmen, 1952

Berry, Herbert, 'A London Plague Bill for 1592, Crick, and Goodwyffe Hurde', *English Literary Renaissance*, 25, 1995

Blake, Robin, *Anthony Van Dyck: A Life 1599-1641*, Chicago, Ian R. Dee, 2000

Boccaccio, Giovanni, *The Decameron*, trans. Guido Waldman, Oxford, OUP, 1993

Boeckl, Christine M., *Images of Plague and Pestilence*, Kirksville, Truman State University Press, 2000

Boghurst, William, *Loimographia: an account of the Great Plague of London in the year 1665*, ed. J.F. Payne, London, Shaw & Sons, 1894

Borg, Alan, *The History of the Worshipful Company of Painters* otherwise *Painter-Stainers*, London, Company of Painter-Stainers, 2005

Bradwell, Steven, *A Watch-Man for the Pest*, London, 1625

Brennan, Michael G., *The Travel Diary of Robert Bargrave Levant Merchant (1647-1656)*, London, Hakluyt Soc., 1999

Brereton, Geoffrey, ed., *Froissart: Chronicles*, London, Penguin, 1978

Brigden, Susan, *London and the Reformation*, London, Faber, 1989

Brown, Rawdon, ed., *Four Years at the Court of Henry VIII*, London, Smith, Elder, 1854

Bruce, Susan, ed., *Three Early Modern Utopias*, Oxford, OUP, 1999

Bull, George, ed., *The Journeys of Pietro della Valle*, London, Folio Soc., 1989

Bullein, William, *A Dialogue both pleasaunte and pietifull wherein is a goodly regiment against the fever Pestilence with a Consolacion and Comfort against death*, London, 1564

Burgon, John William, *The Life and Times of Sir Thomas Gresham*, II, London, Jennings, 1839

Burnet, Gilbert, *History of His Own Time*, London, Dent, 1991

Burrell, Arthur, ed., *Chaucer's Canterbury Tales*, London, Dent, 1908

Byrne, Joseph P., *Encyclopedia of the Black Death*, I, Santa Barbara, ABC-CLIO, 2012

Caius, John, *A boke or counseill against the disease commonly called the sweate or sweatyng sicknesse*, London, 1552

Caldin, Winefride, and Raine, Helen, 'The plague of 1625 and the story of John Boston, parish clerk of St Saviour's, Southwark', *Trans the London and Middlesex Archaeological Soc.*, 23, 1971-2, pp. 90-9

Camille, Michael, *Master of Death. The Lifeless Art of Pierre Remiet*, New Haven & London, Yale UP, 1996

Campbell, Anna Montgomery, *The Black Death and Men of Learning*, New York, AMS Press, 1966

Campbell, Mildred, ed., *The Utopia of Thomas More*, Princeton, Van Nostrand, 1947

Capp, Bernard, *Astrology and the Popular Press: English Almanacs 1500-1800*, London, Faber & Faber, 1979

Capp, Bernard, *When Gossips Meet: Women, Family, and Neighbourhood in Early Modern England*, Oxford, OUP, 2003

Caraman, Philip, *Henry Morse Priest of the Plague*, London, Longmans, Green, 1957

Cardano, Girolamo, *The Book of my Life*, New York, The New York Review of Books, 2002

Carmichael, Ann G., *Plague and the Poor in Renaissance Florence*, Cambridge, CUP, 1986

Cavallo, Sandra, *Charity and power in early modern Italy: Benefactors and their motives in Turin, 1541-1789*, Cambridge, CUP, 1995

Cellini, Benvenuto, *The Life of Benvenuto Cellini*, ed. John Addington Symonds, London, Heron Books, undated

Chandaman, C.D., *The English Public Revenue 1660-1688*, Oxford, OUP, 1975

Champion, J.A.I., ed., *Epidemic Disease in London*, London, Centre for Metropolitan History, Working Paper Series no. 1, 1993

Chester, Joseph Lemuel, ed., *The Reister Booke of Saynte D'enis, Backchurch*, London, 1878

Chester, Joseph Lemuel, ed., *The Parish Registers of St Mary Aldermary, 1558-1754*, Harleian Soc., 1880

Chester, Joseph Lemuel, ed., *The Parish Registers of St. Thomas the apostle. London ... 1558 to 1754*, London, Harleian Society; Parish Registers, vol. VI, 1881

Chew, Helena M., and Kellaway, William, eds, *London Assize of Nuisance, 1301-1431: A Calendar*, London Record Soc., vol. 10, 1973

Clapham, Henoch, *An epistle discoursing vpon the present pestilence*, London, 1604

Clark, George, *A History of the Royal College of Physicians of London*, vol. 1, Oxford, Clarendon Press, 1964

Clark, Linda, and Rawcliffe, Carole, *The Fifteenth Century XII: Society in an Age of Plague*, Woodbridge, Boydell, 2013

Cohn, Samuel K., *The Black Death Transformed: Disease and Culture in Early Renaissance Europe*, London, Arnold, 2002

Cole, Mary Hill, *The Portable Queen: Elizabeth I and the Politics of Ceremony*, Amherst, University of Massachusetts Press, 1999

Cook, Judith, *Dr Simon Forman: A Most Notorious Physician*, London, Chatto & Windus, 2001

Cooke, John, *Unum Necessarium: or, The Poore Mans Case*, 1648

Cool, Jacob, *Den Staet van London in Hare Groote Peste*, ed. J.A. van Dorsten and K. Schaap, Leiden, E.J. Brill, 1962

Cooper, William Durrant, 'Notices of the last Great Plague, 1665-6; from the Letters of John Allin to Philip Fryth and Samuel Jeake', *Archaeologia*, 37, 1857

Cramer, J.A., ed., *The Second Book of the Travels of Nicander Nucius, of Corcyra*, Camden Soc., 1841

Crane, Nicholas, *Mercator: The Man Who Mapped the Planet*, London, Weidenfeld & Nicolson, 2002

Creighton, Charles, *A History of Epidemics in Britain from A.D. 664 to the extinction of plague*, Cambridge, CUP, 1891; Cass, 1965

Cunningham, Andrew, and Grell, Ole Peter, *The Four Horsemen of the Apocalypse: Religion, War, Famine and Death in Reformation Europe*, Cambridge, CUP, 2000

Davies, Matthew, 'Carpenter, John, (d. 1442), common clerk of London', ODNB

Davis, Norman, ed., *The Paston Letters*, Oxford, OUP, 1983

Davis, S., et al, 'Predictive Thresholds for Plague in Kazakhstan', *Science*, 304, 2004

de Beer, E.S., ed., *The Diary of John Evelyn*, Oxford, OUP, 1959

Dean, Katharine R., et al, 'Human ectoparasites and the spread of plague in Europe during the Second Pandemic', *Proceedings of the National Academy of Sciences*, early edition, January, 2018

Defoe, Daniel, *A Journal of the Plague Year*, ed. Cynthia Wall, London, Penguin, 2003

Dewing, H.B., *Procopius*, I, London, William Heinemann, 1914

Dick, H.C., et al. 'Detection and characterisation of Black Death burials by multi-proxy geophysical methods', *Journal of Archaeological Science*, 29, 2015

Dick, Oliver Lawson, ed., *Aubrey's Brief Lives*, London, Penguin, 1972

Dillon, Janette, *Performance and Spectacle in Hall's Chronicle*, London, Soc. for Theatre Research, 2002

Donne, John, *After Our Disposition by the Sickness*, 1625

Drancourt, Michel, et al, 'Detection of 400-year-old *Yersinia pestis* DNA in human dental pulp: An approach to the diagnosis of ancient septicemia', *Proceedings of the National Academy of Sciences*, 95, 1998

Dugdale, George S., *Whitehall through the centuries*, London, Phoenix House, 1950

Duncan-Jones, Katherine, *Shakespeare: An Ungentle Life*, London, Methuen Drama, 2010

Elliot, G.T., ed., Autobiography and Anecdotes by William Taswell, D.D., *Camden Miscellany*, Vol. 2, 1853

Fenn, John, *Paston Letters*, London, Charles Knight, 1840

Fichtner, Paula Suttner, *Emperor Maximilian II*, London and New Haven, Yale UP, 2001

Finlay, Roger, *Population and Metropolis. The Demography of London 1580-1650*, Cambridge, CUP, 1981

Firth, C.H., and Rait, R.S., eds, *Acts and Ordinances of the Interregnum*, London, HMSO, 1911

Fisher, F.J., *London and the English Economy 1500-1700*, ed. P.J. Corfield and N.B. Harte, London, Hambledon Press, 1990

Fletcher, Anthony, *The Outbreak of the English Civil War*, London, Arnold, 1981

Fletcher, John Edward, *A Study of the Life and Works of Athanasius Kircher, Germanus Incredibilis*, Brill, Koninklijke, 2011

Foakes, R.A., ed., *Henslowe's Diary*, 2nd edn, Cambridge, CUP, 2002

Forbes, Thomas Rogers, *Chronicle from Aldgate: Life and Death in Shakespeare's London*, New Haven & London, Yale UP, 1971

Ford, Mark, ed., *London: A History in Verse*, Cambridge, Mass, & London, Harvard UP, 2012

Frandsen, Karl-Erik, *The Last Plague in the Baltic Region, 1709-1713*, Copenhagen, Museum Tusculanum Press, 2010

Freshfield, Edwin, ed., *The Vestry Minute Book of the Parish of St Margaret Lothbury in the City of London 1571-1677*, London, 1887

Furdell, Elizabeth Lane, 'Boorde, Andrew (c.1490–1549)', ODNB

Furnivall, Frederick J. and Percy, eds, *The Anatomie of The Bodie of Man by Thomas Vicary*, London, Early English Text Soc., 1888

Furnivall, Percy, 'The Plague of 1563', *Notes and Queries*, 7th series, vol.5, 12 May 1888

Gabel, Leona C., ed., *Secret Memoirs of a Renaissance Pope: The Commentaries of Aneas Sylvius Piccolomini*, London, Folio Soc., 1988

Galloway, James A., ed., *Trade, Urban Hinterlands and Market Integration c.1300-1600*, Centre for Metropolitan History Working Papers Series No. 3, London, 2000

Gardiner, Dorothy, ed., *The Oxinden and Peyton Letters 1642-1670*, London, Sheldon Press, 1937

Gibb, H.A.R., ed., *The Travels of Ibn Battuta*, II, Cambridge, CUP for the Hakluyt Soc., 1962

Gibbon, Edward, *The Decline and Fall of the Roman Empire*, IV, London, Everyman, 1994

Ginzburg, Carlo, *The Cheese and the Worms: The Cosmos of a Sixteenth-Century Miller*, Baltimore, John Hopkins UP, 1980

Giuseppi, M.S., ed., *Calendar of the Cecil Papers in Hatfield House*, vol. 15, London, HMC, 1930

Glass, D.V., and Eversley, D.E.C., eds, *Population in History*, London, Arnold, 1965

Goeurot, Jean, *The regiment of life, whereunto is added a treatise of the pestilence, with the boke of children, newly corrected and enlarged by T. Phayre*, 1545

Godfrey, W.H., *The Church of Saint Bride, Fleet Street*, London, Survey of London, Monograph No. 15, 1944

Gottfried, Robert S., *Epidemic Disease in Fifteenth Century England*, Leicester, Leicester UP, 1978

Gottfried, Robert S., *The Black Death. Natural and Human Disaster in Medieval Europe*, London, Robert Hale, 1983

Grafton, Richard, *Grafton's Chronicle; or, History of England*, II, London, 1809

Grell, Ole Peter, 'Plague in Elizabethan and Stuart London: The Dutch Response', *Medical History*, 34, 1990

Gwyn, Peter, *The King's Cardinal: The Rise and Fall of Thomas Wolsey*, London, Barrie & Jenkins, 1990

Haensch, S., Bianucci, R., Signoli, M., Rajerison, M., Schultz, M. et al., 'Distinct Clones of *Yersinia pestis* Caused the Black Death', *PLOS Pathogens*, 6 (10), 2010

Hale, J.R., ed., *The Travel Journal of Antonio de Beatis*, London, Hakluyt Soc., 1979

Hale, John, *The Civilization of Europe in the Renaissance*, London, Harper Collins, 1993

Hall, A.R. and M.B., eds, *The Correspondence of Henry Oldenburg*, 13 vols, Madison, University of Wisconsin Press, 1965-86

Halsband, Robert, ed., *The Complete Letters of Lady Mary Wortley Montagu*, I, Oxford, Clarendon Press, 1965

Hampden, John, ed., *Sir Roger de Coverly by Joseph Addison, Sir Richard Steele & Eustace Budgell*, London, Folio Soc., 1967

Hamilton, W.D., ed., *A Chronicle of England during the reigns of the Tudors, from A.D. 1485 to 1559, by Charles Wriothesley*, Camden Soc., 2nd series, vol.11, 1875

Hanawalt, Barbara A., *Growing up in medieval London*, Oxford, OUP, 1993

Harkness, Deborah E., *The Jewel House: Elizabethan London and the Scientific Revolution*, London & New Haven, Yale UP, 2007

Harrison, Mark, *Contagion: How Commerce has Spread Disease*, New Haven & London, Yale UP, 2012

Havran, Martin J., *Caroline Courtier: The Life of Lord Cottington*, London, Macmillan, 1973

Healey, Margaret, *Fictions of Disease in Early Modern England*, London, Palgrave, 2001

Heinze, R.W., *Proclamations of the Tudor Kings*, Cambridge, CUP, 1976

Hirst, L. Fabian, *The Conquest of Plague*, Oxford, Clarendon Press, 1953

Hodgett, Gerald A.J., ed., *The Cartulary of Holy Trinity Aldgate*, London Record Soc., vol. 7, 1971

Holbein, Hans, *The Dance of Death*, ed. Ulinka Rublack, London, Penguin, 2016

Holmes, George, 'Chiriton, Walter (fl.1340–1358)', ODNB

Hope, Valerie, *My Lord Mayor*, London, Weidenfeld & Nicolson, 1989

Hope, Sir William St.John, *The History of the London Charterhouse*, London, SPCK, 1925

Horder, Mervyn, ed., *Memoirs of a Mercenary*, London, Folio Soc., 1987

Horrox, Rosemary, *The Black Death*, Manchester, Manchester UP, 1994

Howarth, R.G., ed., *Letters and the Second Diary of Samuel Pepys*, London, Dent, 1933

Hughes, Paul L., and Larkin, James F., eds, *Tudor Royal Proclamations, Volume I: The Early Tudors, 1485-1553*, London and New Haven, Yale UP, 1964

Hughes, Paul L., and Larkin, James F., eds, *Tudor Royal Proclamations, Volume II: The Later Tudors, 1553-1587*, London & New Haven, Yale UP, 1969

Huizinga, J., *The Waning of the Middle Ages*, Harmondsworth, Penguin, 1965

Hull, Charles Henry, ed., *The Economic Writings of Sir William Petty*, Cambridge, CUP, 1899

Hunting, Penelope, *A History of the Society of Apothecaries*, London, The Society of Apothecaries, 1998

Hyde, Edward, Earl of Clarendon, *Selections from The History of the Rebellion and The Life by Himself*, ed. Gordon Huehns, Oxford, OUP, 1978

Inderwick, F.A., ed., *A Calendar of the Inner Temple Records, I, 1505-1603*, London, Inner Temple, 1896

Inwood, Stephen, *A History of London*, London, Macmillan, 1998

Israel, Jonathan, *The Dutch Republic: Its Rise, Greatness, and Fall, 1477-1806*, Oxford, Clarendon Press, 1995

Jansson, Maija, and Bidwell, William B., eds, *Proceedings in Parliament 1625*, London & New Haven, Yale UP, 1987

Jardine, Lisa, and Stewart, Alan, *Hostage to Fortune: The Troubled Life of Francis Bacon 1561-1626*, London, Gollancz, 1998

Jeaffreson, J.C., ed., *Middlesex County Records*, III, London, Middlesex County Records Soc., 1888

Jewers, Arthur J., 'The will of a plague-stricken Londoner', *The Home Counties Magazine*, III, 1901

Jones, John, *A Dial for all Agues*, London, 1566

Jones, Philip E., ed., *Calendar of Plea and Memoranda Rolls ... 1458-1482*, Cambridge, CUP, 1961

Jordan, W.K., ed., *The Chronicle and Political Papers of King Edward VI*, London, Allen & Unwin, 1966

Kamen, Henry, *Spain 1469-1714: A society in conflict*, London, Longman, 1991

Karlen, Arno, *Plague's Progress: A social history of man and disease*, London, Gollancz, 1995

Karras, Ruth Mazo, *Common Women: Prostitution and Sexuality in Medieval England*, Oxford, OUP, 1996

Keble, N.H., and Nuttall, G.F., eds, *Calendar of the Correspondence of Richard Baxter*, II 1660-1696, Oxford, OUP, 1991

Keene, Derek, *Cheapside before the Great Fire*, London, Economic and Social Research Council, 1985

Keene, Derek, Burns, Arthur, and Saint, Andrew, eds, *St Paul's: The Cathedral Church of London 604-2004*, New Haven & London, Yale UP, 2004

Kelly, John, *The Great Mortality: An Intimate History of the Black Death*, London, Harper Collins, 2013

Kingsford, C.L., ed., *Chronicles of London*, Oxford, Clarendon Press, 1905

Kirby, Joan, ed., *The Plumpton Letters and Papers*, Camden Soc., 5th series, 8, 1996

Knowles, C.C., and Pitt, P.H., *The History of Building Regulation in London 1189-1972*, London, Architectural Press, 1972

Knowles, David, and Grimes, W.F., *Charterhouse: The Medieval Foundation in the light of recent discoveries*, London, Longman, Green, 1954

Lamond, Elizabeth, ed., *A Discourse of the Common Weal of this Realm of England*, Cambridge, CUP, 1954

Laoutaris, Chris, *Shakespeare and the Countess*, London, Penguin, 2014

Larkin, James F., and Hughes, Paul L., eds, *Stuart Royal Proclamations Volume I Royal Proclamations of King James I 1603-1625*, Oxford, Clarendon Press, 1973

Larkin, J.F., ed., *Stuart Royal Proclamations Volume II: Royal Proclamations of King Charles I 1625-1646*, Oxford, OUP, 1983

Latham, R.C., and Matthews, W., eds, *The Diary of Samuel Pepys*, 11 vols, London, Bell & Hyman, 1970-83

Lebeer, Louis, *De Geest van de Graveerkunst in de XVe eeuw*, Diest, Pro Arte, 1945

Letts, Malcolm, *The Travels of Leo of Rozmital through Germany, Flanders, England, France, Spain, Portugal and Italy 1465-1467*, Hakluyt Society, 2nd series, CVIII, 1955

Lewis, W.S., Smith, Warren Hunting, and Lam, George L., eds, *Horace Walpole's Correspondence with Sir Horace Mann*, London, OUP, 1955

Lithgow, William, *The Present Surveigh of London and Englands State*, 1643

Lloyd, T.H., *The English Wool Trade in the Middle Ages*, Cambridge, CUP, 1977

Lodge, Thomas, *A Treatise of the Plague*, 1603

Longstaffe, W.H.D., ed., *Memoirs of the Life of Mr. Ambrose Barnes*, Surtees Soc., L, 1867

Lilly, William, *William Lilly's History of His Life and Times, from the year 1602 to 1681. Written by Himself*, London, 1822

MacGregor, Neil, *Shakespeare's Restless World*, London, Penguin, 2013

Maddicott, J.R., 'Plague in seventh-century England', *Past & Present*, 156, 1997

Magurn, Ruth Saunders, ed., *The Letters of Peter Paul Rubens*, Cambridge, Mass., Harvard UP, 1955

Malden, Henry Elliot, ed., *The Cely papers: selections from the correspondence and memoranda of the Cely family, merchants of the staple, A.D. 1475-1488*, London, Longmans, Green, for the Royal Historical Soc., 1900

Marana, Giovanni P., *Letters Writ by a Turkish Spy*, ed. Arthur J. Weitzman, London, Routledge & Kegan Paul, 1970

Matthews, Henry, *Diary of an Invalid: Journal of a Tour in Pursuit of Health 1817-1819*, 1820, new edn Stroud, Nonsuch, 2005

McClure, Norman Egbert, ed., *Letters, by John Chamberlain*, London, Greenwood Press, 1979 edn

McDermott, James, *Martin Frobisher: Elizabethan Privateer*, New Haven & London, Yale UP, 2001

McMurray, William, ed., *The Records of Two City Parishes*, London, 1925

Medvei, Victor Cornelius, and Thornton, John L., *The Royal Hospital of Saint Bartholomew 1123-1973*, London, St Bartholomew's Hospital, 1974

Minchinton, W.E., ed., *Essays in Agrarian History*, 2 vols, Newton Abbot, David & Charles, 1968

Mitchell, Rosemary, 'Penrose [née Cartwright], Elizabeth [pseud. Mrs Markham] (c.1779–1837), writer', ODNB

Mitchell, Rosemary, *Picturing the Past: English History in Text and Image, 1830-1870*, Oxford, Clarendon Press, 2000

Mole, John, *The Sultan's Organ*, London, Fortune Books, 2012

Montaigne, Michel de, *The Essays: A Selection*, trans M.A. Screech, London, Penguin, 1993

Mullett, C.F., *The Bubonic Plague and England*, Lexington, University of Kentucky Press, 1956

Munkhoff, Richelle, "Searchers of the Dead': Authority, Marginality, and the Interpretation of Plague in England, 1574-1665', *Gender & History*, 11, 1999

Myers, A.R., *Chaucer's London: Everyday Life in London 1342-1400*, Stroud, Amberley, 2009

Mynors, R.A.B., and Thomson, D.F.S., eds, *The Correspondence of Erasmus*, II, Toronto and Buffalo, University of Toronto Press, 1975

Mynors, R.A.B., Dalzell, A., and Estes, J.M., eds, *The Correspondence of Erasmus: Letters 1356 to 1534, 1523 to 1524*, vol. 10, Toronto, University of Toronto Press, 1992

Naphy, William, and Spicer, Andrew, *The Black Death and the history of plagues 1345-1730*, Stroud, Tempus, 2000

Nashe, Thomas, *Christ's tears over Jerusalem, whereunto is annexed A comparative admonition to London*, London, Longman, Hurst, Rees, Orme and Brown, 1815

Nashe, Thomas, *The Unfortunate Traveller*, 1594

Nevinson, Charles, ed., *Later Writings of Bishop Hooper*, Parker Soc., 1852

Nicolay, Nicolas de, *The navigations, peregrinations and voyages, made into Turkie by Nicholas Nicholay*, trans. Thomas Washington, London, 1585

Nichols, J.G., ed., *Chronicle of the Grey Friars of London*, Camden Soc., vol. 53, 1852

Nichols, J.G., ed., *The Diary of Henry Machyn Citizen and Merchant-Taylor of London (1550-1563)*, Camden Soc., 1848

Nicholson, Watson, *The Historical Sources of Defoe's Journal of the Plague Year*, Boston, Mass, Stratford, 1920

Nicholson, William, ed., *The Remains of Edmund Grindal*, Parker Soc., 1843

Nicolson, Adam, *Power and Glory: Jacobean England and the Making of the King James Bible*, London, Harper Collins, 2003

Nohl, Johannes, *The Black Death: A chronicle of the plague compiled from contemporary sources*, trans G.H. Clarke, London, Unwin, 1961

Ormrod, W. Mark, *Edward III*, New Haven & London, Yale UP, 2011

Ozment, Steven, *Flesh and Spirit: Private Life in Early Modern Germany*, London, Penguin, 2001

Packe, Michael, *King Edward III*, ed. L.C.B. Seaman, London, Routledge & Kegan Paul, 1983

Paynell, Thomas, *Moche profitable treatise against the pestilence*, 1534

Pelling, Margaret, and White, Frances, *Physicians and Irregular Medical Practitioners in London 1550-1640*, British History Online Database, London, 2004

Petowe, Henry, *The countrie ague. Or, London her welcome home to her retired children*, London, 1625

Pfizenmaier, Sam, *Charterhouse Square: Black Death Cemetery and Carthusian Monastery, Meat Market and Suburb*, London, MOLA, 2016

Pickering, D., *The Statutes at Large*, VII, London, 1763

Plummer, Alfred, *The London Weavers' Company, 1600-1970* London, Routledge & Kegan Paul, 1972

Poole, H. Edmund, *The Wisdome of Andrew Boorde*, Leicester, Falconer Scott, 1936

Poole, H. Edmund, ed., *Music, Men, and Manners in France and Italy 1770*, London, Folio Soc., 1969

Power, Eileen, *Medieval Women*, ed. M.M. Postan, Cambridge, CUP, 1997

Poynter, F.N.L., ed., *The Journal of James Yonge [1647-1721]*, London, Longmans, 1963

Poynter, F.N.L., and LeFanu, W.R., 'A Seventeenth-Century London Plague Document in the Wellcome Historical Medical Library: Dr. Louis Du Moulin's Proposals to Parliament for a corps of salaried plague-doctors', *Bulletin of the History of Medicine*, 34, 1960

Ramsay, G.D., *The City of London in international politics at the accession of Elizabeth Tudor*, Manchester, Manchester UP, 1975

Ranger, Terence, and Slack, Paul, eds, *Epidemics and Ideas: Essays on the historical perceptions of pestilence*, Cambridge, CUP, 1992

Rasmussen, Steen Eiler, *London: The Unique City*, Cambridge, Mass., MIT Press, 1982

Rawcliffe, Carole, *Medicine & Society in Later Medieval England*, Stroud, Sutton, 1995

Read, Conyers, *Mr Secretary Cecil and Queen Elizabeth*, London, Jonathan Cape, 1965

Renoir, Alain, *The Poetry of John Lydgate*, London, Routledge & Kegan Paul, 1967

Rexroth, Frank, *Deviance and Power in Late Medieval London*, Cambridge, CUP, 2007

Riley, H.T., ed., *Memorials of London and London Life in the 13th, 14th and 15th Centuries*, London, Longmans, Green, 1868

Rudder, Samuel, *A New History of Gloucestershire*, 1779, new edn, Stroud, Nonsuch, 2006

Rye, William Brenchley, *England as seen by foreigners in the days of Elizabeth and James the First*, London, John Russell Smith, 1865, reprinted 2005

Saul, Nigel B., ed., *The Age of Chivalry: Art and Society in Late Medieval England*, London, Brockhampton Press, 1995

Saunders, Frances Stonor, *Hawkwood: Diabolical Englishman*, London, Faber & Faber, 2004

Seaver, Paul S., *Wallington's World: A Puritan Artisan in Seventeenth-Century London*, London, Methuen, 1985

Sellar, A.M., ed., *Bede's Ecclesiastical History of England*, London, George Bell, 1907

Shapiro, James, *1606: Shakespeare and the Year of Lear*, London, Faber & Faber, 2015

Sharpe, Reginald R., ed., *Calendar of Letter-Books of the City of London: F, 1337-1352*, London, HMSO, 1904

Sharpe, Reginald R., ed., *Calendar of Letter-Books of the City of London: G, 1352-1374*, London, 1905

Sharpe, Reginald R., ed., *Calendar of Letter-Books of the City of London: L, Edward IV-Henry VII*, London, HMSO, 1912

Sheppard, F.H.W., ed., *Survey of London, vol. 31, The Parish of St James, Westminster*, London, Athlone, 1963

Shrewsbury, J.F.D., *A History of Bubonic Plague in the British Isles*, Cambridge, CUP, 1970

Skoda, Hannah, 'The 14th century ... when things weren't what they used to be', *BBC History Magazine*, Christmas 2016

Slack, Paul, *The Impact of Plague in Tudor and Stuart England*, London, Routledge & Kegan Paul, 1985

Sloane, Barney, *The Black Death in London*, Stroud, History Press, 2011

Smet, Marjan de, and Trio, Paul, eds, *The Use and Abuse of Sacred Places in Late Medieval Towns*, Leuven, Leuven UP, 2006

Sprat, Thomas, *The History of the Royal Society of London*, 1667

Stow, John, *Annales, or a general Chronicle of England*, 1631

Stow, John, *The Survey of London*, ed. H.B. Wheatley, Dent, London, 1987

Stoye, John, *Europe Unfolding, 1648-1688*, London, Collins, 1969

Stoye, John, *Marsigli's Europe 1680-1730. The Life and Times of Luigi Ferdinando Marsigli, Soldier and Virtuoso*, New Haven and London, Yale UP, 1994

Sturmer, Walter F., *John Lydgate: A Study in the Culture of the XVth Century*, Berkeley & Los Angeles, University of California Press, 1961

Sumption, Jonathan, *The Hundred Years War: Volume II Trial by Fire*, London, Faber & Faber, 1999

Sumption, Jonathan, *The Hundred Years War: Volume IV Cursed Kings*, London, Faber, 2015

Sutton, Anne F., *The Mercery of London: Trade, Goods and People, 1130-1578*, London, Ashgate, 2005

Swift, Jonathan, *Journal to Stella*, ed. H. Williams, 2 vols, Oxford, Clarendon Press, 1948

Symonds, E.M., 'The Diary of John Greene (1635-57)', *English Historical Review*, XLIV, 1928, 1929

Tait, James, ed., *Chronica Johannis de Reading et Anonymi Cantuariensis 1346—1367*, Manchester, Manchester UP, 1914

Taylor, John, *The Fearfull Summer, Or, Londons Calamitie*, 1625.

Thomas, A.H., ed., *Calendar of Plea and Memoranda Rolls ... of the City of London, 1323-1364*, Cambridge, CUP, 1926

Thomas, Christopher, *The Archaeology of Medieval London*, Stroud, Sutton, 2002

Thompson, Edward Maunde, ed., *Chronicon Adae de Usk, A.D. 1377-1421*, London, Royal Soc. of Literature, 2nd edn, 1904

Thomson, Elizabeth McClure, ed., *The Chamberlain Letters*, London, John Murray, 1966

Thomson, Gladys Scott, *Life in a Noble Household*, London, Cape, 1937

Thrupp, Sylvia M., *The Merchant Class of Medieval London*, Ann Arbor, University of Michigan Press, 1989

Thurley, Simon, *Hampton Court: A Social and Architectural History*, London & New Haven, Yale UP, 2003

Trevor-Roper, Hugh, *Europe's Physician: The Varied Life of Sir Theodore de Mayerne*, New Haven & London, Yale UP, 2006

Vergil, Polydore, *The Anglica Historia 1485-1537*, ed. Denys Hay, Camden Soc., vol. 74, 1950

Vincent, Thomas, *God's Terrible Voice in the City*, London, 1667; James Nisbet, 1831

Walker, Julian, *How to Cure the Plague & Other Curious Remedies*, London, British Library, 2013

West, Richard, *The Life and Strange Surprising Adventures of Daniel Defoe*, London, Harper Collins, 1997

West, Richard, *Chaucer 1340-1400*, London, Constable, 2000

Whibley, Charles, ed., *The Lives of the Kings: Henry VIII by Edward Hall*, London, T.C. & E.C. Jack, 1904

[White, Thomas], *A sermo[n] preached at Pawles Crosse on Sunday the thirde of Nouember 1577. in the time of the plague, by T.W.*, London, 1577

Williams, C.H., *English Historical Documents 1485-1558*, London, Eyre & Spottiswood, 1967

Williams, R.F., ed., *The Court and Times of Charles the First*, London, 1848

Wilson, F.P., *The Plague in Shakespeare's London*, Oxford, OUP, 1927

Wilson, F.P., ed., *The Plague Pamphlets of Thomas Dekker*, Oxford, OUP, 1925

Wolbert, Klaus, *Memento Mori*, Darmstadt, Hessisches Landesmuseum, 1984

Ziegler, Philip, *The Black Death*, London, Collins, 1969

Zweig, Stefan, *Montaigne*, London, Pushkin Press, 2015

INDEX